JUNG AND THE
POST-JUNGIANS

JUNG AND THE POST-JUNGIANS

ANDREW SAMUELS

ROUTLEDGE & KEGAN PAUL
LONDON, BOSTON AND HENLEY

for Catherine

First published in 1985
by Routledge & Kegan Paul plc

14 Leicester Square, London WC2H 7PH

9 Park Street, Boston, Mass. 02108, USA

Broadway House, Newtown Road,
Henley-on-Thames, Oxon RG9 1EN, England

Set in 10/11pt Ehrhardt
by Columns of Reading
and printed in Great Britain
by St. Edmundsbury Press Ltd
Bury St Edmunds, Suffolk

Reprinted with corrections 1985
First published as a paperback 1986

Library of Congress Cataloging in Publication Data

Samuels, Andrew.

Jung and the post-Jungians.
Bibliography: p.
Includes index.
1. Jung, C. G. (Carl Gustav), 1875–1961. 2. Psycho-
analysis. I. Title.
BF173.J85S28   1985   150.19'54   84-8353

British Library CIP also available
ISBN 0-7100-9958-4 (c)
ISBN 0-7102-0864-2 (p)

Contents

Preface

This book evolved in my mind in three stages, each emerging from its predecessor. My original intention was to write of the way analytical psychology has developed since Jung's death in 1961. But to achieve that it would be necessary to indicate the starting point for the various post-Jungians whose work I planned to discuss. Therefore the second theme came into being: a critical presentation of Jung's own work. At that stage, there seemed a risk that the project might become too parochial and it felt appropriate to bring in the numerous parallels which exist between Jungian and post-Jungian analytical psychology and psychoanalysis. This third theme spawned its own offspring: an attempt to envision Jung as a pioneer, even the main precursor of changes in psychoanalytic theory and practice since the 1930s. Though Jung's direct influence was slight, I felt that this attempt might help dispel once and for all the credibility gap which has surrounded Jung.

It is impossible to summarise other writers without doing some violence to their views. I can only apologise for this now and add that my hope is to encourage readers eventually to find post-Jungian writings in their original form, if they have not already done so.

This book is not an exercise in psychobiography. I have not asked any of the writers mentioned for information regarding themselves or their relation to Jung. This is because there have been numerous scholarly attempts to show the connections between Jung's life and his work by examining the basic texts now available, such as his autobiography, his letters and the correspondence with Freud. I have been more concerned with questions of validity and applicability.

There have been long-standing obstacles to Jungian psychology acquiring any recognition in either the wider culture or the inner circles of the helping professions, and these are discussed in detail in this book. But recently something has happened to change this state of affairs. There are now over 1,000 Jungian analysts worldwide and the number increases at a great rate; likewise, there are training centres in all the major Western countries. Jungian books sell well and, in many places, Jungian analysts and psychotherapists co-exist in a relatively trusting and mutually supportive manner with psychoanalysts. Analytical psychology has become more respectable.

In the helping professions (and particularly in analysis, psychotherapy, counselling and casework) Jung's ideas are being *used* in a routine and down-to-earth way. It is precisely the combination of the sublime and the universal with a utilitarian and day-to-day approach that is endearing Jungian psychology to so many, whether practitioners or not. Yet the analytical psychology that is summarised in handbooks for students and the analytical psychology that is currently practised with clinical effectiveness and professional respect are very different. This is something that Freudians have to struggle with as well. It seems that only the work of the patriarch is summarised and communicated and it is the constant task and burden of the contemporary practitioner to explain that things are not really quite like that, that we have moved on somewhat. And those who resent most the authority of the master are often the last to appreciate that times have changed.

The selection of themes and the choice of writers is, of course, influenced by subjective factors. But at the back of my mind has been this question of relevance to the therapeutic professions and to the study of psychology. Because of the novelty of its comparative approach and its attempt to be comprehensive, the book should stimulate Jungian analysts, psychotherapists, trainees and scholars. But I am also particularly interested in communicating with analysts, psychotherapists and counsellors who have trained, or are training, in non-Jungian institutes. Such individuals may have had brief contact with analytical psychology as part of their course and want to deepen their knowledge and keep abreast of trends.

In conceiving this book, I have been influenced by a number of personal experiences. First, students and trainees enrolled in courses in analysis, psychotherapy, counselling and human relations have often asked me for guidance about developments in analytical psychology since Jung and for reliable suggestions as to what post-Jungian material they might investigate. Students on psychoanalytic courses, in particular, stated that they had been unable to find any specific statement of Jung's contribution to the theory and practice of psychotherapy and analysis. In addition, there are numerous comparative studies of psychoanalysis but to date nothing of the same kind has been published in the field of analytical psychology.

Second, I have had the experience of helping to found and participating in an international group of senior trainees and recently qualified analytical psychologists (1974-9). As well as giving me insight into, and respect for, a wide range of ways of thinking and working, frustrations in communication and lack of any overview or 'shape' for what we were arguing about amongst these younger Jungians made me feel that bringing together such a book would be worthwhile.

Finally, I have had the chance to be a member of a discussion group which has met monthly since 1975, composed of analytical psychologists, half of whom trained in London and half in Zürich. I want to say that this group has shown me that critical comparison leading to dispute and dialogue is possible and rewarding.

Acknowledgments

I would like to thank the following: my patients D. and M. for permission to write about them (D. for the second time); students and trainees at the Society of Analytical Psychology, Westminster Pastoral Foundation, Guild of Psychotherapists, London Centre for Psychotherapy, Richmond Fellowship, Tavistock Clinic and the Institute of Psychoanalysis for their questions (and answers); the Library of the Institute of Psychoanalysis, London and, in particular, Jill Duncan, Executive Officer, for her good-humoured help with psychoanalytic material and references; Eileen Collingwood, for excellent typing; colleagues and friends who read chapters or sections and made suggestions, or helped with the overall conception: Kay Bradway, Stratford Caldecott (RKP), Giles Clark, Linda Freeman, Jess Groesbeck, Kate Hodgetts, Nonie Hubrecht, Peggy Jones, Alison Lyons, Grant McIntyre, Anne-Lucie Norton, Rosie Parker, Roderick Peters, Sheila Powell, Fred Plaut, Shaie Selzer, Mary Wilson, Vernon Yorke.

There are three to whom I want to offer special gratitude, for their contributions enhanced the book beyond all description:
Bani Shorter, for her careful reading and assessment of the MS, resulting in numerous imaginative and valuable suggestions. She gave generously of her time, her literary ability and her knowledge of analytical psychology;
Kate Newton, for enabling me to keep in touch with the personal and unconscious aspects of writing a book; also for sustained dialogue about its content, and much else besides;
Catherine Graham-Harrison, whose love and support kept me going when I lost my way. She helped me *make* the book.

During the process of writing, I submitted sections of the book for inclusion in professional journals. These appeared as follows: 'The emergence of schools of post-Jungian analytical psychology', *Journal of Analytical Psychology* 28:4 (1983). 'Dethroning the self', *Spring: An Annual of Archetypal Psychology and Jungian Thought*, 1983. 'Beyond compensation: modifying Jung's approach to dreams', *Harvest: Journal for Jungian Studies*, 1983. 'The theory of archetypes in Jungian and post-Jungian analytical psychology', *International Review of Psychoanalysis*, 11:4 (1983). I am grateful to the Editors of these publications for publishing this 'work in progress' and for their editing of it which has been incorporated in the book.

Acknowledgments are due to Routledge & Kegan Paul and to Princeton

University Press for permission to quote from the *Collected Works of C.G. Jung* and to the Editor of the *Journal of Analytical Psychology* for permission to re-use case material from my 'Incest and omnipotence in the internal family' (25:1, 1980) and diagrams from 'The archetypal image of the wounded healer' by C. Jess Groesbeck (20:2, 1975).

A NOTE ON THE INDEX

Those who are not familiar with Jung's ideas, or are not confident of what they do know, may find the Index useful. Bold type indicates where in the text Jung's main concepts are introduced and defined.

UNFAMILIAR NAMES

Where the context does not make it clear, I have tried to indicate the orientation of writers whose names may be unfamiliar.

A writer whose orientation is not mentioned is an analytical psychologist.

1

Schools of analytical psychology

To find one's way around in the contemporary Jungian world is not easy. Jung's standing as a psychological thinker and analyst, rather than guru or prophet, is reinforced by analytical psychologists and the writings of the post-Jungians. It no longer rests solely upon Jung's legacy of the twenty volumes of the *Collected Works* and his commensurate charisma. In a way, Jung needs the post-Jungians as much as they need him if his work is to be extended into the future. The prospect for analytical psychology is a shared concern and the inheritance has become a many-stranded skein of thought which has inspired, influenced, challenged, and, in some instances, infuriated those who followed.

We should note the extent to which post-Jungians have felt able to challenge or attack Jung's work, often arguing with him on the basis of stringent criticisms from non-Jungians, as well as adapting and integrating parallel developments in other approaches to psychology, and also from completely different disciplines. If I constantly draw attention to the various serious objections that have been made to Jung's work it is because these have had a great impact on post-Jungians. Sometimes Jung anticipates, sometimes he influences, but sometimes he gets it wrong, and sometimes another thinker reaches a broadly similar conclusion but does so in a more coherent or better documented way.

In his book *Jungian Psychotherapy: A Study in Analytical Psychology* (1978a), Fordham points out that 'very little has been written on the development of the various schools of analytical psychology that have grown up' (p. 53). I decided to respond to this, bearing in mind Fordham's assertion (ibid., p. ix) that 'analytical psychology is a discipline in its own right . . . its ideas and practices can be assessed without regard to the persons who initiated them.' This has to be a different kind of book from Brown's *Freud and the Post-Freudians* (1961) because, unlike the Freudians, post-Jungians have not yet formed into *officially* recognised schools, though the process has certainly taken place informally. There are schools of analytical psychology in existence with common views, and dogmatism and conflict between these groups has not been avoided. But the reader has less chance of finding out about this from Jungian than from Freudian literature.

DO 'JUNGIANS' EXIST?

To talk of Jungians, of post-Jungians and of schools of post-Jungians, is itself a contentious matter. Jung stated that there simply was *one* Jungian – himself. He eschewed any ambition to start a school of psychology. I imagine he had in mind an attempt to avoid what he considered Freud's excesses of rabbinical authority and the whole painful early history of psychoanalysis which involved so much personalia. Furthermore, as the ideologue of individuation, with its stress on each person becoming himself and differentiating from others, not to mention his observation that a person's temperament and personal psychology play a part in dictating what he believes, Jung was bound to want to leave it up to the personal capacity of an individual as to how 'Jungian' he would be. However, as Henderson points out, 'there is now a basic Jungian body of knowledge which does not permit unlimited experimentation or theorising.' But he goes on to say that Jung 'abhorred systematisation of any kind and this was a reason why his school took so long to be formed' (1975a, pp. 120-1).

In fact, though, Jung was active throughout his life in the politics of psychology. Reading the Freud-Jung letters (ed. McGuire, 1974), one is struck by the pattern in which it is Jung who is constantly putting forward some idea for a coup or alliance while it is Freud (supposedly the more extraverted of the two) who restrains him, diverting him from excessive character attack. Later, in the 1940s, Jung put forward a proposal designed to unify psychotherapists internationally, consisting of fourteen points around which he felt everyone's ideas could coalesce. Given the extraordinary post-war fragmentation in psychology and the psychotherapies, we can now see that this was a forlorn hope, but the relevance of the episode is that Jung does not fit the image of the solitary genius, indifferent to the real world, even, or especially, to his own profession (and see pp. 269-70, below, for a further comment on the fourteen points).

Another noteworthy feature of the gradual formation of Jungians into a broad group is the series of forewords that Jung so often wrote for the books of earlier followers. It was obviously important for commercial and other reasons to receive Jung's imprimatur but, as Fordham has attested (1975, p. 108), Jung seemed to have genuine feelings about doing this. I know of forewords for books by Adler, F. Fordham, M. Fordham, Harding, Hannah, Jacobi, E. Jung, Neumann, von Franz, Wickes, Wilhelm – there are perhaps others.

That suggests that Jung knew perfectly well that for all these writers he functioned as one who introduced them to a wider audience as well as a core or reference point. There is surely nothing shameful or infantilising about this, but the perpetuation of Jung's denial concerning 'Jungians' does seem harmful.

I did not know Jung and I am not disputing that he was hostile to the *idea* of followers or 'Jungians'. But by all accounts he seems to have had an extraordinarily variegated and multi-faceted personality, as well as a very wide range of knowledge and interests. That is why differing points of view have emerged from his original work. My contention has been that, alongside the contempt for followers, Jung developed many of the more expectable characteristics of a leader especially in his wish that they should 'carry on the work' (Adler, 1973, p. 481). In Shakespeare's *Julius Caesar*, when the conspirators were worried that Caesar might not go to the Capitol, Decius suggests that they leave it up to him; he knows just how to handle Caesar. Among his various techniques for manipulating the great man, Decius continually advises him that flatterers betray:

> But when I tell him he hates flatterers,
> He says he does, being then most flattered (Act 2, scene 1).

I am suggesting that we may reverse the proposition: Jung flatters his followers by saying he does not want them. Many post-Jungian books include the by now ritualistic statement that Jung did not want disciples, with the implication that because of this the writer could not possibly be considered a mere follower or disciple. By seeming to eschew his leadership, Jung may have helped maintain it.

In a memoir of Jung to mark the centenary of his birth, Fordham (1975) provided further evidence that Jung was aware of his fatherly role. The analyst members of the Analytical Psychology Club of London, an organisation providing a meeting place for all Jungians but not a professional body, were negotiating to separate and found a professional organisation, later known as the Society of Analytical Psychology. Presumably some members felt left behind and things were not helped when these people were referred to openly as 'the patients'. But it turned out that Jung had actively promoted this conflict because he felt that any 'family' should have its conflicts. I suppose that in this book I am charting the course of Jungian family life with its healthy differences.

TRAINING IN ANALYTICAL PSYCHOLOGY

This leads us to the question of analytical training and here again we must differentiate what Jung said and what he did. There is no doubt that he had mixed feelings about the institution of formal training programmes, whether in Zürich or anywhere else. When that occurred, he was active in helping to devise a syllabus and insisted that there should be examinations (Hillman, 1962, Fordham, 1978a). Jung had bowed to collective standards and permitted changes in the old system, in which vocation, coupled with analysis by himself or a close associate and attendance at his seminars, were all that was required for the formation of an analyst. In this ethos the analysis of the potential analyst was, of course, central. Freud (1912) acknowledged that Jung had been the first to formulate the principle that the analyst should be analysed (in *CW* 4, para. 536). However, A.-M. Sandler dates the *institution* of 'training analysis' in psychoanalysis from 1918 (Sandler, 1982, p. 386).

One more subtle development in Zürich (not, as far as I know, copied elsewhere) is that it is possible to attend certain lectures without making the commitment to becoming an analyst. Many are called but few are chosen and there is now a worldwide trend in which problems of selection for training are engaging the attention of Jungian analytic institutes.

These aspects of Jung's position vis à vis training deserve mention because

3

they serve as a counterbalance to an image of Jung as a spontaneous ordinator of analysts. Jung would have been aware of any difficulties earlier students had got into through lack of a professional basis for their work. And a more formal structure may permit greater rather than lesser freedom by providing exposure to a variety of views, though the risk is loss of spontaneity. So Jung's support for examinations and qualifications may paradoxically foster individual professional development as well as assure greater professional mobility and acceptance.

THE PLACE OF THEORY

Obviously, we have now to consider the place of theory in analytical psychology. It may be profitable to look at Jung's views on the role of theory and then at what some post-Jungians have to contribute on that subject.

Possibly playfully, at one point Jung expresses a preference for dogma over theory because

> for a certain type of intellectual mediocrity characterised by enlightened rationalism, a scientific theory that simplifies matters is a very good means of defence because of the tremendous faith modern man has in anything which bears the label 'scientific'. . . . In itself any scientific theory, no matter how subtle, has, I think, less value from the point of view of psychological truth than religious dogma, for the simple reason that a theory is necessarily highly abstract and exclusively rational, whereas dogma expresses an irrational whole by means of imagery. This guarantees a far better rendering of an irrational fact like the psyche. (Jung, *CW* 11, para. 81)

Elsewhere (*CW* 17, p. 7), Jung says:

> Theories in psychology are the very devil. It is true that we need certain points of view for their orienting and heuristic value: but they should always be regarded as mere auxiliary concepts that can be laid aside at any time.

What is highlighted is the need to establish where Jung really stood in relation to theory. Many of Jung's writings do not develop a body of theory at all but were written as specific lectures – for Swiss pastors, for the Tavistock Clinic in London, the Terry lectures in the United States, for example.

He was constantly aware that, in psychological research, there is more of an overlap between observer and observed than is usually the case and that personal preferences and constitutional factors play a large part. But Jung's overall approach does suggest the presence of the suspect idea of theory. After theoretical formula has been obtained from 'human material', Jung then applies it in 'my practical work, until it has either been confirmed, modified or else abandoned' (*CW* 4, para. 685). Jung goes on to state that the wealth of comparative, often mythological or anthropological, material serves to introduce, illustrate or amplify the theory – *not* to prove it (ibid.). Thus the theory, derived from observation, exists prior to the listing of the confirming material. I find an awareness of this approach enormously helpful in understanding Jung's work. He begins from the human interaction in analysis or from observation of life, develops a theory which is then illustrated by comparative material or further observation. Only then could the mass of imagery and data from many sources be organised. The organisation itself then helps to understand one aspect or other of human behaviour. Thus the process is circular: human material – theory – illustration – application to human behaviour.

The theoretical entities mentioned in this book do not exist. As L. Stein shows (1958, p. 3), a theoretical entity only exists or is contrived to perform a particular task. He points to the physicists' positron, photon, electron, the biologists gene, Freud's id, ego and super-ego and Jung's archetypes. Modern scientists use theory not to advance empirical aims or to describe phenomena; they are attempting to indicate what their statements are about, what they *mean*. What is created is a non-empirical entity which can explain facts. The theory is not inferred or deduced from the facts; it may be tested against them. Stein illustrates this in terms of Newton and gravity. Gravity is a totally contrived invention, because no one has ever observed gravity, only that things do or do not fall. The theoretical entity exists only to do a job, which is its 'heuristic value'.

There are two scientific challenges for Jungian psychology. The first is levelled against all depth psychologies which are held to be unscientific because they deal with unprovable areas. In the sense that no one can finally *prove* the existence of, say, the Oedipus complex, this might be so. But Oedipal theory makes sense of such diverse phenomena as a child preferring one parent to the other, the question of the origin of sexual identity, reasons for perversions, hopeless partner choice in marriage, and so on. We may have to conclude that, in part, psychology is not like *other* sciences.

Jung was particularly keen to assert that psychology was a natural science by arguing that its field of reference is not mental *products* but a natural phenomenon, the psyche. My own view is that for those who demand what they consider to be the highest scientific standards, Jungian psychology will always be wanting – although, as we shall see in the next chapter, the modern sub-atomic physicist and the student of archetypes share more than a commonsense view would presuppose.

The second scientific challenge comes from the Freudians. In this connection I am reminded of a passage in *Psychoanalysis: The Impossible Profession* in which the journalist author comments ruefully on the way regular Freudians dismiss Kleinian views of the early, internal, infantile world as crazy, fantastic and unprovable 'as if their own reconstructions of the castration complex described perfectly ordinary, everyday events' (Malcolm, 1982, p. 35).

In his *Critical Dictionary of Psychoanalysis* (1972, p. ix), Rycroft observes that he 'suffers from the not uncommon constitutional defect of being incapable of understanding Jung's writings.' And Glover concluded that 'from the point of view of scientific exposition, Jung is at the best of times a confused writer' (1950, p. 69). In subsequent chapters I shall be considering these various objections to Jung's ideas but, for all intents and purposes, any attack on

5

depth psychology for being unscientific applies to Freudians as much as it does Jungians.

DANGERS OF THEORY

Clarification of Jung's attitude to theory revolves around how far the practitioner can integrate the theory so that it ceases to be an artificial, imposed, technical, external matter and becomes more an expression of personality. Jung warned against a split between the therapist's knowledge of theory and technique and his personality. *Unintegrated knowledge* is the problem. Here we can see how the apparent divergence between Jung the unsystematic sage and Jung the professor who asks for exams can be understood. The theory must be known and then become personal; this is a matter for analysis, self-analysis and introspection. What we should try to avoid is using theory defensively, so that our own feelings are blocked out, or magically, so that only easy answers are sought – or purely logically in terms of arriving at a diagnosis.

Naturally, theory cannot dictate the process of an analysis; there must be adaptations for each case. Provided the material is allowed to emerge and fill out the theory *if* it will, then the danger of over-intellectualising or over-influencing may be avoided. But it would be an inflated therapist who did not acknowledge the presence of personal influence in therapy as inevitable. Part of the influence must be the therapist's integration of theory. It follows from all this that the cardinal sin is imitation because that would imply pre-determined application of theory. (See pp. 267-9 below, for a continuation of this discussion).

REIFICATION AND ACTION LANGUAGE

Language affects understanding and understanding underpins language. The main problem with the language of Jung, and hence to an extent of the post-Jungians, is that one is tempted to reify it – that is to render as concrete, literal and actual that which is shifting, fluid and experiential, for example, *the* unconscious. Reification not only tempts one to apply a predetermined theory but it bypasses the role of the psyche in psychology. Several ways of getting around this problem have been advanced. Lambert (1981a) suggests that a distinction should be drawn between metaphorical and scientific language – the language of the imagination and the language of the intellect. The former tends to express itself in visual or auditory imagery; the latter uses rational or conceptual approaches. Jung's terms for these two kinds of thinking were 'fantasy thinking' and 'directed thinking' respectively (*CW* 5, paras 11-46). But, as Jung saw, it is possible to conceive of a complementarity or partnership in which the more rational and logical parts of the mental apparatus go to work on imaginal raw material. However personal preference for either metaphorical or scientific language means that the goal of having a model in which both languages play a part may be difficult to achieve (but see Chapter 11).

The problem of reification has been taken up by the American psychoanalyst Schafer (1976) who proposes a switch to an 'action language' which would accentuate the dynamic and fluid nature of psychic activity. And Plaut, in a series of personal communications (1981-2), insists on the values of using verbs (usually gerunds) as opposed to nouns. Thus 'thinking' not 'thought', 'resisting' not 'resistance', 'individuating' not 'individuation', and so on.

USES AND ABUSES OF ANALOGY

Jung, like many who approach the psyche, made continual use of analogy. His concept of libido or psychic energy is itself an analogy taken from natural science. In her paper 'Uses and abuses of analogy' (1973), Hubback argues that the making of analogies is a fundamental, imaginative, mental activity; more than simply a tool for understanding. Indeed, images themselves are a form of analogy because they relate to stimuli which are not currently active. But, as she points out, for Jung, the purpose of analogising is both to make use of and demonstrate the idea that the world may be unitary, the so-called *unus mundus*, a holistic view in which everything connects in some way with everything else. The analogy takes us to a deeper layer of experience of understanding. This is strengthened by the role that hunches, guesses and intuitions play in scientific discovery. An intuition, like an analogy, can bring together two ideas that have not previously been connected.

In analogy, Jung sometimes saw what he did not see before, or saw something from a different angle. Sometimes analogy is closer to psyche than observed reality; often analogy is the opposite of reification. And, I would suggest, analogies with other areas of knowledge may also have had an emotional function for Jung who, like any pioneer, wanted to consolidate his hypotheses.

Hubback quotes Lévi-Strauss: 'By comparison with the natural sciences, we benefit from an advantage and suffer an inconvenience; we find our experiments already prepared but they are uncontrollable. It is therefore understandable that we attempt to replace them with models' (ibid., p. 95). This can be set against an attack on Jung quoted in *Freud and the Post-Freudians*: 'Jung's method . . . is to argue that because A is somewhat like B and B can, under certain circumstances, share something with C, and C has been known on occasion to have been suspected of being related to D, the conclusion in full-fledged logical form is that A=D. As the language of *science* this is meaningless' (Brown, 1961, p. 45).

Hubback's conclusion was that abuse of analogy occurs if there is not mutual agreement concerning the meaning of words used and, above all, the area being focused upon. Analogies can be used defensively to deny differences and hence avoid anxiety. I would say that the primitivity of the analogy is both its strength and its weakness – we are grabbed emotionally but may overstate our case. Nevertheless, effective use of analogy can transform opacity into a wider appreciation.

For example, returning to Jung's use of the terms *libido* and *psychic energy*, the analogy enables Jung to refer to differences in psychological intensity or to express evaluations of psychological experiences. The concepts may be used to communicate about what is experiential or subjective. Energy is not perceived as a force in a mechanical sense.

Diagrams are a special case of analogy, bringing in their wake all the dangers of reification. Their usefulness seems to vary according to the aptitudes and preferences of the observer. One advantage is that the psychological diagram engages us at a more than intellectual level. The conventions of the dividing line between phases of development, or the line which encircles parts, making of them a whole, bring in the risk of over-simplification. Attempts have been made to overcome the hard-edged problems by use of overlapping circles which permit an acknowledgment of blurring and hence correspond more closely to reality (e.g. Lambert, 1981a, p. 194).

Additional problems are shown clearly in, for example, Jacobi's *The Psychology of C.G. Jung* (1942) in which one diagram of the psyche places the ego *at the centre*, relating outwards, first to the personal and then the collective unconscious. Another diagram places the collective unconscious, and specifically that part of it that can never be brought to consciousness, at the centre with the ego *on the periphery*. Of course, both points of view are valid, but the inevitable weakness of the single perspective diagram is that we miss the quality of experience in which sometimes our self-awareness is central and sometimes our basic drives or unconscious motivations take over.

METAPSYCHOLOGY

This term was invented by Freud as a counterpart to 'metaphysics'. It refers to the most theoretical view of psychology and involves a linking of concepts removed from the empirical base which was relevant at one point in their evolution. Earlier, we discussed the idea that theoretical entities do not exist; metapsychology attempts to treat them as if they did.

Freud sub-divided his own metapsychology into its dynamic, topographical and economic aspects. Let us consider what this implies for analytical psychology.

The notion that the psyche is dynamic rather than static is fundamental to Freudian, Jungian and post-Jungian psychology. What is conceived of is an interplay of forces, often instinctual, and the idea of conflict between opposing forces. For Freud, unresolved and unregenerate conflict is the wellspring of neurosis whilst Jung, as we shall see in Chapter 4, regarded the coming together of apparently irreconcilable psychic contents as the basis of healthy development, providing a new position from which the individual can proceed. Perhaps the major dynamic conflict (and Freud and Jung would agree on this even if afterwards variance sets in) is that between consciousness and unconsciousness. This is enhanced in the Jungian view by the proposition that there is also a self-regulatory function within the unconscious. For the moment, the main element we can descry in the dynamic aspect of metapsychology is that parts of the psyche can move together and, conversely, apart. This rhythm of combining and uniting on the one hand, and on the other, separating, differentiating and discriminating, turns out to be an important theme in Jung and a vital one for the post-Jungians in their approaches to the development of personality and to individuating and individuation.

To talk of the topography of the psyche involves identifying sub-systems and placing them either spatially (as Freud did at first) or structurally (as he did later). The roots of the topographical approach lie in anatomy and physiology in which the various parts of the human body have their own location and are connected to other areas and organs. More specifically, attempts continue to be made to locate the place where fantasies originate and so on. The whole notion of the unconscious implies that much is hidden – rather like the foundations of a building – but operating all the same, particularly in psychopathology. Both Freud and Jung perform a dissection of the psyche as a whole to reveal its parts and sub-systems. Topography permits the mode of functioning and main characteristics of a particular sub-system to be looked at in relative isolation, as in the analysis of a complex (see Chapter 2).

The economic approach has been touched on earlier in relation to analogy. As regards metapsychology, the hypothesis is that psychological activity can be expressed in terms of the energy available for any potential process and that this can vary. Perhaps this can best be illustrated from clinical practice. Patients with obsessional symptoms may find themselves unable to cease the symptomatic activity by way of conscious striving. Economically, more energy is invested in the symptom than is available for attempts to overcome it. When we come to consider the interaction of the complexes we shall constantly be making use of this hypothesis.

There is little place in metapsychology for discussion of what is innate or constitutional in personality and what stems from interaction with the environment.

UNKNOWING JUNGIANS

Where interest in Jung has swung away from the arcane and esoteric aspects to an examination of the clinical applicability of his ideas, he is revealed as a surprisingly modern thinker and psychotherapist, who anticipated in a most striking manner many of the ways in which psychoanalytic and other psychological thinking has developed. As Roazen said, in his monumental study *Freud and his Followers*:

> Few responsible figures in psychoanalysis would be disturbed today if an analyst were to present views identical to Jung's in 1913. (1976, p. 272)

And the same may be said for many of Jung's later formulations.

A list of the ways in which post-Jungian analytical psychology is in tune with various developments in psychoanalysis suggests that not only is Jung in the therapeutic mainstream but that there is a sense in which analysis and psychotherapy today are in fact 'Jungian'. We really need a new category – *unknowing Jungians*. During the course of this book we shall look at the interplay between Jung, post-Jungians and unknowing Jungians, mainly in psychoanalysis. We shall, in effect, be providing a detailed substantiation of Roazen's insight (not to mention other, more general, claims on Jung's behalf). Sometimes an idea from analytical psychology can help with a thorny problem in psychoanalytic theory, and vice versa.

My intention is not, as it were, to claim that Jung invented the wheel, or adopt the posture of a fanatical supporter of Jung (there are too many objections to Jung's ideas in this book for that). But my teaching experience and contact with psychoanalytic colleagues suggests that Jung is not yet perceived as a trustworthy figure; there is a credibility gap. By showing that much of modern analysis and psychotherapy has a pronounced Jungian flavour I hope to do something about this credibility gap and interest the reader to explore further those aspects of analytical psychology which he had been prone to dismiss (and see p. 271, below).

I append a list of the changes and developments in psychoanalysis with which I shall be concerned throughout and which reflect this 'Jungian' re-orientation, together with the names of the theorists with whom they are most closely connected:

- stress on early pre-oedipal experience of attachment to, and separation from, mother (*Klein*, the British School of object relations theorists: *Fairbairn, Guntrip, Winnicott, Balint.* Also *Bowlby*).
- a vital part is played in psychological life by innate psychic structures (archetypes) (*Klein, Bowlby, Spitz, Lacan, Bion*).
- there is a creative, purposive, non-destructive aspect to the unconscious (*Milner, Rycroft, Winnicott* on play, and cf. *Maslow* and humanistic psychology).
- symptoms should not be looked at solely in a causal-reductive manner but in terms of their meaning for the patient (*Rycroft* and existential analysis).
- a move in analytic theory away from patriarchal, male-dominated and phallocentric approaches; attention is paid to the feminine (feminist psychology and psychotherapy, *Mitchell, Stoller, Lacan*).
- stress on the clinical *use* of countertransference (most analysts today – e.g. *Searles, Langs, Racker, Little, Winnicott*).
- the idea that analysis is a mutually transforming interaction and hence that the analyst's personality and his experience of the analysis are of central importance (*Langs, Searles, Lomas*, interactionalism).
- the idea that regression in analysis may be helpful and useful, and can be worked with (*Balint, Kris*).
- analysis should be concerned with the self as much, if not more, than the ego; the self is understood as a cohesive expression of the person rather than as one of a number of representations in the ego (*Kohut, Winnicott*).
- there are sub-divisions of personality (complexes) with which an analyst can work (*Winnicott*'s true and false selves, and cf. Gestalt therapy, transactional analysis).
- incestuous fantasy is symbolic (*Bion, Lacan, Mitchell, Winnicott*).

- that issues of personal integration (individuation) are more central than 'sanity' or 'genitality' (*Erikson, Milner*).
- the idea that schizophrenic phenomena have meaning (*Laing* and his colleagues).
- expansion of analytic interest into the second half of life (*Levinson, Parkes, Erikson, Kübler-Ross*).
- the idea that problems between parents find expression in children (family therapy).

SCHOOLS OF ANALYTICAL PSYCHOLOGY

We now turn our attention to the question of the various schools of post-Jungian analytical psychology. It may be regrettable that these divisions exist or it may be healthily inevitable, but they cannot be ignored. This is because theoretical differences do lead to differences in analytical and therapeutic practice, determine which parts of the patient's material gets attention, and contribute to the meaning inherent in the material.

I describe three existing classifications of post-Jungian schools, then my own classification and conclude with a consideration of how broad a spectrum Jungian psychology could or should encompass, with a discussion on eclecticism.

ADLER'S CLASSIFICATION

Adler's system was the first of the three classifications to be published (1967). He felt that it was necessary for analytical psychology to change and develop in much the same way that Jung's own ideas underwent modification; even though this was bound to lead to some confusion, it could not be avoided. Adler describes a continuum ranging from an 'orthodox' to an 'unorthodox' attitude. The orthodox group continue to use Jung's concepts and approaches in more or less the form and manner in which he left them. Clinically, this implies a stress on elucidation of archetypal patterns which give meaning, and, via amplification with comparative data, or by the use of active imagination, into consciousness purposive and teleological elements in the psychic material.

The notion of amplification is a highly developed form of analogy in which the content or story of an already known myth, fairy tale or ritualistic practice is used to elucidate or 'make ample' what might be but a clinical fragment – a single word or dream image or bodily sensation. If the clinical fragment triggers off in analyst or patient the knowledge already possessed then sense can be made of the material. For example, a woman who cannot understand why she does not get on with her mother may dream of meeting a man in an underground place. Amplification may make use of a mythologem of the collective unconscious, i.e. Demeter and Persephone, and thereby accentuate or make apparent sexual rivalry and ambivalent feelings towards the other's sexuality as the reason for the mother–daughter rift. Apart from assisting in

11

the bringing to consciousness of this dynamic, amplification helps the patient to see that she is not alone in her problem, that it is 'typical'.

The idea of active imagination derives from Jung's discovery that the unconscious has an independent symbol-producing capacity. Jung found that this could be used analytically and designated working with such material *active* imagination to distinguish it from passive fantasising and also to emphasise that the patient may have to make choices based on the outcome of his active imagination. Active imagination is a channel for 'messages' from the unconscious by any means; for example, by media such as painting, modelling or writing. These products are not viewed aesthetically but valued for the information they contain about pre-subjective areas of the psyche. Active imagination is therefore a special type of fantasy involving the participation of the ego and with the goal of a connection to internal, objective reality. The ego will hold a psychic fragment, as in the example above, in a contemplative manner and then:

> It is as if imagination begins to stir and a dream of the unconscious begins to unfold. Generally the ego is included in the drama, moving through the scene or asking questions. So with an attitude which acknowledges the reality of the psyche, a conversation begins between conscious and unconscious, and thus one enters the dialectic method which allows the psyche freedom of expression. (Weaver, 1964, p. 4)

The timing of active imagination in the course of an analysis and the type of person for whom it is appropriate are important questions that are entered into in Chapter 6 which is concerned with the analytical process.

Both amplification and active imagination rest on a trust in the dynamic activity of the self which can be repressed just as much as aggression or sexuality can be repressed. If the analysis facilitates the removal of the repression, then initiating the process just outlined will lead to movement.

At the other end of his spectrum, Adler places a second group, the 'neo-Jungians'. This group have modified Jung's ideas by attempting to integrate psychoanalytic concepts (in America from Erikson, in England from Klein and Winnicott). This leads to a departure from Jung's forward-looking approach to interpretation, away from amplification and active imagination in analysis to favour what Adler designates as 'reductive' interpretation. It implies a far greater stress on infantile material, the repetition of infantile patterns in adult life and on the historic child in the adult. Working with infantile material in analysis and therapy virtually forces a concentration on the interaction between analyst and patient because the transference, composed in part of infantile wishes, impulses and forms of psychic mechanisms such as primitive defences, provides the only channel for this material.

Adler's third element in his spectrum is a central group that attempts to combine the two rather different approaches just mentioned and of which he regards himself a member. Adler distinguishes this 'middle group' from the neo-Jungians by asserting that, for this group, the analysis of transference is only one of several instruments available to the analyst. 'Equally, *if not more important* to him, will be the interpretation of dreams (and to a lesser degree the more specialised method of active imagination)' (1967, p. 349, emphasis added). Adler stresses that his conception of transference is far wider than that derived from psychoanalysis, because in addition to the infantile angle is added the possibility of projecting into the analyst unconscious potentials not yet lived.

FORDHAM'S CLASSIFICATION

Fordham, too, perceives that the various post-Jungian schools lay differing emphasis on differing aspects of Jung's work (1978a, p. 50). Fordham does not feel that Adler's use of transference is more than a minor concession (ibid., p. 16) and therefore his classification is at variance with Adler's. His approach is based on geography. For example, he feels that at the C.G. Jung Institute in Zürich it is Jung's later style which is being offered to the students. According to Fordham, this led Jung 'more and more away from analysis and towards studying the possibilities he could discern in the unconscious' (ibid., p. 50). I think that what excites Fordham's criticism is that the teaching in Zürich is not only based on an exaggeration of Jung's later orientation, but that it overlooks the fact that this was never intended by Jung to *replace* his earlier, often more clinical, interests.

Because Jung's own work with patients developed into something highly idiosyncratic and personal to him, very little has been written about what actually happens in 'Zürich-style' analysis. Fordham is also interested and puzzled by the practice of multiple analysis said to be in use in Zürich, meaning either a patient seeing more than one analyst at a time or a process of consecutive analyses with analysts chosen for specific reasons such as sex or psychological type. Fordham sees the Zürich style of analysis as a cultural phenomenon strengthened by the peculiar position of the Institute in Zürich at the centre of a Jungian sub-culture that is not exclusively (or even primarily) clinical. In Fordham's view, the whole emphasis of this school is laid on revealing the myth-like characteristics of the patient's material and applying to the material an already-existing model of the psyche. Thus the material ends up being assigned to one particular slot or other.

Fordham, continuing his geographical survey, comes to London, where, he says, post-Jungians pay attention to transference in a way that differs from the Zürich model so radically that Fordham is prepared to speak of a 'London School'. This roughly corresponds with Adler's 'neo-Jungians'. The London School developed partly because early members were interested in what actually transpired between patient and analyst and partly because Jung's account of maturation in infancy and childhood was felt to be inadequate. Fordham notes that a good deal of interaction with psychoanalysts took place and that 'in particular the Kleinian school, with its emphasis on unconscious phantasy and countertransference, made a fertile interchange possible' (ibid., p. 53).

Rounding off his classification, Fordham notes that similar interchanges with psychoanalysts have taken place in San Francisco and in Germany. But he feels that the use of typological theory in San Francisco is a special feature of post-Jungian work there, whilst in Germany interesting work is being done on countertransference. It should be noted that Fordham's London-Zürich differentiation is more than something conveniently contained by those two centres, and this is a weakness of his classification. It is possible to see 'London' and 'Zürich' influences in many other Jungian centres.

Fordham faced the London-Zürich conflict of his time openly and acknowledged that dogmatism and reaction formation had set in. The situation has been further complicated in London where a second group has emerged with its own organisation and training with the stated objective of 'teaching Jung's psychology in an undiluted form' (Adler, 1979, p. 117). We shall turn in a moment to a consideration of factors that are relevant to this split but I want to continue to discuss previous attempts to classify post-Jungians.

GOLDENBERG'S CLASSIFICATION

The third classification system is that of Goldenberg (1975). She felt that Jungians have not yet formed into schools, thus differing from Fordham and Adler. There is therefore no tradition of self-criticism or evaluation from within – other than interaction between individual analysts. She feels that scholars in other disciplines, such as herself, would have freer access to Jungian concepts and post-Jungian developments, and also that Jungians would be able to communicate with each other and clarify their ideas if some classification were to be made.

Goldenberg divides post-Jungians into two groupings – the second and third generations. She means generations in intellectual history and in relation to Jung as an epistemological core rather than anything to do with the actual age of the contributor. She considers a person a member of the second generation if 'he sees himself as a disciple or teacher of Jung and has tried, in one way or another, to present a coherent account' (p. 203). Goldenberg points out that the terms 'second generation' and 'coherent account' were first used by Jung himself in the foreword to Neumann's *Origins and History of Consciousness* (1954). Goldenberg has therefore also picked up the importance of these forewords in charting the evolution of the post-Jungian mind or, in certain cases, laying the mantle upon the writer.

It is clear that Jung valued attempts to organise his work and to communicate it. And certainly works by second-generation Jungians are extremely popular (perhaps even more popular than Jung's books) because, without expressing any significant disagreement with Jung, they render his ideas into simpler form or express things more clearly than he did. However, Goldenberg would see *both* Fordham and Adler as second generation. She reserves the title of third generation for the school of analysts who define themselves as 'archetypal psychologists' (see Chapter 9 for a full discussion of archetypal psychology). For Goldenberg, this is the first generation of people who do not feel any responsibility to Jung personally although they recognise his influence. I think that this last point is the salient feature of

14

this classification. The question of 'responsibility to Jung' may really be what distinguishes second from third generation post-Jungians.

COMMENT

It is clear that these classifications are mutually exclusive – for instance Goldenberg's third generation are simply not noticed in the other two classifications (though Adler might claim that archetypal psychology was not a force in the late 1960s). And Fordham disputes Adler's claim to the middle ground, while Adler seems almost ready for the neo-Jungians to depart the fold (see below, p. 21). It is a confusing and unpleasant state of affairs and one which perplexes students and current practitioners alike. I am indebted to Clark (personal communication, 1982) for an anecdote concerning a series of seminars he gave for trainee Jungian psychotherapists on the strands in modern Jungian psychology. The students felt these issues so deeply that on occasion tears attested to the anxiety that diversity and schism can cause. The positive side of the story is that the students valued the chance to undertake comparative work.

A NEW CLASSIFICATION

In formulating my own classification I have wanted above all to provide a model that will allow for individual differences whilst describing post-Jungian schools with sufficient coherence and coalescence to be of use in the twin aims summarised by Goldenberg – to provide access into post-Jungian developments for outsiders and to enable a higher degree of structuring, ordering and mutual reflection in internal debate.

My hypothesis is that there are indeed three main schools. We can call these the *Classical School*, the *Developmental School* and the *Archetypal School*. My method is to select three aspects of theoretical discussion and three of clinical practice to which all analytical psychologists relate. I hope to demonstrate that it is the *ordering and weighting* of these that underpin the evolution of the schools.

The three theoretical areas are:
(1) the definition of archetypal;
(2) the concept of self;
(3) the development of personality.
The three clinical aspects are:
(1) the analysis of transference-countertransference;
(2) emphasis upon symbolic experiences of the self;
(3) examination of highly differentiated imagery.

With regard to theory, I think the Classical School would weight the possibilities in the order 2, 1, 3. That is, the integrating and individuating self would be most important, other archetypal imagery and potentials would come close behind and the early experience of the individual would be seen as of somewhat lesser importance. (I imagine this to represent, in general terms, Jung's own ordering of priorities, hence the use of the word 'Classical'.) The

Developmental School would weight these possibilities in the order 3, 2, 1. Importance would be given to the personal development of the individual, which would then involve a consideration of the self, seen as generating its archetypal potentialities and imagery over a lifetime. The Archetypal School would consider archetypal imagery first, the self second, and development would receive less emphasis. Thus the ordering would be 1, 2, 3.

Turning to clinical practice, the Classical School would weight the possibilites 2, 3, 1 or perhaps 2, 1, 3. I am not sure whether transference-countertransference or a pursuit of particularised imagery would come second to the search for the self. The Developmental School would order its clinical priorities 1, 2, 3, or possibly 1, 3, 2. Here again, I am sure that transference-countertransference would be considered a most important aspect, but I am not certain whether experience of the self or an examination of imagery would rate second position. The Archetypal School would probably function in the order 3, 2, 1. That is, particularised imagery would be regarded as more useful than symbolic experiences of the self and both would be more central than transference-countertransference.

Of course there is overlap with the earlier classifications. My Classical School is similar to Adler's 'orthodoxy' and Fordham's 'Zürich School'. My Developmental School bears resemblance to Adler's 'neo-Jungians' and to Fordham's 'London School'. My Archetypal School is termed by Goldenberg 'third generation Jungians'.

I did not select the six themes by accident – theorists of all three schools have reinforced the emphases I have suggested. For example, Adler (Classical School), in a 'personal statement' (unpublished, 1975) wrote:

> We put the main emphasis on symbolic transformation. I would like to quote what Jung says in a letter to P.W. Martin (20/8/45): '. . . the main interest of my work is with the approach to the numinous . . . but the fact is that the numinous is the real therapy'.

As far as the Developmental School is concerned, the editorial introduction to a collection of their papers (Fordham *et al.*, 1974) states:

> the recognition of transference as such was the first subject to become a central one for clinical preoccupation. . . . Then, as anxiety about this began to diminish with the acquisition of increased skill and experience, counter-transference became a subject that could be tackled. Finally . . . the transaction involved is most suitably termed transference/countertransference. (p. x)

That introduction went on to discuss whether the term 'interpretation' has any analytic meaning if unlinked with the past development of the patient.

Hillman, speaking for the Archetypal School, asserts:

> At the most basic level of psychic reality are fantasy images. These images are the primary activity of consciousness. . . . *Images are the only reality we apprehend directly*,

and in the same paper he refers to the 'primacy of images' (1975a, p. 174).

It has been suggested to me (Lambert, personal communication, 1982) that the six elements could be constituted in a grid, similar to that drawn up in psychoanalysis by Bion (1963). This is shown in Figure 1. Bion's grid is designed to help an analyst reflect on problems that arise in analytic practice; it is a method of recording in an abstract manner what he and the patient have been doing, ranging from the most simple to the most elaborate interactions. In fact, I would not suggest that my grid is in any way comparable to Bion's monumental edifice with its forty-eight categories. But the use to which this grid may be put is similar: as part of the professional self-analysis of the analyst, an exploration of the analyst's professional inner world. Even more important, readers of this book may use the grid to orientate themselves in the various post-Jungian debates.

	Transference-countertransference	Symbolic experiences of the self	Examination of highly differentiated imagery
Definition of archetypal			
The concept of self			
The development of personality			

Figure 1

Any classification is, to an extent, a creative falsehood in that there are unlikely to be many individuals who exactly fit the descriptions. For some temperaments, classification is seen as of little value or even as destructive to individuality. Classification is itself suspect as each writer, secretly or openly, favours the group he knows best. But on the other hand, the very existence of classifications such as those of Adler, Fordham and Goldenberg is significant, not to mention catchphrases such as Plaut's 'Klein-Jungian hybrid' (1962) or Hillman's invention of the term 'archetypal psychology' (1975a, pp. 138-47).

I have not presented my classifications in an either/or way; I have made it a central feature that *all* analytical psychologists are likely to use *all* these theories and are interested in *all* these clinical areas at some time and with some patients. Taken altogether, the six headings constitute a large part of the discipline of analytical psychology as a whole – this is the common core or base derived from Jung with all subsequent additions. Following Bion (1965), we may call this the *post-Jungian vertex*, implying an overall point of view or perspective. What defines an analytical psychologist will be whether he relates actively to debates which arise from the differing emphases which may be given to the six headings. Such emphasis, weighting and preference, together with the choices made by individual analysts, constitute the schools. So a classification into schools, carried out in this way, can tell us *as much about what is held in common* as about differences of opinion.

Further, we should expect to find in the schools of analytical psychology more than a common tradition. We may discover something in common in the developments within the various schools, a common ideological and practical future. In Chapter 11 I draw together elements of such a future, but the attempt to do so is a thread running through the book.

I am sure the schools have a 'contra-ideological' component. For example, Hubback has shown how, even in the Developmental School, questions of amplification and active imagination (not usually associated with that school) have been given attention (1980). She comments that it is often a patient, or a group of patients, who provide the stimulus for interest in a particular topic; hence the need for a classificatory approach based on priorities rather than exclusivities.

I mentioned earlier that the schools of psychoanalysis have over time taken on a more formal structure than those of analytical psychology. It is reasonable to suggest that a similar process will take place in analytical psychology and that this has already begun. Thus any temptation to ignore the existence of schools or to minimise their importance is historically unsound, or may hark back nostalgically to an earlier, more unified, period.

In this context we may note what Segal (1979) has to say about the way in which the British Psychoanalytical Society came to organise its training to take account of the reality of differences between schools of psychoanalysis – the 'B Group' composed of Anna Freud and her followers, and the 'A Group' composed of both the Kleinians and what later became known separately as the 'Middle Group' of uncommitted analysts. Segal believes that, after the earlier acrimony during the 1940s, as differences were worked on, things settled down, and that the organisation of the training to take account of the groups not only gives students a firm base in their chosen path but 'also an acquaintance with divergent points of view' (ibid., p. 111).

Segal's account is also interesting for the light it sheds on the way in which the warring factions related to Freud: 'both sides of the controversy quoted Freud repeatedly, but the quotations were different. One could say, Which Freud? Whose Freud?' (ibid., p. 95). And because a key issue was whether Melanie Klein *was* a Freudian, it will not come as a surprise to analytical psychologists (who have, as may be seen throughout this book, their own version of this problem) to hear that:

> to the end of her life [Klein] felt a little bewildered and deeply hurt by Freud's coolness towards her and her work, which she saw as being close to his. Believing that she had developed it in the same ethos and further than any other

living analyst, she found it very difficult to bear that he did not see it that way. (ibid., p. 171)

Perhaps polemic is inevitable. Heraclitus tells us that *polemos*, meaning strife or conflict, is the 'father of all, the king of all'. In addition to ideological factors, the schools of analytical psychology radiate emotional reality and that may be seen as a necessity for an emerging profession.

One complicating factor is that post-Jungian groups have tended to cluster round strong leader figures. I do not think this results from *conscious* fostering, but the erection of leaders, no doubt stemming from a desire to avoid the anomalous and to have ideas arranged in a hierarchy of acceptability, has personalised some of the differences between the schools (cf. Samuels, 1981a).

What is more, the schools are bound to become more, rather than less, powerful in that the various founders are likely to select as trainees those who will be sympathetic to whatever consensus may exist in a particular school.

Returning to my own classification for a moment, a further way to avoid rigidity is to see the schools as overlapping to some extent. That not only allows for individuals who fall between schools but also demonstrates differences within schools. This is shown in Figure 2; the names are arranged alphabetically to facilitate the reader's returning to this chart as he progresses through the book, and the presence of names in the same column implies theoretical similarity rather than a public alliance (though this may exist). Of course there are numerous thinkers on whose work I am not commenting, or with which I am not familiar, or who do not write books and papers; their names cannot appear.

THE LIMITS OF ANALYTICAL PSYCHOLOGY

I have used the term *post-Jungian* in preference to *Jungian* to indicate both connectedness to Jung and distance from him. The questions that will inevitably be asked are: how broad a community should analytical psychology be? Is it possible, or even desirable, that the multiplicity of viewpoints with which we shall be engaged be given *any* common designation? How fluid can practice be with regard to a particular patient before it becomes professionally responsible to refer him to another analyst or even to another kind of practitioner?

Henderson, whom I would think of as a member of the Classical School, touches on these questions when reviewing the collections of papers which have been put out by the Developmental School. He says:

> What readers missed in these papers as they appeared . . . was the sense of adventure to which they were accustomed by the inclusion of large philosophic ideas and the amplification of archetypal images with reference to religion, alchemy and primitive myths such as are to be found in Jungian literature from the pens of such writers as Neumann, von Franz, Adler, Hillman and others.

Now . . . we can see why it was wrong to expect them to be different from what they are. They do not pretend to add much to Jung's teleological (i.e., forward-*looking*) method, with its strong reliance on the language of religious symbolism. . . . It is a part of Fordham's stated claim that Jungian analysis is not incompatible with Freudian analysis, and I think that in certain significant respects . . . this claim has been justified. (1975b, p. 203)

Henderson reminds us that it is pointless to expect something to do more than it is designed to do or to criticise something for not being what it was never intended to be. Accepting diversity means accepting limitations in ourselves and others. However, the idea that Freudian and Jungian analysis may be compatible is, for some Jungians and Freudians, quite unacceptable.

Here, as so often, extremists from both the Freudian and the Jungian camp find themselves in the same bed. In psychoanalysis, Glover attacks any notion of compromise, quoting John Morley:

At the bottom of the advocacy of a dual doctrine slumbers the idea that there is no harm in men being mistaken, or at least only so little harm as is more than compensated for by the marked tranquility in which their mistake wraps them. (Glover, 1950, p. 187)

C L A S S I C A L

DEVELOPMENTAL			ARCHETYPAL		
Carvalho	Abenheimer	Blum	Adler	Guggenbühl	Avens
Davidson	Blomeyer	Bradway	Binswanger	Shorter	Berry
Fordham	Clark	Detloff	Castillejo	R. Stein	Casey
Gordon	Dieckmann	Edinger	Fierz		Corbin
Jackson	Fiumara	Hall	Frey-Rohn		Giegerich
Kay	Goodheart	McCurdy	Groesbeck		Grinnell
Lambert	Hobson	Neumann	Hannah		Hillman
Ledermann	Hubback	Perry	Harding		Lopez-Pedraza
Lyons	Jacoby	Schwartz	Henderson		Miller
Maduro	Newton	Ulanov	Humbert		M. Stein
Plaut	Moore	Whitmont	Jacobi		
L. Stein	Redfearn	Willeford	Jaffé		
Strauss	Samuels		E. Jung		
Zinkin	Seligman		Mattoon		
	Williams		Laughlin		
			Layard		
			Meier		
			Perera		
			Singer		
			Stevens		
			von der Heydt		
			von Franz		
			Weaver		
			Wheelwright		
			Wolff		
			Woodman		

Figure 2

Glover goes on to attack eclecticism which claims to be a commonsense, objective way of going about things. He rejects any gentleman's agreement between opponents. In this he is joined by Adler who objects strongly to Fordham's statement in his obituary of Jung that Jung's personal incompatibility with Freud and the resultant separation appears a disaster from which analytical psychology and psychoanalysis both suffer and will continue to suffer until the damage is repaired. Adler feels that one must accept that we have to make a choice and live with the sacrifice involved (Adler, 1971, p. 114). Adler is speaking both of his rejection of Freudian-Jungian synthesis and of his attitude to internal Jungian diversity – his insistence upon 'undiluted' Jung as mentioned earlier.

Adler is therefore at peace with the idea that Jungian psychology might lose 'on the side of understanding physical phenomena, object relations and some actual therapeutic insights' (ibid., p. 117). The danger for post-Jungians as Adler sees it, is that, with so much diversity, they will be assimilated and so lose their original point of view. As we have just seen, it is now a matter of concern as to what *is* involved in the Jungian view.

In his book *The Art of Psychotherapy* (1979), Storr takes a different attitude to Adler's altogether. He prophesies that soon psychological schools will cease to exist as separate entities because theoretical disputes are storms in teacups which disguise the basic similarity of what analysts and therapists actually do. From an Olympian standpoint, it is possible that similarities outweigh differences, but this proposition may turn out to be more of a hoped-for programme as there are no signs that the schools of depth psychology are losing their appeal (that is, the schools still exert an attraction even though there has been a swing away from analytical approaches in general).

If Storr means that cross-fertilisation is taking place to an unprecedented degree then I am in complete agreement. I would also concur that unbridled devotion to one idea or one man can be destructive. But it is surely necessary for an analyst or therapist to work with conviction, even passion. If this is lacking then something may be lost.

Research material showing that therapists of all persuasions get similar results does not mean, and should not be taken as implying, that it does not matter what you believe. I cannot simply adopt a Gestalt technique – it would be inauthentic and ridiculous for me to do so, given my orientation and training. It follows that choice, arising out of character and conviction, will have to be exercised and we may conclude that questioning and critical acknowledgment of a tradition is a virtue; becoming acquainted with that tradition is then an obligation. However, the requirement of critical choice is not an easy one to fulfil in a complicated and conflict-ridden field.

CONFLICT AND CHOICE

Where does the reader with an interest in Jungian ideas and a desire to update that knowledge go? Popper once said that the place for any beginning seeker after knowledge to go is *where the disagreements are*. If you acknowledge that psychological theory and practice develop organically, by the way of a process, then the point where current practitioners disagree reflects the state of the art. Here you can be sure of being in the presence of the best minds and talents and the most contemporary viewpoints or syntheses of what has gone before and predictions of what might happen next (Popper, 1972).

This notion opposes the apparently more sensible and customary view that we should start with what is known and agreed, and when that has been mastered or at least understood, engage in the grown-up disagreements. Of course the arena where experienced people differ is a heady place to enter, dizzymaking, frightening, fragmentary, but basing a quest for knowledge on *conflict* rather than *consensus* has its points. I have developed these ideas at length elsewhere (Samuels, 1981 a and b), but here I would like to suggest that the main advantage of conflict-oriented rather than consensus-oriented study is that the former continually puts the reader in an *active*, problem-solving situation. He has to decide which of several views is more reliable and suits him best. He will himself be at the tip of a line of inquiry stretching back to Jung and beyond but his first task will be to look into the conflict and then to choose.

Popper says 'we do not know how or where to start an analysis of this world. There is no wisdom to tell us. Even the scientific tradition doesn't tell us. It only tells us where other people started and where they got to' (Popper, 1972, p. 129). So instead of studying the works of Freud, Jung, Klein, Neumann, in a 'sensible' order, one might start with Hillman's attack on the developmental approach (1975a, pp. 5-48) or Fordham's attack on Neumann's views on childhood (Fordham 1981) as in Chapters 3 and 5 respectively. There you have two excellent minds at work; what turns them on, energises them, is worth noticing. Such arcane conflicts are supposed to be too much for the non-specialist to bear. It does not matter if some aspects of the disputes I am chronicling are beyond the grasp of some readers; more will be understood in time and *starting at the beginning is no guarantee of comprehension*.

A pragmatic colouring can be put on most of this. William James said 'ideas become true just so far as they help us get into satisfactory relations with other parts of our experience' (James, 1911, p. xii). So, for example, the psychological theories we are discussing are not to be seen as *answers* to questions of human nature but as *instruments* to guide future action and practice. Pragmatism involves a type of democratic procedure in which a person is free to decide which of various conflicting hypotheses to accept. If his rational examination of the alternatives cannot help him make a decision then he is free simply to follow his own inclination.

One final note on the schools. Those readers whose knowledge of analytical psychology is not extensive should use the classification, grid and lists to orient themselves and find meaning in what follows. Those more *au fait* with the field may, in addition, want to entertain the idea that the schools can also be seen as separate strands existing in the mind of an analyst, sometimes competing and sometimes synthesising. To both groups of readers I would say that the book is, in some sense, in tune with Jung's own thinking when he urged that opposites have to be discriminated before they can be brought together. The schools represent such a discrimination, and the notion that the schools taken together define the discipline represents the combination, the *conjunctio* (see pp. 92–4, below).

22

2

Archetype and complex

In the 'nobody understands me' tone that was characteristic of his last five years, Jung notes in his introduction to Jacobi's *Complex/Archetype/Symbol* (1959) that 'the concept of archetype has given rise to the greatest misunderstanding and – if one may judge by the adverse criticism – must be presumed to be very difficult to understand' (p. x). However, archetypal theory provides a crucial link in the dialogues between nature and nurture, inner and outer, scientific and metaphorical, personal and collective or societal. In the chapter we look first at Jung's theory of archetypes, then at objections to the theory, parallels from psychoanalysis and other disciplines, and then post-Jungian developments. In the second part of the chapter, the focus moves from archetypes to Jung's concept of the complex. In conclusion, I suggest some alternative ways in which these ideas might be used.

ANTECEDENTS

It may be helpful to mention some of the precursors to Jung's theories. Plato talks of original Ideas from which all subsequent matter and ideas are derived. These Ideas are held to be in the minds of the Gods before the world was created; because of this, Platonic Ideas precede experience. But there is a crucial distinction: it is one facet of Jung's approach that archetypes promote basal experiences of life. However, Jung's later formulations do incorporate a transcendent element in which archetypes are in some way beyond time and space.

Kant was another influence; if knowledge depends on perception, then a notion of perception must precede the acquisition of knowledge. From this idea of an *a priori* perceptive 'form', Kant produced an *a priori* schema in which all sensory data could be organised in fundamental, innate categories. Kantian categories are not passive conceptions; they enter into the composition and constitution of whatever is presented to the senses. They are therefore part of experiencing and, in that sense, close to Jung's definition of archetypes. But Kantian categories are also located beyond time and space and lack a connection to bodily realities and everyday experience.

Jung specifically acknowledged his debt to Schopenhauer, referring to him as 'the great find' and crediting him with prime influence on his ideas of the

23

unconscious (Jarret, 1981, p. 195). Schopenhauer wrote of 'prototypes' or archetypes as 'the original forms of all things [which] alone can be said to have true being, because they always are, but never become nor pass away' (quoted in ibid., p. 201).

Jung is at pains to differentiate himself, a psychologist, from these antecedents. He is concerned lest the notion of archetypes become nothing more than a categorisation of cognition or understanding, because this will omit the vital significance of the instincts – 'disguise them under the cloak of rational motivations and transform the archetypes into rational concepts' (*CW* 8, para. 276).

DEVELOPMENT OF JUNG'S IDEAS

The first stage in the evolution of archetypal theory arose directly from Jung's self-analysis and from his work with mainly psychotic patients in the Burghölzli Hospital. He found that imagery fell into patterns, that these patterns were reminiscent of myth, legend and fairytale, and that the imaginal material did not originate in perceptions, memory or conscious experience. The images seemed to Jung to reflect universal human modes of experience and behaviour. Jung designated these *primordial images*, using this term from 1912 onwards, in spite of numerous changes and modifications in the theory. Jung also satisfied himself that no theory of migration could explain the ubiquity of certain cultural motifs, and he concluded that there is a part of the psyche held in common and he called this the collective unconscious. This is different from Freud's idea of the unconscious at that time which emphasised the repression of once-conscious material; Jung called this the personal unconscious. Freud also allowed for the possibility that some elements in the unconscious have never been conscious, a point which, if taken up, would tend toward a concept such as archetype.

To universality and collectivity must be added two further factors – depth and autonomy. The primordial images are like foundations; subsequent imagery is derived from them. And primordial images have a certain independence, can pop up in the mind without warning in dream, daydream, fantasy or artistic creation.

By 1917 Jung was speaking of the collective unconscious expressing itself in the form of *dominants*, special nodal points around which imagery clustered. Here Jung was still using Freudian metapsychology, thinking economically, and the dominant was conceived of as attracting libido or psychic energy to itself. The important thing to note in the move from primordial image to dominant is that the innate structure, whatever it is called, is regarded as more and more powerful, to the point where it becomes actor rather than acted upon. There is a shift in Jung's view of the balance of power between pre-existing structure and personal experience.

Jung was also in reaction to Freud, to psychoanalytic causality and to what remained of trauma theory, so it was therefore important to him to move away from a case history approach and to strengthen his own position in the debate concerning patient recall of childhood experiences. Briefly, Jung felt that certain primal fantasies did not arise from real experience, but were better conceived of as projected into so-called memories. Primordial images and the dominants of the collective unconscious were the sources of these later fantasies (cf. Samuels, 1982).

In 1919 Jung introduced the term *archetype*. Any consideration of the ways in which primordial imagery is transmitted over time runs foul of the Lamarckian fallacy. As applied to psychology, this suggests that fantasies are memories of specific, prehistoric experiences and that their content is inherited from previous generations. In the same way that biologists cannot accept that acquired characteristics are inherited, it is impossible for psychologists to hold that mental *imagery* or other contents can be passed on in that way. However, it is perfectly reasonable to argue that, while content is not inherited, form and pattern are; the concept of archetype meets this criterion. The archetype is seen as a purely formal, skeletal concept, which is then fleshed out with imagery, ideas, motifs and so on. The archetypal form or pattern is inherited but the content is variable, subject to environmental and historical changes.

Far from damaging the idea of the collective unconscious, the notion of archetype strengthens this because it now becomes unnecessary to seek for pictorially similar material. Archetypal themes can be detected even if contents vary greatly; the arguments over cultural transmission are bypassed.

From 1946 onwards, Jung continued to make a sharp distinction between archetype and archetypal image. He refers to the archetype *an sich* (as such), an unknowable nucleus that 'never was conscious and never will be . . . it was, and still is, only interpreted' (*CW* 9i, para. 266). Jung is definite that:

> the archetypal representations (images and ideas) mediated to us by the unconscious should not be confused with the archetype as such. They are very varied . . . and point back to one essential 'irrepresentable' basic form. The latter is characterised by certain formal elements and by certain fundamental meanings, although these can only be grasped approximately. (*CW* 8, para. 417)

The balance between the general archetypal pattern and individual experience was aptly put by Dionysius the Areopagite:

> That the seal is not entire and the same in all its impressions . . . is not due to the seal itself, . . . but the difference of the substances which share it makes the impression of the one, entire, identical archetype *to be different*. (quoted in Jacobi, 1959, p. 34, emphasis added)

We may note that, from the very beginning of archetypal theory, there is a concern for individuality and for personal experience.

The concept of the archetype *an sich* attracted Jung because psychology is assigned an equally fundamental status with biology, morphology and, perhaps, the entire physical environment. Before examining the implications of this, we will look in more detail at the various components of archetypal theory.

ARCHETYPE AS INHERITED DISPOSITION

Because we have the same brain and bodily structure, we tend to function similarly. Birth, nurturing, sexuality, death, are broadly similar experiences for all humans. Our common biology, etc. is inherited. Hence, if the archetypes are also held in common, they, too, must be inherited. Jung was never definite about the exact inheritance of archetypes, i.e. how they are transmitted, but draws parallels to such phenomena as chicks emerging from eggs, birds building nests, and other species-specific behaviour. This biological aspect of the archetype is summed up by the biologist Portmann:

> the ordering of the animal's inner life is controlled by the formative element whose operation human psychology finds in the world of the archetypes. The entire ritual of the higher animals has this archetypal imprint in the highest degree. It appears to the biologist as a marked organisation of the instinctual life. (quoted in Jacobi, 1959, p. 41)

And Jung:

> Critics have contented themselves with asserting that no such archetypes exist. Certainly they do not exist, any more than a botanical system exists in nature! But will anyone deny the existence of natural plant-families on that account? (*CW* 9i, para. 309n)

Jung's catchphrase for archetypal patterns was that they are 'biological norms of psychic activity' (ibid.).

ARCHETYPE AS BLUEPRINT

Certain fundamental experiences occur and are repeated over millions of years. Such experiences, together with their accompanying emotions and affects, form a structural psychic residue – a readiness to experience life along broad lines already laid down in the psyche. The relationship between archetype and experience is a feedback system; repeated experiences leave residual psychic structures which become archetypal structures. But these structures exert an influence on experience, tending to organise it according to the pre-existing pattern.

A simple example shows the feedback system at work. For millions of years of human evolution, human babies have been totally dependent on others, especially the mother, for survival. This is such a regular and predictable happening that eventually a contemporary human baby starts off life with as yet unconscious tendencies – *not* to see his mother as good (pleasurable) or bad (painful), but to organise his individual experience of his early vulnerability around the patterns of 'self', 'mother', 'good', 'bad'. The baby can be said to be structuring his inchoate experiences in accordance with the innate psychological schema in the same way that he 'knows' how to breathe or excrete. In terms of primordial imagery *arising* from this schema, this suggests an image of the Great Mother, nourishing and life-giving on the one hand, depriving and devouring on the other. Jung summarised:

> the collective unconscious is an image of the world that has taken aeons to form. In this image certain features, the archetypes or dominants, have crystallised out in the course of time. They are the ruling powers. (*CW* 7, para. 151)

The baby's apprehension of his experience is structured by innate archetypal forms which force him to reach out and search for corresponding elements in the environment. The interaction between these innate structures and the early environment acquires a positive or negative quality depending on how successful the correspondence is, and this plays a crucial part in the healthy or pathological development of the individual. In this context, Jung refers to the archetype as 'a system of readiness for action' (*CW* 9i, para. 199).

To summarise the foregoing, we may then note: (a) archetypal structures and patterns are the crystallisation of experiences over time. (b) They constellate experience in accordance with innate schemata and act as an imprimatur of subsequent experience. (c) Images deriving from archetypal structures involve us in a search for correspondence in the environment.

The enormous stress laid on what is held in common could seem to limit individuality by seeing it either as 'variation' – or simply part of a romantic metaphysic. However, Portmann's classification of archetypal structures demonstrates a possible balance between the innate and the unique. First, he notes structures that are totally determined by heredity such as 'release mechanisms' in animals. Next come structures in which hereditary dispositions play an open and general role determined more by individual 'imprinting' than by heredity. Finally, we can see structures which result in human familial, societal and cultural organisation (Jacobi, 1959, p. 40).

ARCHETYPE AND INSTINCT

Jung connected the archetypes and their functioning to the instincts. At first, in 1919, he saw the archetype as a psychological analogue to instinct, a 'self-portrait of the instinct . . . the instinct's perception of itself' (*CW* 8, para. 277). Archetype and instinct perform similar functions and occupy similar positions in psychology and biology respectively. Jung goes on: 'the collective unconscious consists of the sum of the instincts and *their correlates*, the archetypes' (*CW* 8, para. 338, emphasis added). We should note that here a primacy is given to instinct which seems to be regarded as more basic than the archetype or archetypal image. Later, Jung revised this to advance the proposition that, far from being 'correlates' of instinct, archetypes are just as fundamental; the division into 'psychology' and 'biology' results from a false distinction. This dispels any idea that analytical psychology is 'anti' the body. Archetypes become seen as psychosomatic entities, occupying a midway position between instinct and image. Jung wrote in 1947:

the realisation and assimilation of instinct never takes place by absorption into the instinctual sphere, but only through integration of the image which signifies and at the same time evokes the instinct. (*CW* 8, para. 414)

There is therefore an interdependence and neither instinct nor image has separate or primary existence in relation to the other. With regard to image the archetype is 'upward-looking', connected to ideas, creative inspiration and the spirit. With regard to instinct the archetype is 'downward-looking' to incorporation in biology and the drives. (The words 'upward' and 'downward' are not exactly devoid of value-judgment but are in current usage – e.g. Jacobi, 1959, p. 38.) It follows that the student of archetypes can follow the downward path and explore the worlds of ethology and biology in the hope of constructing a scientific picture of what it is to be human. Or the upward path may be followed, leading to the world of the spirit. Or a dual path can be taken which emphasises the bifurcated nature of the archetype. Jung developed all three paths but, in his later work, followed the 'upward' direction.

THE ARCHETYPES AND SELF-REGULATION

In her summary of Jung's later concepts, Frey-Rohn (1974) points out how organised fantasy material can be. Jung's ideas about individuation (see below, Chapter 4) involve the notion that this is a natural process, capable of being fostered in analysis, but somewhat similar to an instinct. As man has an instinct to survive so he is driven to become more himself, and the psyche has its own means of promoting these ends. Jung refers to the self-regulating psyche. This does not mean that perfect psychic balance or harmony is attainable or even desirable, but that whatever happens (for example, dreams or symptoms) can be seen as an *attempt* by the whole organism to achieve homeostasis. However, we do need moments of a sense of integration even if this is unattainable as a whole.

Common examples of self-regulation involve very 'masculine' men who dream of being female, or independent types who dream of being babied and cared for. Similarly, a meek and mild person may dream of the aggression which, mixed in with his gentleness, would give more of a balance to his personality.

Psychoanalysis makes use of a similar idea. A sexual perversion, for example, involves regression to infantile sexuality and infantile styles and objects of sexual functioning. A fetish object may represent part of the mother's body, and so on. The point is that the perverted activity blocks transition to genital sexuality and therefore escapes Oedipal punishment with its attendant guilt and anxiety. This would have been worse than the *conscious* feelings of guilt which attach to the perversion. As such, the perversion can be seen as holding the individual's sexual conflict in a momentary balance.

I give this example because it is important to protect the idea of the self-regulating psyche from panglossian excesses, in which everything is seen as being for the best or as part of some giant benevolent plan. Talking to some Jungians, it is often hard to see how anything bad could ever have happened, everything is given a purposive colouring and tragedy is denied. Jung's view was that:

> the archetype determines the nature of the configurational process and the course it will follow, with seeming foreknowledge, or as if it were already in possession of the goal (*CW* 8, para. 411). The conscious mind is extended *forward* by intuitions which are conditioned partly by archetypes. (*CW* 8, para. 175)

We saw earlier how the archetypal image both *represents* and *evokes* the instinct; now we can add a third function – to signify *the goal* of the instinct.

THE POWER OF THE ARCHETYPAL IMAGE

Because archetypal layers of the psyche are, in some sense, fundamental, they tend to produce images and situations which have a tremendous impact on the individual, gripping him and holding him in a grip, often, but not always, with an accompanying feeling of mystery and awe; he will be unable to remain unaffected. We can speculate that turning points in a person's life are in many cases workings out of archetypal activity. Jacobi points out that this power derives from the fact that archetypal images are not invented but 'imposed' on the mind from within; they are convincing by virtue of their immediacy:

> Only when the archetypes come into contact with the conscious mind, that is, when the light of consciousness falls on them . . . and [they] fill with individual content . . . only then can consciousness apprehend, understand, elaborate, and assimilate them. (1959, p. 66)

I would add that archetypal images need to be divested of their power and autonomy by a 'changing of names'; they must be rendered intelligible on the personal level and a polarisation between 'numinous' or awe-inspiring and commonplace avoided. If this happens, if the ego can manage such integration, then the personality is enriched. It is part of analytic skill to foster this transition.

THE PSYCHOID ARCHETYPE

Jung had linked psychology, behaviour, biology and the spirit. He was also to attempt to involve matter as well in the construction of a *unus mundus* or unitary world view. He felt himself to be concerned with an area of the psyche so buried, and yet so fundamental, that it would be an error to regard it as *derived* from man's common instinctual, neurological and morphological base. He called this area the *psychoid unconscious* in 1947 to distinguish it absolutely from all other categories of the unconscious. The psychoid unconscious is a primary ordering agency but its manifestations 'cannot be directly perceived or "represented" ' (*CW* 8, para. 436). It is here that we might hypothesise the origin of fundamental categories of perception such as pain or pleasure. Jung likened psychoid contents to 'the invisible, ultra-violet end of the spectrum . . . it does not appear, in itself, to be capable of reaching consciousness' (*CW* 8, para. 417). From this point of view, concludes Jung, the archetype is unfathomable.

Now some commentators have difficulty with that which is invisible and unfathomable, regarding such notions as unscientific (cf. Rycroft, 1982). But others have accepted Jung's overthrow of conventional epistemological categories (e.g. Bateson, 1979, Capra, 1975), and also his idea that the organism has a form of innate 'knowledge' about its survival and destiny.

To add strength to Jung's intuition, it now seems that the hypothesis in physics of 'action-at-a-distance', originally rejected by Einstein, may in fact be substantiated. This involves the supposed tendency of two very distinct sub-atomic particles to behave harmoniously, as though each 'knew' what the other was doing. If the behaviour of one particle was altered, the other would be expected instantaneously to change in exactly the same way, with no apparent force or signal linking them. Quantum theory predicted this, in contrast to Einstein, and it was reported in the *Sunday Times* science section of 20 February 1983 that experimental verification has now taken place. In that same report, David Bohm, professor of theoretical physics at London University, attempting to assess the significance of the experiment, stated:

> It may seem that everything in the universe is in a kind of total rapport, so that whatever happens is related to everything else; or it may mean that there is some kind of information that can travel faster than the speed of light; or it may mean that our concepts of space and time have to be modified in some way which we don't know or understand. Yet whichever interpretation you choose, the experiment establishes once and for all that physics as we know it is unfinished.

There are those who would say that bringing in any kind of scientific material is futile because this ignores Jung's statement that 'there is no hope that the validity of any statement about unconscious states or processes which will ever be verified scientifically' (*CW* 8, para. 417). Nevertheless, Jung's resuscitation of the *unus mundus* leads to reflections of this nature (and for more discussion of the *unus mundus* see pp. 100, 121, below).

ARCHETYPAL BIPOLARITY

Archetypes express a built-in polarity between positive and negative aspects of experience and emotions. For example, the archetypal image of the father can be divided into the helpful, supportive, strong, admired father, and then the tyrannical, dominating, castrating father (or the weak, useless father). The father image depends to a great extent on the way environmental experience blends with or, to use a more technical term, *mediates* the archetypal imagery. In ordinary development, mediation prevents too extreme a concentration at one end of the positive-negative axis and facilitates the ego's ability to tolerate ambivalence and recognise both loving and hating feelings (cf. Newton, 1965). The all-good father is, of course, an idealisation, and what appears as good to one may not be perceived as good by another.

An individual operating under the aegis of an all-good father image would not be able to handle authority or would feel hopelessly inferior to the paragon father or incestuously bonded to him. An all-tyrannical father promotes a feeling of being pressurised and taken over, whilst a weak father who is imaged as nothing but weak cannot protect a person from human and non-human enemies. If real experiences with father reinforce either extreme then the evolution of a human image of father has broken down. The individual is dominated by and hooked on to one end only of the range of archetypal possibilities; it is a cruel deprivation. (For a further discussion of the relationship between the ego and the archetypes see pp. 58-65, below.)

THE HIERARCHY OF THE ARCHETYPES

Jung organised his archetypes into single entities; thus he noticed that there is a tendency for the unconscious to personify. Attempts to present the archetypes in a plan or hierarchy have proved an irresistible attraction and there are a number of different ways this can be done.

Starting from the outside and looking in is a tradtional way to proceed. In this system, we first meet the *persona*, a term borrowed from Roman drama to indicate the social mask or face we put on to face the world. Without the persona, strong and primitive emotions and impulses would make social living difficult. Social roles such as analyst, banker, lawyer, labourer, produce their own variants of persona. This may be but skin-deep and the danger is of identifying too closely with it, of being fooled by one's own persona.

Continuing inwards, the next discrete archetype is the *shadow*, a word coined by Jung to sum up what each man fears and despises and cannot accept in himself. This is not to say that this low evaluation of what is as yet unlived is correct; it could arise from inhibition or schizoid tendencies. Very often instinctuality is experienced as being in the shadow and, in analysis, becomes more acceptable to the individual. In general, attitudes to the shadow are an interweave of judgment, acceptance and integration – hopefully in that order.

Next, we consider the contrasexual archetypes, *animus* and *anima*, said by Jung to express what is psychologically masculine in a woman and psychologically feminine in a man. We shall go much more deeply into these ideas in Chapter 7, but here I am thinking less of sexuality and more of Jung's theory that these contrasexual archetypes act as a bridge or connection between consciousness and the unconscious (see pp. 212-13, below).

The innermost archetype is the self. Chapter 4 is devoted to this topic; here I would simply note one of Jung's formulations concerning the self: that it is the most central archetype, the archetype of order which organises other archetypal experience. By referring to the 'central' archetype, Jung gives a sanction to this hierarchical form of classification.

Another widely accepted approach (e.g. Jungians quoted by Brome, 1978, pp. 276-7) is that there are four kinds of archetype. First there are the 'shallow' archetypes such as persona and shadow, then 'archetypes of the soul' (animus and anima), then 'archetypes of the spirit' (wise old man and woman), and, finally, the self.

A highly suspect variant on these two approaches is the over-literal adoption of Jung's adage that the archetypes are usually dealt with in analysis in a predictable order – persona, ego, shadow, animus/ma, self.

Another distinction is that between the archetypes of the family (child, mother, father, home) and the self-referring archetypes (self, animus/ma, shadow and persona).

Yet another, less over-concretised, approach is to select an archetypal theme and see how the various archetypes and their imagery cluster round it. An example might be the idea of rebirth or regeneration which has a different feel at different stages of life or when looked at from different perspectives – religious, psychological or otherwise.

L. Stein made a useful contribution to this when he proposed that each archetypal structure has only one 'assignment' (1967, p. 102). Stein made a distinction between these single archetypes and *aggregates* like animus, anima, shadow, which reflect combinations of assignments. He conceived of:

> a framework of planes [which] permits . . . the individual constituents to arrange themselves in pairs of opposites . . . the archetypes . . . are interrelated and this interrelatedness is teleological, i.e., serves the well-being of the individual as a whole. (ibid., pp. 102-3)

I would adapt this slightly so that we can speak of interrelated planes of *imagery*, with a teleological aspect.

CRITIQUES OF THE THEORY OF ARCHETYPES

Refinements, criticisms and objections have been made to the broad outline of the theory and it is possible to see parallels in other disciplines and other schools of psychology. Before turning to these parallels, it will be helpful to introduce a general discussion of some of the problems encountered when we meet with Jung's ideas.

In his review of Jung's *The Archetypes and the Collective Unconscious* (*CW* 9i), written in 1961, Hobson points out that there is a basic confusion between archetype as an explanatory concept similar to that of botanical families, and as a phenomenological concept directly linked to experience. Jung himself saw the difference as akin to that between reading about an illness in a textbook and a real illness one might have. There is, therefore, a distinction to be made between knowledge of the archetype and understanding of the archetype. And, perhaps, this reflects a distinction between theory and practice. Sometimes Jung sticks to the phenomenological approach, observing without external indices of evaluation; sometimes his work revolves around implications of meaning – for instance, the idea that the archetype possesses some sort of foreknowledge.

That an archetype is a formal concept with no material existence and is to be distinguished from archetypal images and representations is central but adhered to by Jung, according to Hobson, only when he discusses the concept in a *thorough* way. 'Unfortunately, however, he often uses the term loosely and carelessly to refer to archetypal forms, to motifs and even to highly elaborated fantasy images' (ibid., p. 70). I have noted a semantic example of the general inconsistency which Hobson is describing in the use of the word 'form'. Sometimes this refers to a specific image (the form the archetype has taken) and sometimes to the form of the archetype, its structure, as opposed to its content, the image.

Hobson wonders if the feeling of strangeness and awe (numinosity) is really essential for an image to be recognisable as an archetypal image. He suggests that the feeling refers more to the experience and less to something in the image. Similarly, archetypal motifs can occur without any numinous feeling. We might elaborate Hobson's point to say that the sense of awe becomes a subjective matter for a person and it follows that some will have a propensity for this type of experience.

It is central to Jung's conception that an archetypal image is quite distinct from a memory image, though the content of both will be similar, due to the ubiquity of the archetype and its effect on memory. But Jung then goes on, unwisely, in Hobson's view, to use the word archetype to refer to specific images such as 'the archetype of the snake' – unwisely because the word snake 'is a perceptual or memory image'. Hobson:

> The anatomical and behavioural properties of the snake are such as to make it an effective analogue of psychic experience involving ambivalence and transformation; and from earliest times in diverse regions, it has been regarded with awe and fascination. It is an apt image for expressing certain archetypal themes and for evoking the typical situations in which these patterns are released. There is no reason to suppose that there could be an image of a snake, of a pearl, or of a woman unless these had been perceptual images. Jung clearly denies that he assumes that there are innate images. These reflections raise the question whether it is appropriate to refer to archetypes by such names as mother, child, trickster, or even rebirth. These names imply a particular matter or content, and it might be that we shall have to evolve abstract formal methods of representation such as are used in mathematics or mathematical logic. (ibid., p. 72)

This is a stimulating criticism and I shall take up some of Hobson's points in a later discussion. Hobson suggests that there are four criteria for an archetypal image, derived from Jung's own guidelines, and almost impossible to satisfy, which must hold before an image can be said to be archetypal: the material must be specific, occur regularly in different people and also in the material of one person; the imagery must appear in different cultures and at different times; there must be a similar meaning whenever and wherever the image appears; there must be no possibility of the imagery being *acquired* through acculturalisation. This leads Hobson to wonder whether myths and fairytales are indeed as culture-free as Jung needs them to be for his theory. They are 'elaborate conscious formulae' (ibid., p. 73) with a social context. And the examples from alchemy and mysticism may, argues Hobson, simply show that groups of people with a similar type of mind occur in different ages.

We should note that Hobson does not refer to biological and ethological evidence (see pp. 36-9, below); however his paper was a book review and hence not intended to bring in new material.

For Glover (1950), the concept of the archetypes is like a Jungian red rag to a psychoanalytic bull. And yet his full-frontal attack contains several important points. He wonders why what is *old* (as the archetypes are stated to be) should be regarded as wise or venerable. The mind of prehistoric man must have been much 'younger' than that of modern man and it would have less collective unconscious to provide wisdom or knowledge. And, Glover asks, 'how can an inherited *tendency* acquire wisdom and experience? . . . Wisdom grows with the development of conceptual forms which depend in turn on word formation and the power of speech' (ibid., p. 51). Glover concludes by reminding us that 'the phylogenetically old was once ontogenetically young, and in fact crude' (ibid., p. 69).

It is unfortunate for Glover's own position that he brings in language acquisition; as we know from psycholinguistics, there is reason to see this as archetypally conditioned (see below). The archetype's relation to instinct and the drives is simply not mentioned by Glover. Nevertheless, his 'phylogeny is crude' point is interesting, as is his accusation that Jung has fallen for the myth of the Noble Savage.

A second suggestion of Glover's is that what appears as so-called archetypal material simply contains left-over parts of a child's pre-reality thinking, residues of primary process activity. Early thought processes are influenced by concrete and predominantly visual mental representations and the inevitability of frustration leads to 'a constant projection onto the world of objects of characteristics pertaining to the subject' (ibid., pp. 35-6). Glover considers it likely that such 'eternities' (ibid., p. 37) as 'experience of instinctual need and gratification, pleasure and pain' influence a baby's reactions more than archetypal activity. It is certainly true that, in primary process activity, images tend to become mixed up and can symbolise one another, while space-time realities are ignored. Hence the risk of domination by, or identification with, an archetypal image. But, once again, Glover leaves a loophole. He has stated that archetypal images result from the projection on to the object of characteristics more accurately pertaining to the subject. But this is *exactly* what does result from our archetypal predispositions in which preconceptions search for and find their content in the early environment (see discussion on archetypes and unconscious fantasy, pp. 42-4 below).

Glover then wonders about the consequences of postulating innate structures. Does he, perhaps, cast half an eye on those battles in the Institute of Psychoanalysis between classical Freudians and Kleinians; the latter group basing many of their conceptions on innate structures? Surely, he posits, innate structures in the psyche lead simply to repetitions and cannot be cumulative. It follows that there can be no progress if the innate predominates. As there has been, if not progress, evolution, then the power of the innate archetype cannot be as great as is suggested. The answer to this is that an archetype is seen as structuring a *potential* which evolves towards its goal over time. A simple analogy would be the way in which genetically inherited phenomena en.erge during maturation – such as bodily changes which occur at the appropriate point in time. It would not be argued that the gene is unimportant because of this.

The essence of what is archetypal is that it is not learnt or similarly acquired. Photographs have become available in recent years showing the foetus sucking its thumb *in utero*. This evidence suggests that theories which claim that the correlation of thumb sucking with pleasure (or the relief of anxiety) has to be *learnt* are misplaced. For the human foetus, sucking and pleasure or anxiety relief are, quite simply, always linked.

Archetypally structured predispositions would come to nothing without a sufficiently precise environmental correspondence, or fit. So applications of archetypal theory to early development require stress on *both* the active contribution of the baby, on the basis of his innate capacities and attributes, and of the mother, using her archetypally informed responsiveness. (See pp. 116-18, 154-61, below for detailed discussion of this.)

Fordham, observing some of his fellow analytical psychologists, is perturbed by tendencies to relate imagery produced by patients to historical parallels only, e.g. from alchemy, mythology or folklore. Too great a concentration on the archetypal content causes one to lose contact with the personal context. It becomes a wide-ranging but primarily intellectual and non-specific exercise:

> The Achilles heel of the historical amplificatory method is this: the patient can never have been present in the historical context. A patient who produces archetypal material with striking alchemical parallels is not practising in the alchemical laboratory, nor is he living in the religious and social setting to which alchemy was relevant. Therefore, it can become unrealistic ... if this is thought of as alchemical ... the patient becomes more divorced than before from his setting in contemporary life. (Fordham, p. 145)

Fordham points out the relevance of Jung's archetypes for a consideration of infancy. Their psychosomatic quality fits in well with the ways in which an infant experiences things through the body. Mind and body are inextricably linked and bodily functions express psychological states. Such activities as eating or excreting *are*, in a sense, projection and introjection.

In terms of the development of ideas, Fordham is prepared to see archetypal patterns at work. He sees precursors of his own theories of infancy in cosmic egg creation myths (1957, pp. 118-19).

Dry (1961) is critical of Jung in a somewhat similar way. She is unhappy about the weight given to myth, legend and fairytale. She points out that there *is* a serious academic debate concerning 'cultural diffusion or psychic unity', and charges that Jung has accepted the latter too uncritically. She quotes Rivers's objection that, as Jung's material is drawn mainly from Indo-European cultures, 'the possibility cannot be excluded that the common tradition reaches the individual in infancy, childhood and youth through the intermediation of parents, nurses, schoolfellows, the overhearing of chance conversations, and many other sources' (ibid., p. 119).

Dry is unimpressed by any connection between the fantasies of children and babies and archetypal motifs. For example, considering a fantasy of attacking the mother and tearing out her insides, she wonders if there is any point in 'invoking' the collective unconscious in the shape of hero myths. She prefers to suggest that the myth is a secondary elaboration of the primary infantile experience. She is therefore not at all in agreement with the idea of an archetype as a blueprint for experience.

There is no doubt that a switch of emphasis has taken place in the Developmental School (and to some extent in the Classical School), so that myth, legend and so on, whilst still studied and regarded as important, have been replaced by a wider personal, social and familial investigation as a basis for archetypal theory. So some of these objections have been integrated, as we shall see in our concluding discussion. Bearing this in mind, we will now examine the parallels from outside analytical psychology that I mentioned earlier.

ARCHETYPES AND ETHOLOGY

There have been numerous attempts to link Jung's archetypal theory to ethology – the science of the study of natural animal behaviour. Archetypal theory would become more acceptable outside analytical psychology if an alliance could be forged with ethology, with its stress on innate characteristics and patterns of adaptation; and it is possible that analytical psychology may have something to offer to ethology. Jung himself drew parallels between archetypes and animal behaviour, suggesting that all natural life has its 'archetypes':

> Let us take as an example the incredibly refined instinct of propagation of the yucca moth. The flowers of the yucca plant open for one night only. The moth takes the pollen from one of the flowers and kneads it into a little pellet. Then it visits a second flower, cuts open the pistil, lays its eggs between the ovules and then stuffs the pellet into the funnel-shaped opening of the pistil. Only once in its life does it carry out this operation . . . the yucca moth must carry within it an image, as it were, of the situation that 'triggers off' its instinct. This image enables it to 'recognise' the yucca flower and its structure. (*CW* 8, paras 268, 277)

The first analytical psychologist who specifically mentions modern ethology seems to have been Fordham. In a paper 'Biological theory and the concept of archetypes' (written in 1949 but published in 1957), Fordham considered that Tinbergen's demonstration of innate release mechanisms (IRMs) in animals may be applicable to humans, especially in infancy. The stimuli which produce instinctive behaviour are selected from a wide field by an innate perceptual system and the behaviour is 'released'. In the same paper, Fordham drew a parallel between some of Lorenz's ethological observations

36

on the hierarchical behaviour of wolves and the functioning of archetypes in infancy.

Jacobi (1959) mentioned Lorenz and his 'innate schemata' in connection with archetypes and also drew a parallel with Uexküll's notion of *Umwelt* – the subjectively perceived environment inhabited by an organism. Von Franz noted that Lorenz agreed in principle with the theory of archetypes, though not with much of the psychological application in detail (von Franz, 1975).

Storr (1973) related IRMs to the innate predispositions with which an infant is born, enabling it to respond to basic stimuli such as parents, the opposite sex, death and so on. Storr quoted Jung as coming close to this when he comments that the whole nature of man *presupposes* woman and his system is tuned into her from the beginning (ibid., p. 49). And presumably the same could be said in reverse.

Stevens (1982) suggests that ethology and analytical psychology are both disciplines trying to comprehend phenomena which occur universally. Ethology shows us that each species is equipped with unique behavioural capacities that are adapted to its environment and 'even allowing for our greater adaptive flexibility, we are no exception. Archetypes are the neuropsychic centres responsible for co-ordinating the behavioural and psychic repertoires of our species' (ibid., p. 17). Following Bowlby (1969), Stevens points out that genetically programmed behaviour is taking place in the psychological relationship between mother and newborn. The baby's helplessness, its immense repertoire of sign stimuli and approach behaviour, triggers a maternal response. And the smell, sound and shape of mother triggers, for instance, a feeding response. To paraphrase Stevens, no learning theorist has taught the baby to suck or the mother to coo; instead the already existing and archetypal system which operates in mothers and babies incorporates the precise instruction: 'Grope for the nipple and when you find it, suck'.

Stevens is aware of the limits of ethology. Not much can be said about experience, sense or meaning. Jung, Stevens reminds us, was essentially interested in those issues and it is to Jung we owe the 'extraordinary insight that we can ourselves perceive our own phylogeny as a personal revelation' (1982, p. 76).

ARCHETYPES AND BIOLOGY

The work I have been describing on ethology is essentially an exercise in parallelism which leaves aside perhaps the hardest question of all for those with a scientific bent. If archetypal structures are inherited, how exactly does this happen and in what part of the human organism are they to be found? Answers to this have been proposed from biology and neurology; we will take biology first. Jung made a number of suggestions concerning the connection of archetypes to genes, particularly in the case of the contrasexual archetypes, animus and anima, which he felt probably do have genetic origins. Later, Fordham made a connection between archetypes and genes, arguing that 'it is only what is contained in a fertilised ovum that is inherited' and concluding that 'when it is said that archetypes are hereditary functions what is meant is that they must somehow be represented in the germ cells' (1957, p. 11).

Stevens is more precise than this, suggesting that it is in DNA itself that we should look for the location and transmission of archetypes. As they are co-terminous with natural life they should be expected wherever life is found. DNA brings a degree of regularity, pattern and order into the natural world. DNA is, says Stevens, 'the replicable archetype of the species' (1982, p. 73).

Stevens's suggestion that DNA may involve archetypes was anticipated by L. Stein in his paper 'Introducing not-self' (1967). In this paper, Stein makes the most precise biological suggestion so far. He begins by asking what an organism must do to survive danger. The answer, in its simplest form, is to recognise what is not itself. This is true in illness as the body fights to throw off an infection or when a person identifies an enemy or, more positively, in a baby's recognition of external caring figures with whom to relate. So, for survival, a pre-existent perceptual pattern, capable of recognising what is not-self must be stirred into action. The organism may take preventive, protective, adaptive action, or no action. This stirring into action is affected by a message in the DNA, carried by a messenger. Stein points out that all the various terms used to delineate the messengers – 'templates, genes, enzymes, hormones, catalysts, pheromones, social hormones' – are concepts similar to archetypes. He mentions archetypal figures who represent messengers such as Hermes, Prometheus or Christ.

Continuing to base his arguments on a consideration of biological defence systems, Stein lists the characteristics of a somatic defence system. It must operate in a whole range of specific circumstances, its agents must be able to go everywhere, the distribution of the agents must not upset the somatic *status quo*, and, in predisposed persons, the agents will attack the self. Stein's proposal is that

> neither the nervous nor the endocrine systems seem to be able to fulfil all these functions. This leads to the assumptions that the biological analogen to the self would appear to be the vast realm of lymphoid stem cells and/or the undifferentiated mesenchyme cells of the reticulo-endothelial systems. (ibid., p. 104)

ARCHETYPES AND NEUROLOGY

Other attempts to discuss the somatic base of archetypes and the method of their transmission come from the field of neurology and studies of brain structure. Rossi (1977) suggests that the now well-established division in function and characteristic between left and right cerebral hemispheres may enable us to locate the archetypes in the right cerebral hemisphere. He cites research indicating that left hemispherical functioning is primarily verbal and associational, and that of the right primarily visuospatial and apperceptive. Thus the left hemisphere is equipped as a critical, analytical, information processor while the right hemisphere operates in a 'gestalt' mode. This means that the right hemisphere is better at getting a picture of a whole from a fragment, is better at working with confused material, is more irrational than the left, and more closely connected to bodily processes.

For all these reasons, Rossi feels that

> the archetype and the related concepts of symbol and collective unconscious may be closely associated with the imagery, gestalt and visuospatial patterns characteristic of right hemispheric functioning. Once expressed in the form of words, concepts and language of the ego's left hemispheric realm, however, they become only representations that 'take their colour from the individual consciousness in which they happen to appear' (Jung). Inner figures such as shadow, anima and animus would be archetypal processes having sources in the right hemisphere. (ibid., p. 43)

In the next chapter we shall look at Rossi's thesis concerning interaction between the cerebral hemispheres; now our concern is with the archetypes and their possible location.

Rossi's formulation has been extended by the neurophysiologist Henry (1977) who felt that it would be less useful to consider cerebral lateralisation, as Rossi did, than Maclean's work on the tripartite brain. Briefly, Maclean conceived the brain as having three phylogenetically differing systems: a sociocultural brain located in the neocortex, the limbic system which deals with instinctually determined patterns and with emotion, and, finally, a 'reptilian' brain located in the hypothalamus and the brain stem, the area responsible for the basic drives. That reptilian brain is an older part of the brain and may contain not only drives but archetypal structures as well. The suggestion is that there was a time when emotional behaviour and cognition were less developed and the older brain predominated. There is an obvious and striking parallel with Jung's idea of the archetypes 'crystallising out' over time. Henry feels that the limbic system and the brain stem taken together may 'be' the site of the collective unconscious.

ARCHETYPAL THEORY AND STRUCTURALISM

Moving on from the hard sciences, we can find a number of parallels between the theory of archetypes and structuralist approaches in psycholinguistics, cognitive psychology and anthropology.

In his work in psycholinguistics, Chomsky describes an unvarying pattern of language acquisition in children. He refers to 'universals' and a distinction is drawn between 'formal' and 'substantive' universals similar to that between archetype as such (structure) and archetypal image.

Similarly, Piaget writes of 'schemata' which are innate and underpin perceptuo-motor activity and the acquisition of knowledge, and are able to draw the perceived environment into their orbit. They resemble archetypes by virtue of their innateness, their activity and their need for environmental correspondence.

Finally, from the field of anthropology, Lévi-Strauss, like Jung, set out to discover the nature of collective phenomena. In his approach to the structure and meaning of myth, Lévi-Strauss concluded that present phenomena are transformations of earlier structures or infrastructures: 'the structure of primitive thoughts is present in our minds' (Leach, 1974, p. 16).

It should be clear by now that such theories as Lévi-Strauss's conception of the unconscious as a 'universe of rules', empty of content, are similar to those of Jung. Indeed, at times Lévi-Strauss sounds remarkably like Jung, especially in his reflections on kinship and incest. But the confusion between archetypal structure and archetypal content tends to persist (e.g. Wilden, 1980, p. 242 and Greenstadt, 1982, p. 486). Greenstadt, a psychoanalyst, claims that 'the archetype is formulated fundamentally as a content rather than as a potentially functional structure'; I hope to have corrected this view.

PARALLELS WITH PSYCHOANALYSIS: LACAN

That the three thinkers whose work I have been summarising (Chomsky, Piaget, Lévi-Strauss) are structuralists implies that they all feel that how we perceive the world is conditioned by how we perceive, what we are biologically capable of perceiving, and by an innate tendency to classify sensory data in accordance with pre-existing classificatory structures. The most openly structuralist *clinical* practitioner is Lacan.

Lacan went beyond the proposition that the unconscious is a structure that lies beneath the conscious world; the unconscious itself is structured, like a language. This alone would suggest parallels with Jung, and Lacan is said to have tried to meet him. Lacan divides the phenomena with which psychoanalysis deals into three 'orders': (1) the Symbolic, which structures the unconscious by a fundamental and universal set of laws; (2) the Imaginary, which approximates to psychological reality, inner world processes (such as fantasy, projection, introjection), attitudes and images derived from, but not the equivalent of, external life. This is considered by Lacan to be our means of coping with the pain of separation (or rupture, as he calls it) – the rupture of birth, of weaning, of growing up; (3) the Real, corresponding not only to external reality but also to what might be called the mystery of reality (to which we will return in a moment).

A case can be made for regarding Lacan's theory as compatible with that of Jung. Lacan's Symbolic and Imaginary orders may be aligned with Jung's archetypal theory (collective unconscious) and personal unconscious respectively. The Symbolic order patterns the contents of the Imaginary in the same way that archetypal structures predispose humans towards certain sorts of experience. If we take the example of parents, archetypal structures and the Symbolic order predispose our recognition of, and relation to them. Images of parents in the personal unconscious are indirectly connected to actual parents, being coloured by the archetypal structure or the Symbolic order. The resultant images of parents are both subjective, in the sense of personal, and objective, i.e. phylogenetic.

But what of the actual parents? Here Lacan refers to the Real order. But he does so in a highly suggestive way. The Real is an 'incommensurable dimension' (Lemaire, 1977, p. 41) which 'no one has been able to attain since

40

humanity began to express itself' (ibid., p. 115). 'One notices that something arranged in a certain manner operates in a more satisfactory way, has a positive result, but still leaves out what one does not understand: the Real' (Lacan interviewed by Lemaire, 1977, p. 116). We do not know the Real because it is pre-verbal, pre-representational and suffers from 'primal repression'. Lacan's concept of the Real therefore approaches Jung's elaboration of the psychoid unconscious, which may be seen as *true* (or even Truth) but cannot be directly known.

Though Lacan tries to keep his three orders apart, they are perhaps better expressed in a circular form in that the Symbolic pervades the Imaginary, the Imaginary makes use of the Real and, as we just saw, the Real plays back into Symbolic laws. In the language of analytical psychology, we are talking here of complexes.

Although the language is quite different, Jung would probably have agreed with Lacan that the unconscious is organised in an intricate network governed by association, above all 'metaphoric associations' (ibid., p. 7). The existence of the network is shown by analysis of the unconscious products: dreams, symptoms, and so on.

PARALLELS WITH PSYCHOANALYSIS: BION

Another psychoanalyst whose work overlaps with analytical psychology is Bion (1963). As we shall see, his concept of 'O' is similar to some aspects of Jung's approach to the self (pp. 130-1, below). What interests me here is Bion's theory of thinking. According to Bion, thoughts precede a thinking capacity. Thoughts in a small infant are indistinguishable from sensory data or unorganised emotion. Bion uses the term proto-thoughts for these early phenomena. Because of their connection to sensory data, proto-thoughts are concrete and self-contained (thoughts-in-themselves), not yet capable of symbolic representations or object relations. That is, they are not yet transformed into specific visual or any other sort of imagery. These *thoughts that precede a thinker* cannot fail to influence what the thinker will think as he develops. The thoughts then function as *preconceptions* – predisposing psychosomatic entities similar to archetypes. Support for this connection comes from the Kleinian analyst Money-Kyrle's observation (1968) that Bion's notion of preconceptions is the direct descendant of Plato's Ideas. Money-Kyrle's understanding of Plato is that any particular object or phenomenon is to be seen as an imperfect copy of an Idea, or general object, in heaven. Money-Kyrle goes further and writes:

> if, by heaven, we mean our own phylogenetic inheritance, it seems to me that Plato was here very near the mark. . . . Our 'phylogenetic inheritance', then, contains . . . an immense amount of potential information . . . which probably comes into being in stages mainly during the first few weeks or months of post-natal life (not counting what develops before). (Money-Kyrle, 1971, p. 443)

At one point Money-Kyrle states that 'Jung's "archetypes" are probably much the same as innate preconceptions in theory.' Although he adds that 'there may be many differences in practice', we shall see in Chapter 6 (on the analytical process) how this is less the case now than previously (Money-Kyrle, 1977, p. 460).

These remarks on Bion leave for later consideration, in Chapter 5, the ways in which the container-contained relationship of mother and infant aids the transformation of proto-thoughts into thoughts proper, and into concepts.

PARALLELS WITH PSYCHOANALYSIS: ARCHETYPES AND
UNCONSCIOUS FANTASY

Jung and Freud revolved their argument over how literally analytical material concerning parental intercourse should be taken around the question of whether an adult could produce what might look like actual memories but which were, in fact, subsequent fantasies. In spite of his insistence on the facts, Freud wanted to know where any later fantasies might come from. In the *Introductory Lectures on Psychoanalysis* (1916-17), Freud wrote:

> There can be no doubt that the sources [of the fantasies] lie in the instincts; but it still has to be explained why the same fantasies with the same content are created on every occasion. I am prepared with an answer that I know will seem daring to you. I believe that . . . primal fantasies, and no doubt a few others as well, are a phylogenetic endowment. In them the individual reaches beyond his own experience into primaeval experience at points where his own experience has been too rudimentary. . . . I have repeatedly been led to suggest that the psychology of the neurosis may have more stored up in it of the antiquities of human development than any other source. (p. 418)

Elsewhere, Freud suggests the existence of *pre-subjective schemas* which might even be strong enough to predominate over the experience of the individual: 'Wherever experiences fail to fit in with the hereditary schema they become remodelled in the imagination' (Freud, 1918, p. 119). We may not agree with Freud's Lamarckian overtones; that is, his suggestion that primal fantasies are a residue of specific memories of prehistoric experiences – but there is little problem for a Jungian analytical psychologist with the concept of pre-subjective schemas.

As a further example of this covert consensus, in *The Language of Psychoanalysis* (1980), Laplanche and Pontalis point out that all the so-called primal fantasies relate to the origins and that 'like collective myths they claim to provide a representation of and a "solution" to whatever constitutes an enigma for the child' (p. 332).

It is Klein's notion of unconscious fantasy, however, that is the psychoanalytic idea most closely aligned with archetypal theory. Although this connection has been accepted by most commentators, some writers have chosen to compare archetypes with internal objects instead (e.g. Dry, 1961, p. 303; Storr, 1973, p. 48). Whilst internal objects must have an archetypal component, they also derive from the external world and hence they are not *structures*, nor do they have the predisposing power of the archetype or innate pattern. I disagree with Storr when, discussing 'highly irrational images', he comments: 'calling these archetypes or internal objects hardly seems to matter' (ibid., p. 44).

First, there is a confusion between archetype and archetypal image. Then it is questionable whether the issue is so irrelevant. Where personal 'facts' come from, the whole status of case histories, and the contemporary struggle in psychoanalysis and analytical psychology between those who favour the empirical and those the empathic modes of apprehending infantile experience – all these issues, vital for beginner and experienced analyst alike, revolve around the issue of the relationship of archetypes to the early environment. Storr polarises what is truly a spectrum when he states that Kleinian analysts 'would derive . . . images for the most part from the infant's actual experiences whereas Jung would have derived them more from inborn predisposition' (ibid., p. 44). In fact, both Kleinians and the Developmental School of post-Jungians postulate an interaction.

We obviously have to look more closely at what the Kleinians mean by 'unconscious fantasy'. In her paper 'The nature and function of phantasy' (1952), the Kleinian analyst Isaacs explains that the spelling 'ph' is used instead of 'f' to distinguish the psychoanalytic usage from the sense of daydream – that is, a fantasy which is known to consciousness. Isaacs feels that it is a further mistake to see fantasy in contradistinction to 'reality' because this devalues the importance of the internal world and omits any consideration of the way so-called reality is built up in the mind. A further point is that unconscious fantasy is normal not neurotic.

The notion of unconscious fantasy derives from an idea of Freud's. The id is in contact with the body and therefore comes closely in touch with instinctual needs, takes them over, and gives them 'mental expression'. Unconscious fantasy is this mental expression of instinct (cf. Jung's 'self-portrait of the instinct'). And, says Isaacs, 'there is no impulse, no instinctive urge or response which is not experienced as unconscious phantasy' (ibid., p.83). This must therefore include sexual *and* destructive impulses (cf. Jung's bipolarity).

Fantasy is seen as the operative link between ego mechanisms and instincts. The instinct is, according to Isaacs, itself a psychosomatic process directed to concrete external objects and, as we have seen, is portrayed in the mind by unconscious fantasy. The image of what would fulfil our instinctual needs not only makes our interpretation of experience subjective, but is also necessary to realise our needs in reality. Similarly, Jung wrote of unconscious fantasies as 'fantasies which "want" to become conscious' and which manifest in the form of images; he also refers to unconscious fantasy as 'creative' (*CW* 9i, paras. 101, 153). The unconscious fantasy derived from instinct *searches* for external objects with which, in Bion's word, to 'mate' (1963).

It is not my purpose in this mainly theoretical chapter to consider the ways these ideas inform our understanding of the whole developmental process, as Chapter 5 is devoted to this. But I do want to play some of these theories back into analytical psychology to show how they have been digested. Lambert (1981a, p. 95), for instance, uses the phrase 'internal *archetypal* object' (emphasis added) to signify the meeting and lodging in the infant's psyche of all these elements: archetypal predisposition (unconscious fantasy), corresponding external objects, incorporation of external objects, 'mating', development of internal archetypal object. This may then be projected at a later point in time on to the external world or on to parts of the infant's own body or to other parts of the infant's inner space. Lambert gives as an example thumb-sucking, which can be seen as a projection of the internal archetypal object (the image of a feeding breast) on to a part of the infant's own body.

Though the external object provides the experiences which are necessary for the construction of an internal archetypal object, the internal archetypal object then paves the way back to a relation to the external world through reprojection and a subsequent exploration (cf. Heimann, 1952, pp. 142-8).

A further, empirical, psychoanalytic parallel to archetypal theory is to be found in Spitz's studies of the first year of life. Spitz found that minimal stimuli produced predictable behaviour in very small infants. This led him to conclude that the internal life of the infant was structured by 'innate organisers' (1965). The production of smiles or fixed stares, stimulated by masks and dummies, has been cited by numerous Jungians as evidence for archetypes (Jacobi, 1959; Fordham, 1969a).

ARCHETYPE: A POWER WORD?

This array of parallels to archetypal theory has an unforeseen consequence. If so many other thinkers and researchers inside and outside psychology have come to broadly similar conclusions, then do we need Jung's theory at all? Does it add anything? For instance, Brome's idea about archetypes is that

> many constituents of the gene pool retain over billions of years part of their old instinctual coding, which gives rise to instinctual drives and primordial reaction formations. The pool of such conflicting reaction formations has acquired the lofty label Collective Unconscious. Thus, it is possible to reduce the Collective Unconscious to what were once called primary processes and thereby strip it of many pretensions. But no self-respecting Jungian would do that. (1978, pp. 284-5)

Some of Brome's objections have been answered in the section concerning Glover. I can agree with the de-mystification that Brome proposed up to a point – and I think that post-Jungians have tended to look at archetypes in a much more *functional* way as structuring our images of, or as metaphors for, typical patterns of emotional behaviour. But, for those who come into contact with archetypal imagery, one element stands out. The individual really is gripped by archetypal experience and imagery; his conscious life experiences and attitudes may count for nothing as they are swept away by pre-subjective schemas.

Jung once said that 'the archetypes are, so to speak, like many little appetites in us, and if with the passing of time, they get nothing to eat, they start rumbling and upset everything' (1978, p. 358). A patient of mine dreamt

44

that she was being cut open and experimented on by scientists. This reflected what she felt about me and the analysis. But the image also derived from her hypercritical father and her own unconscious identification with her mother, who had seemed to be despised and maltreated by her father. No matter what happened in the analysis or in her life, she could not give up the subjective position of victim within a villain-victim structure. In fact, her self-presentation was aggressive and rather domineering. Her sado-masochistic inner dream was 'archetypal' in the sense that it effectively coloured her early and subsequent relationships and, try as she might to break free, her life organised itself around patterns of criticism and rejection.

The problem is that developments in analytical psychology that ignore or go beyond what Rycroft refers to as 'highfalutin', portentous language' do not have wide or popular currency. Rycroft can agree with the proposition that there are 'patterns of mentation', but analytical psychology as a whole loses his sympathy thereafter (1982). From within analytical psychology, Plaut (1982) objects, not so much to the tone of the language, but to the possibility of its redundancy, preferring, on the whole, object relations terminology and other psychoanalytic usage. He asks: 'are we not using "archetypal" as a power word, i.e. in order to lend emphasis to observations which we wish to highlight?' (p. 288). One can hardly dispute that 'archetype' has become a word shrouded in associations, value-judgments and auras; these are therefore reasonable questions.

My own feeling is that it is worth retaining these words. First, because Jung's development of these ideas precedes most of the parallels. Second, because archetypal theory and its language is well-suited both to cultural analysis and to be the clinical variant of structuralism. Third, for a paradoxical reason: one problem with the innate, with structures, is, as we have seen, that the personal element is brought in, not as a factor of equal weight, but rather as a by-product or concomitant. *Archetype theory is useful because of the space and importance it accords the personal dimension.* I refer to the ease with which personal and structural elements may be seen to be blended or delineated. We now look at some post-Jungian attempts to work on the blend or on the delineation.

THE INDIVISIBILITY OF THE PERSONAL AND COLLECTIVE UNCONSCIOUS

This is the title of a seminal paper by Williams (1963a). She questions the validity of the division into collective and personal unconscious. This division she sees as starting with the Freud-Jung split. Jung 'ceded the personal unconscious to Freud' (p. 78) and the collective unconscious and the archetypes became his province.

The split produced a curious situation, which has changed enormously in recent years. The stereotypical Freudian analysand was under 35 and the work concentrated on sexual and social development. The stereotypical Jungian analysand was in the second half of life and, it was assumed, would be more concerned with individuation and with archetypal imagery. Of course, Jung was not unaware that psychotics can produce fine archetypal imagery, and that a weak ego will succumb to its impact; that is, be unable to live a personal life at all, battered between archetypal polarities.

Williams offers two formulations which are designed to produce an integrated personal-collective model of the unconscious. Her first idea is:

> Nothing in the personal unconscious needs to be repressed unless the ego feels threatened by its archetypal power. (ibid., p. 79)

She means that the ego cannot assimilate a purely archetypal content and that unconscious fantasy images need humanising and personalising before they can be integrated; otherwise they will be repressed.

Her second proposition is that:

> The archetypal activity which forms the individual's myth is dependent on material supplied by the personal unconscious. (ibid., p. 79)

She quotes Jung as saying that it is vital to know the personal factor and that that is one reason why he analysed his own personal myth – he could make allowances for his own personal factor when treating patients. And, as we saw in Chapter 1, Jung's insistence that the prospective analyst be analysed dated from before 1912 and hence was present in Jung's attitude to his professional work almost from the start.

IN DEFENCE OF THE IMPERSONAL

It would be a mistake to leave the impression of a commonsense balance between the personal and collective factors. If a personal factor always exists *and can be known* by analysis or any other way, then it follows that the impersonal or archetypal factor can also be apperceived, by a process of subtraction, if nothing else. The distinction between the personal and the collective is still maintained in analytical psychology by spatial formulations, such as Adler's, in which the personal unconscious and the conscious psyche '*rests* on the broad basis of an inherited, universal psychic disposition' (1979, p. 15, emphasis added). Similarly, Jacobi's designation of the collective unconscious is as 'objective' in contrast to consciousness which 'always adopts a personal choice and attitude'. She continues: 'out of the collective unconscious, through the archetypes, speaks the *unfalsified* voice of nature, beyond the judgment of the conscious mind and uninfluenced by the environment' (1959, p. 60, emphasis added).

Although also concerned to underscore the impersonal dimension, Hillman's position is somewhat different. He regards the archetype as the central feature of analytical psychology, arguing in fact that 'archetypal' is the right word to characterise Jung's approach. The archetype is 'the most ontologically fundamental' of Jung's concepts (1975a, p. 142). At one and the same time it is precise (in the image) and, by definition, unknowable and open (in the structure).

Archetypes transcend the individual psyche – they are not just a part of it.

An awareness of the archetypal cannot be acquired simply through focusing upon persons or cases. This eye needs training in addition in biography, the arts, ideas, culture. Hillman is concerned by 'the awesome esteem' we show for the personal psyche (ibid., p. 143). In times past, psychological problems were not dealt with through personal relationships or humanising, but rather the reverse; a connection was sought to 'impersonal dominants' – Gods, spirits, ancestors.

Hillman allows for the personal dimension 'of course' (ibid., p. 179) and regards the interaction between collective and personal as a theme that runs through Jung's work (ibid., p. 161). But:

> on the plain naive level of experience, there is an opposition between individual and collective: I can't be myself when doing crowd things, and the crowd can't function with a unified purpose if it must take into account each individual's styles and needs. The philosophical antimony between individual and universal is itself an archetypal situation. (ibid., p. 179)

This implies that the two can be differentiated. Before Hillman is dismissed as unrooted because of his insistence on this differentiation, I would say that he is actually engaged on a similar search as all the scientists that we discussed earlier. Like them, he is searching for something that can give a quite different perspective on what is personal. Hillman's quest involves examining myths which 'describe the behaviour of the archetypes; they are dramatic descriptions in personified language of psychic processes' (ibid., p. 180, and see Chapter 9 which is devoted to archetypal psychology).

So at the same time that one group of post-Jungians abandons myth in favour of family and body, another group enlarges its mythological interpretive skills. Is this an example of the self-regulation of analytical psychology? It certainly seems that there is a compensatory process at work.

THE AUTONOMOUS PSYCHIC COMPLEX

The concept of a complex was Jung's way of linking the personal and the collective. Outer experiences in infancy and throughout life cluster round an archetypal core. Events in childhood, and particularly internal conflicts, provide this personal aspect. A complex is not just the clothing for one particular archetype (that would, more accurately, be an archetypal image) but an agglomerate of the actions of several archetypal patterns, imbued with personal experience and affect. According to Jung, emotion is organised by 'feeling-toned groups of representations' (*CW* 2, paras 329, 352) which can also affect memory so that 'the entire mass of memories has a definite feeling tone' (*CW* 3, para. 80). A complex is, therefore, not a simple entity; the 'mother complex' contains emotions derived from the interaction of the ego position with numerous archetypal configurations: the individual, the mother, the individual and mother, mother and father, individual and father, individual and sibling, individual and sibling and mother, individual and family, etc., etc.

To avoid the ramifications of such an endless list we need a concept like complex.

Jung reached these broad conclusions between 1904 and 1911 through his Word Association Test (*CW* 2). He analysed responses given by subjects to certain stimulus words in terms of speed of response, hesitation, no response, repetition, and so on. If the list of words were administered again, discrepancies were noted. Tension and anxiety around the key words (complex indicators) gave a profile of an individual's problems. The results were impressive, and of considerable value to Freud as an empirical validation of his theory of repression in the aetiology of neurosis. The test is no longer used clinically, nor is the psychogalvanometer which was introduced later to measure physiological changes, such as skin conductivity. The test has fallen out of use largely because when the clinician has the basic concept of the complex to work with, he can ascertain what the matter is by ordinary therapeutic interaction.

COMPLEX AND EMOTION

A complex results from the blend of archetypal core and human experience and we feel according to our complexes. Sometimes we experience the content of the complex only in projection. Regarded dynamically, the complex may be in conflict with what we consider reality to be or with what we see as ideal – so that psychic activity is interfered with. As Jacobi (1959, p. 15) puts it, such conflict with the conscious ego 'places the individual between two truths, two conflicting streams of will, and threatens to tear him in two.' Structurally, the complex can be studied in relation to the ego. There may be conflict ('two truths') or the ego may repress the complex or, conversely, be overwhelmed by it. The complex can become completely dissociated from the personality, as in psychotic breakdown.

Each complex is in relationship with the other complexes and the ego (see the next chapter). In marital problems, for example, the complex surrounding the member of the opposite sex and that around rejected parts of the personality often relate closely to each other so that elements in oneself that cause anxiety and tension are projected on to one's partner. A further subtlety is that parts of the psyche of a parent may have an impact on the individual; for instance, the driving, ambitious son who is doing it all for his mother (or, rather, for his mother's frustrated animus). There is also the teenage daughter, into whom the father has projected his own sexual conflicts, regarding her as loose and unreliable; so, consequently, he sets unrealistic boundaries to her behaviour.

A further problem lies in distinguishing between unconscious identification with a complex on the one hand and, on the other, feeling overwhelmed by it. Looked at from the standpoint of identification, the mother complex might involve the individual's behaving like the critical or possessive mother he felt he had. From the point of view of being overwhelmed, the person would always feel 'got at' and criticised by others and might be only too willing to offer a hook for such criticisms to hang on by behaving provocatively. Finally, it is possible that the experience of identification with, and that of being overwhelmed by the complex can co-exist.

COMPLEX AND GROWTH

It is important not to see 'complex' as a purely pathological manifestation, though neurotics demonstrate complex theory with clarity. And negative emotions *per se* are not necessarily pathological, while positive emotions can be misleading or self-deceiving. Since the archetypes contain all conceivable potentialities which may be released provided there is an empathic and responsive environment, we should not speak of the small boy as growing into the role of father or leader or wise man; rather he realises or incarnates a potential. As the complex is initially divorced from consciousness, the personality of the boy is enriched by potentials like these becoming conscious and integrated, or impoverished by continued repression.

COMPLEXES AS INDEPENDENT BEINGS

The notion of a complex rests on a refutation of monolithic ideas of 'personality'. We have many selves, deriving from the combination of innate predisposition with experience. However, it is a considerable step to regarding a complex as an autonomous entity, just like a person. In fact, Jung himself wondered whether his theory of complexes might seem to be 'a description of primitive demonology' (*CW* 8, para. 712). Actually, he says, that is quite correct, for when people of ancient and medieval times spoke of possession by a demon, or of loss of soul, they were referring to possession by, or repression of, a complex.

Fundamentally, writes Jung, 'there is no difference in principle between a fragmentary personality and a complex . . . complexes are splinter psyches' (*CW* 8, para. 202). He goes even further: 'Complexes behave like independent beings.' Jung completes that last sentence by adding 'a fact especially evident in abnormal states of mind in which . . . they even take on a personal ego-character' (*CW* 8, para. 253). Sometimes the second half of the sentence is forgotten and, though this is probably not what Jung intended, there has been a rush to render psychic activity as a sort of permanent romance in which complexes and their attendant processes are captured in such simple and clichéd personifications that the structure and subtlety of the activity is quite lost. I mention this because I have had several students and patients who have suddenly announced to me that what is now speaking is their 'wise old man', or their 'anima', or even 'the self'. Very often this is a purely intellectual process involving no emotional contact with the unconscious, though this need not always be the case. In a moment, we shall look at therapeutic use of such personification but, first, some arguments against the idea of complexes as 'independent beings'.

AGAINST COMPLEXES

The psychoanalysts Atwood and Stolorow have developed a thesis which connects theories of personality with the personal life and problems of the theorist (1975, 1979; refs. are 1975). Thus their overall concern is not really with Jung at all – rather their hope is that analysis should free itself from metapsychological reifications which treat the subjective experiences of the theorist as if they were real, thing-like, entities. They would prefer to deal solely with the subjective experiential world of individual persons. If we do this, they assert, we can avoid imposing a subjective mode of experiencing on 'human nature'. But my concern is not to link Jung's personal life to his ideas. This is done competently in a certain manner by Atwood and Stolorow who conclude that 'not surprisingly' there are connections between Jung's often troubled background and his ideas. Nor would I quarrel with the proposition that theory has defensive uses.

Atwood and Stolorow stress the way in which the 'object imago' (by which they mean archetypal image or complex) is experienced as a separate personality, quoting Jung's suggestion that 'one is quite right to treat the anima as an autonomous personality and to address personal questions to her' (*CW* 7, para. 397). Here, Atwood and Stolorow suggest, Jung 'reifies such subjective experiences of object imagos as living personalities' by postulating the existence of autonomous entities (ibid., p. 198). The objects represented by Jung are given extraordinary, often magical and supernatural powers 'as if they were mythological figures sprung forth from the archaic part of humanity' (ibid., p. 198). These archetypal images, say Atwood and Stolorow, are primitive, highly aggrandised, omnipotent objects, and are also split into omnipotently good or omnipotently bad ('divine' or 'demonic'). This is seen by these critics of Jung's as a regressive activation of primitive ways of perceiving and experiencing self and object. Such qualities have nothing to do with reality. This criticism is reminiscent of Glover's point that archetypal material is simply the residue of infantile modes of thinking.

In my view, Atwood and Stolorow omit any reference to Jung's repeated emphasis on the importance of the ego positions of the individual in relation to the archetypes (and see Williams, above). Atwood and Stolorow make far too clear cut a distinction between inner and outer and, finally, the term *object imago* is not an equivalent to *archetypal image* because the mating between inner potential and outer object, characteristic of the latter term, is not implied by the former. 'Object imago' suggests merely an internal representation of what is 'really' external.

Less extravagantly, Dry (1961) urges caution lest metaphor completely supersede argument. She feels that we must be careful not to attempt to divide the complexes completely from one another. She, too, is worried about the philosophical leap we make if we move from the idea that complexes are not within our conscious control to 'personifications of conscious beings, existing over against the subject' (ibid., p. 121).

COMPLEXES – A REVISED VIEW

But support for a revised approach to complexes comes from a similar source, namely, contemporary psychoanalytic self-psychology, deriving from the work of Kohut (1971, 1977). As a Kohutian analyst puts it, 'people use other people as functional parts of themselves' (Goldberg, 1980, p. 4). Goldberg suggests that a person is really a 'collective noun' (ibid., p. 9). He warns against over-simple reification or anthropomorphism, saying we should not think of a 'tiny homunculus inside our head' (ibid., p. 9). But then Goldberg goes on to state that we have now learnt to examine what goes on in a person or between people 'in terms of the significance and meanings that become attached to the "goings on" ' (ibid., p. 9). The emphasis is not on what to name the complex or part of the self, but on what the meaning of it to the individual might be. This is the same as an elucidation of the 'feeling tone'. Psychology, in this Jung-Kohut hybrid, is about meanings, new meanings, hidden meanings. What is needed is an approach that enables us to have a theory of inner agents affecting our lives without unduly reifying or personifying those agents.

We can avoid this by keeping in mind the notion of exchange or relationship. Goldberg gives an example: if a teacher and student are talking, we can often see the child-parent relationship that is also present. The more we know about that student, in particular, the more we know about what sort of child 'lurks in the shadows.' But it is only when we investigate the nature of the exchange that we can ask questions about the effect on either party of it. 'What are the feelings involved?', he asks. 'How does one person expect to alter and be altered by the other? . . . we must consider the nature of the personal experience, the subjective meaning of the interchange' (ibid., p. 7).

Adapted to analytical psychology and its theory of complexes, this amounts to perceiving a complex as an interpersonal or intrapersonal relationship. Thus, it is not a *named* anima, but a network of relationships constellated around anima. In fact we are led back to Hobson's suggestion of mathematical representations because the network becomes too dense.

One implication of this is that 'relationships' are taken to include the whole of object relations, internal, external, 'regardless of whether or not instincts and ego are differentiated from object' (Goldberg, 1980, p. 7). This is an effective reply to Atwood and Stolorow's charge that subjective and objective are confused in Jung. Use is made of the so-called confusion in the construction of as wide as possible a field of reference. Analytical psychology would then become (adopting Goldberg's manifesto for psychoanalysis) 'an introspective investigation of complex [i.e., complicated] interactions, which are matrices of meaning' and the psyche becomes a 'locus of relationships' (ibid., p. 11).

To summarise: two revisions are proposed. The first is concentration on the sense and meaning of the complex to the individual rather than isolation of the complex through naming alone. The second is a re-working of the concept of complex, using it within a broad field of relationships without discrimination between objective and subjective.

THERAPEUTIC USE OF COMPLEXES

From within analytical psychology, Hillman, in particular, has attempted to justify the use of personification of the complexes, not only in theory but also in analysis. He makes the telling point that we reify the complex only if we *infer* it but, as we *experience* complexes all the time, reification is not the primary problem. In fact, the emergence of personifications in analysis is itself a positive sign, indicating that psychic entanglements are gradually being broken down into their more basic components and hence revealing the archetypal core (Hillman, 1975a, pp. 188ff.)

The idea that every personality is multiple can be taken as a charter for regression if the result is dissociation. But multiplicity of personality can also lead to greater differentiation, particularly if the patient is allowed to identify and name the sub-personalities or complexes himself. An analytic, introspective, psychological attitude is therefore facilitated, not harmed.

Hillman reminds us that there is more to our complexes than a feeling that a part of the personality has inflated to take over most or all of the whole. The complex is rooted *in the body* and expresses itself *somatically* (this was the whole point of adding the psychogalvanometer to the Word Association Test). And the complex is active, relating with other complexes, with the ego, with other people, with the 'personality'. It is only when the complex functions psychopathologically that it is like 'an open sore that picks up every bug in the neighbourhood' (ibid., p. 190).

Therapists from other schools continue to make use of complex theory. In Gestalt therapy the patient is encouraged to 'talk to the pain' or to their problem. In Transactional Analysis use is made of the individual's 'parent', 'adult' and 'child' components. Finally, Freudian metapsychological concepts (id, ego, super-ego) are actually examples of complexes. For Jung, the complex was the '*via regia* to the unconscious', the 'architect of dreams and of symptoms'. Actually, said Jung, it is not a very royal road, more like a 'rough and uncommonly devious footpath' (*CW* 8, para. 210).

ARCHETYPE AND COMPLEX: DISCUSSION

I recall Hobson's doubts about naming archetypes, which he feels gets in the way of using the archetype as a formal, utilitarian concept. My own proposals are somewhat different from his. If there *is* an archetypal ingredient in our lives then it is surely sufficient to note, remember and respond to this (and struggle with the emotions caused by it), bearing in mind the impact of that ingredient on *all* situations, experiences and images. We would then ask ourselves with regard to any phenomenon: what is the part played by *the archetypal?* We incorporate the personal dimension but leave the way open for interpretation of the wholly or partially archetypal. We avoid retreat into nature-nurture argument by assuming a constant layer of nature, which is surely what all the scientific and other parallels to archetypal theory have been telling us is at work.

This may be what some post-Jungians do already – that is, abandon discrete archetypes altogether and assume the existence of an omnipresent archetypal component with greater or lesser impact upon the individual depending on his circumstances and his ego strength. Images and experiences can then be considered phenomenologically; in practical analytic terms this means with the *minimum* of preconceived categorisation.

For there is a general move in analytical psychology away from single, big, decorous, numinous expectations of archetypal imagery. The archetypal may be said to be found in the eye of the beholder and not in that which he beholds – an eye that interacts with images. The archetypal is a *perspective* defined in terms of its impact, depth, consequence and grip. The archetypal is in the emotional experience of perception and not in a pre-existing list of symbols. In a similar vein, there is a tendency to abandon any schema, hierarchy or programme of archetypes and archetypal images. Themes, patterns, behaviour, interlace with images and the imaginal, and these then mingle with emotion, instinct and body. Thus a continuous and seamless field of reference is created with no pre-existing or prescribed focus or locus of interest. That is elected by the individual, or by the context, or by the field of reference – or simply elects itself.

For example, I recall a case discussion group in which one participant told of a patient who had been caught in bombing raids during the 1982 Israeli advance into Lebanon. The patient had numerous terrifying dreams about being bombed. There was a more or less predictable interchange about what this might mean for the patient, how internal or external the bombing really was, what view the analyst might take, and so on. Later in the group, the same participant described her reaction to being in the group. She said the group was 'wordy' and went on to say that she had always had trouble with words as a child and had only recently overcome this problem. The effect on the group was dramatic and highly unpredictable.

Some group members felt that they had been attacked, others identified with the speaker's problems in communicating, others attacked her, asserting that she had certainly not overcome these problems. The point is that, at that particular moment and in that context, whatever was involved in 'bombing' was not archetypal in terms of depth or grippingness. Whereas what was involved in a woman's struggle with words certainly was. But *wordy* seems far less 'archetypal' than the terrifying image of *bombing*. Of course, the truth of the matter is that *wordy* was, just then, an archetypal image.

Jung warned that 'it is a well-nigh hopeless undertaking to tear a single archetype out of the living tissue of the psyche' and goes on to refer to the archetypes as 'units of meaning that can be apprehended intuitively' (*CW* 9i, para. 302). I would also see archetypes not so much as organisers or pattern makers, but in a cybernetic manner, more as linking agencies containing the possibility of sense. Taking archetypal theory as a whole, we can see three types of sense-making link: *polarity* – the positive and negative, or personal and collective, or instinctual and spiritual, spectra of the archetype; *complementarity* – the relative balance noticeable in psyche; *interaction* – the interplay of planes of imagery.

The reader must judge for himself whether the scientific work on Jung's archetypes does justice to Jung's psychoid elaboration of the concept and its assumption that the archetype is ultimately unknowable, or whether such work is one-sided, looking downwards to the world of biology and the instincts. There is a tension between accepting archetypal theory on a personal, experiental basis and the desire for more certain knowledge.

3

The ego

Relating to the archetypes depends upon consciousness and I want now to outline Jung's ideas about the ego (*CW* 6, para. 706; *CW* 9ii, paras 1-12; *CW* 8, paras 343-442). These need to be seen against a general background of Freudian psychology because in his various formulations Jung challenged the Freudian conception of the ego and of ego-consciousness. In fact, Jung also adopted a good deal of early, pre-1920 psychoanalytic speculation concerning the ego, particularly in regard to its roots in bodily functioning and brain activity, along with the approximate date at which an ego could be said to exist in the developing child; as Jung stated it, it was during the third or fourth year. Because of the interweave between Jungian and Freudian psychology, it might be a good idea to summarise the main features of the 'Freudian' ego.

For Freud, the ego was the central agency of the personality, mediating between instinctual drives and infantile urges (the id) on the one hand and the dictates of conscience (the super-ego) and of external reality on the other. The ego can bring a set of largely unconscious defensive mechanisms into play to protect the person from an excess of anxiety. The origin of the ego lies in the conflict between the drives and external reality and also through the personality moulding itself by identifications with other persons, mainly the parents. This means that a person's conscious attitudes and ways of behaving are, to some extent, learnt through contact at an intense level with others who are important to the child. For Freud, the ego is the repository of reason and he compared its relations with the id to those of a rider and horse.

Some psychoanalysts dispute Freud's concept of an ego emerging from an undifferentiated id and regard the ego as the whole psyche; others take an existential view and regard the ego as the part of us that experiences ourselves as 'I'. Another psychoanalytic idea which will be seen to be similar to Jung's is Glover's notion of the ego forming via a fusion of fragmented ego-nuclei (1939). Jung wrote of the coalescing of islands of consciousness (*CW* 8, para. 387).

Jung points out that though it might be assumed that the ego is the psychic entity we know most about, it is in fact a mystery, full of obscurities. The ego and ego-consciousness exist in a complementary relationship with the unconscious, so that what is known tells us something about what is not. The ego, in Jung's phrase, is a mirror for the unconscious.

Jung commented that one of the consequences of twentieth-century psychology has been a relativisation of consciousness in general and hence the ego in particular. Here he refers to Freud's work on the unconscious. Jung's argument is that while it is in order to see the ego as the centre of consciousness, it cannot any longer be regarded as the centre of the psyche. Here he goes beyond Freud to incorporate his own work on archetypes and the self (see the next chapter).

One difficulty here is that Jung uses 'ego', 'ego-complex', 'ego-consciousness' and 'consciousness' interchangeably. Another problem is his use of ambiguous metaphors: the ego is both the skin stretched over the unconscious (*CW* 18, paras 122) and at the same time the centre of consciousness (*CW* 6, para. 706). It is therefore helpful to consider Jung's ideas about the ego under three headings. (a) The ego may be seen as an archetypal core of consciousness and we will speak of an ego-complex with a set of innate capacities. (b) The ego may be seen as an element in psychic structure in terms of its relations with the self. (c) Finally, Jung sometimes adopts a developmental perspective from which to view the shifting demands made on the ego at various stages in life.

Jung resisted the temptation to say what proportion of the psyche is taken up by the ego or how dependent the ego is on the psyche as a whole. He contented himself with saying that it is fettered and dependent in many ways. For instance, for some people the ego is dominated or overwhelmed by the unconscious. Others will undervalue the unconscious with equally psycho-pathological results. And elsewhere Jung remarks ironically that often the right balance can be achieved only by first living through and examining the consequences of a wrong balance.

Jung said that the ego arises from the clash between the individual's bodily limitations and the environment. Subsequently, the ego develops from further clashes with the external world and also with the internal world. Jung appreciated that any definition of the ego must be merely formal and is rather difficult. This is because it is the ego that is doing the defining and also because to make a too-precise definition would be an insult to the human individuality which is the essence of the ego and of ego-consciousness. The elements of 'ego' may be structurally similar in one person or another but the feeling tone and emotional colouring will vary (and, of course, people are constitutionally dissimilar and have different backgrounds). One other obstacle to precision is that the ego is not a constant and unvarying entity but is thoroughly mutable both in sickness and in health. Thus in mental illness there may be disturbances of ego functioning and in healthy maturation there will also be changes in style and emphasis. These changes may be accelerated by analysis.

THE CENTRE OF CONSCIOUSNESS

In the main, Jung stresses the ego as an entity at the centre of consciousness. This entity is responsible for identity and personal continuity in time and space; hence memory is a prime ego function. The ego is also concerned with action and ultimately with will power and free will. The ego is surrounded by and embedded in unconscious complexes and images of various kinds. As we were discussing in Chapter 2, the principle of a complex emphasises the variegated nature of psychic activity and psychic experience. More important for our present discussion is the idea that complexes are engaged in a series of ongoing transactions with the ego.

The ego, too, is derived from the combination of inner and outer and it, too, has a relatively autonomous life within the psyche. The ego may itself be regarded as a complex. The ego-complex and the other complexes may suddenly connect so that something which has been powerfully at work in an individual may force itself to the conscious attention of that person. This does not mean that the internal content will simply go away; rather it will now have a *specific* relation to the ego-complex. Jung gives the example of St Paul on the road to Damascus. His unconscious Christ-complex had been in existence independently of his ego-complex. His conversion symbolises the coming together of unconscious complex and ego-complex. It might be argued that his Christ-complex overwhelmed his ego-complex, given his subsequent extremism, as Jung suggested, referring to Paul's epileptic fits as evidence that the move from Saul to Paul had not gone as smoothly as all that (*CW* 9ii, para. 276).

Although many of the autonomous complexes will interact with the ego-complex on their way into consciousness, Jung is very careful to draw a line between saying that the ego is 'the centre characteristic of our psyche' and saying that it is the central *point* (*CW* 8, para. 582).

We have been considering how the various autonomous complexes interact with ego-consciousness. This interaction becomes more intense when the ego is interfered with by psychic fragments that have not yet become sufficiently organised as complexes.

For example, a young woman patient of mine could not understand why she could not attract or hold a boyfriend. She was beautiful and talented and I could not understand this either. We discussed how she related to young men and it emerged that she usually began by telling them all her troubles and expecting or hoping that they would offer a solution. This might be something mundane like how to move some possessions from one part of town to another or much more personal such as seeking advice on contraception or asking the boy why he thought she had tried to kill herself. At first I speculated that this was a search for a father but, as her anxiety had the flavour of a desperate search for reassurance that 'everything will be all right' rather than for specific solutions, I tried to make connections with what she had told me about her childhood. Her mother had had to deal with her alcoholic father and the children were constantly admonished not to do anything which might upset the father. The parents went away on holidays together so that the father could take a cure. Although she could not remember feeling deprived of maternal attention, it was clear that, in practice, her image of her mother was not that of an emotional resource. But there was no figure in her mind (in dreams or fantasies) to give some life to the image of the neglectful mother. Then she dreamt about taking an axe to an older woman who would not listen to her; the discussions we had about this helped her to see that she had been asking potential boyfriends to carry out maternal functions which had clearly terrified them. It took a long time for her to work through this insight and either contain her anxiety, or bring it to me, or to her parents.

Jung emphasised that the ego-complex takes time to develop. That this process is sporadic reflects the piecemeal way in which experience accumulates. Consciousness may then be seen as a precarious potential, unfolding and developing over time.

Jung's stated wish for analytical psychology was that it should react to an over-rational and over-conscious approach which will isolate man from the natural world and from his own nature and so limit him. But he insists that the fantasy images and material from the unconscious (dreams and so on) cannot be used in a *direct* way as if they were a sort of revelation. They are symbolic, a raw material which must be transmuted into the language of consciousness. He conceives of the ego co-operating with the complexes and with archetypal images, and designs a model to show how this happens.

THE EGO AND THE SELF

Jung saw the ego arising out of and functioning in the service of something greater than itself. He called this entity the self and used the word in a number of different ways (see the next chapter). His argument is that because the ego is only the centre of consciousness, because the ego-complex is but one complex among many, and because the unconscious is 'bigger' than the conscious, there is a need to hypothesise something behind, beyond and underneath the ego. The relation of the self to the ego is compared to that of 'the mover to the moved'. The self, like the unconscious, is postulated to have been present always. Jung states that the self is an unconscious prefiguration of the ego – that is, the ego is merged with and then differentiates from the self. Jung describes a fundamental interdependence: the self is supreme, but it is the function and fate of ego-consciousness perpetually to challenge that supremacy. And what is more the self needs the ego to make that challenge. The ego must try to dominate the psyche and the self must try to make the ego give up that attempt.

As the self advances the ego will feel a sense of defeat; but without the establishment of the ego no experience of the self is possible. Ego formation and transformation takes place over a lifetime and the perception of their interdependence and of the ultimate 'surrender' of the ego is central to analytical psychology (cf. pp. 116-18, below).

THE TRANSCENDENT FUNCTION

Let us assume that an individual has a conscious attitude which is preoccupied with sensual things, with the flesh and with having a good time. The opposite attitude to this sensuality – spirituality – will be present as a potential in the unconscious. For some reason (such as the difficulty in living a totally bodily life lacking depth and meaning) the individual's spirituality forces itself up from the unconscious and enters the field of ego-consciousness. The ego will be torn between these two opposites of sensuality and spirituality and will try to keep to the middle ground. This middle ground then becomes tremendously important because the combination of spirituality/sensuality which forms is a genuinely new product. The existing extremes of spirituality and sensuality will try to take over the new product and one of two things will happen. Either the ego will favour one side or the other and the new, mediatory product will be destroyed, the split in the person's psyche remaining unhealed. Or the ego may become strong enough to protect the mediatory product which then becomes, as it were, superior to the two old extremes. At this stage in the process Jung makes what is, for him, a fundamental point. The strength of the person's ego will help the mediatory product or middle position triumph over the two extremes. But *the very existence of the mediatory product actually strengthens the ego*. A new attitude is available for conscious living and, at the same time, ego-consciousness itself is strengthened.

Jung called this process the 'transcendent function' to emphasise how opposites that *could* dialogue with each other and engage in mutual influence might actually do so by transcending their old positions in consciousness and unconsciousness and finding a new position, attached to the ego. The ego is holding the tension of the opposites to let a mediatory symbol come through – a facilitation of the processes of the self which permit the unconscious-conscious transcendence. The symbol presents a way of moving from 'either-or' to 'and' by going beyond the limitations of logical discourse or commonsense; the symbol communicates its message in a way which can be seen as the only possible one. The experience of 'and-ness' is central to psychological change. What is involved is more than a crude combining of two possible solutions to a problem. Rather the transcendent function mediates between a person and the possibility of change by providing, not an *answer*, but a *choice*. Apart from the moral courage which is necessary to face change, making a choice involves discrimination by the ego of the possibilities and then some sort of balanced assessment of these.

Jung stresses these two facets of consciousness. First, discrimination. This is the capacity to distinguish ego from non-ego, subject from object, positive from negative and so on. For it is impossible to talk of bringing opposite positions together without first having distinguished them as opposites in the first place. Without ego-consciousness there would be no such discrimination and, therefore, in Jung's view, nothing but blind instinctuality. Without an experiencing ego there could be no experience whether of higher or lower things. The second facet of ego-consciousness is its capacity to hold the various choices in some sort of balance once they have been discriminated and to facilitate the production of new psychic contents, and hence new conscious attitudes.

In the illustration of the young woman I mentioned earlier, the first stage of analytical work revolved around an image that could only be hypothesised because it was not present in consciousness – that of the mother who did not listen. Her conscious memory was of a normal, attentive mother. The imagery of the axe dream contradicted her memories of her mother and presented her with a choice: to try to stop asking for help from every boy she met. In this case the mediatory product took the form of a change in behaviour rather than a specific symbol. But the idea that the existence of a third, new element strengthens the ego in itself is demonstrated. Containing her anxiety or taking it to appropriate parent figures gave her opportunities to internalise helpful parental images which then became part of a process of ego strengthening.

Neurological support for Jung's intuition of a transcendent function came from Rossi (1977). We saw in Chapter 2 that there are psychological consequences of the brain's division into two cerebral hemispheres. The integration of hemispheric functioning may be analogous or even similar to the transcendent function. Jung described two ways for the transcendent function to express itself – the 'way of creative formulation' (undirected thinking, metaphorical language) and the 'way of understanding' (science, concepts, words). The former is associated with the right and the latter with the left hemispheres. Rossi says 'just as the cerebral hemispheres are in a continuous process of balancing and integrating each other's functions on a neurophysiological level, Jung describes a similar regulation' (ibid., p. 45).

On the other hand, Atwood and Stolorow (1975) saw the idea of the transcendent function as an expression of Jung's denial of the conflicts in life and his unconscious search for symbiotic reunion or merger with an idyllic object. The ego or conscious content represents the infant and the unconscious content represents the mother. However, Jung was careful to state that the transcendence of the inner-outer division is momentary and that the new product is then once again challenged from within. So if there is a merger, it is to be seen as the starting point for a further dynamic. I would agree, though, that the notion of transcendent function can be used to avoid working through conflicts by proclaiming their sudden resolution.

SUPER-EGO OR INNATE MORALITY?

Because Jung uses 'consciousness' and 'ego' interchangeably, it is difficult for him to conceive of the ego as anything other than completely conscious and totally within consciousness. But this is problematic because Jung then has no equivalent to the psychoanalytic metapsychological construct of a super-ego. Nor can he say much about ego defences, which are also unconscious in operation (see p. 74, below).

In psychoanalytic thinking, the super-ego functions as a judge or censor of the ego leading eventually to conscience, self-observation and the forming of ideals. At first psychoanalysis saw the super-ego as the 'heir to the oedipus complex' arising out of internalisation of parental prohibitions and demands but subsequently a much earlier date was adopted for super-ego formation. The super-ego is now seen by object relations theorists as an introjection of a breast made persecuting by projection of the infant's own aggression, or by his fear of an abandoning mother. There is also the possibility of a diversion of excess aggression on to the self. Finally, an overactive super-ego may result from over-strict, prohibitive parenting. The super-ego is held to evolve from the earliest moments in life (Segal, 1973, p. 2).

Jung asserted that ethics and morality, when they are more than blind adherence to collective standards, are *innate*. He suggested that an innate form of conscience must precede either the forming of a moral code or super-ego formation because there can be no guilt without a pre-existing fundamental capacity of the psyche to feel guilt (*CW* 10, paras 825-57). Grinnell (1971) has suggested that there is a 'moral archetype', neutral in itself like all archetypes, and hence capable of underpinning good or bad conscience. The function of the moral archetype is 'the extraction of the moral factor from the amoral archetypes in general', he says (ibid., p. 175).

Jung comments that, in addition to biological, mental and spiritual channels for psychic energy, there is also a moral or ethical channel (*CW* 8, 108-11) so that energy itself has ethical as well as biological, psychological and spiritual aspects (*CW* 11, paras 105-8). But the morality in such a channel is somewhat primitive and cruel and could exacerbate splitting into wholly good and wholly bad and accentuate the tension of opposites by promoting a striving for perfection. Then, as Newton (1975) points out, the function of the mother becomes not to 'supply' the super-ego, but rather to moderate and modify the operation of the baby's primitive morality and perfectionism by signalling her acceptance of him as a whole.

Hillman also reflects on such primitive morality. He establishes the difference between inhibition (innate, from within, a built-in balancing tendency, part of the self-regulating psyche) and prohibition (from an external, authoritarian source). Inhibition is inherent in all impulses, suggests Hillman, and its function is to promote fantasy activity, hence making the instincts psychological and bringing the individual into dialogue with them (1975a, pp. 105-25).

Amongst psychoanalysts, Winnicott stressed that a child is simply not born amoral, and immorality can be taken to mean *complying* with external authority at the expense of a personal way of life or sense of integrity. And Searles has pointed out that humans have an innate need to help others. These views suggest that Jung's notion of an inborn moral sense may not have been as wide of the mark as a first assessment could imply.

There is also much suggestive ethological evidence concerning the innateness of morality. For instance, the white-fronted bee-eater (a common East African bird) demonstrates complex patterns of friendship, kinship and clanship. The bird lives in burrows dug deep in the river bank. Each burrow is the property of a clan of from two to eleven birds. Not all the birds in each clan breed but all roost together and help one another to make the burrow, defend it, incubate the eggs and feed and protect the young. The clan members jointly hold a foraging territory with boundaries respected by other clans; they commute to this territory which is some miles from the burrow. The real surprise is that the clan is not composed of relatives, nor is it based on chance associations. Instead, 'a clan consists of a complex and ever changing set of friends, relatives, past mates and associates who come, go, and reappear in a manner that could provide a plot for a television soap opera' (*Nature*, vol. 298, p. 264, quoted in *The Times*, 21 July 1982). Why are these birds not more selfish? How do they keep track of who has helped whom and when this help should be repaid? The suggestion is that this capacity for social and community living rests on an innate morality (cf. Marais's extraordinary book *The Soul of the White Ant*, 1937).

Jung's suggestion of an innate human morality also speaks to theologians, who conduct their own extensive debate on the subject. Interest has therefore been excited at both ends of the scientific-spiritual spectrum.

THE OPERATION OF CONSCIOUSNESS – PSYCHOLOGICAL TYPES

Jung was interested in illustrating how consciousness works in practice, and also in explaining how it is that consciousness works in different ways in different people. He formulated a general theory of psychological types, hoping to distinguish the components of consciousness. This theory was first published in 1921 (*CW* 6).

Some individuals are more excited or energised by the internal world and others by the external world: these are *introverts* and *extraverts* respectively. But in addition to these basic *attitudes* to the world, there are also certain properties or *functions* of consciousness. Jung identified these as *thinking* – by which he meant knowing what a thing is, naming it and linking it to other things; *feeling* – which for Jung means something other than affect or emotion, a consideration of the value of something or having a viewpoint or perspective on something; *sensation* – which represents all facts available to the senses, telling us that something is, but not what it is; and, finally, *intuition*, which Jung uses to mean a sense of where something is going, of what the possibilities are, without conscious proof or knowledge. A further refinement is that these four functions divide into two pairs – a *rational* pair (thinking and feeling) and an *irrational* pair (sensation and intuition). As we shall see in a moment, what Jung means by these categories and, in particular, his use of the word 'feeling' are problematic issues.

We are now in a position to describe a person's overall style of consciousness and his orientation towards inner and outer worlds. Jung's model is carefully balanced. A person will have a primary (or *superior*) mode of functioning; this will be one of the four functions. The superior function will come from one of the two pairs of rational or irrational functions. Of course the person will not depend exclusively on this superior function but will utilise a second, or *auxiliary* function as well. This, according to Jung's observations, will come from the opposite pair of rational or irrational functions depending on whether the superior function came from the rational or irrational pair. Thus, for example, a person with a superior function of feeling (from the rational pair) will have an auxiliary function of either sensation or intuition (from the irrational pair).

Using the two attitudes and the superior and auxiliary functions, it is possible to produce a list of sixteen basic types. Jung sometimes represented the four functions on a cross-like diagram (Figure 3).

The ego in the middle has energy at its disposal which can be directed into any of the four functions; and of course the extraversion-introversion possibility provides another dimension. Jung felt that the number 4, although arrived at empirically and psychologically, was symbolically apt for the

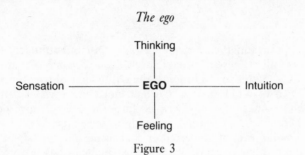

Figure 3

expression of something intended to be as encompassing as a description of consciousness.

Jung then puts forward a proposition which transforms his typological theory from being merely a descriptive, academic exercise into something of value in diagnosis, prognosis, assessment and in connection with psychopathology generally.

We have so far allotted two of the four functions of consciousness; what of the other two? Jung observed that the other function from the pair that provided the superior function often caused a good deal of difficulty for the individual. Let us say that an individual has a superior function of feeling. If Jung is right, then he may have a problem with the other function from the same, rational, category – namely, thinking. We can see how this approach of Jung's works out in practice. We all know of people who have a mature, balanced attitude to life and seem stable; they are at home with emotions and value personal relationships. But they may lack the capacity for sustained intellectuality or systematic thinking. They may even regard such thinking as a terrible thing, hate logic and proudly talk of themselves as innumerate and so on. But the pride may hide feelings of inadequacy and the problem may not be so easily resolved. Jung names the problematic function the *inferior function*. This will be the area of consciousness that is difficult for a person. On the other hand, the inferior function, which exists for long stretches in the unconscious, contains enormous potential for change which can be brought about by attempts to integrate the contents of the inferior function into ego-consciousness. Doing this, realising one's inferior function, is a prime element in individuation because of the 'rounding out' of the personality that is involved.

It is important to realise that Jung is applying his theory of opposites in the construction of this system (see the next chapter for a more detailed discussion of that theory). Within the broad category of 'rationality', thinking and feeling are opposites and this fact struck Jung more forcibly than the more obvious opposition between rational and irrational, e.g., between thinking and intuition. It is the very *link* of their shared rationality that enables thinking and feeling to be conceived of as opposites. Jung felt that, as a person is more likely to be rational *or* irrational, the important question typologically would have to be answered from within either the rational or the irrational category. The point needs stressing because, in a way, it conflicts with commonsense which would assert that the true opposites would be rational and irrational tendencies.

Jung speculated that in maturation and individuation these various

63

typological opposites merge so that a person's conscious attitudes, and hence a great part of his experience of himself, will become richer and more variegated. One interesting question is the chronology of type formation. Jung describes a two-year-old child who would not enter a room before he had been told the names of the pieces of furniture there. Jung took this as, amongst other things, an example of early introversion. The idea of timing leads to the conundrum of how fixed or changeable a person's type is and this has attracted the energies of several post-Jungians, as we shall see (in Appendix, below).

Jung thought that the functions have a physiological base with a psychic component which is partially controllable by the ego. To some extent a person can choose how to operate, but the limits are probably innate. No one can dispense with any of the four functions; they are inherent to ego-consciousness. But the use of one particular function may become habitual and exclude the others. The excluded function will remain untrained, undeveloped, infantile or archaic and possibly completely unconscious and not integrated into the ego. But it is possible for each function to be differentiated and, within limits, integrated. Nevertheless, for social or familial reasons one function may become one-sidedly dominant in a way that is not in tune with the person's constitutional personality.

THE PSYCHOPATHOLOGY OF EGO-CONSCIOUSNESS

It is now time to turn our attention to Jung's statements concerning the psychopathology of ego-consciousness.

The *first* possibility is that the ego will not emerge satisfactorily from its original unity and identity with the self; hence there will be little discrimination or ego-consciousness and the personality will be run by the competing autonomous complexes.

The *second* possibility is that the individual will allow his self, or total personality, to become limited by identification with the ego – which thereby becomes inflated. He will behave as if there is nothing but ego and ego-consciousness in himself. The unconscious and the complexes will protest at being denied in this way and a tension between ego and self far greater than the healthy norm will develop, with destructive consequences.

Moving on from this, the *third* possibility is that the ego may identify itself with an extreme conscious attitude, forsaking a mediatory position and cutting off the rest of the spectrum of possibilities. To do this, the ego will 'select' from emotional data so that elements which do not fit in with the conscious pattern are denied or split off.

The *fourth* possibility is that the ego-complex may find itself unable to relate in a fruitful and imaginative way to the other complexes so that the personalisation and differentiation of the complexes that Jung regards as vital for growth cannot take place. The individual either cannot bring up fantasy images or cannot relate to them if he does.

The *fifth* possibility is that the ego may get overwhelmed and carried away by an inner content.

The *sixth* possibility is that the ego-complex may be too weak to preserve the individual's unity and integration so that these crack and cannot hold under the impact of the multiplicity and primitivity of the unconscious.

The *seventh*, and final, possibility of ego-psychopathology has to do with the inferior function described in the section on typology, above. The inferior function may be so unintegrated and unavailable that it makes a nonsense of conscious intentions.

EGO AND SHADOW

Jung used the term *shadow* to signify and sum up what each man fears and despises in himself. The shadow also expresses that for mankind as a whole, or for a particular culture at a particular time. While it is possible for the ego to become conscious of what is located in the shadow, this can never be a total consciousness. The paradox is that making something conscious also constellates unconsciousness because the one is always in relation to the other. When ego-consciousness illuminates something, what is on the periphery is in darkness. Jung put it thus:

> we come to the paradoxical conclusion that there is no conscious content that is not in some other respect unconscious. (quoted in Hillman, 1979b, pp. 12-13)

It follows that the more differentiated the ego, the more problematic the shadow. Indeed, for one with a high level of ego-consciousness, the shadow may take the form of the unconscious itself. Pathology results from what *could* be healthy elements of the ego remaining unconscious, and hence operating in a distorted way, or in projection. This last possibility, projection of the shadow, interferes with close relationships on the personal level and, on the communal level, with harmonious living. In both instances, it is tempting to shove what is not wanted outside where it can be condemned at leisure. Beams and motes, in other words.

Jung went on to stress that the shadow should not be regarded as a 'bad thing'. The dark side of man is, after all, a side of man. So there is a compelling *moral* aspect to integration of the shadow: to unblock personal and communal relationships and also to admit the inadmissible, yet human. The aim of such an integration is greater psychological wholeness (meaning completion not perfection). The designation *shadow* is not the same as that of *sin*. In fact, Jung asserted that everything of any substance or solidity (hence of value) throws a shadow.

Jung's positive evaluation of the shadow is shown most clearly in connection to instinct:

> assimilating the shadow gives a man body . . . the animal sphere of instinct, as well as the primitive or archaic psyche, emerges into the zone of consciousness. (*CW* 16, para. 452)

Jung commented that man's 'specious unity' breaks down under the impact of the unconscious and a conflict commences between ego and shadow:

> so long as the patient can think that somebody else (his father or mother) is
> responsible for his difficulties, he can save some semblance of unity. . . . But
> once he realises that he himself has a shadow, that his enemy is in his own heart,
> then the conflict begins and one becomes two. (*CW* 16, para. 399)

But such a conflict with the 'other' will lead in analysis, Jung continued, to the
possibility of a transforming and unifying third position, if the ego can achieve
the necessary integration.

The wholeness, or completeness, or sense of these, to which integration of
the shadow leads is vital if man is to develop. First, Jung concluded, he must
see that *he* is the problem. It is not a question of getting rid of the shadow, but
recognising it and integrating it; this is a dangerous task for ego-consciousness
because the ego is brought into direct contact with the archetypes and may opt
for an incestuous retreat and duck the moral confrontation (see pp. 166-7,
below).

Used as a metaphor in relation to a culture, the shadow includes those
outside the social system (criminals, psychotics, misfits, scapegoats) as well as
national enemies. These individuals are people who do not fit in with the
prevailing tendency of a culture which, in turn, may be seen as failing to
assimilate its shadow. If this failure continues then the societal shadow may
erupt, as in fascism, or in racial hatred, or in a senseless and destructive war.

A SYMBOL FOR THE EGO

It follows from this presentation of shadow that ego-consciousness may be
symbolised by light or illumination. But there are other ways in which,
according to Jung, ego-consciousness finds cultural or personal expression.
From the earliest times the symbol of ego-consciousness with which man has
been most able to identify is the hero. The larger-than-life nature of the hero
stands for man's aspirations, and his various struggles and conflicts aptly
express the uneven course of human existence. The hero's journey as
expressed in myth and legend 'signifies a renewal of the light and hence a
rebirth of consciousness from the darkness' (*CW* 5, para. 558).

It is possible to list a number of features which can be observed in heroic
stories. (That is not to say that every heroic tale – Perseus, Herakles, Oedipus,
Moses, Arthur and so on – will display *all* these features.) The common
features are: the hero's mother is a royal virgin. His father is a king and
related to his mother. The circumstances of his birth are unusual and the
hero is said to be a son of a god. At birth his father or his maternal
grandfather try to kill him but he is spirited away and reared by substitute
parents in a far-off country. After a victory or series of victories over a giant,
dragon or wild beast and/or a king he becomes the king and marries a
princess. All goes well for a while and the hero-king draws up a series of laws
but eventually he loses favour with either the gods or the populace and is
driven from throne and city. After this he meets with a mysterious death, often

at the top of a hill. His children, if any, do not succeed him and his body is not buried. Nevertheless he has one or more holy sepulchres.

Lord Raglan, in his book *The Hero* (1949), tells us that out of a possible 22 features Oedipus scores 22, Theseus 20, Romulus 18, Perseus 18, Herakles 17, Jason 15, Moses 20 and Arthur 19.

The invariable maleness of the hero is to be taken symbolically. Because of Jung's stress on the personalising of the complexes, his own cultural biases and those of the time, he was content to let consciousness be symbolised by male figures. It does not follow that women are excluded from consciousness or have 'less'. Nevertheless, the dubious idea that consciousness in a woman lies in her 'masculine' side remains (cf. Stevens, 1982, p. 189). This issue is discussed fully in Chapter 7.

One particular personification of ego-consciousness should be noted and that is Job; Jung wrote a psychological commentary on the Book of Job (*Answer to Job, CW* 11). Although Job is theoretically inferior to Yahweh, he gradually becomes aware of Yahweh's power shadow; that is, he achieves consciousness in a way that a God never can. Yahweh behaves in a disturbed and distorted way. His jealousy and grandiosity are infantile; Job is like a parent, pressed beyond 'mortal' patience in his explosive outburst. Job does not represent mature ego-consciousness for there is still no mention of connection to the feminine which remains split off. And, as Lambert points out (1977), he is not an Everyman figure, rather a metaphor for a phase of the development of consciousness.

CRITIQUES

We have seen how hard Jung finds it to accept that the organ and centre of consciousness is not in fact aware of its own operation. Thus Jung says very little about ego defences and has no conception of defences such as those Anna Freud enumerated in her now famous classification (1937). On the other hand, some of Jung's ideas do come closer to definitions of earlier defences as proposed by object relations theorists (see pp. 151-2, below). The main problem is not simply that the idea of *defence* is undeveloped but that insufficient stress is laid on *anxiety* as the reason for defences in the first place. Analytical psychology benefits from psychoanalytic classifications of anxiety; for example, persecutory and depressive anxiety, or anxiety resulting from super-ego activity.

Jung's view of ego-consciousness does not allow for much variation in the quality and intensity of consciousness. Gordon points out that there are two meanings of consciousness – being aware or awake, and being self-aware. Self-awareness has two meanings as well – 'primary self-awareness' in which 'one knows and is aware of what one does and experiences' and 'reflective self-awareness', a deliberate focusing on mental processes (Gordon, 1978, p. 173).

Jung does not link the development of ego-consciousness to any schema of personality development or maturation. He regards the ego as developing far later than is probably the case and sees children as living in their 'notorious unconsciousness' in which 'there is as yet no clearly differentiated ego' (*CW* 17, para. 83). Following from this, Jung leaves open the question of the structure of the ego itself and also the issue of its origin and the way it actually does cohere. In particular, there is little stress on the role of frustration in the genesis of the ego, and the symbol of the hero is regarded by some post-Jungians as inadequate or unsuitable. Jung does not examine in great detail the role of the ego in personal relationships nor the role of personal relationships in the formation of the ego.

Glover's reaction to Jung's views on the ego is that Jung seems to have abandoned any sense of an evolution from unconscious to conscious and the psychoanalytic account of the way in which the 'originally dynamic unconscious evolves into later structural formations' (1950, p. 47). The concept of conflict, says Glover, is reduced to a conscious level and there is no sense of infantile mechanisms being present in the unconscious. We have already noted that Jung's failure to see that the ego has unconscious elements such as defences has unfortunate consequences. But Jung *is* constantly concerned with the relations between conscious and unconscious. These can include conflict but many other modes are also possible. Glover therefore inadvertently fits the unfair stereotype of the Freudian seen by Jungians as regarding the unconscious as an *enemy*.

Glover feels that he can demonstrate that Jung has also abandoned the concept of repression – 'the keystone of the Freudian system of mental economy' (ibid., p. 78). He quotes repeated references from Jung which suggest that repression is something under conscious control (suppression, in other words). I think this may reflect a weakness in Jung or it may be a linguistic problem – certainly no post-Jungian would argue that you can decide what to repress or whether to repress it.

Glover's further criticism is that, by stressing the autonomy of the complexes, Jung is trying to keep the ego 'clean' and wants to project less pleasant infantile material into the autonomous complexes, thereby giving up conscious responsibility for it. We can clarify the position by saying that, as well as its innate core, each complex has in it bits of personal infantile history *and* ego elements (e.g. ego-nuclei, Glover's own concept).

Jung's typological theory has become controversial and has been challenged by Glover and by many others. Glover's objections are that all mention of development is omitted and that the question is left begging as to whether type is to be considered innate, even accidental. I think that Jung has tried to discuss this but has fought shy of stating unequivocally that type is inborn. Glover feels that extraversion and introversion are ridiculously simple labels and 'cannot give the slightest hint of the elaborate and complicated dynamic and structural developments that give rise to these end-results. Consequently they are useless' (ibid., p. 103). Glover's methodological objection is that Jung is dealing with *end-products* when he should be dealing with *processes*.

Storr (1973), in a critical look at Jungian typology, has put forward an interesting theory which connects Jung's ideas of extraversion and introversion with those of Fairbairn, a psychoanalyst of the object-relations school. Fairbairn sees extraversion in terms of ego defences against depression; extraverts are depressive because, being so involved with external objects and other people, they live close to the fear of loss. Introverts are basically more primitive because they are in flight from the external world. Fairbairn, Storr says, felt that personal development played a great part in this, and would criticise any idea that psychological attitude is innate or genetically determined.

Storr goes on to argue against Jung's balanced view of extraversion and introversion which, value-wise, places them both on an equal footing. Storr feels that extremes of extraversion are less pathological than extremes of introversion (ibid., p. 73). He reaches this conclusion because the schizoid state he associates with introversion precedes in development the depressive state he associates with extraversion. Only the extravert relates to whole other persons (presumably because only the extravert has reached the depressive position or stage of concern). The introvert, in extreme form, is schizophrenic. Schizophrenic withdrawal, involving the individual inhabiting a world of his own, is a more serious illness than depression.

It is difficult to know how to evaluate this idea. It is to be welcomed that an attempt has been made to make clinical use of these concepts of Jung's but I am not sure that many would regard introversion as a more pathological state than extraversion.

The position can be clarified somewhat because Storr picks up on a basic difference between Jung and psychoanalysis in general, which can be expressed in terms of the ego. Jung, summarises Storr, sees the ego 'poised between inner and outer, between subjective and objective, with an equal need to relate to each world' (ibid., p. 74). In Storr's view, psychoanalysis, on the other hand, sees the inner world as infantile or, if overpresent in the adult, as psychopathological. Storr's synthesis is to suggest that the inner world of fantasy images is both infantile (and hence pathological in an adult), and also biologically *adaptive*. He points out that man's means of adaptation is partially internal anyway, through concepts, symbols and dreams or reveries. Hence, the internal world has a part to play in external adaptation.

In the quote above, Storr seems to equate inner with subjective and outer with objective. But the emphasis of psychodynamic psychology is to suggest that inner activity has the force and impact on the individual of objective truth and, conversely, that what is felt to be real in the external world of relationships and objects is often highly coloured by subjective factors. The whole issue can be clarified by the use of a term such as *subjective reality*.

Storr noted a problem with Jung's use of the word *feeling*, which is confused. Jung tried to distinguish feeling from emotion or affect but complications arise because one aspect of feeling is the detecting and registering of emotion. Willeford proposes a solution to this problem: feeling is *relatively* different from emotion but both are derived from the underlying affective organisation of the personality (1976, p. 131).

THE POST-JUNGIANS: INTRODUCTION

We now turn our attention to the ways in which these themes have been taken up and developed by the post-Jungians, and to a look at the debate on the topic of ego-consciousness that is taking place in analytical psychology today. There are two main issues in this debate. The first has to do with the relevance, applicability and appropriateness of the hero motif as a symbol for ego-consciousness. The second has to do with whether the ego may be better seen more as an ally or more as an opponent of imagination. As we shall see, there is a common feature to be observed in both these debates: *there is no such thing as ego-consciousness but rather a number of varieties or styles of ego-consciousness*, deriving from the internal and external circumstances of the person.

THE HERO MOTIF

Neumann worked on the image of the hero as a metaphor for ego-consciousness and is associated with the idea that there are archetypal stages to be observed in the development of the ego which follow the various stages of the hero myth. Neumann felt that he had avoided the trap of too facile an analogy between the development or evolution of the human species with that of an individual man or woman by using myth as metaphor, which is why he seeks for amplificatory material in what can be called the 'folk history of consciousness', rather than from empirical data. This is justified by Neumann's statement that:

> If, in the course of our exposition, we 'personify', speaking of the hero's own experience, or describing a mythological situation from the feminine point of view, it is to be understood that we are speaking figuratively and in abbreviated form. Our retrospective psychological interpretation corresponds to no point of view consciously maintained in earlier times: it is the conscious elaboration of contents that were once extrapolated in mythological projections, unconsciously and symbolically. (Neumann, 1954, pp. 150-1)

It follows from the notion that the individual ego passes through archetypal phases or stages of development that at each stage of its evolution the ego will enter into a new relationship with the archetypes and complexes. Thus the power and range of ego-consciousness increases. Neumann stresses the creative power of consciousness, seeing it at the border between individuality and collectivity. What follows is my attempt to synthesise the various statements of his model that Neumann has made (1954, 1959, 1973).

Neumann calls the first stage of the development of consciousness the *uroboric phase* after the ancient symbol of the circular snake that bites its own tail. He remarks that the uroborus 'slays, weds and impregnates itself. It is man and woman, begetting and conceiving, devouring and giving birth, active and passive, above and below, at once' (1954, p. 10). The uroboros is a representation, not of childhood or infancy as a whole, but of the state of consciousness characteristic of that time. The uroboros is an image which captures in one bound the essence of infantile omnipotence, solipsism and relative lack of conscious differentiation. (For a full discussion of Neumann's approach to the mother-infant relationship, see pp. 155-61, below.)

The second phase of the development of the ego, the *matriarchal phase*, is dominated by the maternal side of the unconscious, the Great Mother, who, in her control of the food supply and in other manifestations of her power and protectiveness, forces the ego to play a passive role at first. According to Neumann, there is no differentiation as yet between infant and mother, ego and non-ego, masculine and feminine, or active and passive. The parents are seen as undifferentiated and merged rather than as two separate individuals who have united in a marriage.

The earliest acts of the ego involve the use of aggressive fantasy to make a separation between infant and mother and, subsequently, between mother and father. After that other pairs of opposites will emerge. This separation of what was merged and one into two opposites offers the possibility of further development of consciousness along the lines of Jung's classic description of two psychic contents combining to produce a third, new, product.

Making these differentiations is, says Neumann, a heroic act. 'Through the heroic act of world creation and division of opposites, the ego steps forth from the magic circle of the uroboros and finds itself in a state of loneliness and discord' (1954, pp. 114-15).

The hero, symbolising ego-consciousness, embarks on a journey or quest which will involve him in numerous conflicts and struggles. These struggles represent the ordinary hurdles of growing up. But what seems ordinary, general and to be anticipated by the observing adult is exciting, terrifying and tremendously important to the child.

What is the hero trying to do in his quest and his struggles? Neumann distinguishes three psychological goals. First, the hero/ego is trying to separate from the mother and the maternal environment. Second, the hero is trying to identify and discriminate the masculine and feminine sides of himself, so as to integrate them. Third, he is looking for values and modes of psychological functioning to offset and balance the over-directed and exaggeratedly conscious manner he has had to develop to break out of the embrace of the Great Mother. The ego has to behave in this over-stressed and stereotypically masculine way to free itself precisely because being in the thrall of the Great Mother is not always a horrid experience. The pleasant floating sense of having no responsibilities is known to us all; it is a highly seductive path of regression. The one-sided 'masculinity' can then be seen as necessary and inevitable, and in need of its opposite, namely the princess or similar feminine figure and the treasure. That may be seen more as a goal that is different in quality from martial achievement or other traditionally masculine processes.

The treasure also represents a quite different world-perspective from that of ego-values. Neumann can be summarised as saying that the necessity for separation between the evolving ego and the matriarchal world leads to a temporary loss of depth (of soul) and to espousal of conflict and struggle. The soul-maiden redresses the balance in her marriage with the hero. When the hero possesses the captive he is enabled to give up incestuous fantasies of marriage within his family and can look outside it. For if this tendency were not facilitated, human culture would remain stuck in the family of origin, static and sterile.

Neumann reminds us that the hero meets helpful figures on his journey. For example, Perseus is given the gift of invisibility by Hades, a sword by Hermes and the reflective shield which is necessary for the killing of Medusa by Athene. From Perseus' point of view they were helpful parent figures who had an investment in the successful ego development of their child and are therefore a necessary antidote to any inflated idea that the hero has the whole world against him. In real life, parents can see that their children have to grow up and away, even if this may bring pain for all parties.

The battle between the hero and the king (the *patriarchal phase*) is seen by Neumann to have a different meaning from that between the hero and the dragon-monster. This represents nothing less than the perpetual battle between the generations, between young and old, new and established. Neumann does not accept Freud's view that the impulse to kill the father is based on sexual rivalry and he works hard to differentiate his argument from Freud's by concentrating on the cultural aspects of the hero-king conflict. It seems more likely to me that the sexual and cultural dimensions are two sides of a whole picture (see pp. 166-9, below, for a fuller discussion of the Oedipus complex in analytical psychology).

To summarise: Neumann has identified the main elements as the hero himself, the dragon and the victim/treasure. The dragon, though often androgynous, is contiguous with the mother and the mother archetype. It is certainly with *her* that the hero must fight. Victory over her will regenerate the hero-ego because the treasure offers the various rewards outlined above and because the *deliberate* exposure of the ego to the dangers of conflict with the dragon or monster is a vital testing out of strength.

Entrance into the cavern, threatening contact with the mother, transforms the ego. The outcome is enhancement of ego-consciousness. Then the 'feminine' aspect of the victim-treasure plays its part in readjusting the style of ego-consciousness to a more balanced mode.

The hero is the bearer of the ego with its power to discipline the will and mould the personality, and the whole conscious system is now capable of 'breaking away from the despotic rule of the unconscious' (Neumann, 1954, p. 127).

EGO DEVELOPMENT: AN ARCHETYPAL FANTASY

Giegerich (1975) criticised Neumann for trying to trace the development of an archetype, thus breaking one of the 'rules' of analytical psychology which is that archetypes, as fundamental structures, simply do not develop. Giegerich also felt that Neumann's concept of stages of ego development is an archetypal fantasy of Neumann's, which may be why Neumann's approach has captivated so many analytical psychologists.

Giegerich argues that, while there *are* stages in the development of consciousness, and myths which amplify these stages, each myth, as a *style* of ego-consciousness, is working continuously and contemporaneously, and that all the styles are in a constant state of interaction. The ego is best conceived of, in other words, as a series of styles of consciousness with patterns of interaction between them.

I would ask the reader to hold this notion in mind – *ego styles which do not grow old and do not fade away* – as this will emerge as a common theme in post-Jungian thought about the ego.

Giegerich's central argument is that to utilise culture to link ego-consciousness to phylogeny is absurd because phylogeny precedes man's known cultural history by thousands of years. Giegerich felt that Neumann took his stages far too concretely, did *not* use them as metaphors, and hence rendered concrete what should be left imaginal.

EGO DEVELOPMENT IN INFANCY

Fordham agreed with Giegerich that Neumann has misused the concept of archetype. But his *main* criticism of Neumann's speculations concerning the development of consciousness, in his paper 'Neumann and childhood' (1981), is that they are adultomorphic, that is, infantile phenomena are looked at from the point of view of an adult. Though children know less about adult living than adults, there is no evidence that the child is absolutely unconscious or passive in the way Neumann describes.

Fordham quotes studies that demonstrate that in some respects a baby's reality perceptions are more differentiated than an adult's. Visual, auditory and tactile functions and perceptions are present at birth and a small baby has a fairly wide imitative range. Much has also been learned about intrauterine life in which the foetus 'develops quite sophisticated skills and interacts with his containing aquatic environment.' Most important of all, the new-born baby is equipped to undertake approach behaviour which is initiatory and not simply reactive or reflexive. This approach behaviour, says Fordham 'can be understood best by considering its effect on the mother . . . it seems that his looks, his cries, his movements are so constructed as to play on his mother's affects and attach her to him' (1980a, p. 317).

Fordham feels that there is a growing consensus that there are organised perceptual ego-functions at birth and 'there does not now appear to be any basis for assuming that infant endowment is unorganised, but this view is still current, so needs mentioning' (1976, p. 46). But, as we shall see in the next chapter, Fordham does not attribute this organisation *primarily* to the ego or to ego-consciousness, but rather to the organisation of the self.

Fordham's examination of ego functions is of considerable interest for it demonstrates a modern view based on some of Jung's formulations. The ego functions are: (a) Perception – though not all perceptions cross the threshold of consciousness. (b) Memory. (c) Organisation of mental functioning (presumably using the two attitudes and four functions of consciousness delineated by Jung). This would also include the part played by the ego in integrating fantasy. (d) Control over mobility. This is important for two reasons: first, because the ego is shown to be rooted in the body and second, because the ego resonates to actual separation from the mother. (e) Reality testing. (f) Speech. Here what is important is the way in which words such as

'I', 'you', 'he' have different meanings at different developmental stages and are used with greater or lesser frequency. (g) Defences. Fordham's list of defences, and his division into earlier and later defences, follows conventional practice based on developments in psychoanalysis. But he makes the point that ego-defences, which have tended to be seen negatively and as dispensable in a state of mental health, are now understood as a part of maturation. Provided defences are not too rigid and a person does not become excessively dependent on one particular type of defence, they cannot be seen as psychopathological. If the ego does not use such mechanisms as projection, introjection and identification, it can neither protect itself from anxiety, nor add to itself. (h) Capacity to relinquish its controlling and organising functions. Fordham lays considerable importance on this and his paradoxical proposition would be that only a strong enough ego can allow other parts of the psyche to flourish (1969a, pp. 93-6).

We should note that Fordham, too, when he speaks of an ego that gives up its own strengths, has moved away from any unitary view of the ego.

Because Fordham is not prepared to accept the use of myths and ideas about myths to tell us about infantile functioning, he is highly critical of Neumann's stages for the development of ego-consciousness. The problem with the stages is that they are claimed to represent the development of the internal structure of an archetype or an aspect of an archetype. Like Giegerich, Fordham claims that it is conceptually wrong to assert that an archetype is capable of development and proposes instead the idea that *it is consciousness which is necessary for development in the first place* (1981).

COMMENT: (1)

These are highly technical questions which do not bear on the usefulness of the hero motif as a metaphor for ego-consciousness and, in particular, on the relevance of the hero for questions of moral choice. Archetypal metaphors do change with the passing of each generation; this does not imply change in the archetype as such. New metaphors do receive cultural acknowledgment and each subsequent generation has a different store of images on which to draw. For example, the generations following the Women's Movement will meet a quite different constellation of images around *woman*. Another aspect of the image has become accessible; the image has 'turned' or we have walked around it.

In addition, archetypal manifestations occur in differing forms at different moments in life. Thus the demands made on the ego in early life and those of old age will be different. And it should be remembered that a weak ego is not necessarily a childish ego; the issue is not a comparison between the ego of childhood and that of adulthood but rather an evaluation of the phase-appropriateness of ego strengths and weaknesses.

MYTH, INFANCY AND IMAGINATION

However, Giegerich is as unsparing of Fordham's scientific approach as he was of Neumann's mythological concretism. Both, according to Giegerich, are essentially non-psychological because they are both embedded in the Great Mother myth to the exclusion of all other possibilities: Neumann because he is caught up in the Great Mother–hero struggle and Fordham because he is over-committed to heroic ego-laden empiricism, and therefore cut off from the imagination and the imaginal.

Giegerich feels that the notion of a heroic ego is a tragic one because

> it can only continue to separate, dissolve, analyse, and kill, but never again find connectedness, not because such connectedness is altogether impossible, but because it has no place within a myth aiming for separation and violence. The 'premise' of the vision structured by the hero archetype is war, opposition, severing. (1975, p. 125)

Here I suspect Giegerich himself has failed to see that it is precisely to achieve connectedness that the heroic ego is led to search out the anima-victim.

Exaggeratedly one-sided heroic ego activity *is* tragic. But neither Fordham nor Neumann is *advocating* this as far as I can tell and Giegerich may have set up an Aunt Sally here.

THE EGO AS THE ENEMY OF IMAGINATION

In his essay 'The Great Mother, her son, her hero, and the *puer*' (1973), Hillman questions whether the ego must always be seen in relation to the mother; in fact he would say it is vital to see the ego in terms other than those which relate it to the mother archetype because the child can just as easily be seen as representing a 'movement of the spirit' as it can an entity struggling to separate itself from the mother. But in hero myths the hero is unthinkable without the opposition of a Great Goddess in some form. For Hillman the act of the emergent ego in killing the dragon is interpretable in terms of the killing off of the imagination and this will lead to ego-ic one-sidedness. The dragon is an imaginal entity (as is the hero) but it is the hero who has become dominant in our approach to and love of ego-consciousness.

Hillman asserts that the heroic way of thinking splits spirit and matter (represented respectively by the anima-treasure and the dragon-mother). This split is demonstrated by the way the anima has to be hewn bloodily from the maternal material, as it were. Hillman opposes this with the possibility that matter and spirit, far from being polarities, are in fact complementarities. At first it might be argued that this idea involves Hillman in 'stopping' the mythic hero story before the point is reached at which the hero marries the captive anima or spirit. But stopping the story at the critical point to see what it tells us, what it suggests to us, is exactly what Hillman wants us to do to appreciate the parallelism and relativity of the psyche. Each time the story is stopped one can apperceive a different imaginal strand running through it. The story may reveal one style of ego functioning to be predominant at any one point, only to be superseded by another style. Or more than one ego style may be in operation at any one time.

Because, continues Hillman, most analytical psychologists conceive of oppositional conflict and struggle as the fundamental prerequisite for growth, direct and easy access to the spirit is denied as a possibility for the ego. What is required and insisted on is heroic struggle and dramatics, and by going along with this view, far from separating from the Great Mother, we fall right into her lap/trap. Hillman suggests that the way to 'solve' the mother complex would not be to 'cut from Mom, but to cut the antagonism that makes me heroic and her negative' (ibid., p. 98). Distortion sets in when we *prefer* the hero myth as a model for ego-development. What would happen, asks Hillman, if we did not conceive of ego development via the heroic model involving conflict and strength and constantly seeking light? Is that the only way to consciousness and culture?

Hillman quotes Jung to illustrate his point: 'Unfortunately, however, [the] heroic deed has no lasting effects. Again and again the hero must renew the struggle, and always under the symbol of deliverance from the mother' (*CW* 5, para. 54). As long as psychotherapy remains to do with ego, then, it will always be about mother and not about psyche. For example, the very name of the arch-hero Herakles means 'glory of Hera'. In spite of her attempt to kill him at birth, Herakles himself claims that it is Hera who *drives* him to heroic extremes. So the path of ego development is not away from the Great Mother or mother but rather towards her. If the ego-complex is conceived of as arising from a conflict with the Great Mother then the ego is nothing more than 'the mother complex in a jockstrap' (Hillman, 1973, p. 107).

So, for Hillman, following the principles of his archetypal psychology, we arrive at the proposition that the heroic ego, far from being about separation from the mother, simply leads us back to her. A side effect is the destructive consequence of this for imagination.

COMMENT: (2)

A riposte to Hillman's argument would rest on the fact that ego-styles have an age-appropriate element in them. That is, development and ego-consciousness affect each other so that it is foolhardy to drive a wedge between personal growth and the development of ego-consciousness. But, as we have seen, Hillman and Giegerich have already dismissed such an approach as reductionist.

I think that Hillman's impatience mars his thesis. If he could see the ego as *growing* in some sort of facilitating setting then the other things he hopes for may come to pass. It is important to say this to try to build a bridge between Developmental and Archetypal approaches. For few would disagree with Hillman's view that 'assertive masculinity is suspicious. Somewhere we know it must be reactive to feminine attachment' (1973, p. 105). My feeling is that there is a normal human split between a desire to grow and a desire, or need, to regress (see p. 167, below). We may say, with Hillman, the more heroic the more a mother's boy. But it is also true that, the closer the incestuous bond with mother, the more the hero is needed to initiate object relating and becoming a separate person.

It could also be said that an ego engaged only in separating from the mother by defeating her is but a phase of ordinary ego development characterised by the Kleinian term 'paranoid-schizoid position'. I am referring to the ego taking an 'either/or' line (split or schizoid functioning) in response to imaginings of maternal persecution and threat (paranoid functioning). An ego that is not destructive to the imagination is one that can function on something other than an either/or basis, being able to handle ambivalence, emotional fluidity and the multi-faceted nature of the imaginal world. Such an ego would share the characteristics of the depressive position in which mixed feelings about self and others can be tolerated, aggression owned, fantasies of damage repaired, and concern for the mother as a person replaces the convenience of splitting her into bad and good so as only to attack the bad and love the good.

THE EGO AS THE ALLY OF IMAGINATION

Hillman and Giegerich have been stressing the imagination and the imaginal as if these were in some way opposed to ego-consciousness. On the other hand, Plaut (1966) advanced the idea that ego-consciousness is an essential precondition for imagination, where the latter is seen as different from fantasy (meaning the expression of frustrated wishes). Plaut reached the conclusion that 'the capacity to imagine constructively is closely related to, if not identical with, the capacity to trust'; *that* capacity depends on the quality of ego-consciousness and ego strength. Both trust and the capacity to imagine can be damaged by defects or problems in early relationships. Plaut reached his conclusions by considering patients in analysis who, apparently, cannot imagine.

Plaut's examination of how the ego experiences the products of imagination rests on an earlier exploration of his (1959) in which he tried to answer the question: who or what experiences anything prior to the ego being established? Plaut's theory was that the infant's bodily experiences must get attached to, or attracted by, bits of ego which he called 'zonal ego elements'. Over time, these cohere to form ego-consciousness as such. But if there is a problem in early relationships then this does not happen, and we witness the formation of what Plaut, by chance using the same term as Neumann, has called an 'emergency ego'. This *seems* strong, but in reality is merely brittle and incapable of allowing passage for, or relating to, the products of the imagination. These are then either experienced as overwhelming the ego, or become self-indulgent pretty pictures.

Behind the zonal ego elements Plaut perceived an 'archaic ego', which is present from birth but which will never become conscious. The archaic ego will continue throughout life and is not to be conceived of as prenatal or primitive. Plaut feels this idea is reinforced by what we now know about the activity of infants (see p. 73, above).

I would select two features of Plaut's argument which strengthen my notion of an underlying analytical psychological approach to the ego. First, the archaic ego is present from birth. This is something that continues throughout life, in much the same way as primary and secondary processes are said to coexist in Freudian theory. Second, that there are enormous differences in the quality of ego-consciousness depending on which zone is centred upon. I want to underline the idea of different ego styles.

A coherent central ego must be established to permit the passage of contents from inner to outer world in an assimilable way – true imagination will then flourish as opposed to relatively passive fantasising in which the mental contents are not owned by the individual but just happen to him. This passivity is a form of alienation arising from a defect in ego-consciousness caused by a missing feeling of having been held in the maternal environment.

Plaut felt that his formulation was in line with Jung's idea of the transcendent function in which a permeable ego sits midway between the person's individuality and his connection to the unconscious collectivity. He commented that in the development of Jung's thought a change seems to have taken place between the writing of 'The transcendent function' in 1916 and *Mysterium Coniunctionis* in 1955-6. In the earlier work Jung identifies two complementary ego functions – allowing material to flow by means of creative formulation and, then, the necessity of understanding such material. In the later work Jung talks of the need for a shift from a 'merely perceptive, i.e. *aesthetic*, attitude to one of *judgment*' and remarks that this is 'far from easy'. Plaut summarised Jung as calling for independent judgment by the ego of the internal content but, at the same time, for the ego to release its control to let such internal content reveal itself.

In the facilitation of ego-consciousness, Plaut regards the role of the analyst as analogous to that of the mother. He supplies a setting which can hold exciting experiences and let them be felt and shared, and also helps in finding and developing imagery which, if expressed in words, becomes linked to the conscious part of the ego. This last function could be referred to as lending the patient a bit of ego.

The proposition is that the mother/analyst lends his ego to the child/patient so that he may draw exciting experiences together into a central ego and hence feel a unit. It follows that what lies *beyond* the boundaries of the ego – that part of psychological experience so sought after by Hillman and Giegerich – may now be discussed in a realistic manner. Plaut distinguishes this realism from 'joint enthusiasm about interesting imagery (fantasy) which may not be firmly enough linked with the ego core' (1966, p. 136).

POST-JUNGIANS: RECAPITULATION

We have looked at Neumann's working out of the detail of the hero myth as an archetypal metaphor for consciousness. He stressed the way in which inevitable one-sided 'masculinity' is balanced by a new connection to the 'feminine'. Fordham objected to this primarily because of Neumann's insistence on a wholly unconscious, passive state at birth which is contradicted by empirical, scientific study of infants. Fordham followed Giegerich in disputing Neumann's picture of an archetype that can develop. But Giegerich regarded both Neumann *and* Fordham as caught up in genetic fantasy about infancy and childhood. Giegerich and Hillman saw in the heroic ego something inherently hostile to the imagination. Hillman pointed up the paradox in which, because hero and Great Mother are inseparable, heroic ego activity will lead directly back to the maternal world, rather than effecting a separation from mother. Plaut, far from perceiving the ego primarily as an opponent of the imagination, regarded a fully flexible or permeable ego as a prerequisite for the development of the imagination.

We may comment that the heroic ego, in exaggerated form, can be seen as an age-appropriate ego style. But that in itself begs the questions: how many ego styles are there, and what are they? The point is that seeing the ego as an ally of imagination underscores the inadequacy of the hero – or any other single image – as a representation of ego-consciousness. For example, only a non-heroic ego can dispense with its strengths to permit integration of the products of the imagination.

STYLES OF EGO-CONSCIOUSNESS

I mentioned a moment ago the notion of each bodily zone generating a different style and quality of ego-consciousness. We shall look at this now, because from it we get the clearest picture of a schema underpinning a wide range of styles of ego-consciousness. Lambert (1981b) has drawn a picture of an ego with at least six quite different styles derived from zonal development and from object relations theory and, I would add, each with its own mythology. The first three styles were mentioned initially by Abenheimer (1968).

The first style arises from the infant's response to frustration and his reaction to early separations. He tries to bridge the separation to get his demands met. The needs to be fulfilled are primarily oral and so we could call this an *oral style* of ego functioning.

Then, as the infant becomes aware of his growing independence, he explores his own capacities, attributes, power and productivity. Abenheimer, following Freud, sees defecation as the prime expression of this; the infant can do this by himself and the excretion experience focuses his awareness: the *anal style* of ego functioning.

What prompts a third style is that the child starts to control his inner contents to such a degree that the ego can develop its own interests, relatively divorced from the exigencies of want, need and vulnerability. This corresponds to the individual's free will, his capability to be the subject of actions. At this point the child is separate enough from the mother for this style of ego functioning to take the form of a turning away from her and from her femininity and acquiring a quite different character – hence a *phallic style* of ego functioning.

What is central for us is that Abenheimer points out that each style of ego functioning not only exists alongside the others but *is also in conflict with them* at any one time. The oral ego wants to be dependent and to regress, the anal ego is engaged in a search for self-esteem, and the phallic ego seeks to avoid (or perhaps kill) the mother altogether, and perceives its ideal as masculine.

Lambert feels that in addition to the three modes Abenheimer has outlined, he might have added one derived from the move from two-person to three-person functioning in an individual's development in his family; we could call this the *Oedipal style* of consciousness and I imagine it would concentrate on feelings of rivalry, possession and exclusion and the working out of guilty sensations. Lambert can also differentiate a style of ego-consciousness derived from fully *adult genital* functioning.

But the biggest omission for Lambert is that Abenheimer does not refer to changes in the quality of consciousness brought about by the shift in the infant from primitive split functioning to his having a real concern for the mother as a person. We discussed the differences such as these between the paranoid-schizoid and depressive positions earlier (cf. p. 77, above). This leads Lambert to postulate a *depressive position style* of ego functioning.

We can now identify six different styles of ego functioning: oral, anal, phallic, Oedipal, adult genital and that stimulated by the achievement of the depressive position (or stage of concern). Lambert concludes: 'we may postulate that any negotiation with these six positions must activate the degree of self-awareness that is appropriate to each one of them' (1981b, p. 10).

Lambert's further observation is of the importance of frustration. Lambert wonders if the tendency for frustration and discomfort to promote ego-consciousness has an archetypal base. He refers to the figure of the devil, Satan, the Adversary, as a 'spontaneous critique of the *status quo*' (1981b, p. 15). Lambert links the Adversary with such diverse phenomena as Popper's principle of falsifiability as a scientific yardstick, and the presence of a 'loyal opposition' in the British political system. Ego-consciousness seems to need this 'other', this archetypal thou. We can see this even more clearly in Zinkin's work which is discussed in a moment.

COMMENT: (3)

We are dealing with paradoxes: the ego is fundamental in forming attachments and relationships, yet is concerned with separation and boundary. The ego is necessary for imagination to be integrated, yet can annihilate the imaginal.

Are there stages of ego development exemplified by the stages of the hero myth? Is the hero – or any other one-sided image – adequate to express the multiplicity of ego styles? Is it possible to link the idea of a variegated, imaginal ego to zonal reference points and to good enough mothering?

The reader will recall a hypothesis of mine from Chapter 1. I suggested that the differences between the schools may also reveal the common base of the discipline of analytical psychology. Differences there are but also strange alliances and bedfellows. And polemic there certainly is – to the point of outrageous generalisations such as Hillman's charge that all comments about development of ego-consciousness are retrospective fantasy (1972, p. 243), or Lambert claiming that Hillman wants to do away with the ego altogether (Lambert, 1981a, p. 6).

I have been struck by the way in which analysts of the Developmental

School, such as Plaut with his concept of a permeable ego, Fordham with an ego that can give up its powers, Lambert with his six ego styles, can be compared with Hillman and Giegerich of the Archetypal School which sees the ego as operating under the aegis of many myths in parallel. Where does this leave Neumann and the Classical School which has been attacked by members of both the other two schools? I would suggest that Neumann, with his central image of re-connection to the feminine, may not be as monolithically heroic as all that. So there is a 'Jungian' approach or point of view with highly important differences of opinion between schools.

Kohut provides a reference point from psychoanalysis. He sees the ego as identified with a 'maturation morality' which has got Western civilisation in its grip. This was brought about largely by Freud who placed 'knowledge values' at the top of the tree of human capacities. This means, above all, the ability to discriminate between inner and outer, no matter how painful. What has evolved in psychoanalysis is too *rigid a distinction* between inner and outer (Kohut, 1980, pp. 480-1).

The work of the post-Jungians on ego-consciousness is part of a general modification to the value system of psychodynamics. Based on Jung's work, the post-Jungian synthesis can contribute to current re-evaluation of the ego.

DIALOGUE PRECEDES SELF-AWARENESS

An example of this synthesis is to be found in Zinkin's paper 'The collective and the personal' (1979). Zinkin felt that Jung's division of the psyche into personal and collective tends to see the individual in relation to the large collective group, and not in terms of one individual in relation to another. Jung always refers to 'the external world' as something lying beyond the individual psyche rather than as a world of other persons. And his idea of the ego as the centre of consciousness 'despite its great organising powers, is simply not the "I" that addresses, or recognises itself when addressed by, another person' (Zinkin, op. cit., p. 235). And although Jung made the self the centre (and sometimes the entirety) of the psyche, he gave 'no special consideration . . . to it having a function in relating to other people . . . his model did not allow of this possibility' (ibid.). So neither the ego nor the self is responsible for relations with other people!

Zinkin draws on Martin Buber to place the principle of *dialogue* as the central distinguishing feature of personal relationships. Zinkin says:

> my own view is that the experience of dialogue with another person from the beginning of life, primarily with the personal mother (or mother-substitute) is at the root of all other forms of dialogue – whether it be with God, with stones, with the outside world, or with 'contents of the unconscious'. (ibid., p. 237)

Zinkin summarises Buber as distinguishing three ways of perceiving another person. These ways are named by Buber as observing, looking on, and becoming aware. If we observe another person then we are taking an objective and dispassionate attitude towards them. If we look on another person then we open ourselves to his transmissions to us. But if we become aware of another person then we enter into a true and deep two-way dialogue with him. Zinkin's adaptation of Buber enables him to include personal relating within the sphere of the ego and also to differentiate what sort of ego activity is occurring. Here again, we may note that ego functioning is conceived of in terms of a number of differing styles.

Zinkin then takes a step of fundamental importance. He challenges the basic Jungian idea that consciousness 'arises' from the unconscious. Using data from studies of mother-infant interaction to support his idea, he suggests that 'in the very first weeks of life an early form of "conversation" takes place between mother and infant – sometimes called "proto-conversation" ' (ibid., p. 237). The inference is that it is false to state that the baby *first* experiences a Great Mother collective image, and only then an actual mother differentiated by consciousness.

Zinkin wonders if the child may not first experience his personal mother and then generalise this into an idea of mother-ness. If so, then the personal – in one way of looking at it – precedes the collective. Zinkin tries to resolve the issue by analogising with the field of language studies. There are two points of view about the development of language. Some workers think that a child observes an entity and then abstracts a general class from that, and others say that we have an innate sense of category and recognise an entity that fits into the category. But it seems possible that both these processes may go on *simultaneously*. So, argues Zinkin, the personal-first hypothesis could co-exist with the more generally agreed view that consciousness of the personal mother arises from the collective unconscious.

One of Zinkin's section headings in the paper I am discussing is 'Dialogue precedes Self-Awareness'. This catchphrase is based on Buber's '*a priori* of relationship' idea. Dialogue with another precedes dialogue with oneself. Dialogue with the other world or with oneself is imaginary, says Buber, and only with another person can true dialogue take place. No analytical psychologist could agree that dialogue with oneself is 'imaginary', if that is meant pejoratively, and Zinkin is no exception. But the interaction between dialogue with another and self-awareness is certainly a major factor in the development of ego-consciousness (and see pp. 182 ff., below, for a consideration of this in relation to analysis).

HERO AND ANTI-HERO

Finally I would like to turn to an attempt by Redfearn to take Neumann's thesis further whilst avoiding the pitfalls noted by Fordham and others. In his paper 'The captive, the treasure, the hero and the "anal" stage of development' (1979), Redfearn raises the possibility of enlarging our whole idea of ego-consciousness so as to rid it of its elevated, superior (and possibly compulsive) tone. He sees an anti-heroic strand in the hero metaphor:

If we consider what the 'treasures' of the unconscious are, they are the 'treasures' of incest, the 'treasure' of sadism and other negative pre-genital

82

impulses, the 'treasures' of all the parts of the personality repudiated and abhorred (the opposite of 'treasured') by consciousness.... They are only available 'behind the mother's back' and they are, as we find in our clinical material, phantasised as the 'treasures' of the mother's insides or backsides. Of course these 'treasures' have to be transformed into acceptable forms, and this is usually the work that has to be done by the hero helped by the wise mother/anima/sister. (ibid., p. 190)

Redfearn reminds us that 'Jung dug deep into the well of his own unconsciousness, and he and his unconscious psyche worked hard to convert the filth and rubbish he found there to treasures of universal value' (ibid., p. 190). Jung himself specifically connected the hero's quest for the treasure and the feminine to an excremental dimension:

> if a much venerated object is related by the unconscious to the anal region, we have to conclude that this is a way of expressing respect and attention, such as a child feels . . . we might also mention the intimate connection between excrement and gold in alchemy, the lowest value allies itself with the highest. (*CW* 5, para. 276)

Redfearn visualises the hero image as essentially compensatory to feelings of dependence (normal dependence, that is). He does not agree with Fordham that the hero represents a manic defence (Fordham, 1981, p. 117). Rather the heroic stance and style of ego-consciousness is part of growing up and Redfearn links the hero image to the infant's active part in feeding and in making demands generally.

So the hero is also an anti-hero. My own view is that, because of developments in consciousness and experiences in this century, such a shift in definition is possible. This is observable in developments in literature generally and in the novel in particular. For instance, the American literary critics Fiedler and Wise have given us, respectively, the metaphors of 'the bum as American culture hero' and 'the *schlemiel* as modern hero' (1955, 1971). The modern hero, the modern image of ego-consciousness is, as Redfearn hints in his paper, adrift in a world he did not create, yearning for a more than earthly power. The hero wonders if he can achieve a separate and individual destiny and we can see this in the adventures of today's picaresque heroes in the novels of Kerouac, Mailer, Bellow, Updike, Heller and so on.

This hero drifts in and out of love affairs, friendships, jobs and groups; in a way he is searching *for* a dragon to fight as a way of getting started on the path to soul-relatedness. Everywhere he feels the imprisoning effects of the terrible mother. He needs order and meaning but often finds chaos and meaninglessness. This search may be said to constitute the social expression of the quest of ego-consciousness for the anima. We can see it in generational politics of protest or in explosions of interest in 'humanistic' psychology – i.e. the psychology of relating to others.

Appendix to Chapter 3
Developments in typology

This subject is placed in an Appendix because of its technical nature and the risk of obscuring the lines of the debates on the ego, and not because the topic is unimportant.

It would be tempting to agree with Storr that 'whilst the dichotomy of extraversion versus introversion has proved valuable and continues to stimulate research, the quaternity of the four functions has been discarded by all except the most dedicated Jungians and is, I suspect, little used even by them' (1973, p. 79). This is not born out by the results of a survey conducted by Plaut (1972) into the views of Jungian analysts on the usefulness of Jung's typology in clinical practice, and the importance of typology to Jungian psychology generally. Half of the analysts who replied found typology helpful in clinical practice and three-quarters thought that typology is of importance to Jungian psychology. Of course, as Plaut admits, there are huge disadvantages in such a survey. For example, the analysts not interested in typology may simply have chucked the questionnaire away. But the results, coupled with the large numbers of articles appearing in the *Journal of Analytical Psychology* on the subject, seem to indicate an extensive interest. Similarly, Bradway and Wheelwright found that 74 per cent of analysts use typology with 5 per cent or more of their patients (1978). The motivation for some, but not all, of these post-Jungians seems to be to try to put one area of Jungian psychology on to a more scientific base by improving tests that measure the functioning of consciousness.

Plaut sees the contemporary debate as:

> a confrontation between the ideas of fixed types versus the symbolism constituted by a psychological framework within which movements (possibly accelerated by the process of analysis) do occur. (1972, p. 147)

I do not intend to go into the precise mechanisms and details of the construction, administration and scoring of the tests. The two main tests are the Gray-Wheelwright test (1964) (known as the GW) and the Myers-Briggs Type Indicator (1962) (known as the MBTI). Both of these tests use rather closed questions posed in the form of alternatives; in this way, it may be objected, several of Jung's hypotheses are *built into the tests designed to evaluate them*. For example, Loomis and Singer (1980) conducted an experiment in which they rewrote the two classical tests so that fixed choice questions were eliminated. For example, in GW there is a question:

At a party I   a. like to talk
                b. like to listen.

This question was replaced by two items covering the same ground but separated in the test. The participants were asked to use the 'old' test and the 'new' test in the same session and some staggering results emerged. The discrepancy between the old and new was 61 per cent regarding something as basic as superior function and 48 per cent of the subjects did not have an inferior function opposed to the superior function in the traditionally expected manner.

Loomis and Singer wonder why the superior/inferior polarity has to be stressed when it has so little validity when looked at empirically. Is not this contrary to the basic Jungian idea that opposites can be transcended? They wonder why 'sensation and intuition, or thinking and feeling, or introversion and extraversion, *never* appear paired as the two most highly developed functions in any profiles obtained by inventories measuring Jung's typology' and conclude that this is more than a result of a forced choice question structure (1980, p. 353). There has been a failure to consider the polarity stressed by Jung in a critical way. They add that more research is needed but, especially for creative people, the polarity can be seen as no more than an *assumption*. Loomis and Singer have inadvertently provided support for one of the most common Jungian 'howlers' made by students. Earlier, we saw that Jung was more interested in opposition *within* the rational or the irrational pairs of functions rather than that *between* rational and irrational tendencies within a person. This was because he felt that true opposites shared a common base. Students often challenge the idea that the inferior function must be from the same side of the rational/irrational divide as the superior function and may, for many years, have been right to do so (and see the next chapter for more discussion of the theory of opposites).

Bradway and Detloff (1976) replaced the distinction between rational and irrational pairs of functions by one between *judging* and *perceiving* – terms less subject to misunderstanding, as Jung noted. (This is a distinction brought out in a similar way in the MBTI as well.) The irrational functions deal with perceptions, with the discovery that things *are*, while the rational functions provide judgment on the raw material. As a further revision of Jung's theory, Bradway and Detloff feel that making a sharp distinction between superior and auxiliary functions is problematic. These authors found that the Gray-Wheelwright test did not successfully differentiate between the two predominant functions so that, when using it, the list of sixteen basic types could be reduced to eight. This is achieved by coupling what had previously been divided into superior and auxiliary. For example, a person who previously was described as superior thinking/auxiliary intuition would now be referred to as using thinking and intuition and the same terminology would describe one who previously was held to have superior intuition/auxiliary thinking.

Bradway and Wheelwright also found that, while the Gray-Wheelwright test failed to distinguish superior and auxiliary functions, self-typing may be more accurate in that respect (1978). It will be noted that Bradway and Detloff/Wheelwright are not quite as extreme in their revisionism as Loomis and Singer, in that the latter pair of writers challenge the basic oppositionalistic structure of Jung's theory. Nevertheless, they anticipated Loomis and Singer's undermining of the concept of the inferior function. When Bradway and Wheelwright examined the results of self-typing compared to those achieved with the Gray-Wheelwright test, they found that almost 25 per cent of the Jungian analysts carrying out the self-typing did not state their inferior function as the opposite of their superior function in the way Jung's theory requires. That is, the inferior function was said to be the opposite of the superior function in terms of a rational/irrational divide.

Perhaps the most extreme view amongst post-Jungians is that of Metzner *et al.* (1981). They regard the four functions as able to operate without reference to any particular overall pattern in combinations of superior, auxiliary and inferior depending on the situation. They also dispute that there is a verifiable distinction between judgment and perception and claim that categories of 'experience' and 'judgment of experience' serve better. They propose a twelvefold typology in which each of the four functions could have any of the others as 'inferior' (in a new use of the word; what they mean is that a feeling type, for example, will have an amalgam of the other three functions less prominent in his make-up). They feel, like Storr, that the cross-shaped mandala-like representation of the four functions, though emotionally satisfying, is far too restrictive.

In summary, there are three main proposed modifications for Jung's typology: Loomis and Singer wonder if either the two rational or the two irrational functions in combination might not give a clearer picture of the conscious orientation of a person. Bradway and Detloff advocate desisting from attempts to differentiate sharply between superior and auxiliary function. Metzner, Burney and Mahlburg regard all four functions as capable of serving in any capacity or combination.

The maelstrom is such that it is almost a relief to come across Meier and Wozny (1978) who used a sophisticated computerised approach to devastate all the tests. The results of this are that the tests seem only to measure three rather basic things: extraversion-introversion (but in a superficial way), the divide between introverted thinking and extraverted feeling (extreme polar opposites in Jung's original model), and the general band of sensation-intuition can be differentiated – that is, sensates can be distinguished from intuitives.

As Plaut suggested, some post-Jungians are using typology in a different way: to argue various theses about the nature of man and the structure of his psyche. Adler proposed that typology is not so much a schema for the testing of personality as it is of value in revealing the dynamic interplay of opposites which has much to do with the self-regulating psyche (1979, p. 92).

The question of the clinical applicability of typology remains a crucial one and has been pressed most strongly by Fordham (1972). He points out that there is an ambiguity in Jung's work on types between considering them as something eternal and given in the personality – a sort of equivalent of archetypes in consciousness – and seeing types as capable of undergoing alteration and integration during analysis and individuation. But, adds Fordham, it is the eternal rather than the dynamic aspect of typology that Jung and most post-Jungians have stressed. Nevertheless, in his memoir of Jung, Fordham (1975) recalls that most of those who went to see Jung for one or two appointments (which was a great number of people due to his fame and the established ritual of new 'Jungian' analysts paying a visit to the master) were staggered at how intuitive he was. Fordham wonders if, far from guessing, Jung was using his theory of types in those one-off sessions to search for the hidden unconscious content, i.e. the inferior function, which, as yet undiffereniated from the unconscious, was likely to be a thorn in the flesh.

Von Franz's formulations (1971) do help us to see how typology might be used in clinical practice, perhaps more as a point of orientation for the analyst than anything else. She feels that the superior function (how we usually approach the world) arises from a biological predisposition coupled with a natural tendency for people to play to their strengths and develop what they are best at. Over time, the promotion of the already stronger way of proceeding may lead to a degeneration of the rest of the conscious personality. Sometimes a child is forced to be other than he is, or a family member is assigned a function within the family, and the resultant distortions present specific problems.

The underdeveloped side of the conscious personality remains in the unconscious as a slow, infantile and tyrannical element (to paraphrase Jung). This is what people are referring to when they claim they 'just can't' do such and such a thing or that they are 'no good' at something. For example, an extreme intuitive will find filling in even a simple form an extraordinary burden and will have to spend hours on it. Some people are virtually innumerate, others clumsy and inept at mechanical tasks like typing and so on. In general, the person may experience this undeveloped side of himself, this inferior function, as destructive and a nuisance to ego-consciousness.

But there is a positive side. Von Franz tells of fairy tales in which there is a king with three sons. The youngest son is a complete fool when compared with the others but it is he who finds success in whatever task or problem is facing the country – and this is after he has been ridiculed for even thinking of trying to help. This youngest son is, it should be noted, the fourth person in the fairy tale and, portrayed as a fool, is a representation of the inferior function. He stands for 'the despised part of the personality, the ridiculous and unadapted part, but also that part which builds up the connection with the unconscious totality of the person' (ibid., p. 7).

So the inferior function of consciousness acts as a link between the ego and the unconscious and needs assimilating into the ego. One particular consequence of this is that a one-sidedly introverted person may have to develop an extraverted inferior function in order to grow, making a demand on that person to become *more* worldly or materialistic. This needs to be said because the individuation process in over-simplified form seems to involve nothing but introspection. Individuation for some people may mean a reorientation outwards.

Although the problems caused by the inferior function can be got rid of temporarily by projection, the special relationship between the shadow and the inferior function means that this cannot last for ever. Developing the inferior function can lead to breakdown, but this may be worthwhile if the one-sidedness is rectified.

Finally von Franz quotes Jung quoting the legendary alchemist Maria Prophetissa: 'One becomes two, two becomes three, and out of the third comes the one as the fourth.' Realisation of the inferior function helps in the realisation of the whole personality and this is why it is necessary to attempt to integrate the inferior function into ego-consciousness. The scene is now set for the next chapter on the self and individuation in which issues of oneness and multiplicity are paramount.

4

The self and individuation

Freud may have challenged our conception of consciousness but he elevated the centre of consciousness, the ego, to the highest position. Jung, as we saw, was concerned not to overestimate the importance of the ego, seeing it as arising out of, and subordinate to, the self. Jung's use of the word *self* is different from everyday usage and from psychoanalytic uses; in addition the term has an inclusive quality. I have tried to pick out the main themes.

The structure of the chapter is as follows: first the central features of Jung's attitude to, and use of, the concept of the self are discussed and then his theory of individuation is examined. Next, I review some of the general problems that have been perceived in Jung's ideas. Moving on to the post-Jungians, their extensive contributions are analysed and commented upon. Finally, I give some psychoanalytic parallels.

THE SELF AND MEANING

Throughout this chapter on the self the reader will find a repeated use of such words as unity, order, organisation, wholeness, balance, integration, totality, regulation, pattern, centrality and synthesis. Such a variety of terms would have little weight were it not for the fundamental connection of the self to questions of meaning.

What, in Jung's conception, is the self in pursuit of? His answer was the discovery of meaning and purpose in life. When we speak, therefore, of self-realisation we mean more than a clinical goal. Jung did not deny the existence of meaninglessness but asserted that life without meaning is not worth living. Traditionally, questions of meaning have been the province of organised religion, with a tendency to see meaning in dogmatic and moralistic terms, though, of course, for many it does not feel that way.

When we speak of 'balance' or of 'pattern' we do not do so as if Zeus has laid down a precise schema to be followed obediently. There is always Hermes, prankster and messenger of the Gods, to exploit mankind's incorrigible disobedience. Put in other language, we need to distinguish between the structure of the self, which *is* to do with the patterning and balancing of different parts into an integral whole, and the content of the self, an infinite variety of shapes and images.

A bodily parallel would be the glands; they each have their own organising function, but in health they are regulated or balanced in relation to each other by a dynamic in the whole body. Without that their specific organising function is useless. In maturation, sometimes one predominates and sometimes another, e.g. sex hormones. So the picture is not one of static 'order' but rather a dynamic integration. Similarly, archetypes have their own organising function but need to be related to the whole.

As Jung stressed, consciousness is the factor that gives the world a meaning and he points up the individual nature of such meaning. Jung's point was that it is illogical to speak of 'life' as if it preceded 'meaning'; in fact the two are indissolubly linked (*CW* 9i, para. 67). And, as Jaffé put it:

> no answer is the final one and none of them can answer the question of the meaning of life completely. The answer changes as our knowledge of the world changes; meaning and unmeaning are part of the plenitude of life. (1971, p. 11)

EGO AND SELF

Jung was alerted to something greater than the ego by his personal and clinical experiences, by contact with Eastern religions, and by discovering what appears to motivate the transcendent function. We looked at the part played by the ego in integrating a 'mediatory product' formed by a synthesis of conscious dynamics and unconscious contents. That quality of the integration depended on the strength of the ego and, reciprocally, strengthened the ego. But the self is responsible for the capacity to produce any blend (the mediatory product) in the first place. Initially, Jung regarded the self as comprising the conscious and unconscious, but later he differentiated self and ego as follows:

> The ego stands to the self as the moved to the mover, or as object to subject, because the determining factors which radiate out from the self surround the ego on all sides and are therefore supraordinate to it. The self, like the unconscious, is an *a priori* existent out of which the ego evolves. (*CW* 11, para. 391)

The relationship between the ego and the self is a subject that several post-Jungians have worked on extensively. Here we may note that a mutuality is implied, that neither self nor ego exist independently in spite of the supraordinate nature of the self. A familiar tag for Jungians is that the self needs the ego as much as the ego needs the self, hence the term 'ego-self axis' (see pp. 116-18, below).

SYNTHESIS AND TOTALITY

A working definition of the self as Jung envisioned it would be: 'the potential for integration of the total personality'. This would include all psychological and mental processes, physiology and biology, all positive and negative, realised or unrealised potentials, and the spiritual dimension. The self contains the seeds of the individual's destiny and looks back to phylogeny as well. The definition stresses integration because the self functions as a container for all these disparate elements. Such synthesis is relative in practice; we are concerned with an ideal – the culmination of the self-regulating psyche and of the psychosomatic, teleological archetypes. The self involves the potential to become whole or, experientially, to *feel* whole. Part of feeling whole is feeling a sense of purpose and so a vital element in integration is sensing some goal. Part of wholeness, too, is feeling that life makes sense and having an inclination to do something about it when it does not; a religious capacity. Jung says:

> The self, though on the one hand simple, is on the other hand an extremely composite thing, a 'conglomerate soul', to use the Indian expression. (*CW* 9i, para. 634)

THE CENTRE OF PERSONALITY

In the same passage, Jung refers to the self as a 'centre' of personality' – a distinction from the 'total personality'. Similarly, he conceives of the self as the central archetype or centre of an energy field. This double definition (centre and at the same time totality) makes for a problem, but Jung confidently asserts that 'the self is not only the centre but also the whole circumference which embraces both conscious and unconscious' (*CW* 12, para. 44). The formulation that the self is the centre *and* the circumference of the personality may be compared with the idea that the ego is the centre *and* the totality of consciousness.

It is clear that Jung's idea of the self is different from ordinary feelings of selfhood or the psychoanalytic concept of personal identity; these important qualities Jung locates in the ego. The idea of a centre, of having a centre, of being motivated or regulated by a centre, may be the most accurate description of what is involved in a *feeling* of wholeness. There is a sense in which a definition of the self emphasising wholeness and totality can be seen as a conceptual hypothesis (ideal), whereas feelings of having a central self-core express the experience of the self.

91

BALANCE, PATTERN, ORDER

A further quality of the self as a centre of personality is that it permits a suggestion of pattern, balance and order, without implying any cessation of the dynamics of the psyche. In Chapter 2 we looked at archetypal patterning and the question was raised: 'What patterns the archetypes themselves?' My partial answer was that, by conceiving of an archetypal ingredient rather than particular archetypes or archetypal representations, we automatically include a teleological element; what is archetypal involves goals. Jung preferred sometimes to consider the self as an archetype whose special function is to balance and pattern, not only the other archetypes, but *all* of a person's life in terms of purposes as yet unconsidered and unlived. The impact of this archetype could be observed in such collective phenomena as the development and symbolic use of numbers – for example, one to symbolise unity, two dialogue, three the Trinity (or the Oedipus complex), four the totality of something – the four points of the compass, the four humours, Jung's own four functions of consciousness, and so on.

It is difficult to see what the precise function of the self archetype would be, given that all the archetypes have such a patterning function. The concept would be redundant but for two special, additional properties of the self that raise it above the ordinary rank of archetypes. These are (a) the self functioning as a synthesiser and mediator of opposites within the psyche, and (b) the self as the prime agent in the production of deep, awesome, 'numinous' symbols of a self-regulatory and healing nature. These special aspects of the self lead some post-Jungians to use a capital 'S'; lower case is used in the *Collected Works* to avoid the appearance of esotericism.

THE SELF AND THE OPPOSITES

We have already discussed the bipolarity of archetypes. For Jung, bipolarity is of the essence; it is a necessary condition for psychic energy and for a life lived at a level other than that of blind instinctuality. Opposites are required for the definition of any entity or process – one end of a spectrum helps to define the other, to give us a conception of it. And sometimes the conflict is such that we 'suffer' the opposites. Jung suggests that it is fruitless to search for the primary member of a pair of opposites – they are truly linked and cannot be separated; they involve each other. The General Index to Jung's *Collected Works* (*CW* 20) contains a list of pairs of linked opposites which repays contemplation, for it demonstrates the basic part played by oppositionalism in Jung's psychological theories and in his way of thinking generally. For example: ego/self, conscious/unconscious, personal/collective, extraversion/introversion, rational/irrational, Eros/Logos, image/instinct. In fact, virtually all of Jung's major ideas are expressed in a manner involving opposites.

A non-Jungian may want to say that of course life is defined in terms of opposites, what is so extraordinary or particularly psychological about this recognition? Jung's insistence on the fundamental nature of oppositionalism can be further attacked by arguing that it reflects over-dependence on Germanic philosophy – e.g. Hegel's thesis-antithesis-synthesis. It is certainly true that Jung was influenced by Hegel, that he did conceive of psychological process in terms of discrimination and then synthesis of opposites. The experience of synthesising the opposites involves a process of balancing or self-regulation. Jung refers to this as *compensation* – implying the automatic rectification of an imbalance or one-sided attitude. Compensation may initially appear in the negative guise of symptoms. It is not to be thought of as implying that balance is regularly or easily attainable. Neurosis can then be seen as unbalanced or one-sided development arising out of the dominance of one of the two sides of the pair.

As we suggested just now, Jung tends to conceive of the psyche itself in terms of balance or imbalance. This can be further spelled out to demonstrate psychopathological consequences of imbalance:

ego/self – pathologically the self overwhelms the ego, or the ego inflates and identifies with the self.

ego/persona – confusion between genuine identity and social role.

ego/animus-anima – the ego may reject contrasexuality (see Chapter 7) leading to stereotypical one-sidedness; in a man, 'macho' behaviour, ruthlessness, over-intellectualism; in a woman, fluffy or 'hysterical' behaviour. Or the ego may identify completely with the contrasexual element, expressed because of its primitivity initially as a stereotype, leading in a man to moodiness, sentimentality, lassitude and effeminacy, and in a woman dogmatism, competitiveness and insistence upon the literal or factual. It should be emphasised that the contrasexual archetype functions in such stereotypical terms only when there is an ego/animus-anima imbalance.

ego/shadow – pathologically, a rejection of instinctuality, hence a depotentiating of the personality, or a projection of unacceptable facets of the personality on to others (and see p. 65, above). It is also possible to identify with the shadow – a form of negative inflation such as self-depreciation, lack of self-confidence, fear of success (and a peculiar 'analytic' state in which everything is put down to dark and nasty unconscious motivations).

typology – Jung's description of the attitudes and functions of consciousness rests on these ideas about opposites. However, as extraversion and introversion seem largely inborn, it is not really possible to speak of them as opposites within a person, save *in potentia*. But as an explanation for much interpersonal friction they come into their own as representing opposite world views. There is also a possible tension to be observed between the inborn extraversion-introversion position and that which is habitually used. Finally, in individuation (see p. 101, below), a balance between the two attitudes might develop. The four functions, on the other hand, are redolent of opposites. They are aligned in pairs of opposites – each pair contains a further pair of opposites, and so on.

In the appendix to the previous chapter we noted that there is doubt about the validity of such an oppositional hypothesis. On the other hand however,

Apter, in his non-analytic theory of psychological reversals (1982), suggests that motivation and other aspects of psychological functioning are best expressed in terms of 'bistability' and 'reversal theory'. Similarly, Lévi-Strauss refers to 'binary oppositions' as underpinning human thought and culture (cf. Leach, 1974).

This picks up on Jung's view that the tension of opposites re-allocates psychic energy. But in addition to this, and to defining each other, opposites can also constellate one another; a strong light calls forth a strong shadow. This explains the phenomenon in which a polar extreme suddenly reverses and assumes exactly the opposite character. This tendency for any extreme position to swing to the opposite Jung referred to as *enantiodromia*, borrowing the term from Heraclitus. Jung defined *enantiodromia* as 'the emergence of the unconscious opposite in the course of time' and quotes Heraclitus as saying that 'it is the opposite that is good for us' (*CW* 6, paras 708-9). As we shall see, post-Jungians from the Developmental School have shown how Jung's attitude to opposites can be seen as relevant to personality development (see pp. 115-16, below).

FROM SIGN TO SYMBOL

The second of the self's two functions that distinguish it from the other archetypes concerns representations and symbols that, in the light of Jung's theory, can be seen as of the self, leading to personal experience of it. Before considering this, it is important to understand what Jung means when he refers to symbols.

Jung's own definition of symbol can be summarised as referring to the best possible formulation of a relatively unknown psychic content that cannot be grasped by consciousness. Mattoon (1981) illustrates this by the symbol of the 'kingdom of heaven'. This image becomes a symbol because it refers to something unknown which could hardly be described by a simple, single statement. Specific metaphors can be used to 'circumambulate' the symbol, but the symbolic image 'points to a meaning that is beyond description' (ibid., p. 135). For Jung a symbol is not a *sign*; that refers to what is already known (a road sign, a sign for the lavatory, and so on). The psyche spontaneously produces symbols when the intellect is at a loss and cannot cope with an inner or outer situation. A symbol is not an analogy which simply illuminates or translates (though Frey-Rohn, 1974, p. 256, refers to symbols as 'psychic analogies').

L. Stein (1973) tells us that the word symbol derives from the Greek words *sym*, meaning together, common, simultaneous, and *bolon* – that which has been thrown. Hence, symbol as the throwing together of things which have something in common (ibid., p. 46). Jacobi (1959) finds an examination of the German word *Sinnbild* worthwhile. *Sinn* means sense or meaning and *Bild* means image – hence, symbol as meaningful image (ibid., p. 95). Edinger (1962) demonstrates a correspondence to our modern idea of a tally; Greek traders would cut notches in a stick to show the quantity of goods being dealt with. When buyer and seller parted the stick would be split vertically and each

94

participant would then hold an identical record. Hence, symbol as a healing of a split in man (ibid., p. 66). Westmann (1961) suggested that the split stick was divided between an initiate in a cult and he who initiated him; a further prospective association.

Analytical psychologists reiterate the differences between Jung's approach to the symbol and that of Freud. Freud saw a symbol as a translation of one image into another, necessitated by repression, usually of sexuality. So 'skyscraper' symbolises 'penis' which cannot be allowed into consciousness *per se* for fear of castration. Symbols are therefore primarily defensive in Freud's view and not the purposive, healing psychic inventions of Jung's conceptualisation. The most often quoted nexus of the difference between the two approaches is their attitudes to incestuous imagery. Freud is said to take this literally; Jung to see a desire for re-connection to roots and for personality enrichment. We shall see in the next chapter that psychoanalysts have gradually moved closer to Jung's attitude, both to sexuality in general and to incestuous imagery in particular. Jung felt that Freud's approach to symbols was too rigid – though he does himself ascribe relatively fixed meanings to some symbols, e.g. water for the unconscious. But the full meaning can only be revealed through amplification and is, therefore, not fixed (but see Hillman, p. 118, below). And Jung's idea of the symbol as expressing a conflict in a way that helps resolve it has no parallel in Freud.

There are various special aspects of Jung's approach to symbols which are more or less taken for granted by contemporary analytical psychologists; an enumeration of these may help the reader to empathise with the background to post-Jungian approaches to symbols.

(1) Symbolic meaning permeates the vehicle that carries it. This means that the form of the symbol will be appropriate to its meaning. Sometimes one image will be both sign and symbol – Mattoon suggests that the cross fits this description.

(2) Symbols transcend opposites but some symbols take this further to embrace the totality; these are symbols of the self. As an illustration of the movement from diversity to unity, a patient of mine dreamt that he saw a box of insects copulating; there were hundreds of them, male and female. The process of reproduction was so rapid he could observe it. But instead of increasing the population of the box the reprodutive activity seemed to be leading to fewer and fewer, larger and larger, more and more human forms. The dreamer awoke before any conclusion was revealed but he speculated whether the end would have been one insect or one human or two insects or two humans. We took this to symbolise his increasing integration.

(3) The self symbolises the infinitude of the archetype and anything that a man postulates or conceives of as being a greater totality than himself can become a symbol of the self – Christ or Buddha, for example.

(4) Central to all the schools of analytical psychology is the idea that the main question we ask of a symbol is its *meaning*, rather than its derivation or an enquiry into the precise composition of the image. This has led to stress being laid on a symbolic approach or attitude as being of paramount importance. This is emphasised by Jung (*CW* 6, paras 818-9), but developed further and made more fundamental by post-Jungians (e.g. Whitmont,

1969, pp. 15-35).

(5) Although some symbols will do their work irrespective of conscious attitude, others require a particular attitude before they are perceived and experienced as symbols at all. Note – this attitude is more than simple consciousness which can be all-too literal and unsymbolic. What is referred to as a symbolic attitude can be facilitated in analysis, though carefully and cautiously. We shall see later in this chapter how the formation of a symbolic attitude can also be hindered or facilitated in developmental experience (p. 120, below).

(7) Symbols work towards self-regulation and on behalf of a natural amplitude of the personality.

Jacobi (1959, p. 82) makes the point that the more universal the stratum of the psyche from which the symbol derives, the more forcefully it impacts on the individual. Images such as fire, water, earth, wood, salt, with far-reaching implications for man, become powerful symbols. Similarly, the symbols of the house ('personality'), and blood ('passion') are also stronger than usual. So we are faced with a hierarchy of symbols – as well, it should be noted, with some rather fixed meanings.

Jacobi goes on to question whether the idea of 'self-portrait of the instinct', usually applied to images, is applicable to symbols. She concludes that this is not the case because the symbol is 'upward-looking', involving a spiritual meaning. Nevertheless, there seems to be a general connection between symbol and instinct in that the transcending symbol, the third factor in any polarised conflict, has the capacity to transform energy by switching its direction into new channels. Then, as we have seen, the ego either will or will not be able to sustain the new energy pattern and the symbol.

SYMBOL IN SERVICE OF SELF

We can now return to our discussion of symbols of the self which may lead to experience of it. Such symbols refer to something above and beyond the individual, or at the centre of the individual, or suggest *depth*. In all cases, there will be a feeling of integration, coupled with a sense of place in the scheme of things; the personality is enriched. It is possible to distinguish symbols that refer to the self *per se* from symbols of the self as an ordering agency, though the same symbol may exist in both categories. For example, the image of the child may function as a *symbol of the self* (child as totality, integration, potential), or as a *compensatory symbol* for an over-adult person, putting him in touch with areas from which he is cut off.

Symbols of wholeness are exemplified by mandalas; this is a Sanskrit word meaning 'magical circle', referring to a geometric figure with more-or-less regular sub-divisions, divided by four or multiples thereof, and said by Jung to express the totality, radiating from a centre. Mandalas may be drawn during Jungian analysis and the character of them can be interpreted. Mandalas may serve as images of compensatory wholeness for people who are fragmented or be used defensively.

Symbols of the self not only *express* potential integration or order, they also *contribute to it,* and also to the psyche's self-healing capacities. Symbolic experiences are often stated by Jung to be *numinous* – that is, powerful, awesome, enriching, mysterious – but not capable of being described exactly. Not only symbols of a pictorial nature can be numinous – states of bodily feeling or, on the other hand, confrontations with works of art or natural phenomena can promote this type of experience. This is close to what some humanistic psychologists (e.g. Maslow) call 'peak experiences' (Samuels, 1979; Mattoon, 1981, p. 194). This rather bald summary of mine cannot hope to describe experiences of this nature and we must remember that there is considerable room for self-deception. However, we can connect this type of experience to ordinary human emotion. I am thinking of the feeling of having been created, of being a creature rather than a creator, or of being in the presence of something one did not create oneself, which is a part of numinous experience. This is a more differentiated version of the sense of discovery of otherness that accompanies a move out of infantile grandiose fantasies of doing without the other. As Bateson (1979) says, the discovery of difference is a 'joyous shock' (= numinous).

Jung and his closer collaborators have schematised the imagery that forms self-symbols (e.g. Jacobi, 1959, pp. 139ff.) but, it has been suggested, in so doing have made it more difficult for a person to find his own position by predefining the symbolic meaning of an image (see p. 118, below). It is the personal implication of symbols of the self that promotes growth, not knowledge or classification of them; only a personal experience of the symbol leads to a reconciliation of the opposites.

A patient of mine dreamt of a pitchfork of the type used on farms to bale and stack hay. Her associations to this image were that the fork's tines were sinuously curvey like a woman's body, that its prongs were sharp, and that such a fork is used on the land in a food-productive way, and not in a domestic garden. The image of the fork with its two prongs suggested that two tendencies were being worked out in the dream. The feminine curves, so soft and gentle, contrasted with the two spikes. These, the dreamer felt, were two horrific nipples and yet, at the same time, oddly reassuring in that they complemented the soft femininity, gave it 'a point' (pun suggesting goal, or end product).

The fork image encapsulated two different reconciliations. First, the dreamer's mother was now felt to be feminine as well as phallic and threatening (in reality the mother was a successful career woman); the sharp nipples were reconciled by the curviness and the connection to fertility. Second, the dreamer, who was herself also involved in a career structure as well as being a mother, had been unsure whether the two could be combined and had unconsciously held herself back at work (she was a lecturer). She automatically felt that her male colleagues were brighter, and refrained from contributing to discussions and so on. The fork image suggested that not only could the two sides of her life be 'held' together but also that this could be productive in a wider context. The result was that she was able to finish her book, which became a standard work, and undertake a highly successful lecture tour.

THE TRANSPERSONAL SELF: (1) THE GOD-IMAGE

Mention of 'otherness' leads to a consideration of the self as a transpersonal entity. This can best be examined by a division of transpersonal aspects of the self into three. The first (discussed in this section) conceives the God-image in man as a symbol of the self. In the same way that, say, Christ, represents a personality greater than the average man, Christ, as a symbol, represents something greater than the average ego – the self (*CW* 11, para. 414). Jung is not saying anything categorical about God's existence; that cannot be stated in any empirical way. He is referring to feelings that a person can have of being part of a divinity, or of being connected to a divinity, understood as something greater than himself and outside the usual order of things. Jung comments that religions arise naturally and can be seen as an expression of a religious 'instinct' (*CW* 17, para. 157). Stripped of dogma and intellectualising, religions rest on experiences of the awesome – visions, revelations, transformations, miracles, conversions, and so on. These are more profound than attempts to see God as a glorified parent or anthropos which simply reflect needs of the ego to see things 'out there', in projection.

Symbols of the self and symbols of the God-image in man are really the same thing, Jung says:

> As one can never distinguish empirically between a symbol of the self and a God-image, the two ideas, however much we try to differentiate them, always appear blended together, so that the self appears synonymous with the inner Christ of the Johannine and Pauline writings. . . . Psychologically speaking, the domain of 'gods' begins where consciousness leaves off, for at that point man is already at the mercy of the natural order. . . . To symbols of wholeness that come to him from there he attaches names which vary according to time and place. (*CW* 11, para. 231)

As Frey-Rohn (1974, p. 215) comments, both forms of awareness – psychological experience of the self and religious experience – are based on the same thing, namely something experienced as a comprehensive, integrated unity.

Jung saw Christ as a symbol of the self in his reconciliation of the divine/human and spirit/body pairs of opposites. And in Christ's resurrection he transcends and mediates the opposites of life/death. But to be an even fuller symbol of integration, Christ would have to be linked to the Antichrist, to evil as well as good.

Christ as a religious symbol does differ from Christ seen from a psychological point of view. For whereas psychologically he represents the paradigm of individuation in that he lived out his nature and destiny to the very end, he does not represent the perfection which has been emphasised in the conventional church. This formulation got Jung into difficulty with theologians who saw in Christ only what is good and regarded evil as *privatio boni*, merely the absence of good. Another aspect of Christ's incompleteness to Jung was the missing feminine element, which does not appear in representations of the Trinity but which is incarnated by the Virgin Mary (see p. 229, below).

Similarly, the development from the sadistic, omnipotent view of God in the book of Job to the intervention of the suffering Christ of the New Testament demonstrates movement within the God-image itself. This is analogous to the way the self can be seen as a repository of potential yet to be lived, but which emerges and unfolds over time.

THE TRANSPERSONAL SELF: (2) SELF AND OTHERS

Mattoon comments that Jung's conceptualisation of the self is a relatively closed system which does not reflect much on the interrelation of self and others (1981, p. 112). My feeling is that the transpersonal self *can* be viewed in terms of relations with others. The self is the primary source of phenomena such as empathy. Human capacity to put oneself in the shoes of another implies something more than an extrapolation from self-referent data, which is then applied to the situation of others. Empathy is a form of psychological interpenetration, a deep link between people; the mother-infant relationship is both a special example of this and a model for empathy throughout life. We are talking of ways in which people absorb the lessons of experience and this, it may be argued, depends on the sense-making capacity of the self which is more than ego-learning.

A further transpersonal function in connection with self and others concerns the tendency to seek a merger with something 'greater' than oneself that was briefly mentioned in Chapter 2. If the self, as an integrate, is a form of oneness, then regressive impulses in adult life such as desires to re-unite with the uterine environment, nostalgia, blissful oceanic feelings, and similar phenomena, are connected to the self. This is a Jungian slant on the death instinct. As conceived of by Freud, the hypothesis of the death instinct refers to an attempt by the organism to reduce excitation and tension to zero by achieving an inorganic state as in death.

Jung may have been thinking of Goethe's *Faust* when he spoke of 'a deadly longing for the abyss, a longing to drown in [one's] own source, to be sucked down to the realm of the mothers' (*CW* 5, para. 553). There he points out that he does not mean just the personal mother, rather mother implying 'the gateway to the unconscious, the Eternal Feminine' where the 'divine child slumbers, patiently waiting his conscious realisation' (*CW* 5, para. 508). The self, manifested in 'death-instinct' form, has to do with experiences of merger, fusion, oneness. A combination of psychoanalytic and analytical psychological approaches suggests that the death instinct has a purpose; namely to act as a necessary antidote to the pain and anxiety resulting from rupture and separation so that, in the peace and quiet of an integrated state of oneness, the boilers of creativity can be re-stoked.

Conscious striving for perfection may be seen as a malign regression under the aegis of the death instinct, but the unconscious return to an original unitary condition as a preparation for psychological rebirth is the positive aspect of the death instinct and a necessary prelude to growth (see p. 167, below for a reworking of these ideas in terms of the development of personality).

THE TRANSPERSONAL SELF: (3) THE *UNUS MUNDUS*

The idea that the world is one world was destroyed by the Newtonian scientific revolution and by the Enlightenment. The image of a form of divine intelligence permeating all creation could not survive the rise of empirical observation and the systems, sub-systems and principles that gradually emerged. The death of God was also the death of this *unus mundus*, but Jung revives the notion when he speculates on the *psychoid unconscious*. He writes:

> Since psyche and matter are contained in one and the same world, and moreover are in continuous contact with one another and ultimately rest on irrepresentable, transcendental factors, it is not only possible but fairly probable, even, that psyche and matter are two different aspects of one and the same thing. (*CW* 8, para. 418)

Here he restates the idea of the *unus mundus*, not so much in the sense that everything obeys the same *rule* as that every stratum of existence is intimately linked with all the other strata. Jung likened the unitary integration of an individual with that of the world and thus his ideas about the self and his speculation about the nature of the universe belong together (*CW* 14, para. 664). Jung's approach is, therefore, holistic (though he does not use the word) in its concern for the whole, always greater and more interesting than its parts. From a historical perspective, Jung is also (implicitly again) a systems theorist in that action at one point of the *unus mundus* has implications throughout the entire system.

Jung anticipated many of the philosophical consequences of developments in modern physics which have changed the way we look at such basic concepts as time, space, matter and cause and effect (cf. Capra, *The Tao of Physics*, 1975). Jung's insistence that what makes psychology different from the other sciences is the participation of the observer, leading to a subject-object overlap, is strikingly similar to the modern scientific stress on observer bias and interrelation with the observed phenomena. The paradoxical world of sub-atomic physics, with its accent on the rapid interaction and interchange of matter across the whole field, and relativity theory, resembles the psyche in its fluidity and 'symbolic' functions. Psychology walks a constant tightrope between the general (the typical, the collective, the syndrome) and the individual or unique which is also captured in the jargon of physics concerning 'probability'. Finally, when the sub-atomic physicist can accept that something can be simultaneously a particle (confined to a precise and small volume) and a wave (which covers a wide area) it is easier to come to terms with Jung's notion of the self as centre *and* circumference.

Those sceptical of Jung's revival of the concept of the *unus mundus* may ponder the implication of reports, such as those in *The Times* science section on 25 January 1983, of experiments which seem to substantiate the theory that there is an underlying force in nature, unifying the four forces which are

100

known to control the universe: electromagnetism, strong and weak nuclear forces, and gravity. This should be added to our earlier remarks about 'action-at-a-distance' and the psychoid archetype (see p. 30, above).

SYNCHRONICITY

In his search for what lies beyond the rules of time, space and causality, (a search he insisted arose from repeated experiences that the world does not always obey these rules), Jung coined the term 'synchronicity'. This he defined in several ways: as an 'acausal connecting principle', as referring to two events meaningfully but not causally connected (i.e. not coinciding in time or space) and finally as referring to two events that coincide in time and space but are then seen to have other, more meaningful, connections. Jung chose to try to demonstrate the synchronistic principle by examining a possible correspondence between astrological birth signs and subsequent marriage partners. He concluded that there was neither a statistical connection, nor was the pattern due to chance; so synchronicity was proposed in 1952 as a third option (*CW* 8, 'Synchronicity: an acausal connecting principle').

The experiment has been much criticised. The sample was based on people who believed in astrology and was therefore not random, the statistics have been challenged, and, most important, astrology, whatever else it may be, cannot be claimed to be acausal! It is the supreme difficulty of demonstrating acausality that has bedevilled attempts to put synchronicity on a scientific basis. Nevertheless, most people have experienced meaningful coincidences or detected some sort of tide in their affairs, and it is in connection with that type of experience that Jung's synchronicity hypothesis may have use.

However, Jung applied synchronicity to a wide range of phenomena that are, perhaps, more accurately seen as psychological or parapsychological. A down-to-earth example of this type of activity might be the coenesthetic level of perception – an example of which is mother-baby communication, as mentioned earlier. As conceived of by Redfearn, for example, that is certainly not synchronicity:

> There is an intimate connection between sensory data, i.e. from the mother's body or facial image, thence via the organisation of such data by one's perception processes . . . to one's affects and motor expressions . . . integrated in a not necessarily conscious neurological structure . . . the self at this level is a body self. (1982, p. 226)

JUNG'S CONCEPT OF INDIVIDUATION

This consideration of Jung's idea of the part played by the self in psychic processes leads us naturally to the part played by those processes in the gradual realisation of the self over a lifetime. This Jung called *individuation*.

The essence of individuation is the achievement of a personal blend between the collective and universal on the one hand, and, on the other, the unique and individual. It is a *process*, not a state; save for the possibility of regarding death as an ultimate goal, individuation is never completed and remains an ideal concept. The form the individuation process takes, its style and the regularity or fitfulness of it, depends on the individual. Nevertheless, certain images express the kernel of the individuation process; for example, a journey, death and rebirth, and symbols of initiation. Jung found parallels in alchemy. Base elements (the instincts, the ego) are transformed into gold (the self). (See pp. 178ff., below, for a fuller discussion of alchemy.)

Individuation, as expounded by Jung, has to be differentiated from individuality or the attainment of an individual ego-identity. Sound ego functioning may be necessary for individuation but it is not co-terminous with it. Jung developed his theory out of his experience with patients in the second half of life. In the first half of life, in Jung's conception, the heroic ego struggles to be free from the mother and to establish its independence; this leads to an inevitable one-sidedness which the psyche will seek to redress. This may take the form in mid-life of a person re-evaluating his life in a private, introspective way, divorced initially from the world of relationships. After this, the result of the re-evaluation will feed back into personal relations, leading to greater clarity and satisfaction. The task in the second half of life is to go beyond ego-differentiation and personal identity to a focus on meaning and suprapersonal values; for this, ego stability has prepared.

These preliminary remarks set the scene for presentation of the main elements of the individuation process as Jung most often wrote of it, that is in terms of the second half of life. That this restriction is no longer accepted by all analytical psychologists will become clear.

INDIVIDUATION AND THE SELF

Individuation can be seen as a movement towards wholeness by means of an integration of conscious and unconscious parts of the personality. This involves personal and emotional conflict resulting in differentiation from general conscious attitudes *and* from the collective unconscious (*CW* 6, para. 762).

This suggests becoming oneself, the person one was intended to be, achieving one's potential. That implies a recognition and acceptance of parts of oneself that are initially repugnant or seem negative, and also an opening up towards the possibilities presented by the contrasexual element (animus-anima) which can act as a gateway or guide to the unconscious, as we shall see in Chapter 7. This integration leads not only to a greater degree of self-realisation, but also to the awareness that one has a self.

Jung refers to the 'achievement of a greater personality' (*CW* 7, para. 136) by such integration, though he acknowledged that the integration of the shadow, implying acceptance of rejected, repressed and as yet unlived aspects of oneself is painful, particularly when what is involved is the withdrawal of projections on to other people. The self becomes an image not only of a more complete person but also of the goal of life and in this context we can rightly speak of attaining or realising one's self:

empirically, the self is an image of the goal of life spontaneously produced by the unconscious, irrespective of wishes and fears of the conscious mind . . . the dynamic of this process is instinct, which ensures that everything which belongs to an individual's life shall enter into it, whether he consents or not . . . (*CW* 11, para. 745)

Jung emphasises that the quality of consciousness makes a decisive difference and adds that, before the bar of nature, unconsciousness is never accepted as an excuse – 'on the contrary there are very severe penalties for it'. The self is located on a 'higher moral level' and a man must 'know something of God's nature if he is to understand himself' (*CW* 11, paras 745-6). It is now clear why Jung was so concerned to equate self and God-image.

Individuation can also be taken to mean 'becoming oneself', that is, who one 'really' is. This suggests a balanced or optimum development, involving an incorporation of personal idiosyncrasies so that a person's own true nature is not damaged by repression or, conversely, by exaggeration or hypertrophy of any one side. This involves a sense of self-awareness, together with an accurate self-image as devoid of self-deception as possible. The ego-ideal is abandoned in favour of self-acceptance and, more importantly, the super-ego, in its negative form of blind adherence to collective norms, is replaced as a moral arbiter by the self acting as an inner guide. What we are describing is separation from the collective, together with an assumption of responsibility for oneself and a developed attitude towards past and future. Separation from the collective may extend into a withdrawal of investment from relationships and I think it is true to say that the tone of Jung's ideas on individuation emphasises the dialogue between the individual and the collective unconscious rather more than that between the individual and others.

We have noted how the self develops symbols to compensate one-sided conscious attitudes and to bring together opposites. A specific example of this is in the field of typology. In Jung's conception of the individuation processes, the various functions of consciousness start to operate in a less hierarchical manner. The inferior function, in particular, becomes more integrated. This is the aspect of the individuation process most open to idealisation. The psychological tension of the opposites within a person is not ejected or substituted by individuation; it may even be accentuated as the ego withdraws its support from the habitual mode of consciousness. Thus a conflict between, say, rational and irrational impulses, may spring up; prior to this one side may have been held down. Work on 'the opposites' is a central part of analysis and a final reconciliation is impossible. Individuation is not, in Jung's view, an elimination of conflict, more an increased consciousness of it, and of its potential.

Our discussion of complexes showed how the psyche is to be conceived of as a multiple entity; yet we have been talking about integration and wholeness. The balance between these two tendencies (themselves complementary opposites) is a key theme in post-Jungian psychology. We have also noted the ways in which the psyche uses compensation in its self-regulating attempts to keep a balance. These mini-compensations gradually cohere in individuation, and what is revealed to the person is the plan, pattern and meaning of his life (*CW* 8, para. 550). We could regard this as a form of self-regulation; the various parts of the personality become related round a centre, the self.

When we talk of opposites we imply that ego differentiates between the two halves of the pair. In this respect, the individuation process is dependent on ego function. But it is central to Jung's conception that symbols and images occur independently of the ego which then attempts to integrate them.

The implications for analysis are that progress is achieved by the facilitation of symbols and images which derive from self and accompany the individuation process. There is, therefore, relatively less importance given in the Classical School to outward manifestations in the life of the patient or to the therapeutic interaction (but see pp. 187 ff., below). A correlation of this is that symptom removal cannot be a yardstick of change or development. Indeed, as Jung was fond of pointing out, for some patients the nature of their problems *requires* the emergence of symptom or symptoms. Be that as it may, the ego plays a continuous part in individuation and is not subsumed by the self. (See pp. 118-19, below, for a full discussion of 'symbol' and 'image' and pp. 58ff., above, for discussion of the ego's role vis à vis symbols).

There are a host of metaphors for and summations of individuation: differentiation, realisation of potential, awareness of one's 'personal myth', coming to terms with oneself. There are others but this selection gives the flavour.

GENERAL CONCEPTUAL PROBLEMS

Glover's objections to Jung's idea of the self are characteristically trenchant (1950). He wonders if the self is to be conceived of as something one works towards or makes, or as something one is developing out of or from. The answer is, of course, both, but Glover's question illuminates these twin trends in analytical psychology: those who see life more as an unfolding of what was always there and those more interested in pursuit of a goal. Next, Glover wonders about the relation of the self to the outside world. He points out that if all energy is in the totality there will be none left for outside relationships. Responding to this weakness, post-Jungians have tended to view object relations and personal relationships as more connected to individuation than Jung seems to have done. Finally, Glover is concerned lest emphasis on divinity makes of the self a morally binding imperative. This, says Glover, exposes a contradiction because, if individuation involves a replacement of super-ego dominance by self-directed activity, a moral instruction to individuate coming from outside the person would offend the principle. Here we must concede that Glover has a point and the notion that individuation may be directed is a contradiction in terms. But what of individuation assisted in analysis? Admittedly, everything depends on the degree of inner-directedness, but the existence of the very idea of individuation will cause material to gravitate towards it.

Storr takes up the point about external relationships, commenting that much of Jung's writings seem unconnected with 'day-to-day problems, neurotic symptoms, sexual difficulties, and all the other matters which may make a person turn to books on psychology and psychotherapy' (1973, p. 91). One of my central concerns is that Jung's ideas can and are being used in *therapy* all the time (and not only by 'Jungians'). However, Storr is referring to the lengthy, often interminable, discussions and disquisitions on religious, alchemical and other symbolism, which may alienate modern readers from Jung. Elsewhere, he comments that Jung writes 'next to nothing about the effect of analysis on the patient's life in the world or upon his personal relationships' (ibid., p. 90). Again, even if this is true of Jung, it has been rectified by post-Jungians.

Ironically, Dry (1961) comments on the extraordinary fragmentation of Jung's writings on individuation, and also notes the introversion of his way of thinking. She feels that in comparison, say, to James's ideas about religious conversion, individuation is a rather played down, discreet sort of activity, lacking in zest and *joie-de-vivre*. This reflects the view of several post-Jungians who feel that Jung's description is altogether too static.

Atwood and Stolorow (1975) assert that, as the prime personal danger for Jung was dissolution of the personality and being overwhelmed from within, the establishment of a stiff and stable self-representation is a necessity. This is to take place via individuation – the gradual filling out of the personality cuts down the room available for anxiety. They detect three ways in which this 'cramming' of the personality is achieved. The first is by making the unconscious conscious, the second by way of the transcendent function, and the third by making a distinction between personal and collective contents and thus enabling contact with universal themes, which provide additional stability. But Atwood and Stolorow completely neglect the role played by the ego in relation to the transcendent function and make far too sharp a division between collective and personal contents, eliminating the possibility of formulations stressing personal *experience* of universal *contents* – which is central to Jung's idea of individuation. Nevertheless, what they see as the defensive reduction of the empty space in the self, and the connection of this to a lessening of anxiety, does suggest the possibility of false individuation, characterised by an inundation of symbols unmatched by increased self-awareness and genuine integration.

I mentioned earlier the problem of seeing the self as a central point and also as a totality. In this regard, Fordham (1963) felt that Jung developed two incompatible theories of the self. If the self means (a) the whole personality, he asserts, then it can never be experienced because the ego, as the agency of experiencing, is 'in' the totality. If the self refers to (b) a central *archetype* then it cannot also refer to the totality which includes the ego, for Jung is clear that the ego and the archetypes are to be distinguished. The self in this second definition would exclude the ego altogether. Fordham prefers to conceive the self not as an archetype, but as *beyond* archetypes and ego, which are then seen as arising out of or 'deintegrating' from the self. In this formulation it is possible to avoid complications caused by seeing ego and self as two quite different systems.

Fordham postulates a primary self integrate, present at birth, which, on meeting a correspondence in the environment, commences a rhythmic cycle of deintegration and reintegration. The ego, as the conscious element of the self, is attached to the entirety of the archetypal contents of the self for, otherwise, no experiencing would be possible. Fordham's ideas about deintegration and individuation (cf. 1957, 1976, 1978a) have become important in contemporary analytical psychology and are further discussed in the next section of this chapter; his model of personal development is summarised in Chapter 5, pp. 154ff., below).

Newton (1981) suggests that it is still reasonable to see the self as a special archetype, a 'transcendental archetype' which is different from other archetypal manifestations. She concludes that the dynamic of the self (its stress on states of integration, wholeness, reconciliation of opposites) affects our experience of the other archetypes. At the same time, Jacoby (1981) feels that, though there might be a contradiction in logic, there is no experiential contradiction in seeing the self both as a part of the whole and the whole.

In fact, Jung re-wrote his definition of self in 1960 (*CW* 6, paras 789-91), taking account of this apparent contradiction and emphasising that the self is a special transcendental concept. Although the new definition strengthens the idea of the self as the total organism, the transcendental element allows for an oscillation that permits the self also to function as the archetype of unity.

Humbert (1980) points out that the deceptively simple problem of recognising oneself as a subject is one which many philosophers regard as a meaningless snare. He prefers a much more personal definition: 'the self is the inner voice which tells me frequently and precisely how I shall live'. He goes on to stress that what is meant by 'totality' is the *relationship* of conscious and unconscious, not just an addition (ibid., p. 240). Humbert represents a trend towards conceiving the self as a system composed of relating sub-systems.

Redfearn (1969) is concerned to tease out differences between the Jungian self and other usages. He feels that there are two everyday uses of *self* – for simple identifications of oneself (who I am factually), and referring to a subjective experience (roughly, what is in, or felt to be in, my body). Jung uses *ego* to refer to both of these feelings. As regards the self, Jung is concerned with the expression of self and self-realisation rather than representations of oneself as appearing in the ego. This is the crucial distinction between analytical psychology and orthodox psychoanalysis. The latter has seen *self* as a particular kind of representation in the ego and nothing more, at least until quite recently (see pp. 123ff., below).

THE SELF: A RELATIVE CONCEPT

Many post-Jungians have turned away from an exclusive consideration of integration to examine partial states, representations of parts of the self; they see the self as a barren and overvalued concept when used to deny the multiplicity and polycentricity of the psyche. The intriguing thing is that analysts following this route come from all the schools using different but compatible ways of expressing themselves.

Hillman, in his paper 'Psychology: monotheistic or polytheistic?' (1971,

1981), quotes Jung's equation of self with monotheism, animus-anima with polytheism. In the same way that polytheism is a pre-stage of monotheism, animus and anima are precursors of the self. Jung concluded that the self is 'the archetype which it is most important for modern man to understand' (*CW* 9ii, paras 422-70). Although Hillman makes much of the mono/poly issue, I want to focus on what little he says about the self; the polytheistic argument is found in Chapter 9.

Jung's preference for the self, says Hillman, unduly narrows a psychology that in every other respect stresses the plurality and multiplicity of the psyche, the archetypes and complexes. Are we to assume that differentiated complexes are less important than the self? If so, then everything in therapeutic analysis except the self and its products is relegated to second place. All explorations of consciousness become preliminary to experience of the self. So we would spend our time looking for, and at the conjunction of opposites, mandalas, the *unus mundus*, synchronicity, etc.

To talk of opposition between the pluralistic psyche and the self (integrated and whole) is itself a monistic activity, because either/or contradicts pluralism (thou shalt have no other Gods . . .). That there is a place for unitary experience within a pluralistic perspective is shown in Lopez-Pedraza's comment on Hillman's paper: 'the many *contains* the unity of the one *without losing* the possibilities of the many' (1971, p. 214). This radically revises Jung's notion of the one containing the many, as represented by mandalas, for example.

Hillman goes on to ask where in psychology the *superiority* of the self is demonstrated? The place of the self as the repository of integrated experience may be maintained but this would be one style of functioning among many. Other post-Jungians, e.g. L. Stein (1967), have stressed that integration is but one psychological option. Jung's valuation of the self may be considered as an expression of a 'theological' temperament, as much as of introversion. As Hillman notes, Jung regarded the monistic tendency as introverted, the pluralistic, extraverted (*CW* 6, para. 536).

In addition to the self's being deflated, there are ways in which it functions that are themselves inadequate. The self cannot handle 'a multiple field of shifting foci and complicated relations' (Hillman, 1981, p. 112); its tendency will always be towards a synthesis which may require shoving psychic data into a *complexio oppositorum* that restores harmony at the expense of spontaneity. Hillman suggests we suspend our habitual thinking about unity, about stages, about psychological development, a *fantasy* of individuation which 'character-ises it mainly as movement towards unity, expressed in wholeness, centering, or in figures like the Old Wise Man or Woman' (ibid., p. 113). Lopez-Pedraza refers, in this connection, to the 'endless discussion at the Jung Institute' in Zürich on Yahweh and Christ as symbols of the self (1971, p. 212).

But Jung *did* use a polycentric model of the psyche. He did write of a multiplicity of partial consciousnesses like stars or divine sparks, 'luminosities' (*CW* 8, paras 388ff.). This supports a polycentric psychology, and Hillman's proposal was that we aim less at gathering the sparks into a unity and more at integrating each spark 'according to its own principle' (Hillman, 1981, p. 114); we should accept multiplicity of voices without insisting on unifying them into *one* figure. It follows from this that the dissolution process is as valuable as the unifying process. Closer interest in psychological variety instead of psychological oneness will produce deeper insights into emotions, images and relationships. This will not satisfy those who must see individuation as an impelling movement from chaos to coherence and ultimately to wholeness. But is chaos always less useful than wholeness? And cannot wholeness appear in chaos?

According to Hillman, wholeness, in a truly psychological sense, means seeing a phenomenon *as a whole*, as it presents itself. He contrasts this with wholeness in a theological sense which means *the one*. There are

> two views of completion, a psychological wholeness where individuation shows itself in multiple relations, and a theological wholeness where individuation shows itself in degrees of approximation to an ideal or unity. (ibid., p. 116)

Individuation may mean disintegration and splitting (or may involve those processes), but there is more than one myth or meaning of individuation.

To sum up, Hillman's favour is less towards 'identity, unity, centredness, integration', and more towards 'elaboration, particularising, complication'. The emphasis is not on transformation but rather on 'deepening what is there into itself' (1981, p. 129).

Guggenbühl-Craig presents a similar re-evaluation of the self (1980). For him, Jung's view of the self is simply too positive and leaves out 'invalidism'. This recognition of pathology and incompleteness in ourselves is the true opposite of wholeness and yet is nowhere to be found in Classical views of the self in analytical psychology. When we talk about the self:

> there is too much said about qualities like roundness, completeness, and wholeness. It is high time that we spoke of deficiency, the invalidism of Self. I have always had difficulty with the fact that mandalas are regarded as symbols *par excellence* of the self – they are much too whole for my taste. . . . Completeness is fulfilled through incompleteness . . . admittedly, it is difficult to sustain the image of completeness and wholeness and, at the same time, to accept invalidism. (ibid., p. 25)

Guggenbühl-Craig wonders if Jungians have become involved in a 'cult of perfection'. For instance, we avoid asking whether a psychopath, lacking morality, has a self. If so, is it an immoral self?

Plaut (1974) has also examined Jung's luminosities or multiple aspects of consciousness, but from the point of view of object relations and part-object psychology which characterises the Developmental School. In infancy the nipple may be termed a part-object, standing in for the whole object and giving off the same aura to the infant as the whole object. At times the part-object may represent the entire external world. For these reasons, the part-object is likely to be experienced as gripping, fascinating and awesome. The part-objects of childhood, and the luminosities, function in a way that contributes to the relativisation of the wholeness of the self that we have been discussing.

Plaut felt we quite naturally behave as if parts were wholes, and endow particular things and themes with the depth and life of totality (1975). He argues it would be mistaken to undervalue a less than whole object which still expresses early splits (e.g. into good and bad). In such an object there would have been no 'fusion of characteristics', i.e. of good or bad images of the mother, which would enable us to speak of *object constancy* (ibid., p. 208). What Plaut refers to, in contradistinction, as a *constant object* could well be one-sided and regarded by the individual without any healthy ambivalence. But such an object is valuable and necessary for many people and can function as an 'alternative core' round which experience can coalesce and be assimilated. Such an object can be 'fascinating and awe-inspiring, in short, numinous'. Plaut concludes: 'as such, it may be identical with Jung's self' (1975, p. 214). Plaut supports his idea by pointing to the connections between sexuality (as expressed in pictorial images of sex organs) and creativity or spirituality. Furthermore, people who have single-mindedly invested themselves in a 'deity, a muse or an ideology' are all partaking of the numinous, luminous nature of what is less than whole, less than the self.

We can draw a parallel between Guggenbühl-Craig's attack on perfection and Plaut's acceptance of the constant object. Invalidism and something less than whole are seen as compatible with, but also as a moderating influence on, the self. Coupled with Hillman's insistence on a move away from the over-valuation of integrated states, we can observe how radical is the shift from Jung's starting point.

Fordham also feels there is too much stress upon the integrating functions and capacity of the self. He regards a precarious and dynamic state as a *sine qua non* of human life, whether physiological or psychological. This is particularly true in the case of psychic structures: 'sometimes they are predominantly stable (integrated), sometimes they are unstable (deintegrated).' Continuing this comment on Hillman's 1971 paper mentioned earlier, Fordham understands Hillman to be arguing for the inclusion of deintegrated states within the individuation process and he is in agreement with this (Fordham, 1971, pp. 211-12). What Fordham is aiming at in his own work on deintegrates (e.g. 1976) is rather similar to Hillman's target: both insist upon the polycentrism of psyche. Exclusive emphasis or resolution of chaos into pattern is simply not feasible, whether in infancy or throughout life.

In the paper 'The self as an imaginative construct' (1979a), Fordham reminds us that no symbol can represent the whole self because, in order to form images at all, the self has to divide into that part that makes imagery (the unconscious) and the part that observes and interacts with imagery (the ego). The ego, he asserts, must, to a degree, always be 'outside'. Fordham comments that we have moved from the grand archetypal forms and from mysticism to be able to consider the self as composed of parts, each felt equally to be 'myself'. He refers to part-selves, such as the social self and the ethical self, for example.

As there are states of integration and deintegration, there are bound to be two forms of the self: the whole self (integrate) and these part-selves (deintegrates) which are stable enough to be expressed and experienced. Fordham then makes a point which, effectively, aligns him with Hillman on this matter. He states that his model is *neutral*; part-selves are not less important than the whole self, which remains an unrepresentable abstraction.

Fordham and Hillman are each proposing a situationist, relativised, pluralistic self in which clusters of experiences carry the feeling of 'being myself' rather than that of being or feeling 'whole'. If the part-self or psychic fragment is lived out fully, then wholeness will take care of itself. It should not be forgotten that the feeling of being oneself is often extremely uncomfortable and thus fulfils Guggenbühl-Craig's objections to the idealised, perfect self.

Finally, in this review of the current standing of 'integration', I would like to include L. Stein's point that, if we are talking of structure in the sense of 'archetypal structures', then to speak of order is a tautology. The *a priori* archetype does its 'ordering' in the sense of patterning in any case. But to equate such order or pattern with harmony is quite wrong: chaos may be orderly; conservatism is not necessarily harmonious and states of unintegration may persist. We must, concludes Stein, distinguish between a theory of macro-order and an experience of micro-instability (L. Stein, 1967).

It would be wrong to leave the reader with the impression that the swing away from a stress on integration involves all post-Jungians, however. Adler (1961), while noting that there is a disintegrative drive in the unconscious, feels that there is 'an empirical unity in which even the "negative" unconscious has a hidden tendency to integration' (p. 37n). Regarding mandalas, they express 'the unity of the psyche and its totality' (ibid., p. 56). Elsewhere, Adler feels that 'the circle, the roundness, symbolises wholeness and integration, and as such the self' (1979, p. 21). Similar statements can be found in Jacobi, 1959; Edinger, 1960; Whitmont, 1969; Frey-Rohn, 1974; Mattoon, 1981.

There is therefore a genuine debate which is more than a question of accentuation or emphasis. Gordon's reasonable comment is that the self, as a concept, has two aspects. Used metapsychologically or in a portrait of psychic structure, it does refer to the wholeness of the psyche, including conscious, unconscious, personal and archetypal experiences and capacities. The self can also be used in an experiential model, as part of making sense of our experience (Gordon, 1978, p. 33). I would add that 'making sense' is a different proposition from ordering, organising and even integrating.

INDIVIDUATION: A DEMOCRATIC PROCESS

It is difficult to know who Jung addresses when he talks of individuation. He likens individuation to a drive such as sex or hunger, postulating an instinct in man to grow psychologically, similar to ordinary physical maturation. *Individuation is, therefore, a natural tendency*. At the same time, he says that, before individuation can be taken as a goal, a necessary minimum of 'adaptation to collective norms must be first attained' (*CW* 6 para. 760). This might mean that individuation is only for those with 'strong egos', with good social adaptation and who are functioning genitally. This suggests that *individuation is for an élite*, and Jung may be able to justify this with his view

110

that nature, after all, is aristocratic (*CW* 7, paras 198, 236; *CW* 17, paras 343, 345).

Jung refers to people having a 'vocation' for individuation (*CW* 17, para. 300): 'Only the man who can consciously assent to the power of the inner voice becomes a personality' (ibid., para. 308). But he goes on to say that the necessary task is to translate the vocation into one's own individual reality (thereby, incidentally, validating the part played by the ego in individuation).

But the use of the word *vocation* and many other references equating individuation with a religious or spiritual attitude can lead to conceiving individuation as a mystical summons rather than a psychological necessity and process. Individuation does imply an acceptance of what lies beyond the individual, of what is simply unknowable but not unfelt. In that sense, individuation is a spiritual calling but, as the realisation of the fullness of a personality, it is a psychological phenomenon. A search or quest for individuation grips many people and the process itself is sometimes symbolised as the grail rather than the grail as its goal.

Finally, there is a need to question Jung's idea that individuation is a process pertaining exclusively or more markedly to the second half of life. It is argued by the Developmental School that individuation is a life-long activity and, in all its essential features, can be observed in children. This has led to a distinction being made between individuation 'proper' in the second half of life and individuation in childhood and then throughout life. Because of the contradiction I mentioned earlier in which individuation is said to be both natural and for few, we need a tripartite classification: (a) individuation as a natural process occurring throughout life; (b) individuation as a natural process taking place in the second half of life; these two as distinct from (c) individuation worked on and brought to consciousness by way of analysis. We can only regret that the last idea of individuation (individuation in analysis) dominates popular notions of analytical psychology as involving alchemical, religious, mystical, and other arcane symbolism. And, not the least problem, although all post-Jungians talk of individuation *processes*, the appellation 'individuated', implying a *state* of being, is still used.

If individuation means becoming the person you are, or were intended to be, this may well include all sorts of sickness and personal wounds resulting from accidental dispositions of archetypal factors and/or environmental disaster, as Guggenbühl-Craig has suggested (1980). Are we to say that an orphan cannot individuate? Or a paraplegic? Or a pervert? Just as the implication that the Self involves nothing but integration has been challenged, equivalent objections have been made to too pristine a definition of individuation.

We can regard against this background Fordham's theory of individuation in childhood. He takes as his starting point Jung's remark that 'individuation is practically the same as the development of consciousness out of the original state of identity . . . the original non-differentiation between subject and object' (*CW* 6, para. 762). This latter development occurs in infancy. Similarly, the differentiation from 'collective, general psychology' (*CW* 6, para. 757) can be equated with the infant's separation from his mother. Fordham holds that this differentiation is concluded by the age of two. After birth the

111

primary self deintegrates, and the infant then takes steps towards the achievement of a state of identity with the mother (1976, p. 37); out of this identity the infant develops object relations and individuates in accordance with Jung's definition. Of course, nobody fully separates from mother in an emotional sense; a 'continuity of union makes possible recurring and fruitful fusion with others in later life' (ibid., p. 38). In Fordham's view the state of identity with the mother then becomes the basis of the animus-anima, persona, and 'the superordinate personality' (ibid., p. 38).

Before the second year, the infant achieves a fair degree of bodily mastery, anal and urethral sphincter control, and a sense of his own skin boundary. He has also made emotional progress in terms of concern for others and the development of a rudimentary conscience. And, above all, he is using symbols – whether transitional objects or in other play (ibid., p. 21-3). All the essential ingredients for individuation are there, and nothing more is required than ordinary good mothering (ibid., p. 40). The process is vulnerable and may go wrong, but can be repaired at any point. Opposites such as good and bad, inner and outer, have been reconciled, and a conscious/unconscious integration quite different from the original organismic integrate at birth has been achieved.

It could be said that this is merely a description of maturation rather than individuation. There are two possible ways to consider this. The first would say that the features outlined above are a special part of maturation, having to do with the uniting of diverse strands in the personality and with symbolic experience. Maturation is the larger term, individuation a special part. The second reply would welcome maturation as individuation, going on to stress that we now have a model for individuation as a *natural* process which, because attainable by all in infancy and childhood, is potentially attainable by all in later life. By stressing how natural the process is, Fordham democratises individuation.

Jung might well *not* have agreed with Fordham's idea of individuation in childhood:

> again and again I note that the individuation process is confused with the coming of the ego into consciousness and that the ego is in consequence confused with the self, which naturally leads to a hopeless conceptual muddle. (*CW* 8, para. 432)

At stake here is Jung's conception or preconception of what individuation is or should be. Jung was so concerned with a particular kind of self symbol and of symbolic experience that he sometimes lost sight of his initial insight that individuation is like an instinct or drive, and hence natural.

Once again, Hillman spots the same problem from a different angle by suggesting that, rather than *I*ndividuation, we should talk of a multiplicity of individuations deriving from 'our internal multiple persons. Therefore an individual cannot provide a norm *even for himself*' (1975b, p. 88). Each of us has many Gods to obey, and our various inner norms are expressed in this internal pantheon. Global assessment is pointless.

Individuation is an archetypal fantasy in Hillman's opinion. In its classical definition it is the work or product of one archetype, the self. It is not the only way to proceed. Individuation is itself a particular way of seeing which automatically involves fantasies of development, progress, or order. Hillman's proposal is a ceaseless interweave involving numerous modifications worked by the archetypes on each other. But there should be no definition of what individuation *is*.

Meltzer, speaking out of his Kleinian psychoanalytic background, has written in remarkably similar terms:

> Mrs Klein described, in effect, what you might call a theological model of the mind. Every person has to have what you might describe as a 'religion' in which his internal objects perform the functions of Gods – but it is not a religion that derives its power because of belief in these Gods but because these Gods do in fact perform functions in the mind. Therefore if you do not put your trust in them you are in trouble, and this trouble is the trouble of narcissism. (1981, p. 179)

Hillman's iconoclasm (*individuation is just one way of looking at things*) can be added to Fordham's democratisation (*requiring nothing more than ordinary good mothering*) to give the flavour of a post-Jungian synthesis.

Another factor to be considered is the inclusion of close personal relationships within the purview of individuation. It is possible that a gathering in or integration of the parts of the personality might lead to a natural withdrawal from personal relationships. But for some people the proposition can be reversed, and the quality of relationship to others becomes central (cf. Plaut, 1979).

For in the area of personal relations, even more than in any other, individuation cannot mean perfection. We may have to talk, as Guggenbühl-Craig does, of *individuation marriages* which by 'normal standards' are quite crazy but which represent the optimum self-expression of a relationship (1980). Such individuation qualities as tolerance, sense of otherness, and so on are bound to be tested in a two-person relationship – and, as nobody is perfect, pathology must be taken into account. This links with the necessity to involve psychopathology in our views of individuation.

I would think that the next step will be to connect individuation with group and social functioning. Many Jungians 'cannot cope with groups' (or so they say); at the same time there is a growing cross-fertilisation between analytical psychology and group psychotherapy (see p. 205, below). There is no theoretical reason I can think of why the central elements in individuation, particularly as modified and reconstrued by post-Jungians, should not apply in social life generally.

When discussing individuation, it is important to remember that Jung was careful to distinguish this from an 'unconscious wholeness', a false individuation. 'Conscious wholeness', in contrast, is a 'successful union of ego and self so that both preserve their intrinsic qualities' (*CW* 8, para. 430n).

HOW OPPOSITE IS OPPOSITE?

Post-Jungians have also modified Jung's structuring of his psychology of the self round opposites and their reconciliation. In Freudian psychoanalysis, the opposites, such as active/passive, phallic/castrated, masculine/feminine, are seen as permanently incompatible. One cannot lead to the other in a synthesis, or similar dialectical process; rather the pair itself expresses a permanent conflict. Classical Jungian analysis makes much of 'the opposites': 'above all, getting a clear and objective view of the self entails having it out with the opposites' (Hannah, 1967). Sometimes the opposites become almost miraculous in their operation: 'the best chance of the atom bomb not being used is if enough people could stand the tension of the opposites in themselves' (ibid.).

Willeford (1976) considers that not all psychological phenomena express underlying polarities. He feels that it could be a mistake to have a model which stresses polarity/reconciliation dynamics because this overlooks the 'mutually supportive interplay of functions that can but do not always oppose one another' (p. 116). Concentration on the opposites leads to neglect of slight gradations and subtle transitions of difference; the concept is simply too global. This is a point also made by Dry (1961) who objects that the pairs of opposites most used by Jung (conscious/unconscious, masculine/feminine, instinct/spirit) are far too complex to be *ultimate* units of mental life. She appreciates that the tension of opposites becomes a hypothetical necessity to explain the creation of psychic energy but feels that this is too exclusive an explanation. What about the energy in the bodily zones, for instance? I would go further, and, in common with modern trends in psychoanalysis, question whether we need a concept of psychic energy at all. Energy, as we saw in Chapter 1, is an analogy developed from the physical world and easily becomes a metapsychological reification. Conversely, the notion of energy, even if taken nowadays purely as a metaphor, helps to explain differences in perception.

Hillman rejects oppositionalism as a basis for psychology. His image for psychology is rather something circular 'thriving on . . . cycles of return to the same insoluble themes' (1975b, p. 213). Oppositionalism is a useful tool but it can become the master, Hillman continues. Although none of Jung's oppositions are logical oppositions (they are *empirical* oppositions) there is a tendency to behave as if they were. What really structures Jung's whole conception of the psyche is oppositional antagonism and complementarity.

Hillman's further suggestion is that, in any psychic event, the opposite can be regarded as already present: 'every psychic event is an identity of at least two positions.' Only when we look from one side do we see oppositionalism (1979a, p. 80). Provided the categories under consideration are in some way connected, we may assume an identity of opposites. It follows that we must consider everything in relation to its opposite at all times. Reconciliation is not the work of consciousness, it rests on the pre-existing identity of opposites. The child contains the mother and vice versa; they are not opposites. Similarly, child and adult are identities, deeply involved with one another. In sum, oppositionalism is yet another metaphor for one particular way of looking at things. Above all, it is a metaphor for perception that helps and encourages the ego with its limited holistic but greater analytical skills.

Of course, Hillman's 'identity of opposites' idea is itself a metaphor for a way of perceiving and, it may be argued, he has extended rather than contradicted Jung's thesis that opposites may be united, synthesised or reconciled. And there is a real tension between the child and the adult parts of a person which is creative, and hence important not to deny.

Post-Jungian typologists have also been critical of Jung's theory of the opposites, as we saw in the Appendix to the last chapter. If opposites can be transcended, why stress polarity, wondered Loomis and Singer (1980)? And Metzner *et al.* propose what amounts to a pot-pourri of attitudes and functions (1981).

Drawing this material together, we can see that we are offered three differing models for psychological activity:

(1) pairs of conflicting opposites (Freud);
(2) potentially reconcilable opposites (Jung);
(3) circularity and the identity of opposites (Hillman).

A fourth approach, deriving from Jung, is to visualise psychological activity and development as a *spiral*. The spiral is a system with opportunity for new elements to enter, though not *ad lib*. In the spiral, the same elements interact with each other but at a different place with each repetition in the ascent. (For example, ego and self relate differently at different points.) The spiral also illustrates the way in which components of the psyche are operated upon by environmental demands. Circularity and oppositionalism will present as phase-appropriate phenomena in the spiral. Zinkin (1969) has suggested that the spiral can be used to illustrate a two-person field (e.g. analysis) and can be tight or open. The interpersonal dimension is not ruled out by Jung's theory of opposites but the apparently real figures with which the ego may be in conflict are usually seen by him as external manifestations of inner processes. For example, conflict with *anima* rather than *wife*.

Shorter (personal communication, 1982) feels that the essence of the theory of the opposites is that their tension and clash calls for a resolution by action, meaning psychological change. The opposites, and what we do about them, inform our attitude to our lives, whether we discern meaning or not. Above all, tension between conscious and unconscious underlines the need for synthesis.

THE OPPOSITES IN DEVELOPMENT

Jung's general approach to the opposites, apparently so abstract and quasi-philosophical, has been used as a base for speculations about ego and self in infancy by members of the Developmental School. These ideas reflect the manner in which ego and self are experienced as separate: 'indeed at times they may be experienced as opposed to each other' (Gordon, 1978, pp. 32-3). The ego sums up all that is involved in separation, sense of boundary, personal identity and external achievement 'with all the images associated with one's own body and one's own personality' (ibid.). From the self we derive 'the need for fusion and wholeness – with the associated phantasies of re-entry into the mother's breast or belly . . . or a re-fusing with Mother, Nature or Universe' (ibid.).

The interplay between the two psychic systems of self and ego has also been emphasised by Strauss (1964) who felt that resolution of the conflict between tendencies to separate (ego) and unite (self) is crucial for the development of personality in infancy and throughout life. Strauss distinguished between two different states which are both implied in Jung's concept of the self. First, an innate, integral, merged, undifferentiated wholeness and, second, the self as a conjunction of opposites. Pre-existing states of wholeness, the primary self, or simply the organic fact of man, are not the same as unions formed out of two or more differentiated entities or parts of the personality.

Elsewhere (Samuels 1982), I have commented that discrimination of the opposites in infancy has something to do with aggressive biting and with fantasies of dismemberment and with symbolism of the teeth. Such fantasy represents the process of differentiation into opposites that may then unite, as just outlined. The image that an infant develops of his parents' marriage may be the first *union* of differentiated opposites that he experiences. First he must consciously differentiate the merged parents, and biting helps him in this attainment; then he must overcome his jealousy and envy of them to 'allow' them to have a fruitful marriage or union.

Many analysts of the Developmental School (e.g. Redfearn, 1978) have stressed that the outcome of discrimination of the opposites depends on the individual's capacity to contain the tension caused by break-up of his earlier attempts to maintain a unitary world construction. Such containment is an ego function whose early roots are in the quality of the mother's 'holding' of her conflicted baby (see Chapter 5).

In analysis, discriminating *and* reconciling opposites (the one connected with the ego and the other with the self) can co-exist. Newton presented case material (1965) illustrating how, for one patient, analytical work involved a *discrimination* of herself as separate from the analyst, and also a *reconciliation* of all-good and all-bad images of the analyst/mother.

Whatever the status of the theory of opposites, *qua* theory, its application to personal development and to clinical work is an interesting product of one of Jung's basic interests. It will have been noted that all the writers on this particular topic scarcely mention self without mentioning ego, and vice versa. We now turn our attention to that relationship to look at it in more detail.

THE EGO-SELF AXIS

Edinger (1960, 1972) comments that the classic formula *first half of life ego-self separation, second half of life ego-self reunion* needs revision. He suggests that ego-self separation and reunion proceed in an alternating cycle throughout life. Ego-self relatedness takes three forms – ego-self identity, ego-self separation and ego-self alienation. In ego-self identity, ego and self are one, which means that the ego is absorbed. Ego-self separation is never fully achieved but implies a high degree of conscious awareness of both the ego and the self. The ego-self axis (which is a term coined by Neumann (1959) but used with greater precision by Edinger) functions as the gateway between the conscious parts of the personality and the unconscious. If the ego-self axis malfunctions in some way (e.g., if there is an unconscious content that is so threatening that the ego shuts the gateway in terror), then an alienation between ego and self results.

Edinger comments that it is difficult in practice to distinguish between ego-self separation and ego-self alienation. Alienation results from the fact that the real parent simply cannot accept all the aspects of the child's personality that are contained in the self.

Following Neumann (1973), Edinger feels that the self can only be experienced at the beginning of life by being projected on to parents – it cannot emerge without a concrete parent-child relationship to function as a 'personal evocation of the archetype' (Neumann, 1959, p. 21). Neumann went further than this to regard the mother as the 'carrier' of the child's self, and, sometimes, of the mother 'as' the child's self:

> the development of the later ego-Self axis of the psyche and the communication and opposition between ego and Self are initiated by the relationship between mother as Self and the child as ego. (1973, p. 17)

What Neumann has done is to develop the proposition that the baby/ego separates from the mother/self. Fordham (1981) has pointed out that, if self means the totality, there would then be no baby. Or, viewed from another angle, if the mother *is* the baby's self, there would be no mother. Fordham feels that all he can accept is that to the baby, his mother is a part of the self (1976, p. 54).

This difference of opinion between Fordham and Neumann may be seen as part of a wider divide between empirical, scientific approaches to the study of infancy as distinct from those based on metaphor and empathy. Neumann's idea that the mother carries the baby's self links with modern psychoanalytic theorising about the importance of mirroring, and the whole issue is detailed in the next chapter. In terms of the post-Jungian debate about integration and pluralism, Neumann's conception of the self follows Jung's rather than leading to an idea of a polycentric psyche, whereas Fordham's approach, as we saw, permits of more variety.

This issue of the mother functioning as the baby's self, as opposed to the baby's self deintegrating in relation to the mother, raises a good deal of heat in analytical psychology. Newton and Redfearn make two useful bridging suggestions. First, images that appear in clinical material of the mother-infant relationship do *symbolise* the relations between the self and the ego:

> just as the self initiates, comprehends and transcends zonal drives and part-object relations, so, if all goes well, the quiet 'holding' mother initiates the feeding relationship and sustains and supports her infant through the vicissitudes of the emotional conflict associated with his oral drive, through her capacity to keep in touch with him as a 'whole person'. (1977, p. 299)

From this general connection between self activity stemming from within and maternal activity stemming from without, a second, more precise parallel can be drawn. Inner feelings of harmony and purpose (experiences of the self) can be envisioned as internalisations of the maternal environment and especially the presence and 'feel' of the mother (ibid., p. 310). An analogy would be with the way the personality of a head teacher permeates a school. The individual's ego-self position reflects what has transpired between him and his mother. This is perhaps a more satisfactory way of utilising the ego-self axis than the over-simple, reified 'mother as self' formulation. It is interesting to note how far the relativisation of the self has now travelled – *the centre of the personality, archetypal to its core, depends for its individual incarnation on the feeling experiences of infancy.* This is one of the key points of theoretical rapprochement in post-Jungian psychology, where the nitty-gritty of analysis of infancy and the 'greater personality' of the self finally touch.

FROM SYMBOL TO IMAGE

The impact of post-Jungian modification of Jung's fundamental theories is seen with clarity in connection with symbols. I intend to show how Jung's initial differentiation between 'sign' and 'symbol' has been extended to make a distinction between 'symbol' and 'image'.

A Classical analytical psychologist such as Adler would be emphatically opposed to the application of specific meanings to symbols and, as far as I can tell, all the post-Jungians follow this in principle. Adler went further and found a positive advantage in the 'inexactitude of symbols' (1979, p. 11). This ambiguity is appropriate for, and reflects the nature of, life, he says. Further, if we adapt the physicist Bohr's 'principle of complementarity' to psychology, we will know that statements of interpretation which are too clear and distinct are absolutely bound to contain something false. If we are dealing with psyche then we had best be indirect.

But in spite of repeated warnings and prohibitions, symbol dictionaries exist. On the flyleaf of Cirlot's *A Dictionary of Symbols* (1962), we find the following claim: 'the basic aim of this work is to create a centre of general reference for symbological studies by clarifying the *unvarying essential meaning of every symbol*' (emphasis added). In the foreword, particular credit is given to Jung (p. xii). Analytical psychology can disclaim this type of venture, but there are repeated attempts to 'fix' the symbol. For instance, in the introduction to *The Origins and History of Consciousness*, Neumann is at pains to argue that what might look like a *personal* symbol is in fact transpersonal, hence collective and fixed (1954, p. xxiii). Later, he refers to personal aspects of the symbol as 'secondary personalisations', with the implicit devaluing of individual variation from the primary version (ibid., pp. 335-42). Von Franz was to be heard on BBC radio on 23 August 1982 saying that 'birds always mean spiritual intuitions – that's why the Holy Ghost is always represented by a bird.'

It is a way of speaking all too common in some circles of analytical psychology: definite, dogmatic, self-contained, creating and maintaining an in-group who *know* and, hence, schism and split.

The angriest outburst against this type of approach has come from Hillman (1977, 1978). He bases his diatribe against symbols on what he knows is being

118

done in some Jungian analysis (method), as opposed to statements of principles (methodology). As a one-time Director of Studies at the Jung Institute in Zürich, he can be expected to know. His position, in plain language, is that symbols have been worked to death: 'they no longer hold my attention' (1977, p. 62). What has been developed is a knowledge of symbols that has, symbolically, killed them. (Cf. Fordham, 1957, p. 51, where the same image of killing the symbol is invoked.)

Before something can become a symbol it has to be an image (cf. Samuels, 1982, p. 323). But looking at symbols in an academic manner, as part of a thesis or dissertation, makes them into something less than images by removing them from any specific context, mood or scene. Images are both reified and minimised. It follows that some so-called symbols, because now not authentic images, cannot even be regarded as symbols. If we look at an image from a symbolic viewpoint, we instantly limit it by generalisation and convention. This sounds at first to be a confusion by Hillman between sign (à la Freud) and symbol (à la Jung). Hillman's rebuff rests on the difference, already noted, between methodology and method: the fact that analytical psychologists do look up symbols in Jung or elsewhere demonstrates that such entities are not images and hence cannot be true symbols.

But do images need to become symbols? Jung said that the 'symbolic process is an experience *in images and of images*' (*CW* 8i, para. 82) and that there would be no symbols without images. But we have seen that, in Hillman's view, symbols tend to erase the characteristic peculiarity and plenitude of images. In a way, we suffer because of the work that Jung and Freud have done; by abstracting symbol from image, image has got lost. For present-day analysts the symbol is not as mysterious as it was. Symbols have become 'stand-ins for concepts' (Hillman, 1977, p. 68). The once-forgotten language of the unconscious had been largely reclaimed by the founding fathers and by the second generation. The taste of the third generation, according to Hillman, is for the rescue of image from symbol.

In Hillman's imagistic approach, image is concentrated upon in its relation to image; this is reminiscent of my 'archetype in the eye of the beholder' fancy in Chapter 2. We saw that one result of this is that it is not necessary for archetypal images to be 'big' – that is 'symbolic'. Whether an image is archetypal or not depends on what one gets out of it. The move is from immanent symbol to pragmatic image. The implication for analysis is that interpretations cease to be 'right' or 'wrong' and will be made in parallel, their efficacy assessed by the richness of what flows from them. This is remarkably similar to the Kleinian analyst Meltzer's notion of an 'interpretative atmosphere', in which a two-way discussion of the meaning of images and interactions takes place rather than a 'translation' of image into symbol by the analyst.

Comparing Hillman's remarks on image to those of Fordham's on symbol twenty years earlier (1957), we need to remember that, for Fordham at that time, *symbol* was still a word with a positive connotation so that what he castigates as unsymbolic is similar to what Hillman regards as unimagistic. The point is that both theorists deride definitory approaches, or attempts to apprehend symbols/images as distortions that must be dissected and corrected. There is to be no pre-conceived dictionary of instant inter-pretations.

DEVELOPMENT OF THE SYMBOLIC ATTITUDE

The symbolic attitude, whilst a universal potential, may be arrested or interfered with in early development. This leads to speculation on whether a person who has not brought together early opposite images of good and bad breasts or good and bad mothers can be capable of the symbolic combination of opposites later. Before an infant can develop the capacity to symbolise he must first be able to make and sustain a conscious distinction between himself and his inner world, himself and his outer world, and inner and outer worlds. In practical terms the question is whether or not a baby can get a sufficiently stable internal image of his mother to give him a feeling of security and confidence when she herself is not there. That is, whether he can employ a symbol of her in his imagination. We have considered that the symbolic attitude develops via use of transitional objects and play (see p. 112, above). Here we should note Fordham's observation that Jung came to many of his intuitions through play with stones and pebbles – this helped him to intuit a way of linking, via symbols, his 'two' personalities (1976, p. 23).

Gordon (1978) has delineated the various stages through which the symbolic attitude develops. Basing her ideas on those of Segal (1973), she differentiates between a symbolic 'equation' and the true symbolic function. Both of these are based on a layer of sensory data and inchoate sense impressions. But there is a crucial difference; in the symbolic equation there is no 'as-if' element, no sense of metaphor. Segal's famous example is of the schizophrenic violinist who could not play because it *would be* masturbating in public. On the other hand, for my patient who had the pitchfork dream, there was no question that she believed her mother's nipples to have been anything other than *as if* prongs.

Gordon suggests that there are three possible explanations why some people cannot benefit from the as-if experience. These are fear of death (often apparent as attraction to death), problems and fears of separation, and greed. All of these are opposed to the development of psychological variety and hence antithetical to metaphor. Death is an inorganic, unvariegated state; problems with separation imply denial of boundary realities and otherness; and greed is an attempt to get everything inside oneself.

It follows from a consideration of Gordon's hypothesis that it is *the self itself that interferes with the development of the symbolic attitude* in that all these problems are essentially a clinging to oneness. But the self is also responsible for the meaningful element in symbols. We have either to conclude that there are two kinds of self – one which promotes and the other which destroys the symbolic attitude – or that we are dealing with dysfunctions of the self. Or, putting these together, that we are observing natural functions of the self, but possibly working destructively in the specific circumstances of an individual. These natural functions may be referred to as defences of the self.

DEFENCES OF THE SELF

Fordham (1974a) expanded his idea of primary self to include the notion that the self, just as much as the ego, has mechanisms of defence. These come into play when there is a lack of a sufficiently empathic 'fit' between baby and mother so that the usual deintegrative processes do not flow freely. Elsewhere (1976), Fordham has commented that lack of a capacity to symbolise arises from a 'basic catastrophe' in the relation between baby and mother so that, although actual feeding may take place, there has been no emotional communication. This lack, together with more tangible deprivations such as illness, early death of mother, twin-trouble, and so forth, can be seen as leading to the retreat into oneness expressed in the absence of the as-if capacity. We are forced to posit a capacity of the self to form an absolute barrier between self and not-self when required or impelled through anxiety or threat. This is an important theoretical point: it is not simply trauma or disappointed expectation that destroys the capacity to symbolise. There are also defence systems which can react to insensitively presented not-self as if it were a vicious enemy which must be neutralised by any means.

Lambert suggests that what is being described is a personality that is truly shattered but held together by cast-iron defences. The result of the shattering is that no ego can cohere and form alongside deintegrative-reintegrative processes; hence the experience in many situations (e.g. relationships) will be of disintegration (1981b, p. 196). Jung, from his own different viewpoint, refers to an individual generating a 'specious unity', in which everything that is wrong is located outside himself, or the presence of the personal shadow is denied. But when this specious unity has contact with the unconscious (i.e. images), it shatters (*CW* 16, para. 399). Plaut used the term 'emergency ego' to refer to the same phenomenon, a rigid and characteristically brittle ego (1959), and Newton suggested that fantasy images of mother-infant interaction that merged the two persons into a blissful or horrific oneness are performing a similar function (1965).

My own emphasis is on the individual's use of incestuous fantasy to contract the available area for interpersonal experience so that others are treated as parts of the self. Omnipotent control of inner and outer worlds is thereby preserved (Samuels, 1980a). The term I used then was 'uroboric omnipotence' to describe the defensive *aim* of infantile fantasies of omnipotence – a return to a less threatening object-less oneness.

THE *UNUS MUNDUS*: CLINICAL PERSPECTIVES

The last aspect of the self to consider from the point of view of post-Jungian psychology is the usefulness, or otherwise, of the *unus mundus* for clinical practice. To avoid exaggerated claims, it is important to distinguish between acausality as such, concepts of a connected universe and special examples of 'strange' connectedness quoted by analytical psychologists from work in non-psychological scientific fields. (Cf. Gammon's use of relativity, 1973, and Keutzer's use of biology, 1982.) It is because the subject matter of psychology is so hard to grasp that analytical psychologists are constantly making these excursions into other fields to help them pin down their material.

The disadvantages of the *unus mundus* for analysis and therapy are obvious: a retreat into a spurious, defensive holism that, by 'transcending' reality avoids any attempt to reach deeper levels. This would not be activity of the self but defensive use by the ego of a distorted version of the self. Regarding the *advantages* for clinical practice, Williams suggested that having synchronicity in mind rescues the analyst and the patient from:

> the twin perils of the opposing attitudes: (1) I am the pawn of fate, i.e., of supernatural powers; and (2) I, the ego, have done it, i.e., performed magic. The analyst is also rescued from falling back on purely causal explanations which usually serve only to debunk the experience instead of letting it work towards change. (1963b, p. 138)

Williams's approach is strengthened by Fordham's remark that synchronicity is *not* a theory about parapsychology or other unusual causation, but is an attempt to define a problem in which phenomena said to be thrown up by chance are not in fact caused by chance (but rather by synchronicity). Jung is trying to cut across the chance-cause duality (Fordham, 1957, pp. 35-6).

Jung suggested that so-called synchronistic phenomena may be more prevalent when the level of consciousness is low. They could then be seen as compensatory, possibly directing therapeutic attention to problem areas which, because unconscious, will not be known of. What may be even more important is the way in which coincidences deepen therapeutic interaction and the connection between analyst and patient (see my case illustration in Chapter 10 for examples of this).

Interesting research has been done in this area by Dieckmann and three other German analytical psychologists who formed a research group to look at countertransference and, in particular, to record the analysts' associations to the material of the patients at the same time as recording the patient's comments. In relation to associations to dream imagery

> the most astonishing result for us was the psychological connection between the analysts' chains of association and the patients'. For the psychotherapist it is, of course, self-evident that the chain of associations should be connected together in a psychologically meaningful way. So it was to be expected that this connection would be found not only in the patient's chain of associations but in the analyst's as well; what we had not expected was that the two chains would again be connected with each other so that they again corresponded meaningfully all along the line. Perhaps the situation may best be characterised by the spontaneous exclamation of one of our members: 'The patients continually say what I am thinking and feeling at the moment!' (Dieckmann, 1974, p. 73)

Dieckmann concluded by referring to Spitz's proposal of a coenesthetic perceptual system, based on phylogenetically older perceptual systems in the sympathetic and parasympathetic nervous systems (ibid., p. 82) – reminiscent of Henry's observations about the location of the archetypes in the hypothalamus, the older, 'reptilian' brain (Henry, 1977, p. 39, above).

The last use of *unus mundus* in clinical work that I want to mention is the questionable resort in analysis to systems such as that of the *I Ching*, Tarot or astrology. It is perhaps, worth reflecting on what Jung wrote to Frey-Rohn in 1945 about the *I Ching*:

> I found the *I Ching* very interesting. . . . I have not used it for more than two years now, feeling that one must learn to walk in the dark, or try to discover (as when one is learning to swim) whether the water will carry one. (quoted in Jaffé, 1979)

PSYCHOANALYTIC PARALLELS

In recent years, psychoanalysts have developed an interest in the self and self-psychology. This arose out of clinical necessity and, particularly, work with more disturbed patients for whom the orthodox structural theory and object relations approaches alike seemed inapplicable. Theorists from many diverse backgrounds have started to work in this field so the situation is extremely confused. But, because I am sure that post-Jungian self-psychology and psychoanalytic self-psychology creatively cross-fertilise, I want to look at the work of three major psychoanalytic theorists: Kohut, Winnicott and Bion.

At the same time as agreeing with Jacoby (1981) that there is little point in crowing over the fact that psychoanalysts are treading ground crossed by Jung fifty years ago, I have a good deal of sympathy with Gordon's view (1980) that, precisely because Jungian analysts have been working with ideas of the self for such a long time, they are unaffected by psychoanalytic factionalism in this area.

KOHUT'S SELF-PSYCHOLOGY AND ANALYTICAL PSYCHOLOGY

Kohut, who was based in Chicago, produced the most comprehensive psychoanalytic self-psychology (e.g. 1971, 1977) and has applied his findings, leading to changes in clinical emphasis and technique. Kohut can be seen as reacting against three quite distinct streams in psychoanalysis. First, against Freud's psychobiological approach, which seems to Kohut mechanistic and to concentrate on modification of the pleasure principle, so that Freud's view of narcissism is fundamentally derogatory. Second, Kohut is in reaction to ego-psychology with its concentration on defences against drive-based anxiety. The part played by psychic *conflict* in internal processes is disputed by Kohut. Finally, Kohutian self-psychology is different in kind to object relations psychology and the Kleinian approach because the latter involves no metapsychological construction and, more important, rests on a division between internal and external that, according to Kohutians, contradicts experience (Tolpin, 1980).

In fact, as we shall see in the next chapter, Kohut disputes that the object relations approach to early developmental experience is psychoanalytically valid! Concisely, this is because an objective point of view is being applied to inner activity. Though an observer may detect conflict, this is not necessarily being experienced as conflict by the infant subject, who is simply getting on with his maturation. Kohut prefers his own empathic methodology. But we shall also see how, even in object relations theories of personality development, a place has been found for the concept of the self (see pp. 161-2, below).

There are two principles which underpin Kohut's thought. To begin with, narcissism can be looked at as something which persists throughout life rather than something that exists in a primary form and then dissolves into healthy libidinal relations with others. For Kohut, narcissism implies positive involvement and investment in oneself, the development and maintenance of self-esteem, and the erection and attainment of ambitions and goals. Put like this, there is no way narcissism can remain pathological, in the sense of a failure to relate to other people or to external objects. Narcissistic development becomes a life-long task. Kohut's second principle is that a psychic centre other than the ego is necessary to explain, not *phenomena*, but *feelings*. Initially, Kohut, like many psychoanalysts, used the term self to refer to a representation of the person and of identity as this appeared to, and in, the ego (e.g. Jacobson, 1964). Later, the self was said by Kohut to be a psychic system of its own, with its own dynamic and structure.

Let us examine briefly the bones of Kohut's idea about how the self develops. Narcissistic development proceeds along its own separate pathway, in the same way as object relations are conceived of as having a distinct path of development. It is important to note that there is no fundamental reason why narcissistic development should damage object relating capacities – the reverse is probably true in that positive self-development leads to positive relations with others.

Narcissistic development also has its own set of objects, called self-objects. To start with, a 'mirroring' self-object, usually the mother, allows an unfolding and expression of a baby's 'exhibitionism' and 'grandiosity'. That is to say, she permits him the illusion that he runs the world and is its centre. She does this, not only by her empathic responses to her baby, but by her joyous acceptance of him. The baby gets an idea of what he is like as a person (later on, self-esteem) by what he sees in the mirror of the mother's face and the way she communicates her attitude to him.

Gradually, the mother introduces acceptable levels and types of frustration which modulate the grandiose and omnipotent illusions/delusions of the baby. She lets him down gently, and not too soon. Kohut refers to this deflation of a loving kind as one of a number of 'transmuting internalisations'. The grandiosity is transformed into fundamental *self-assertiveness, goals and ambitions*. What this means is that one can cope with being deflated if the person doing that radiates love and acceptance while so doing. Kohut regards the capacity to do this as a natural part of motherhood.

At the same time, the baby will tend to idealise his self-objects, at first the nipple and breast, and later the mother. He does this for two main reasons –

because of projection of his own grandiose goodness and also because he needs to conceive of a greater good outside of himself, a self-created stimulus to reach out to the world. The principle of transmuting internalisation applies equally to these idealised self-objects as to the grandiosity. They are also gradually internalised – as *ideals and values*.

Taking the two processes together, a bipolar self emerges in which archaic grandiosity and exhibitionism have been transformed into goals and ambitions (one pole) and archaic idealisations have become inner ideals and values (the other pole). Together, the two poles form what Kohut calls the 'nuclear self'. This is said to be the earliest complex mental structure.

Although questions of psychopathological development and analysis will be dealt with in the next two chapters, the implications of Kohut's model of the development of the self for treatment need a brief note. Transmuting internalisations, through the working out of self-object transferences in analysis (mirroring or idealising) can repair damage done to the nuclear self by parental psychopathology, environmental defect or a poor fit between the infant and mother. If the twin developments arising from grandiosity and idealisation go awry the result is a mixture of inability to attain goals and ambitions and to enjoy any activity and a diminished capacity to relate to instinctual life and order experience in terms of value. This expresses itself in a form of cut-offness or unreachability, in the making of unreasonable demands, in exaggerated self-sufficiency, fear of exploitation, and so on. Kohut, amongst other psychoanalysts, described this condition as narcissistic personality disorder.

Kohut's ideas about timing are particularly interesting. Somewhere between two and four years grandiosity is transformed into ambition; somewhere between four and six years idealisation shifts over into values and principles. The self is therefore created by the parental self-object being able to regard and treat the baby as if it had a self (Kohut's term is 'virtual self'). Gradually, the baby's assertiveness and healthy rage, accepted by the mirroring self-object, secures the establishment of the self. Rage is conceived of as a positive response to a sense of having been injured.

It will be noted that the self as Kohut describes it is both a metapsychological structure and an experiential entity. Whilst this does not satisfy the logicians (in much the same way as Jung's centre and circumference formulation), there are considerable advantages in having this twin viewpoint: objective structure and subjective experience. The self can be seen as an ordering of feelings about oneself that have developed in infancy which does not require ego-comprehension to take effect. The self may remain inaccessible to the ego.

Returning to our task of critical comparison, there has been a debate within analytical psychology concerning differences and similarities between Kohut's theory of the self and that of Jung's. We may note at the outset that if the self is envisaged as being *created* during development, as in Kohut's view it is, then this is antithetical to Jung's archetypal theory and in particular to Fordham's post-Jungian conception of an *a priori* primary self. On the other hand, as Jacoby has pointed out, Kohut does talk of a 'blueprint for life' being laid down in the nuclear self (Jacoby, 1981, p. 23) and of the 'unchanging specificity' of the self (Jacoby, 1983, p. 108). There is a problem here of language and of background. For an analyst with a Freudian background, 'blueprint for life' rings bells connected to psychic determinism and the primacy of actual early experience in the formation of later personality. So, for Kohut, events occurring at age four that affect someone at age forty might well constitute a 'blueprint'.

My own opinion is that Kohut does *not* talk of the self as something there from the beginning – his view is more that the self is a result of numerous communications between mother and baby. However, the idea that the mother mirrors the baby's grandiose self implies that she must in some sense be in communication with it (what is the 'self' that creates self-objects?), and therefore it is possible to stretch Kohut's theory to involve the idea of an innate self. But it is Kohut's reference to the infant's earliest self forming *at a point in time* which contradicts the idea of a self in the Jungian sense.

Nevertheless, Kohut's description of the way in which the self is created by, and forms out of, the empathic communication between the infant and his self-objects fills a gap in Fordham's theory, which is less focused on *experiences* of the self and of selfhood. We could aggregate the two theories to regard Fordham's deintegrates as an explanation of the way in which self-objects are themselves constructed; Kohut's theory then illuminates ways in which infant/self-object relations cohere into a feeling of selfhood.

Jacoby suggests that a further parallel can be drawn between Kohut's use of self-object (the mother) and Neumann's idea that the mother carries or incarnates the baby's self (Jacoby, 1981, p. 21). I would place Kohut's theory of development midway between Fordham's and Neumann's. 'Kohut's baby' is strong, effective, independent, active, vigorous, with a feeling of 'normal entitlement' or 'primary confidence' which is not extinguished by everyday small-scale frustrations and anxieties:

> The baby's capacity to root, suck, swallow, refuse and push away the nipple, grasp, touch, cry, scream, kick, struggle, propel himself with swimming movements, look, listen, move in synchrony with the human voice, etc., are in-phase autonomous capacities. (Tolpin, 1980, pp. 54-5)

This sounds more like Fordham with his emphasis on the *active* contribution of the infant, than Neumann – but what is missing is the vital suggestion that these capacities are part of an organised integrate that exists at the start of life. At the same time, the mother's response that mirrors the baby's continuity and integrity also strikes a chord with the way that Neumann conceives the primal relationship between the baby and the mother who carries his self.

Continuing our discussion of whether Kohut's self theory is compatible with that of Jung, Schwartz-Salant (1982) tended to disagree with Jacoby and noted four basic differences. Kohut's self is so wedded to development that it reflects but one archetypal pattern – the '*puer-senex* archetype', meaning growth and maturation towards wisdom. Only the child/adult opposites in the personality are involved. Next, Kohut's self radiates a defensive quality; it is more a defense of the self than the self in a Jungian sense. Third, the exhibitionism-idealisation polarity is only one of many possibilities, leaving out, for example, integration of the contrasexual archetype. Finally, the Kohutian self is largely positive; negative emotions such as hate, envy, rage and so forth, are 'disintegration products' of 'poor empathy' (ibid., p. 21).

For Jung, the self involved all possibilities, positive and negative, spiritual and instinctive. Schwartz-Salant feels that the sympathetic attitude towards Kohut amongst some post-Jungians has to do with his purposive approach but that, for him personally, it is in their clinical application that he finds value in Kohut's ideas. He is not convinced by Kohut's many utterances of a 'cosmic' nature.

Jacoby did indeed take Kohut's references to 'cosmic narcissism' more seriously (1981). Kohut is on record as saying that 'the self is the centre of the individual's psychological universe' and that it is a centre for initiative; we have already noted the metaphor of a 'blueprint for life'. Finally, Kohut is positively 'Jungian' in his confession of the limits of self-psychology:

> The self as the centre of the individual's psychological universe, is, like all reality – physical reality . . . or psychological reality . . . – not knowable in essence. We cannot, by introspection and empathy, penetrate to the self *per se*; only its introspectively or empathically perceived psychological manifestations are open to us. (1977, pp. 310-11)

This aspect of Kohut's thesis does throw up numerous similarities and some thought-provoking differences. As we saw, Kohut's explanation of the self arising out of processes of mirroring and idealisation can usefully be added to Fordham's theory of a primary integrate with innate (archetypal) organising powers. For those with a pictorial bent, Fordham talks essentially of a big blob self that breaks up; Kohut of little bits that gradually form the blob. The tension between the two theories is that between the self as viewed by an external observer and a first-person experience of a self.

Self-psychology attempts the philosophically difficult task of trying to express how another person feels about himself and what his inner world and his experiences *mean* to him. As we noted when discussing complexes, self-psychology is a psychology of meaning. The philosophical problems can be appreciated when it is remembered that we also need to know how the individual feels about what others feel about him.

Within psychoanalysis itself there has been considerable disagreement between object-relations theorists and the group of analysts connected to Kohut. Speaking for the Kohutians, Tolpin considered that all object relations approaches are skewed by being based on conflict, whether between internal world and external reality or between different internal agencies. There is, she continued, a basic error which confuses a child's normal psychology with an adult's mental disintegration products. Object relations theory does not explain

> normal workings of the mind, central regulations of a conflict-free sphere [which] are part and parcel . . . of a cohesive self, an independent centre of initiative which is capable, within human limits, of using its own functions for regulating the self. (Tolpin, 1980, p. 59)

Tolpin concluded by noting that debates within psychoanalysis like these – 'fruitless "controversial discussions" over early object relations theory' – have 'compounded a split' in an already divided psychoanalytic profession (ibid., p. 60).

So there may be a case for arguing, along with Gordon (1980), that analytical psychology *can* bridge self-psychology and object relations theory. If narcissism is to be seen as healthy self-love, then we must ask with Gordon: 'who is this "I" that I love?' While it is the case that a self-object communicates something to the baby that helps him to develop a feeling about himself, that same self-object is also in part an emotional construction of the baby's, about which he has a wide range of feelings. Such construction of a self-object arises from the operation of the early defence mechanisms (e.g. projective identification, splitting and idealisation) and, especially, from deintegration of the self. In brief, the post-Jungian contribution is a model which can incorporate *innate* potentials, *inner* processes and *external* objects, using both a *subjective* and an *objective* perspective.

We are dealing with a mating of the highest and lowest. The self is the supraordinate personality, the totality, the God-image. It is *also* something the baby experiences in the presence and feel of his mother, to use once more that phrase of Redfearn's. Though we may attempt to distinguish these two aspects of the self, they tend to constellate each other and a degree of confusion is probably inevitable. What would be a pity is a situation in which analytical psychology or psychoanalysis espouses but one of these two perspectives; this would be as futile as attempting to live by either primary or secondary process alone or, in Jung's terms, to use either directed or undirected thinking at the expense of the other.

WINNICOTT AND THE SELF

Winnicott is another psychoanalyst (1958, 1965, 1971) whose work is frequently compared with Jung's. We know that Winnicott had contact with analytical psychologists, contributing a review to the *Journal of Analytical Psychology* and participating in numerous 'ecumenical' meetings of the British Psychological Society involving psychoanalysts and analytical psychologists. However, he staunchly refused to grant credence to the concepts of analytical psychology and scarcely mentioned the work of the Developmental School going on in London at the same time as he was writing many of his papers. Winnicott's influence on analytical psychology has been great (and acknowledged), especially his ideas about the developing mother-infant relationship. In this chapter we are more concerned with Winnicott's attitude to the self.

At the start of life, according to Winnicott, there is no self and no self-consciousness. It is only when the latter develops that we can talk of a 'self'. The 'person' begins in the forming ego and Winnicott tends to refer to the self to overcome the deficiencies of orthodox Freudian drive and structural systems, which leave out an experiencing person who can contribute to his own experience. These contributions take the form of an inner reality, which is conceived of as clustering round a central self or core of personality:

the central self could be said to be the inherited potential which is experiencing a continuity of being, and acquiring in its own way and at its own speed a personal psychic reality and a personal body-scheme. (Winnicott, 1965, p. 46)

The self is seen as a more or less isolated core embedded in, and surrounded by, inner reality. It develops through a recognition of otherness and difference; the self is defined by the other. The baby begins life in a relatively unintegrated state and, depending on the quality of maternal care, progresses towards integration and 'unit self' status. In addition to the role of the mother in promoting such integration, Winnicott also notes the continual elaboration in imagination and fantasy of bodily activity. In other words, integration is a joint product of the maternal environment and the baby's own psychic processes.

If the 'fit' between mother and baby is not 'good enough' then the baby will experience the environment as persecuting and invasive, impinging on him. What happens in such circumstances, according to Winnicott, is that the baby's True Self is outraged, angry, anxious at the premature destruction of his omnipotence and goes underground. The baby then presents to the world a coping and compliant False Self. In adult life, the False Self is experienced as emptiness, meaninglessness and inauthenticity.

There are two parallels with Jung. First, Winnicott's False Self is similar to Jung's persona when that functions pathologically. And second, whilst the ego is scarcely a False Self, an ego that does not reflect some of the purposefulness of the self will experience life in terms of the meaninglessness characteristic of the False Self.

Whatever the True Self/False Self vicissitudes, it is clear that, for Winnicott, it is object relations and the infant's relationship to his mother that alter and affect his sense of self rather more than the contribution of the self to object relations. For Winnicott, unlike Jung, Fordham and Neumann, usually depicted the self as the *end product* of an evolution from unintegrate to integrate.

Winnicott himself saw a way of closing the gap between his approach and that of analytical psychology. In one of his references to analytical psychology, he notes that analytical psychologists feel that there is a 'primitive self which looks like environment' arising out of the archetypes, something more than the operation of instinct. Winnicott felt that:

we ought to modify our [i.e. psychoanalysis'] view to embrace both ideas, and to see (if it is true) that in the earliest theoretical primitive state the self has its own environment, self-created, which is as much the self as the instincts that produce it. (Winnicott, 1958, p. 155n)

I am not sure whether any analytical psychologist has ever claimed that the environment *is* the self; the bone of contention is whether we can theorise about a self existing *in its own right* in relation to, and interdependent with environment. Here, Winnicott is feeling his way towards this point of view, which is different from his more developed notion of a created self arising out of activity between the individual and his environment.

Winnicott's stress on the self as an organ of meaning, his observations concerning man's need to transcend himself through creative action, are also close to Jung's idea of the self. Perhaps the clearest parallel is in the degree of trust given to unconscious processes, viewed, not in terms of potential conflicts and neuroses, but as life-enriching, even numinous. Winnicott's stress is on the quality of living rather than on abstractions such as mental health or sanity, and this aspect of True Self process resembles individuation.

A further area of Winnicott's work which may be compared with analytical psychology is his notion of transitional objects, leading to symbol formation and a 'third area', the 'area of experience'. This is distinct from the other areas of inner and outer reality. It operates symbolically and its origin can be observed in the infant's use of tangible objects (such as blankets, teddies, or its own hand and fingers), initially as a defence against separation anxiety and depression, and later on as symbols of the absent mother. Winnicott used the phrase 'the first not-me possession' to imply that transitional objects occupy a special point on a self-other spectrum – an intermediate point which reflects the parlous state of a baby's ability to recognise and accept reality (1971). The workings of the transitional area, its synthesising functions and its bridging of inner and outer, are reminiscent of Jung's transcendent function in which symbols can hold together contents which the intellect cannot. For Winnicott, use of symbols, at first tangible but later psychological, is a way of getting in touch with inner psychic reality. Winnicott regarded symbols as dealing with a transcendence of the polarity between 'external world phenomena and phenomena of the individual person who is being looked at' (1971, p. 168).

Winnicott's interest in play links directly with Jung's personal experience of its creative potential (Jung, 1963). The essence of play is that the rules of the ego may be broken; category differences, hierarchy, reality, normality, decency, clarity, and so on, all may be discarded. If we accept that playing operates out of the self-system rather than the ego-system, then it is in Winnicott's connection of play, and the ethos of play, to religion and creativity that forms the clearest link between him and Jung. Jung refers to a religious instinct or drive and playing is also ubiquitous and natural. Religion and creativity thrive on transcendence, on symbols, and on 'not-me' types of experience, and all these elements are present in a child's play.

BION'S CONCEPT OF O

The third and last psychoanalyst whose ideas I am comparing with Jung's is Bion. Here again we must be selective and inevitably do injustice to Bion's entire edifice (cf. Bion, 1977). It is Bion's concept of O that bears resemblance to several of Jung's usages of the self. O can be defined as:

> Ultimate reality, absolute truth, or unknowable psychic reality in the Kantian sense, which can only be known through its transformations. (Grinberg *et al.*, 1977, p. 145)

In any observation, Bion stated, we are not concerned with static phenomena but with transformations between one state and another. In analysis, the patient's associations expressed in words are transformations of thoughts and emotions; these in turn are transformations of internal or external, past or present events. These are based on certain 'original facts' – in the context of an analytic session, these unknowable facts are O. O therefore implies psychological reality. According to Bion, O can only be known indirectly, by observing transformation. First, *from* O, for instance in the analytic session as described. Second, *in* O, implying that O itself contains a dynamic. Transformations in O are said always to be disruptive. Finally, there is a sense in which phenomena *become* O – that is, re-connect to their ultimate base. Because O can only be inferred and not known directly, a faith or commitment is necessary to get close to O. This could be the conviction of a scientist or that of a mystic.

We can see the parallels with Jung and with analytical psychology. Jung also insists on the self as ultimately irrepresentable, observable only via its manifestations. The disruptions in O are reminiscent of the deintegrative process. The process of becoming O is paralleled by the impulse to return to 'the world of the Mothers', the ground of one's being. And the conviction and passion to know O as closely as possible is similar to Jung's individuation instinct. Knowing the *manifestations* of O can be achieved by the senses and by the ego; knowing O is a matter of faith.

Fordham felt that O does correspond to his own concept of a primary self and that O as ultimate truth corresponded to Jung's self or God-image (1980b, p. 203). Plaut suggested that Bion's insistence on the analyst leaving his conscious intentions and desires out of account so as to focus 'analytic intuition' (Bion's term) on what is happening in the session implies something akin to an ego-self dynamic; O would then occupy the self end of an ego-self axis with the analyst's more active intervention at the ego end of the axis (1972).

It seems to me that the main point of similarity is that both O and Jung's self do not evolve as such, but are seen as containing all potentials. What evolves is the state of knowledge about, and closeness to, O or the self. Thus, where a person is in his emotional development (how individuated) informs his perception and experience of O and the self alike.

PSYCHOANALYSIS AND INDIVIDUATION

I had thought to draw a sharp distinction between psychoanalytic ideas and analytical psychology's concept of individuation. This was not to be; in psychoanalytic discussion about what does and does not constitute 'normality', we find parallels with post-Jungian thinking about individuation.

Joseph (1982), in his paper 'Normal in psychoanalysis', observed that, from his experience, 'normal' was not synonymous with *regular, standard, natural, typical*, as the dictionary suggested. Rather, what is normal is determined by subjective evaluation. Freud (1937) had talked of 'normality in general' as an 'ideal fiction' and, Joseph concludes, Freud equated normality with analysability and with the outcome of a successful analysis. Joseph drew attention to the work of Offer and Sabshin who, in their book *Normality* (1973) distinguish four different aspects of the word-idea 'normal'. These are: normal as health, normal as average, normal as ideal, normal as process.

Such an undogmatic approach was also taken by Jones who proposed in 1931 that normality could be assessed in terms of 'happiness', 'efficiency' and 'adaptation to reality'. Klein, in a similar vein, wrote of normality as involving the harmonious interaction of several aspects of mental life such as emotional maturity, strength of character, capacity to deal with conflicting emotions, a reciprocal balance between internal and external worlds, and, finally, a welding of the parts of the personality leading to an integrated self concept (1960).

What lies behind these psychoanalysts' explorations of normality is an idea very similar to individuation – consider Klein's list. Psychoanalysts, in their turn, may perceive that, far from being a mystical quest, the concept of individuation in analytical psychology relates to a concern of theirs.

CONCLUDING NOTE

I want to end by gathering in the main definitional problems I have mentioned around the use of the word 'self'. First, there is confusion between self as an experience (myself) and the use of the word objectively, in psychological theory. Next, there is a problem between self as centre (archetype of unity or balance) and self as the totality of the personality. Finally, we need to distinguish self *per se* from self-representations and symbols.

The reader will have noted the gradual change of emphasis: nowadays the self and individuation tend to be discussed in a more relative tone. Regarding the self, we have seen this in terms of a debate on integration, an examination of the theory of the opposites, stress on the interdependence of self and ego, and a rejection of the symbol dictionary approach. Individuation has also been made less absolute and expanded to include psychopathology – an emphatic reconnection to a natural psychology.

5
The development of personality

We have reached the point where it is appropriate to discuss the development of an individual personality. Both ego and self arise out of the articulation of innate potentials in response to environmental factors encountered by the individual. If the ego is sufficiently strong to permit free passage of unconscious contents then it itself is strengthened; much of this depends on the quality of early relationships, and the establishment of trust. Central to this is the way in which frustration is met by mother and child. The self, meaning here a subjective feeling of being, continuity and integration, is first experienced by the individual in terms of the presence and feel of his mother as she accepts him as an integrated whole; he experiences his personal wholeness in her perception of his wholeness, in her relating eye. Her capacity to hold together his multiplicity of being and to give him a sense of meaning provides him with a base for subsequent psychic integration. He, in turn, brings to the situation an innate potential to feel whole in himself.

The traditional view is that Jung was not much interested in the personal development of the individual, that his theory of early development is therefore inadequate and that this has had to be rectified by wholesale borrowing from psychoanalysis. While it may be true that Jung's interests were often more keenly engaged in such areas as phylogeny and an examination of psycho-cultural development, it is by no means true that he left no theory of development in infancy and childhood. His writings on this subject are scattered and many of his most suggestive theses are *not* found in the volume of the *Collected Works* entitled *The Development of Personality* (*CW* 10). This is because Jung moves so rapidly from the personal and ontogenetic to the transpersonal and phylogenetic that, rather than a coherent statement, we find numerous references and it is our task to form these into a consistent thesis.

It has been part of my intention to show that Jung's writings represent such a consistent theory and that, once again, both the areas of concern he mapped out, and his overall attitudes, anticipate by many years what happened in psychoanalysis, as Roazen confirmed. Analytical psychology has had its own internal debates, and this book records them, but in certain key areas the cast of thought inspired and pioneered by Jung enables analytical psychologists to move smoothly onwards where psychoanalysts experience internecine conflict and the problem of loyalty and responsibility to Freud. We noted this in relation to combining of self-psychology with object relations theory and we shall see it again in relation to personality development.

Because of the scattering of Jung's writings on the subject of development, and because I do not want to write a history of psychoanalytic thought, the structure of this chapter is different from the previous chapters. There, the following elements were kept separate: Jung's contribution, critiques of this from outside and inside analytical psychology, the post-Jungian corpus and debate, parallels in psychoanalysis and other diciplines, and my own commentary. Here these elements have to be intermingled.

THE INFLUENCE OF INFANCY

We may want to know more about Jung's reticence in drawing together his thoughts on early development. In this regard, he seems to have undergone at the outset the same intellectual process as later generations of Freudians. Roazen noted that Jung was arguing that neurosis was not necessarily a matter of fixation 'years before the rise of ego psychology' (1976, p. 272).

The main reason why Jung could not put energy into developing a coherent theory has to do with an over-reaction to Freud. Jung often mentioned that he used Freudian (and Adlerian) theories when this was appropriate for the patient, and the implication was that such theories were adequate. Jung's early modifications of Freud in such works as 'The theory of psychoanalysis' written in 1913 (*CW* 4) do not disguise the enormous debt owed to his mentor. And, as we noted with reference to the ego in Chapter 3, there are moments when Jung functions like a most authentic Freudian (perhaps like the Freud he knew), particularly with regard to the chronology of the various psychological events in infancy.

Perhaps Jung, quite consciously, decided to leave the 'nursery' to Freud and, again consciously, he wanted to differentiate himself by finding quite other directions to explore – many of which had interested him since his student days before his encounter with psychoanalysis or even psychiatry. For example, in a volume of Jung's papers given to the Zofingia student fraternity at Basle University in 1895, we find hints of several aspects of his later work on religion, the nature of science, psychology, and other matters (Jung, 1983). At the same time, Jung cannot bring himself to ignore the issues Freud and he explored together, and finally parted over. This is substantiated by the ubiquity in Jung's writings of statements concerning many of the flashpoints of disagreement with Freud about early life, for example, the question of the literal or symbolic nature of memories, and also the Oedipus complex; or the relative importance of the parents in the destiny of the individual; or, crucially, the pros and cons of reductive and constructive (or synthetic) approaches. All these matters are discussed in this chapter.

Another important reason why Jung did not codify his ideas about early development is that he would have run the risk of obscuring his vision of a psychology of the whole of life which he created in contradistinction to Freud's concentration on infancy and childhood. We shall be looking at this later on.

Jung saw the use of reduction as central to Freud's method of attempting to reveal 'elementary processes of wishing or striving, which in the last resort are of an infantile or physiological nature' (*CW* 6, para. 788). Jung is critical of the reductive method because the *meaning* of the unconscious product (symptom, dream image, slip of the tongue) is lost. By attempting to connect such an unconscious product with the past, its value to the individual in the present may be lost. Jung's further objection was the tendency of reduction to over-simplify, eschewing what he saw as a deeper understanding.

Jung questioned the operation of psychic determinism and causality in an individual. That is:

> The psychology of an individual can never be exhaustively explained from himself alone: a clear recognition is needed of the way it is also conditioned by historical and environmental circumstances . . . no psychological fact can ever be explained in terms of causality alone; as a living phenomenon, it is always indissolubly bound up with the continuity of the vital process, so that it is not only something evolved but also continually evolving and creative. (*CW* 6, para. 717)

Jung went on to point out that what he refers to as the 'final standpoint' is usually taken for granted in everyday life where we tend to disregard the strictly causal factor. For example, if a man has an opinion and expresses it, we tend to want to know what he means, what he is getting at. We are less interested in the origin of his idea. But Jung states that the causal and final perspectives can also co-exist. Discussing our understanding of fantasy, he said that this

> needs to be understood both causally and purposively. Causally interpreted, it seems like a *symptom* of a physiological or personal state, the outcome of antecedent events. Purposively interpreted, it seems like a *symbol*, seeking to characterise a definite goal with the help of the material at hand, or trace out a line of future psychological development. (*CW* 6, para. 720)

Jung is less than fair to the reductive standpoint. He gives as an example of the reductive approach an interpretation of a dream of a sumptuous feast in terms of the dreamer having gone to bed hungry! Here Jung's conception of 'reductive' is somewhat prosaic. We may glean many other possible meanings from this dream, still reductively but less stolidly, perhaps. Why a 'sumptuous' feast? Is this compensation for earlier oral deprivations? Or an inflation? Or a wish? And is the dreamer host or guest? Was it a traditional celebration or a one-off occasion? A christening or a funeral? I would not consider this list of questions as exhaustive either, but the difference is that the reductive approach, as I understand it, does not imply an archivalist mentality; it also requires imagination. It is not a question of simply *reconstructing* infancy and childhood. In those questions reference is made to fantasy and to the current state of the dreamer, emphasising a *prospective* connection to the past.

Psychoanalysis has experienced a parallel internal debate about causality. Freudian psychoanalysis had developed the concept of psychic determinism. Any psychological event is seen as the inevitable outcome of preceding psychological events. These preceding events function as causes and the phenomena under discussion are the effects of these causes. Rycroft, surveying the field of psychoanalysis from within, gives numerous indications that this analogy with natural science is disputed. For instance:

> I refer ... to the doubts which have been expressed by Szasz, Home, Lomas, myself and others as to whether the causal-deterministic assumptions of Freudian theory are valid, i.e., whether it is really possible to maintain that human behaviour has causes in the sense that physical phenomena do or that human personality can really be explained as the result of events that happened to it as a child. (1972, p. ix)

This quote from Rycroft comes from the introduction to his *Critical Dictionary of Psychoanalysis* which is an extremely useful book. In that introduction, Rycroft went on to show how other lacks in Freudian theory have been met by ego psychologists, object relations theorists and existential analysts. The similarities between these three groupings and analytical psychologists, Jungian and post-Jungian, is what we are discussing. That this can be done at all is particularly pleasing since Rycroft has claimed to suffer from 'the not uncommon constitutional defect of being incapable of understanding Jung's writings' (ibid., p. ix).

What Rycroft wrote regarding causality may be further compared with this of Jung in 1921:

> a scientific psychology must ... not rely exclusively on the strictly causal standpoint originally taken over from natural science, for it has also to consider the purposive nature of the psyche. (*CW* 6, para. 718)

Returning to Rycroft – he states that he and the analysts he mentioned feel that Freud's crucial contribution was to see symptoms as *communications*:

> Advocates of this view argue that theories of causality are only applicable to the world of inanimate objects and that Freud's attempt to apply deterministic principles derived from the physical sciences to human behaviour fails to take account of the fact that man is a living agent capable of making decisions and choices and of being *creative*. (1972, p. 89, emphasis added)

It is in connection with being creative (in all senses) that we now turn to look at what Jung means by the synthetic or constructive approach which he contrasts to the reductive, and then at how this affects his ideas about early development. My point is that, unless Jung's commitment to the idea of synthesis in interpretation is understood, his ideas about infancy and childhood make less sense.

THE SYNTHETIC METHOD

Jung used the terms 'synthetic' and 'constructive' interchangeably but the former is preferable because of a confusion with psychoanalytic terminology in which 'constructions' refer to attempts to achieve a factual reconstruction of the patient's past which is, of course, exactly the opposite of what Jung meant in his use of constructive, seeking to imply 'building up' or moving on (*CW* 6, para. 701).

It is important to note what Jung said in connection with the synthetic method because his statements are open to idealisation. Jung stated that he saw unconscious products as symbolic and as anticipating some psychological development which has not yet occurred. For instance, a symptom that relates to overwork may appear as a compensatory symbol calling attention to the need to rectify the situation.

A patient of mine who fitted this description found himself falling asleep at his office desk with some regularity; this led him to take pills to keep his energy level high. Soon his dose was above what was safe and we had to discuss the whole position. Focusing on the question of sleep produced a memory (which may not have been factual, not the point here) of sleeping with his head on his mother's lap when going on holiday in a train when in his early teens. He had been sleeping like this because he felt travelsick. Without going into much detail, this led him to share his business worries with his wife who was, to his surprise, helpful and, together, they worked out a less demanding routine for him. He stopped trying to protect his wife and asked her for the succour symbolised by the image of his mother's lap. His fantasy that he was protecting his wife (and serving her interests by his overwork) contained his own need for maternal care in a projected form. I give an example like this to make the point that the synthetic approach can function in a down-to-earth way.

Jung summarised this approach by referring to a 'prospective function of the unconscious'. We have already discussed how the self regulates the psyche in a manner that suggests the organism 'knows' what is best for it. This is evidence of the 'prospective function'. Because the products of the unconscious are conceived of as expressions 'oriented to a goal or purpose' (*CW* 6, para. 701), it follows that our interest is less with the *sources* of unconscious material but rather more with the meaning. The problem then becomes one of how to elucidate this meaning and this is where Jung justified his use of comparative data and of amplification (see Chapter 1, p. 5, above).

The feature of the synthetic method which is most directly relevant to our considerations of early development is the way in which the unconscious expresses itself in 'symbolic language'. It was Jung's understanding of the synthesising nature of symbols, and his insistence on it, that provided the intellectual fuel for the break with Freud.

REAL PEOPLE OR SYMBOLIC FIGURES?

It is well known that Jung refused to accept the Oedipus complex as a literal, factual event. He recognised the archetypal component and saw in the child's desire for the mother a regressive longing to re-enter her body and return to a state of early contentment. Jung also stressed, as we shall see in detail later, the personality-enhancing outcome of such a return.

It is relatively well known that Freud was forced to accept Jung's thesis concerning retrospective adult fantasy in relation to the primal scene, for example. Jung, according to Laplanche and Pontalis in their *The Language of Psychoanalysis*, 'shattered' Freud's argument (1980, p. 332). Freud continued to maintain that perception or misperception played a part but came very close to postulating the functioning of an archetype, as we saw in Chapter 2 (p. 42, above).

It is less well known how far Jung developed his idea that what seemed to be 'real' to the patient when he spoke of parent figures was, in fact, a reference to symbolic figures formed out of the interaction of archetype and experience, or just the result of archetypal identification. For instance, referring to the child, Jung wrote:

It may not be superfluous to point out that lay prejudice is always inclined to identify the child motif with the concrete experience 'child', as though the real child were the cause and pre-condition of the existence of the child motif.... The empirical idea 'child' is only the means to express a psychic fact. Hence, by the same token the mythological idea of the child is emphatically not a copy of the empirical child but a *symbol* clearly recognisable as such and not ... a human child. (*CW* 9i, para. 273n)

Or, with reference to the struggle between the hero and the monster-mother, Jung did not regard the latter as symbolising the real mother:

It is not the real mother who is symbolised, but the libido of the son whose object was once the mother. We take mythological symbols much too concretely.... When we read: 'His mother was a wicked witch', we must translate it as: the son is unable to detach his libido from the mother-imago, he suffers from resistances because he is tied to his mother. (*CW* 5, para. 329)

And not, presumably, as 'his mother was a witch.'
Or, with reference to the parents:

the parents are not the 'parents' at all but only their imagos: they are representations which have arisen from the conjunction of parental peculiarities with the individual disposition of the child. (*CW* 5, para. 505)

In all these extracts, reference *is* made to the real person, i.e. the 'empirical child', the 'parental peculiarity'. So Jung has not ruled out a part that might be played by the real events of childhood in contributing to the adult psyche. In effect, he provides a framework which enables contemporary analytical psychologists to take *all* the material that their patients bring as 'real', without undue concern whether the material is factual or an account may be taken as reliable. Distortions of childhood memories and archetypal motifs are treated with the same phenomenological respect as so-called facts. We shall see presently how analysts of the Developmental School have been liberated by this but first we must attempt to clarify one area of Jung's thought where he quite signally failed to blend the archetypal and empirical approaches. This has to do with the nature of the child's psychology.

The problem can be stated simply as follows: are we to see a small child as an extension of the psychology of its parents or as being recognisable as itself? The question has to be put because here Jung contradicts himself. In the transcript of an interview filmed in 1957, Jung makes the following two statements:

> Already in earliest childhood a mother recognises the individuality of her child, and if you observe carefully you can see tremendous differences even in very small children.

And

> in any case of a child's neurosis I go back to the parents and see what is going on there, because children have no psychology of their own, in the literal sense. They are so much in the mental atmosphere of their parents ... they are imbued with the paternal or maternal atmosphere, and they express these influences. (Jung, 1978, p. 274)

In case it might be thought that the spoken word has contributed to this contradiction, Jung shows the same confusion in other places. In his Introduction to Wickes's *Inner World of Childhood* he wrote:

> What is the thoughtful reader to make, for instance, of the puzzling but undeniable fact of the identity of the psychic state of the child with the unconscious of the parents? ... There is nothing 'mystical' about identity ... [it] derives essentially from the notorious unconsciousness of the small child. ... Unconsciousness means non-differentiation. There is as yet no clearly defined ego, only events which may belong to me or to another. (*CW* 17, para. 83)

But elsewhere we find that:

> the preconscious psyche – for example that of a new born infant – is not an empty vessel into which ... anything can be poured. On the contrary, it is a tremendously complicated, sharply defined individual entity which appears indeterminate to us only because we cannot see it directly. (*CW* 9i, para. 151)

My suggestion is that this weakness contains a potential strength. The individuality of the child does derive from more than what Jung refers to as his 'accidental parents' (*CW* 17, para. 93). But the child will not grow without parenting and, in some cases, this will be inadequate. In the majority of cases there will be a satisfactory linkage between the child's individuality and the environment into which he is born. 'Satisfactory' does not mean 'perfect', however. As we have seen, frustration is of the essence in the development of consciousness. Jung has stumbled on to what may be seen as the fulcrum, or

139

essential feature of a modern developmental approach. The child, a separate person, has to get to terms with his parents to survive, while they, in their turn, will have to adapt to his individuality.

THE POST-JUNGIANS AND DEVELOPMENTAL PSYCHOLOGY

The picture I have sketched shows Jung at his most ambivalent. Not surprisingly, this lack of certainty has stimulated a variety of debates between schools of post-Jungians and, in the case of the Developmental School, within the school itself.

There are two main areas of disagreement. The first concerns whether an approach to analysis which utilises developmental theory is based on anything other than 'genetic fantasy' (Giegerich, 1975, p. 125). The second debate (confined more to the Developmental School) presents the problem: when we talk about 'the child' do we refer to an empirically observable situation in childhood or to images derived from our empathy with the child parts of an adult? Let us consider these two issues in turn: first, the value, or lack of it, of a developmental approach.

DEVELOPMENTAL PSYCHOLOGY: TRUE OR FALSE TO PSYCHOLOGY?

Giegerich, who used the term 'genetic fantasy', felt that any backward looking is un-Jungian because, for Jung, the 'whence' is less essential than the 'whither'. Giegerich was actually attacking Neumann's attempt to delineate stages of ego development but he extends this to include 'empirical verification, scientific truth and systematisations' (ibid., p. 125).

Giegerich derives support from Hillman's statement that the child functions as a screen on to which the developmental psychologist 'may freely propound [his] fantasies without contradiction' (Hillman, 1972, p. 243). Or, put another way: 'Freud's fantasy of the little girl's mind becomes a Freudian fantasy *in* the little girl's mind' (ibid., p. 243).

What Giegerich and Hillman are trying to say is that it is *the attempt* to describe and theorise about early childhood that is of interest rather than any verifiable data. The attempt is, of course, an archetypal quest or questioning and the goal is knowledge of origins. The findings of developmental psychology constitute nothing more than contemporary creation myths. Again, Rycroft, coming from a totally different background, points out that developmental theories are *historical explanatory concepts* which attempt to explain the 'clinical present'. It follows that:

> concepts which have been arrived at by backward extrapolation from adults tend to be formulated in terms of the forward development of a theoretical construct, 'the infant' or 'the child' who looms so large in the analytic literature. (Rycroft, 1972, p. xxiii)

This does not demean the efforts of those who analyse or observe children, which we shall discuss. But it remains true that we are dealing with a tendency to talk of events which are 'inferred to have occurred' (ibid.).

Hillman is quite right to suggest that the notion of the completely objective analyst or objective observer of children is absurd. Therefore any remarks we make about the child or childhood are not simply about the child or childhood. He goes on to explain that our culture's view of the child has changed over the centuries and that this can be seen by evolving images of children in painting and sculpture. Further, it is only recently that the idea of childhood as a separate entity 'requiring special attention and facilities' has been developed (1975a, p. 10).

But behind Hillman's assertions to the contrary, there is a model of development in his work which is different from a linear model (stages etc.) on the one hand and, on the other, from the notion of development as a spiral. The spiral idea implied that the same elements in the personality find repeated expression but at different points, and in differing relation to ego and self, along the spiral. *The bias is therefore towards an idea of growth*, and this Hillman wants to do without, preferring his circular model (see p. 114, above). What is meant by circularity is that every element in personality is seen as always present and as always having been so, and that development is construed as development of something into itself, into the nature that was always there.

I would like to be provocative here and suggest that the circular approach, promoted within the Archetypal School by Hillman, could be summed up by the use of the word 'unpacking' which is usually associated with the Developmental School (e.g. Lambert 1981a, p. 193). The contents of the self unpack over time and 'tangle' with the environment. Hillman stated, in his essay 'Senex and puer' (1979b) that the senex, the wise old man, the archetype of meaning, is there at the beginning 'as are all archetypal dominants' (p. 21). Hillman therefore approaches the idea of a primary self (which, as we saw, does not lead us inevitably to stable and organised states). Hillman sees the senex as a *potential*, ready to be incarnated when the right developmental stimulus is provided; this does not have to be in old age as there are age-appropriate forms of the wise old man present in the small child. One can think of the child's curiosity, respect for knowledge and capacity to learn from experience as evidence of this, and even of childlike 'wisdom'.

The similarity between Hillman's model of development and that of the Developmental School has to do with the perception that development is generated, to a great extent, by *something already there in the child*. This may be compared with Jung's emphasis on the prospective, the final viewpoint and the synthetic approach. Strictly speaking, there is no incompatibility between these two points of view (the circular and the prospective). A person's goals will themselves always have been there. But there is a difference of emphasis. Once again, as with the varieties of ego style, and in the democratisation and relativisation of the self and individuation, we can see that the two wings of the post-Jungian world join forces to attack the centre, the Classical School.

I do not mean to contradict Hillman's statements of his overall view which is openly anti-developmental, but rather to point up these similarities. He

141

would, perhaps, claim to rest his ideas on those of Jung, especially when Jung refers to 'the age-old son of the mother' (Jung, 1963, p. 153) and reiterates the theme of the two-million-year-old man who is present in a baby (Jung, 1978, p. 99).

We now turn our attention to a different assessment of the importance of personal development.

THE IMPORTANCE OF DEVELOPMENT

Giegerich and Hillman have expressed their Archetypalist view that developmental psychology is fantasy. As might be expected, the Developmental School cannot agree with that. Fordham has suggested that the whole point of analysis is to break down complex structures into simple forms and systems so as to explore the basic behavioural patterns and mental functioning of the patient. Fordham asserted that it is 'in infantile states of mind [that] the nucleus of later structure is to be found' (1978a, p. 59). Besides this analytic intention, Fordham also suggests that it is therapeutic in its own right to discuss and explore infancy and childhood. There is no reason to rule out an analysis of the personal history in conjunction with the social and cultural context of the person.

Fordham goes on to discuss the question of how 'historical' the process of analysis is to be considered. He aims at as complete as possible a reconstruction of the patient's development. But he also acknowledges that this is, of necessity, incomplete. Reconstructive work has the advantage of giving analyst and patient a perspective, yet Fordham emphasises that in time such reconstructions may be revised or discarded.

For example, a patient may change his opinion of his parents. A patient of mine regarded his father as a 'crap out', a complete failure, but also a bully and a tyrant. When his father died, the patient had the task of communicating this to his uncles, aunts and cousins. He had never met any of these people previously, though he knew that, because of the timing of his grandfather's death, and also a gap of seventeen years between his father, the youngest, and his father's brothers and sisters, his father had been disadvantaged familially and materially. His father had lived a working-class life; the other children had led upper-middle-class, professional lives. It was by having to talk to these others that my patient began to appreciate something of his father's life experience and see his own childhood as less tortured or persecuted and more as part of a wider context of tragedy. Somehow, in this process he forgave his father.

Fordham discussed the question, raised by Jung and mentioned earlier, of whether reductive analysis is destructive to the unconscious:

> reduction of human behaviour to a number of primary entities is not the end of human beings with their unpredictable creative capacity. . . . [That] is an illusion that can just as well be attributed to those who lay excessive emphasis on types . . . or archetypes. (1978a, p. 60)

142

Lambert (1981a, p. 106) made the paradoxical but important point that it is the aim of freeing the patient from excessive entanglement with the past that makes an examination and, where possible, reconstruction of the history desirable. He refers to such clinical phenomena as a tendency to react with a gross and inappropriate emotional response to a current situation. The patient may be functioning with the impatience and nervousness of a baby, perhaps, and with a baby's global style of functioning. Or a patient may present a very one-sided personality, with a fixation at some earlier point which interferes with adult functioning – excessive dependency or jealousy, perhaps.

With regard to the cultural dimension, Lambert has suggested that such aspects as the social system at the time the patient is growing up, the fashion in child-rearing, the religious attitudes of the parents, may have to be taken into account. But Lambert is also emphatic that the analyst-as-historian is different from an ordinary historian because the past with which the analyst deals is still alive.

In his paper 'The significance of the genetic aspect for analytical psychology' (1959), Neumann suggested that analytical psychology should attempt to combine the personal and the transpersonal, the 'temporal genetic' with the timeless and impersonal. Since that paper was written a considerable amount of attention has been given to just that question. Neumann's own contribution was expressed in his term 'the personal evocation of the archetype'. Taking the child's dependence on the mother as an example, Neumann pointed out that such dependence is *both* on the mother *and* on the archetypal image of mother. The transpersonal, timeless archetype cannot be activated save by a personal encounter with a human being. Yet, because the evocation of the archetype takes place on the personal level, there is the possibility of disturbance and pathology.

Neumann hoped he had found a position midway between a developmental orientation and an archetypal one. In this hope he has something in common with the Developmental School with which, as a Classical analytical psychologist, he is so often in conflict, largely because his concept of development is dissimilar. Neumann's conclusion:

> Neither ferreting out personal data during the anamesis nor amplifying only the archetypal material leaving childhood unconsidered could be appropriate. (ibid., p. 129)

Redfearn, writing on the subject 'Can we change?' (1974), made the point that, for most people, even quite substantial changes do not interfere with a feeling of 'dynamic continuity'. That is, events and experiences which seem to have altered one's life do not change the essential person. As far as our discussion of development is concerned, this suggests a medial position. Dynamic continuity implies that material can be looked at reductively or synthetically or in the here and now – or in combinations of these perspectives depending on which viewpoint seems more useful with the material in hand or at the time.

As an illustration of such pragmatism, Redfearn offered a personal memory from his late adolescence when he always seemed to be searching for something such as a visual image, like a jewel, or the perfect girl, or an ideology or ideal. He wrote:

> We might look at these objects of quest as different versions or derivations of an idealised breast or mother or some other lost psychological state. There is no harm in using these terms as long as one is not thereby discouraged in the quest. For it is only through the search for these goals that life and change can go on. (ibid., p. 1)

EMPATHY AND OBSERVATION

I suggested that there has been a second debate amongst the post-Jungians, this time within the Developmental School. That concerns the relative merits of a model of infancy derived from empirical observation of real mothers and babies (such as that proposed by Fordham in 1980), and a model involving empathic extrapolations from material obtained in adult and child analysis. The proponents of the former view feel that they avoid adultomorphic fantasy in which later psychological states, occurring in regressed or ill adults, are confused with what may be observed as normal in infancy. Those who have favoured empathic extrapolation feel that they are better equipped to penetrate the internal life of a baby by finding out about the feeling experiences of the *baby in the adult*. Many who have formulated hypotheses concerning what happens in early infancy agree that at an early stage the infant operates, and, crucially, is related to by his mother, as if he is in a state of psychological identity, or metaphorically speaking, *oneness* with his mother – e.g. Freud's 'primary narcissism', Mahler's 'normal autism', Winnicott's 'illusion of omnipotence'. Though there are differences between these ideas, there is a degree of overlap. Similarly, work with adults in analysis throws up fantasies of idealised or horrific oneness with the analyst. What are the connections between these two sets of phenomena? In neither case is it objectively true that there is anything present other than two persons. But, metaphorically *and* emotionally speaking, in both instances an atmosphere of psychological oneness prevails. The question is to what extent such fantasies in an adult are regressive in the sense that they hark back to what was actually experienced and felt in infancy. Or are such adult fantasies merely wishes that infancy had been like that, sentimental or sympathy-seeking, depending on whether the state of oneness is pleasant or unpleasant?

The debate has revolved around the question of whether or not it is helpful to state that mother and baby function in accordance with the baby's subjective perception of their relationship. Or, to put it another way, if a very small infant has no clear perception of boundaries or the objective rupture or separation between his mother and himself, how valid is it to refer to a phase of psychological oneness of limited duration and existing *alongside* the separateness noted by the observer?

From the observational standpoint, there is no such thing as this oneness. Mother and baby start life together as two separate beings and gradually find each other and enter into a relationship. The entire process involves the active participation of both. It is conceded that in the course of this relationship the infant may become identified with his mother, even muddled up, but this is a temporary illusion on the part of the baby and should not be permitted to offset our understanding of the objective separateness of the two (Fordham, 1976, p. 54).

From the empathic standpoint, both infant and regressed adult, in their different phase-appropriate ways, are struggling towards the establishment of boundaries and the integration of awareness of the separateness which is objectively the case. But for the baby the illusion of oneness or of omnipotence is normal and provides the base for satisfactory ego-development. For the adult, such illusions are illusions in the pathological sense but speak to us of *his experience of normal illusion* in his infancy. As these fantasies will also affect his current relationships and emotional state, they are a potent bridge between past and present. As Newton put it:

> The reality of the infant's separateness does not tell us about his subjective experience . . . I would like to distinguish between infant observation and work with the infant in the adult. Jung said that each phase of development becomes an autonomous content of the psyche. In adult patients, images relating to infancy derive from autonomous complexes with a personal and archetypal dimension. . . . The analyst, who is participating in the relationship . . . will be in touch with, and use, his own subjective responses. . . . In infant observation, the observer is a non-participant . . . presumably he aims at objectivity and keeps his subjective responses to a minimum. The differences in these two approaches can enrich each other, or they can lead to misunderstanding. (1981, pp. 73-4)

The notion, mentioned by Newton (quoting Jung), that each phase of early development becomes and continues to be an autonomous content of the psyche in adult life is of enormous significance. At any one moment, earlier phases of development, or rather of experience, have the possibility of becoming operative within a person. This suggests that there is an incredibly complicated mosaic of potential images. These phases-become-autonomous contents influence each other and the ego, hence constituting a system which accounts for distortions and other problems that may affect objective reconstruction. In addition to subjective bias, we have to conceive of later images as influencing earlier ones as ego-integration occurs; the rules of time may not always apply.

We can say that personal experiences of infancy and childhood that have evolved in this way function in the adult as complexes, cores around which adult events cluster, and which dictate the emotions and feelings such events engender. Images of infancy in adult life need to be regarded as symbols, as well as referring to the historical infant. One key issue is the balance between interpersonal and intrapsychic factors. In infancy, archetypal determinants, innate expectations, affect the infant's experience of his interaction with his personal mother. And, in turn, interpersonal activity stimulates intrapsychic imagery. In an adult, images arising from this interpersonal/intrapsychic matrix affect his adult relationships.

The fact that these contents are expressed in the form of images is a useful bridge to the polycentric, imagistic tone of archetypal psychology; once again the two apparently opposite Schools show a similar face. Because of this, we do seem to have the tools to achieve the balance between the personal and the archetypal that Neumann sought in 1959.

For example, a patient of mine who had to go into hospital for a minor operation was sure that her mother's cancer would enter a terminal phase. She fantasised that the mother would time this occurrence deliberately. It later happened that way. The patient had to leave her hospital bed minutes before her operation to rush to her mother's bedside. The image the patient had evolved of her mother during and since childhood involved a particularly negative sense of oneness between the two of them. On this occasion, the image was first the core of her fantasy and then played itself out in reality.

Psychoanalysis presents its version of the debate. Kohut (1977, pp. 267-312) asserted that the essence of psychoanalysis, its uniqueness among the sciences, is that it has acquired its raw material on the basis of introspection and empathy. The 'world is defined by the introspective stance of the observer' and there is a 'unity of observer and observed'. Indeed, Kohut suggested that phenomena may only be regarded as *psychological* if the mode of observation is based on introspection and empathy:

> Empathy is not just a useful way by which we have access to the inner life of man – the idea itself of an inner life of man, and thus of a psychology of complex mental states, is unthinkable without our ability to know via vicarious introspection – my definition of empathy – what the inner life of man is, what we ourselves and what others think and feel. (ibid., p. 306)

The empathic approach to observations is different from the empiricism of the natural sciences. Even when such empiricism is applied by developmental psychologists with an analytic outlook, what is involved is an observer who occupies 'an imaginary point *outside* the experiencing individual' (ibid.). On the other hand, the empathic and introspective mode of observation places the observer 'at an imaginary point *inside* the psychic organisation of the individual with whom he empathically identifies' (Kohut, 1971, p. 219).

Observations leading to empirical data belong to the social sciences: they are not analytic. Kohut says of the formulations of Spitz (1965) and Mahler (1975) that they are not wrong. Rather they are 'experience-distant', because they are not derived from a prolonged empathic immersion into the inner life of the observed. In fact, the degree of externality is so great that Kohut condemns such observational work as being dominated and contaminated by the 'traditional value judgments of Western man' (1980, p. 450).

This last point about Western values is one that resonates with some of Hillman's critique of a developmental stance in relation to the ego (see pp. 75-6 above). Kohut suggests that the stress in Mahler's work on 'separation' and 'individuation' (meaning something different from Jung's use of that word) reflects an already existing scale of values: clinging dependency is 'bad', uncomplaining self-sufficiency is 'good'. This is to be contrasted with a stress in Kohut's work on 'inner feeling states' of which independence is but one (Kohut, 1980, p. 451).

What is implied in Kohut's repeated use of the word-picture *empathy?* Empathy involves putting oneself in the place of, or inside, another person without losing sight of who one is. The other person may help one to empathise as when an analysis is proceeding well and patient and analyst are working together. Or the patient may erect defences to the analyst's empathy. And empathy *can* be used in observations of children (e.g. Winnicott's poetic musing about a baby's inner feelings in an attempt to put these into words – 'Hello object', and so on). The difficulty here is that, for many people, to empathise with a child is problematic because of the need to activate their own child-selves *without* imposing their patterns of experience. It can be seen how different this is from 'objective' observation of infants in which the child-self of the observer is, optimally, under control. Though most infant-observers know such objectivity is unattainable, few would follow Kohut in his encouragement of an apparent confusion between self and other.

Kohut is at pains to distinguish empathy from compassion on the one hand, and, on the other, from intuition. Empathy need not be compassionate, though it is necessary for true compassion. Psychological warfare is based on empathy, and so are the tricks of the skilled salesman. As far as intuition goes, the distinction is more difficult to make. All parents and most analysts have had the experience of an association to the patient's material prior to the patient arriving at just that point (cf. Dieckmann's research into counter-transference, p. 122, above).

The main reason why these phenomena are not based on intuition is that the process by which they take place is *susceptible to rational investigation, whereas intuitive acts and experience are not.* Kohut observed that

> No one, of course, will speak of intuition with regard to our ability to recognise the face of a friend. But how about the single-glance diagnosis of some illness by a seasoned clinician; the seemingly unreasoned choice of an, to others, unpromising direction of scientific investigations that ultimately leads to a great discovery by a gifted researcher; and yes, even the decisive moves of certain great chess players, military strategists, politicians, and diplomats? In all these instances talent and experience combine to allow either the rapid and preconscious gathering of a great number of data and the ability to recognise that they form a meaningful configuration, or the one-step recognition of a complex configuration that has been preconsciously assembled. (1980, pp. 450-1)

Kohut is aware that observation of the external world can proceed in a far more detailed way than observation of the inner world. But, within the limitations of observation of the inner world, not only is empathy important, but it ensures that the highest standards *appropriate to inner world investigation* will be maintained. There is no difference in principle between non-empathic investigation of the external world and empathic investigations of the inner world. It is simply that empathy makes the latter possible in the first place. The reader may note the similarity with Jung's definition of empathy which stressed the 'animation' of the object and the possibility of the active use of empathy (*CW* 6, para. 486).

JUNG'S CONTRIBUTION TO DEVELOPMENTAL PSYCHOLOGY

Following these preliminary discussions, I want to concentrate on Jung's contribution to our understanding of early development. In addition, I draw parallels with theories of development in psychoanalysis. In the subsequent section post-Jungian contributions are discussed. I can delineate eight areas in which Jung's contribution is striking or noteworthy; some of these have been discussed elsewhere and I provide cross-references.

Emphasis on the mother. Jung was among the first to spell out the primary importance of the relationship of infant and mother in terms recognisable today. This has to be compared with Freud's insistence that it was the Oedipal triangle that imposed its aura and vicissitudes on later relationship patterns. Jung wrote in 1927:

> The mother-child relationship is certainly the deepest and most poignant one we know ... it is the absolute experience of our species, an organic truth. ... There is inherent ... [an] extraordinary intensity of relationship which instinctively impels the child to cling to its mother. (*CW* 8, para. 723)

Equally, we have to bear in mind the centrality of the need to separate from the mother (and the limitations of that effort):

> With the passing of the years, the man grows naturally away from the mother ... but he does not outgrow the archetype in the same natural way. (*CW* 8, para. 723)

Jung stressed three aspects of the child's relation to the mother. These are, first, that throughout maturation there will be regression; second, that separation from the mother is a struggle; third, that nutrition is of prime importance.

Regression comes about because of the demands made on the baby to adapt; such demands may be external or internal. Regression is not only to the personal mother, a sort of recharging or respite from life's demands, but also to the unconscious archetypal image of the mother because 'regression ... does not stop short at the mother but goes beyond her to the parental realm of the "Eternal Feminine".' Here we find 'the germ of wholeness' waiting for conscious realisation (*CW* 5, para. 508). This is reminiscent of the psychoanalyst Balint's distinction between benign and malign regression in which the former offers the chance for a 'new beginning' (Balint, 1968).

Jung's second emphasis was on the struggle of the child to separate from the mother. One might ask why separation is conceived of as a struggle. Jung never disputed that the individual wants (is programmed, almost) to separate; but he was aware that other volitions or temptations exist. Remaining merged with mother beyond an age-appropriate point is attractive because, for instance, oedipal conflicts are avoided. A further idea of Jung's sheds light on

148

why the use of the word struggle is justified. He suggested that separation from the parents is also an initiation into a new state. But:

> Even if a change does occur, the old form loses none of its attractions; for whoever sunders himself from the mother longs to get back to the mother. This longing can easily turn into a consuming passion which threatens all that has been won. The mother then appears on the one hand as the supreme goal and on the other as the most frightful danger. (*CW* 5, para. 352)

This is the essence of the hero's predicament that we discussed in Chapter 3. Jung has identified a split in human nature: one part wants to grow outward and onward and the other wants to return to origins for strengthening. One part seeks to assimilate new experiences 'out there', the other searches for a new and regenerative meeting with elemental psychological forces. This split is the essential premise of any concept of Life and Death instincts. Though the Death instinct finds external manifestation in aggression and destructiveness, we have seen that its true object is to reduce the known world to a preconceived state that, from the standpoint of psychology, would be inorganic (cf. p. 120, above). This is why man's unconscious seeking for regression is also dangerous.

The third of Jung's emphases concerning the mother-baby relationship is on the importance of feeding in the early years. Jung, intent on separation from Freud, insisted that this is a non-sexual area. Freud, noted Jung in 1913, observed that feeding was pleasurable and exciting and concluded that sucking had a sexual quality. Jung's riposte was that all such an observation tells us is that both sex and sucking are exciting: '*Obtaining pleasure is by no means identical with sexuality*' (*CW* 4, para. 241). Jung went on to observe that in man, as in most of the rest of nature, there is an exclusive concentration on nutrition and growth for some time. Both intra-uterine and the immediate extra-uterine periods of infancy belong to this stage of the life processes (*CW* 4, para. 237).

Jung followed this important point by making what now seems like a misjudgment. He argued that, if there are both sexual instincts and nutritional instincts, then we should not claim that feeding is sexual lest someone claims the opposite, that sex is based on feeding. We know now that much sexual dysfunction occurs precisely because of unfulfilled feeding impulses or bad experience. In short, sexuality and nutrition do influence each other.

There are several reasons for this mutual influence. There is bodily contact and intimacy in both activities and both involve the penetration of something by another. Both produce excitation and, eventually, discharge of tension. Mix-ups between the oral (nutritional) and the genital (sexual) take many forms. Projections of oral aggression lead to a man's fantasies of teeth-lined vaginas. The incorporating mother or the invasive mother become either the swallowing-up vagina or the woman's fantasy of an intrusive and controlling penis. (Such zonal confusions are not all between orality and genitality. Sex is spoken of as dirty (anal/genital confusion), or it is experienced as a struggle for power, with imagery derived from the anal tensions of infancy.)

Jung seemed to be opening the door upon these formulations but closed it by dismissing his own argument as 'juggling with concepts'. He cannot accept that the two separate instincts of sexuality and nutrition can co-exist in the infant. He concluded that

> The co-existence or separate manifestation of the two instincts is *not* found in the infant, for one of the instinctual systems is not developed at all, or is quite rudimentary. . . . The co-existence of two instinctual systems is a hypothesis that would certainly facilitate matters. (*CW* 4, para. 241)

However, Jung did go so far as to say that there are 'many intimate connections between the nutritive and the sexual functions' (ibid., para. 291). I am convinced that had Jung not been in the grip of as one-sided an attitude (no sex in infancy) as Freud's (nothing but sex in infancy) he would have been able to explore this further.

Regarding the psychopathology of the mother-infant relationship, Jung describes the result of an archetypal expectation not being met. In this instance it is an archetypal expectation held by the infant. If personal experience fails to bring about a humanising of the archetypal image, the individual is forced to try to achieve a direct connection to the archetypal structure which underpins the expectation, to try to live on the basis of the archetypal image. Pathology also results from confirmation by experience of only one pole of the available range of positive/negative possibilities. Thus, if bad experiences predominate in infancy over good, then the 'bad mother' pole of the range of expectations is activated, and there is no counterbalance. The individual may be said to be 'possessed' by the image of the bad mother. Similarly, an idealised image of the mother-infant relationship can lead to only the 'good' end of the spectrum being experienced, and the individual will never come to terms with the disappointments and realities of life.

If we turn to current psychoanalytic theories of the infant-mother relationship, we can see that the nuances expressed in Jung' work are also present, though sometimes couched in different terms. In her book *Narcissus and Oedipus: Children of Psychoanalysis* (1982, p. 28), Hamilton teases out the various strands in psychoanalytic child psychology and charts these views of the child ranging from a *passive and negative* orientation to an *active and positive* orientation. At the extreme passive end we find Freud with his idea of primary narcissism (out of which the reluctant infant has to be 'tempted'), Mahler (symbiosis of mother and infant) and Kohut. In Hamilton's account, all these theorists see the child as having a relatively passive attitude in his early relationships. Moving along the chart we find object relations theory such as that advanced by Klein. Next come ideas of intense relatedness between mother and infant (Balint). Finally there are the more 'active' theories of 'interactional synchrony' (Bower) and Winnicott's stress on mutuality.

Jung straddles Hamilton's chart, though he did not develop any of these ideas as much as did the psychoanalysts she mentions, in his conception of the child both as dominated by its parents' psychology (passive) and as an active individual. One criticism of Hamilton's chart is that she does not distinguish clearly which theorists use an intrapsychic perspective, which an interpersonal perspective, and, if any, which use both.

Early psychological mechanisms. Jung gave descriptions of psychological mechanisms, some of which he applied to infantile states, but all of which anticipate object relations theory.

The first mechanism is splitting, which is usually seen in Kleinian psychoanalysis as an early defence involving control of the object by dividing it into a good and a bad part-object. Similarly, the ego is also divided into good and bad (Segal, 1973, p. 128). The individual may enjoy the good or attack the bad on the basis of the split with less confusion and with less fear of punishment or loss.

Jung talks of splitting in relation to the mother or, to be more precise, the image of the mother. Jung referred to the 'dual mother' (in 1912) and this can be understood in two ways: first as the duality between the human, personal mother and the mother archetype, and, second, as the duality between good and bad versions of either the real or the archetypal mother (*CW* 5, paras 111 and 352). We should probably place 'real' and 'archetypal' in quotes because the real mother has an archetypal ingredient and the archetypal mother requires personal evocation. We can present the dualities schematically:

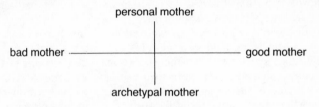

Figure 4

A second mechanism is referred to by Jung as 'primitive identity'. By this he means an *a priori* likeness based on an original non-differentiation of subject and object. Such identity, for instance as experienced by the baby in relation to the mother, is unconscious and a 'characteristic of the mental state of early infancy' (*CW* 6, paras 741-2). In 1921, then, Jung had depicted a stage of development similar to Balint's 'area of creation' (1968) and Mahler's normal autistic phase (1975). In all these, stress is laid on the relative lack of subject-object differentiation. Jung's contribution is noteworthy for its stress on an *already existing* likeness, an innate tendency to identity, rather than a similarity that is *discovered* through experience or achieved through fantasy. He, and most other theoreticians, would regard that as identification (cf. Laplanche and Pontalis, 1980, p. 205).

More important than primitive identity is Jung's use of a special kind of identity for which he uses the term *participation mystique*. This is a phrase he borrowed from Lévy-Bruhl, the anthropologist. In anthropology this refers to a form of relationship with an object (meaning 'thing') in which the subject cannot distinguish himself from the thing. This rests on the cultural notion that the person and the thing – for instance a cult object or holy artefact – are *already* connected and when the state of *participation mystique* is activated this connection comes to life.

Jung used the term from 1912 onward to refer to relations between *people* in which the subject, or a part of him, attains an influence over the other, or vice versa, so that the two become momentarily indistinguishable to the subject's ego. In more modern psychoanalytic language, Jung is describing projective identification in which a part of the personality is projected into the object, and the object is then experienced as if it were the projected content. For example, a baby may project his aggression into the mother's breast. If he does so with sufficient intensity then he will identify the breast with his own aggression, and feel attacked or persecuted by the breast. The content is *projected* on to or into the object which is then *identified* with the content.

Projective identification or *participation mystique* are early defences which also appear in adult psychopathology. They enable the subject to control the object, or at least retain the illusion of control by having defined the external object or 'coloured' it according to the inner world view of the subject. In this way the archetypal inheritance of the infant exerts its influence on the external world so that we can speak of subjective schemas of experience or of archetypal objects (see pp. 43-4, above).

There is also a similarity between *participation mystique* and Kohut's notion of a self-object in which the usual division of self and object is challenged (see p. 124, above). A further link may be made to Bion's idea of 'mating' between what is innate and what is environmental.

Jung made use of the idea of *projection* and *introjection* (*CW* 6, paras 767-68, and 783-4). There is no need to discuss his use of these terms in detail for it is relatively unidiosyncratic. Nevertheless, we may take account of his notion that projection can consist of collective as much as personal contents, his stress on the role of 'active projection' in empathy, and his remarks on the diminishment of the person caused by projection and leading to the eventual need to recollect projections (and cf. von Franz, 1980).

The pre-oedipal libido. We have been discussing Jung as a pioneer of pre-oedipal developmental psychology. He provided a number of ideas concerning libido and how it might be described as functioning prior to the Oedipus complex. What Jung did was to accentuate the emotional counterpart to the specifically instinctual libidinal process. He noted that the affect of a child is as intense as that of an adult, which is, incidentally, another reason for disputing an exclusively sexual definition of libido, the latter emphasising the contrast between infantile and adult libido.

Jung went on to refer, in 1913, to an 'alimentary libido' (*CW* 4, para. 269). Elsewhere, he noted that, if a venerated object is related to the anal region by a child, then this must be seen as a way of expressing respect. Jung has therefore perceived the connection between anality and creativity which many other theorists have developed.

Jung's focus was upon the *transformation* of libido and, in particular, on the movement of psychic energy 'upward' from instinct to the areas of value-making and spirituality. The problem was, and remains, how to keep the links between instinct and spirit without losing a sense of the differences.

Psychoanalysis has also become concerned with the transformation of instinctual libido. But, in addition to spirituality and value-formation, more emphasis is placed on the transformation of libido into *relatedness*. Rycroft suggests that

During the last thirty-five years or so, Freudian analysts of all schools have increasingly tended to regard [the erotogenic zones] as vehicles by which the child's relationships to its parents are mediated. (1972, p. xxiv)

Rycroft on the anal phase:

[this] is now regarded not simply as a period during which small children are preoccupied with their anal functions, but also as one during which they are learning mastery of their body and are being confronted with the problem of rendering their behaviour acceptable to adults. (ibid., p. xxv)

Differentiation. This is a term used a great deal by Jung, and in a number of ways. In his major definition in 1921 (*CW* 6, para. 705), he talked of differentiation as the separation of parts from the whole. For example, concentrating on and being aware of the relatively separate existence of the complexes or the organs of the psyche.

A second use is in connection with individuation. Here a person may be said to have differentiated himself from others. Or, put another way, to have differentiated *himself*, a differentiation of the whole person beyond one-sidedness or unnecessary division.

The notion of differentiation can be used in connection with infancy and childhood not least because it permits talk of its corollaries: undifferentiation and predifferentiation. These are psychological states (undifferentiated) where adequate boundaries have not been maintained. Predifferentiation suggests a normal aspect of early development; undifferentiation is more of a psychopathological category.

A psychosomatic schema. In 1913 Jung advanced a model of psychosomatic growth which connects physiological maturation and psychological symbolism in a remarkable way (*CW* 4, paras 290-1). He suggested that, throughout childhood, the libido is slowly moving towards a sexual form. Jung saw as the central feature of this process the way in which sucking ceases to be a function of nutrition and becomes a rhythmic activity aiming at pleasure and satisfaction. Such rhythm becomes the basis or template for manual stimulation of the various parts of the body. Eventually, the 'rubbing, boring, picking, pulling' hand reaches the genitals and masturbation ensues. The key element for us in this description is the way in which the later manual rhythm is said to derive from, which means *symbolise*, the earlier sucking rhythm. We are justified in using the term symbolic because masturbation in childhood points ahead to full genital sexuality and is therefore a prospective activity and not only a substitute for the experience of sucking in the past.

A model such as this also permits us to postulate regression as well as progression along a spectrum: nutritional sucking – hedonistic sucking – manual exploration of body – manual genital stimulation – genitality. We may also see the phase of exploration of the body as connected to the formation of a skin boundary.

For the sake of completeness, I want to note some other features of Jung's contribution to the psychology of early development which have been discussed fully elsewhere; his theory of *ego formation* arising from islets of consciousness (see p. 68, above) and his approach to *symbols* (see pp. 94ff, above). We can connect Jung's approach to Winnicott's (1971) use of the idea of transitional objects. As we saw, the paradoxical formulation that such objects are the 'first not-me possession' fits exactly the function that Jung marks out for a symbol: that it should link apparent irreconcilables in a unique way.

Jung's divided view of child psychology has also been discussed in this chapter. The view of the child as an individual underpins child analysis. The child can be strengthened to survive a difficult home environment, even hostility to the treatment, precisely because he is an individual with his own strengths. On the other hand, the view of the child as a repository of parental psychopathology underpins family therapy; prominent practitioners in that field acknowledge the debt to Jung (see pp. 165-6, below).

To recapitulate: we have looked at areas where Jung's contribution to theories of early personality development is distinctive. They were:
– emphasis on the mother
– description of early psychological mechanisms
– theory of the pre-oedipal libido
– differentiation
– a psychosomatic schema
– theory of ego formation
– symbols

Because of the solidity of this, I do not think we can go along with Glover when he refers to Jung's 'drawing-room version of psychic development' (1950, p. 50) or asserts that Jung has rejected any theory of individual mental development (ibid., p. 41).

Now I want to show how the post-Jungians have proceeded from all this, what they have rejected or adapted in this model, and what they have adopted from elsewhere.

POST-JUNGIAN VIEWS OF EARLY DEVELOPMENT

Readers will have noted that there is opposition between the theories of Fordham and Neumann. For instance, we saw in Chapter 3 how different were their views about ego-consciousness. In Chapter 4 it became clear that both thinkers have a different conception of the self. To a degree their theoretical opposition stems from the paradoxical fact that both men elected to make good the deficiencies that they perceived in analytical psychology stemming from Jung's reluctance to codify his ideas about early development. Nevertheless, *mutatis mutandis*, Fordham and Neumann stand in conflict as representatives of the Developmental and Classical Schools respectively.

As the intellectual basis of the differences between these two writers is their dissimilar approach to infancy and childhood, I would like to present their ideas in a parallel, comparative form. Although I have depended upon my own understanding of the work of both men, my specific sources are Neumann's *The Child* (1973, published posthumously in German in 1963 and, Mrs Neumann informs me, written 1959-60), Fordham's 'The emergence of child analysis' (1980a) and Lambert's clear understanding of Fordham's views in his book *Analysis, Repair and Individuation* (1981a). I must emphasise that both Fordham and Neumann have written far more widely than this concentration on early development might indicate.

I have selected four headings to facilitate the comparison: (1) the earliest states, (2) the mother-infant relationship, (3) the maturational processes, and (4) psychopathology.

Fordham	Neumann

(1) THE EARLIEST STATES

F.'s views on early development stress their derivation from objective observation of mothers and infants; he seems, therefore, to occupy the empirical end of the empiricism-empathy dichotomy. But F.'s views contain a substantial subjective element in that they also derive from analytical material from work with adults and children.

F. postulates a primary self, existing in a sense before birth, and containing all psycho-physiological potentials. These take the form of archetypal expectations of the environment and predispositions – ways of perceiving, acting on and reacting to the environment. The primary self also contains the potential for ego-consciousness but in a fragmented form. Most important, the primary self carries what might be categorised as innate, individuating propensities. This would include a tendency towards growth, a teleological factor, a homeostatic facility and various self-protective functions. The tendency towards growth is encapsulated in the capacity of the primary self to deintegrate and then reintegrate in a rhythmic manner (see below in the section on maturational processes). Deintegration involves more than a growing relation

N.'s conception of early development is derived primarily from subjective sources, namely an empathic extrapolation from adult material and he states specifically that he is trying to view early development from the inside, as the baby experiences it. At the same time, as with F., we find that this is not the whole picture. N. also claims to use an objective viewpoint, deriving from the use of mythological material, not related to any one person, as metaphors for psychological phenomena.

N. refers to a second, psychological, birth of the infant which takes place towards the end of the first year. (He also refers to a third birth when the child enters the prevailing culture.) He calls the early stages extra-uterine embryonic phases, implying that the infant is not fully formed as a person and the self may best be conceived of as embedded in a maternal, acquaceous setting. N. holds that the various stages of development are archetypally conditioned and there is, in general, relatively little stress on the environment as a receptor of archetypal elements. The initial stage of development is further characterised as non-ego or pre-ego and N. uses the image of the uroboros to express the characteristics of this stage. It will

Fordham	Neumann
with the environment; we must remember that differentiated parts of the self enjoy their own set of intra-psychic relationships.	be remembered that the uroboros served as an image of infantile omnipotence, denial of having a mother and lack of a sense of boundary. As the earliest state, the uroboros excites a special form of regression, akin to a longing for unconsciousness on the one hand and, on the other, to a desire for merging with a creative mother. Although the ego is not at all active in the uroboros, it exists in a passive form, as not yet awakened ego nuclei.

The infant is conceived of as separate from his mother from the moment of conception and he remains a separate person. His job is to establish relationship with his mother and this remains true even when the earliest relationship is of a fused or *participation mystique* character. The infant has well-developed perceptual capacities (cf. pp. 73-4, above) and he is conceived of by F. as an active infant in his ability to attract his mother's sensibilities and attach her to him.

He is born able to adapt; adaptation should not be taken to mean acquiescence but involves the ability to influence and master the external world so that, eventually, infant and mother know each other as a whole. In spite of the fact that full object relations are not in operation, the scene is absolutely human; even part-object functioning is personal.

As we saw in the preceding chapter, N. sees the mother as 'carrier' of the child's self or, sometimes, 'as' the self of the child.

(2) THE MOTHER-INFANT RELATIONSHIP

F. stresses that the mother is not omnipotent but rather one half of a relationship. The outcome of early development will be satisfactory with nothing more than ordinary good mothering and it is important not to idealise the role of the mother. The mother facilitates growth, especially by her capacity to contain her baby. This may be seen as an extension of *in utero* containment and as expressed in the physical act of holding. However, more is implied.

N. refers to this as the 'primal relationship', characterised by the infant's total dependence on the mother. The infant's instinct of self-preservation will try to keep this bond in existence. The mother's body is the world in which the infant lives and, in the earliest stages, the child has little more than a 'body-self' which, in any case, is captive in the primal embryonic relationship. This is further described as a 'dual union' in which mother and baby,

Fordham	Neumann
Containment is also expressed in the mother's looks, her talk and her general presence. In addition, her preoccupation with her baby provides a form of mental containment (he is *in* her thoughts) and makes sense of the world for the baby. The mother lets herself be affected by her baby and uses her empathic capacities in relation to him. She takes the baby's emotions into herself, understands them and then hands them back, transformed and intelligible. The mother and baby are in a systemic relationship and each affects the other. But this is by no means a symbiotic relationship.	objectively separate, are functioning psychologically as one. The mother is seen as the 'good Great Mother', she contains, nourishes, protects and warms her child. N., rather alarmingly at first glance, refers to her as non-personal, anonymous, transpersonal, archetypal. On examination, he is merely referring to her instinctiveness *qua* mother.
	Nevertheless, N. rules out the possibility of the mother's being seen as a human *person* by the baby; this does not occur for quite a while in N.'s view and it is only towards the end of the first year that the various maternal functions are humanised and experienced in the person of the mother. An I-Thou relationship can then come into being between mother and baby *but* even then 'the primal relationship is still the entire field of the child's life . . . even then the mother remains all powerful' (1973, p. 25).
	N. sees the *participation mystique* of mother and infant as existing from birth and not as something to be achieved. He also notes that control and regulation of child development are at first exerted exclusively by the mother (contrast F.). At the same time, N. also seems to recognise the triggering effect an infant has on his mother; he quotes research work on such topics as the shape of the baby's head stimulating a maternal response.

(3) THE MATURATIONAL PROCESSES

Fordham	Neumann
F. sees a process of continual development. This is based on deintegration-reintegration movements as the various archetypal	N.'s conception is quite different from F.'s. Following the uroboric phase, he suggests that the child experiences a matriarchal and then a

Fordham	Neumann

elements in the primary self 'mate' with the environment.

When, for instance, the archetypal expectation of a predisposition to relate to the breast reintegrates from the primary self, it will, hopefully, meet an actual breast or teat. After this matching has reliably taken place over a sufficient period of time, the self will be able to reintegrate something rather different from the original deintegrate. The infant now has the basis for a true internal object.

The earliest relationships are purely part-object and the whole rhythmic process may be likened to breathing. As time passes and development proceeds, more and more objects will be internalised. There will always be archetypal potentials that are not realised as well as archetypal images that affect behaviour but have not, or not yet, found a satisfying environmental correspondence.

The infant does not, of course, *know* that he is deintegrating but he will be aware of experiencing something, usually in connection with a bodily zone and accompanied by excitation. On the other hand, reintegration involves sleep or sleepy states of quietude. Reintegration is a time when the infant needs to feel separate as he assimilates and digests the exciting deintegrative process. He will react negatively to invasions of his privacy.

As far as the impact of the father is concerned, F. suggests that the key element is the switch from two-person to three-person functioning. It is triangulation which is the novel

patriarchal stage of development.

The fundamentals of the matriarchal stage embrace 'shelteredness in the continuity of existence' (1973, p. 39). There is a gradual development of a two-person relationship which serves as the basis for all subsequent relationships. The uroboros masked the twoness of mother and baby; in the matriarchal phase this becomes paramount and includes the capacity to integrate negative experiences. This leads to formation of an integral ego which has some defensive capacities; in particular negative feelings are abreacted or discharged. But this integral ego does not exist prior to the start of the second year.

N. uses Jung's idea of 'animus' (see Chapter 7, below) to explain the presence of the father. He is at first found in the phallic aspect of the mother, which means that he is still subordinate to the Great Mother. Gradually the figure of the father emerges, often as an ideal (cf. Kohut's idealised self-object) and guardian of spiritual values within the family. N. suggests that weaning, taken as other than a literal event, represents the transition between these two quite different stages. If the child's inner schedule of development is followed, weaning will not be traumatic, particularly if the mother makes up for the reduction in other bodily contact by kissing and caressing the child.

N.'s view is that the father and mother images are immediately in tension. He makes a distinction between 'masculine' attributes (consciousness, activity, motion,

Fordham	Neumann
element and not some radically dissimilar style of consciousness.	aggression, destruction, penetration) and those of the 'feminine' (unconsciousness, protecting, sheltering, swallowing up) but leaves the way open for these attributes to be mixed in the actual parental figures.

(4) PSYCHOPATHOLOGY

F.'s accent is on to what extent the infant can tolerate the inevitable clash between archetypal expectation and the real, external world. A degree of friction is necessary and stimulates increased consciousness. But if there is such a feeling of rage and disappointment at the less than perfect situation that the infant cannot bear it, he will feel fragmented and unable to deal with either his internal impulses or with external demands. Psychopathologically, there are two possibilities: the individual grows up with a weak ego or the individual will overorganise his feelings and armour himself against the world with omnipotence, with superior presumptions of how the world should be, and by narcissistic defences (cf. defences of the self, p. 121, above).

N. makes a similar point to F.'s with his conception of a 'distress-ego'. This occurs when the protective atmosphere of the uroboros and the matriarchal stage is prematurely broken and the infant's ego is awakened too soon, 'driven to independence by the situation of anxiety, hunger and distress' (1973, p. 77). This is the origin of narcissism, seen by N. as involving an incapacity to tolerate negative experiences. The distress-ego remains permanently dependent and will call out stridently for the satisfaction of its demands which tend to be seen by the subject as greater than they really are.

A second consequence of a failure in the primal relationship, a failure leading to activation of the distress-ego, is a heightened tendency to aggression and a concomitant sense of guilt. This aggression is quite different from healthy ego assertion. N. has hereby linked a weak ego with narcissism, with over-demandingness and with aggression. They flow from a disruption of the primary mother-infant relationship.

COMMON GROUND

The most obvious area of common ground would be the question of 'responsibility to Jung.' We saw how Fordham has aligned his concept of the primary self with Jung's ideas (p. 112, above). Neumann's debt to Jung is equally obvious. I would select one feature in particular. The twin aspect of the uroboros as a form of personal, psychological death and, conversely, signifying spiritual regeneration, is in line with Jung's thesis that regression to the mother is horrifying and attractive at the same time.

The men also share a determination not to idealise motherhood (though Fordham accuses Neumann of idealising childhood). Neumann states that the mother is replaceable by a substitute in certain circumstances (1973, p. 21), and his whole accent on the automatic nature of the processes of development stresses how much of what the child sees in the mother stems from the child's current psychological needs.

Fordham, in his criticism of Neumann, provides a summary of Neumann's ideas in psychodynamic language (1981). He does this (he says) to see whether there is something of value in them. Fordham's summary:

> there are passive, mainly perceptive but possibly reflective and active, mainly motor, stages of the ego to begin with; next phantasies develop in which subject and object are not well defined and magic-like affects follow; that state may lead to manic (warlike) attempts to triumph over adversaries . . . later the ego develops, and activity that is relatively free from conflict. (p. 117)

The question that interests me is whether such a summary destroys the essence of Neumann's theory. One can see quite clearly that the differences between scientific and metaphorical language do not aid mutual comprehension. The picture is complicated by Fordham's insistence that he is *also* interested in empathy and Neumann's claim that he is *also* empirically objective. It is possible to say that each theory is half of a whole. Viewed together, Fordham's and Neumann's models enable us to speak of a 'Jungian' approach to early development with important differences of opinion expressing themselves in the Schools.

If the Jungian approach is compared to contemporary psychoanalysis, Fordham's theory stresses the activity of the baby and hence gives impetus to ideas of 'interactional synchrony' and puts them *within a metapsychology* (the primary self and its deintegrates); this has not yet been done in psychoanalysis.

Neumann, on the other hand, may claim to be one of the pioneers in the formation of ideas about mirroring in infancy. His proposition (1959) that the mother carries the baby's self, meaning a sense of the baby's wholeness and acceptability which is then passed back to the baby, may be compared to several psychoanalytic formulas. I am thinking of Winnicott's description of the mother's face as the baby's first 'mirror' of himself (1967), Kohut's picture of the mother as a 'joyful mirror' of the baby (1977) and Lacan's *stade du miroir* (1949) in which, it is asserted, 'self-recognition in the mirror takes place somewhere between the ages of six and eight months' (Lemaire, 1977, p. 79). Such psychoanalytic views have been summarised by Dare and Holder (1981):

> the mother can be understood as . . . reflecting the first qualities of the infant's

self onto the infant . . . we would speculate that the first disjointed experience of what is later to become the 'self' are essentially affective, deriving from bodily sensations and interactions with the mother. (p. 327)

I am not forgetting, when making this claim on Neumann's behalf, that the self of analytical psychology and that of psychoanalysis exhibit differences. But in Chapter 4 we observed that even in its most 'elevated' form, the self rests on what has happened in early development. It is fitting to conclude this comparison of Fordham and Neumann with these suggestions about their achievements.

ANALYTICAL PSYCHOLOGICAL AND OBJECT RELATIONS

The Developmental School has encountered both the Kleinian School of psychoanalysis, also based in London, and several British object relations theorists, themselves influenced by Klein, but not members of her group. I do not propose to do more than show how such a rapprochement and influencing could have come about. This is because it must be a mystery to many Classical Jungians how such events ever came to pass and, consequently, the movement has been viewed as a departure rather than a development (see Adler's attitude to the 'neo-Jungians', p. 21, above).

Briefly, Freud's conception of hypothetical energic forces, arising from the stimulation of the nervous system via the erogenous zones, was felt by some psychoanalysts to be inadequate. Instead, development was conceived of increasingly as revolving around experiences and relationships with 'objects', meaning parts of persons, persons or symbols of either. This brings psychoanalysis closer to life as it is lived and also permits changes in technique to match the theory.

In a penetrating paper entitled 'British object relations theorists' (1980), the psychoanalyst Sutherland touched on Klein's work and examined that of Balint, Winnicott, Fairbairn and Guntrip in some detail. He saw Klein as an inspired theoretician who did not sufficiently systematise her work; in addition the role of the external object (the real mother) is drastically under-emphasised. Sutherland tells us that Balint and Winnicott 'refused to become psychoanalytic heretics by attempting to formulate . . . [a] revised structural theory'; this means that they leave us metaphorical description instead of an explanatory theory (ibid., p. 833).

Fairbairn and his associate Guntrip do try to develop a new meta-psychology. For instance, in place of zonal development (oral, anal, genital) Fairbairn wrote in terms of the changing quality of dependence and of early relationships, and gradually abandoned libido theory based on erotogenic zones. As the other theorists mentioned have also done this, though less specifically than Fairbairn, we can see how common ground was easily forged with Jungians.

Although Fairbairn originally referred to a unitary ego at the start of life he soon followed Guntrip in referring to this as a 'self' which 'seeks relationships as its primary need' (Sutherland, 1980, p. 847). A distinction between

Fairbairn's self and that of analytical psychology (whether Jung, Neumann or Fordham) is that, for Fairbairn, the self is essentially a 'reactive matrix' rather than an initiatory agency.

Does the idea of the self as a source of archetypal potential add anything to psychoanalytic theories of the development of object relations? We have seen that Sutherland feels Klein failed to embrace simultaneously the world of internal unconscious fantasy and the world of the real mother and infant, over-emphasising the inner world. Now we have noted that the other object relations theorists fill 'their' self with material derived from the infant's reaction to *external* objects. There is, therefore, a middle position which is open and attractive to developmental analytical psychology.

Sutherland felt that the task of understanding 'what it is for a person to be an agent' (ibid., p. 854) is difficult. He adds that we are not helped in this by Fairbairn's insistence that the inner world is created to make good the deficiencies of the outer one (ibid., p. 854).

Sutherland goes on to say that 'to imagine an organising principle at work does not necessarily take us into innate forms' (ibid., p. 855). I would reply: 'what does it matter if it did?' If we speak of innate structures in the psyche, we are not deprived of speaking at the same time of the personalisation through experience of those structures, or of the need for personal input from mother and baby to realise, or evoke, such structures.

Sutherland concluded that we may consider the self as:

> a supraordinate structure of great flexibility and perhaps in the nature of a 'field force'. Its primary function is to contain and organise motives from all the subsystems that have differentiated from it. (ibid., p. 857)

I do not see much quarrel with that from the viewpoint of analytical psychology, nor with Sutherland's verdict that

> The value of the self conceptualised as the overall dynamic structural matrix is that . . . we can allow for the self to be dominated at different times and in different situations by any of its subsystems, such as the superego. (ibid.)

This is a remarkably similar point to that made, and noted in Chapter 4, by Fordham, Hillman and Plaut concerning the way in which a part of the self (part-self, image, luminosity, constant object) may function, quite healthily, with the self's full capacity to create purpose and meaning.

There now follows a series of sections on specific aspects of the development of personality: the father, the family, incest, and the psychology of the whole of life.

A NOTE ON THE FATHER

Contemporary developmental analytical psychology has been as neglectful of the role of the father in early development as psychoanalysis (cf. Burlingham's remarks on the lack of literature concerning the father and the pre-oedipal child, 1973). In spite of Freud's interest in the father as a threatening and prohibitive figure, post-Freudian study has focused more and more on the mother. Although Jung did write one paper on 'The significance of the father in the destiny of the individual' (*CW* 4), this is an early (1909) psychoanalytic paper with later additions stressing the father *archetype*. We therefore have to look more widely at Jung's work to tease out the following ideas about the father:

- father as the opposite of mother, incarnating different values and attributes.
- father as an 'informing spirit' (*CW* 5, para. 70), as a representative of the spiritual principle and as the personal counterpart of God-the-Father.
- father as a model persona for his son.
- father as that from which the son must differentiate himself.
- father as the first lover and animus image for his daughter.
- father as he appears in transference in analysis.

I shall be discussing gender and sex in Chapter 7 and the question of whether there *are* 'masculine' and 'feminine' attributes belongs there.

Von der Heydt (1973) comments that, in psychology as a whole, the personal mother has been over-emphasised to the point where all subsequent psychological trouble is laid at her door. (And, therefore, the image of woman as an erotic being, or as existing in her own right and separately from man, has been under-employed). She links the elimination of the father from psychology to social and cultural developments. No longer is the father the unchallenged head of the family, no longer is he the sole breadwinner as the Welfare State and the working wife share this burden. And, I would add, no longer are traditional stereotyped male characteristics so highly valued, largely because of the Women's Movement. Von der Heydt concludes that, even in religion, the fatherly God is no longer such a central figure. These phenomena form the background to our modern world with its moral anarchy and relativistic ethics.

Seligman (1982) gives a psychological name to this general picture: 'the missing father'. She means a father *experienced* as unavailable by both mother and child. She asks whether the father is excluded, or whether he excludes himself. The father may be excluded by a woman in the grip of an androgynous fantasy who wants to deny the role of a male 'other' in the production of the child (cf. Samuels, 1976) or, as Seligman suggests, mother and child may work together to prolong their intimacy and postpone the vicissitudes of the oedipal triangle, hence excluding the father.

Where the father excludes himself, this derives from his own background and temperament. This justifies referring to a lack of 'paternal empathy' in the home. Seligman makes the further point (1982, p. 19) that a missing father is likely also to be an absent husband; she sees such a marriage as 'dilapidated' and requiring the children to play out surrogate father behaviour in relation to the mother.

The psychological aspects of the cultural changes mentioned by Von der Heydt were examined further by Dieckmann and he focused on the question of authority (1977). Dieckmann distinguished three levels of authority: based on violence and power, reputation and prestige, and on knowledge and wisdom. In family life, the father uses all of these to bring about instinctual inhibition in the child. In Dieckmann's words, 'the father mediates between the child's primitive natural being and his social surroundings and his highly differentiated inheritance' (ibid., p. 234). Dieckmann looked at a substantial number of initial dreams (i.e. the first dream told to the analyst) brought to him by patients during the first ten years of his own practice when, it might be assumed, he presented himself as less of an 'authority'. Images of authority in these dreams were overwhelmingly of negative or destructive authority.

Dieckmann is concerned for our civilisation because the sado-masochistic authority image is a 'part of the inner psychic system not only of the members of the ruling class, but also of those people who rebel against repression' (ibid., p. 240). Dieckmann acknowledges that analysis can only affect individuals but argues that the search for a source of authority less contaminated by violence and power is vital.

Blomeyer also expresses a cultural concern (1982, pp. 54ff.). How can one challenge authority or the father without suffering the fate of Oedipus – sleeping with one's mother? Blomeyer has no answer save that of an increase in consciousness which will enable an individual to become aware of the connection between revolt and regression. For instance, the link between anti-authoritarianism and drug taking; drugs induce passive and regressive states (in bed with mother). Blomeyer informs us that in 1919 the psychoanalyst Federn was already speaking of the 'fatherless society', with reference to the contemporary political scene following the First World War. Lyons has suggested that current interest in the father and the missing father may reflect cultural and social consequences of the two great wars with many countries under military discipline, and with many fathers actually, and in some cases permanently, missing (personal communication, 1983).

Kay (1981) focused, in contrast, on fathers who, for reasons of their personal psychopathology, insist on providing their offspring with the first mothering experience. If a man

> has serious doubts and confusion about his sexual identity and potency, the arrival of an infant, particularly a first-born beautiful male child can have a very powerful and crucial effect. (p. 215)

Kay gives an example in which a father idealised his son, seeing him as a 'divine child hero' and as a 'healing for his own wounds'. The child was compelled to fulfil the father's needs and was not permitted to differentiate. That child became Kay's patient; however, by a coincidence, the father in question had also had analysis and Kay's reconstruction of the father's personality could be confirmed by the father's analyst!

Carvalho (1982) enumerated the ways in which the father facilitates the psychological development of the infant. The father is the first representative of masculinity and the first significant other apart from the mother. He therefore promotes social functioning. In addition, he is vital for the formation of generational and gender identity. If the father is emotionally absent, the onus of differentiation falls on the child. This may then be fantasised as destructive because there is no chance of reconciliation or reparation. The fantasy would be one of oedipal victory for a boy and of oedipal rejection for a girl. One further point is that, if in normal development the father symbolises the 'capacity for agency and for manipulating the environment' (ibid., p. 344), then his absence will impair a sense of the possibility of such achievement in the child.

My own contribution (Samuels, 1982) stressed the infant's ability to discern mother and father as separate entities so that, subsequently, he can see them as united in a primal scene. I was concerned with the way mother-infant imagery invaded primal scene imagery past an age-appropriate point. That is, it is inevitable that there will initially be some projection of the infant's own frustrations and gratifications into his image of his parents' marriage. If this persists, then future relationships will be at risk. Gradually there needs to be a recognition by the infant that the two relationships of mother-infant, on the one hand, and mother-father (husband-wife), on the other, are distinct.

Finally, special attention is being paid to the influence of the father on the psychology of his daughter. Shorter points out that, as far as her initiation into adult womanhood is concerned, for the daughter

> her own father figure will be *decisive*, the one whose conscious participation, like that of Zeus [in relation to Persephone], fulfils or denies incest resonsibility with consequent effect on the psychological maturation of his girl-child, however their relationship is ritually contained, represented and interpreted. (1983, p. 8)

If, Shorter adds, her father fails her in this respect, a woman may either strive to *become* an authority, or convert a man into a fatherly authority for herself and serve him. She may flee from her sexuality, or maltreat her body, as in anorexia nervosa. Or she may fail to separate from her father, and live with him (or a substitute) as wife-surrogate, nurse, secretary, or muse.

The reader will note that several of the contributions I have been discussing have been written since 1980. We may speculate that a new phase in analytical psychology's exploration of early development is under way. In Shorter's phrase, a 'clarion call to the father' has been issued.

ANALYTICAL PSYCHOLOGY, FAMILY THERAPY, FAMILY DYNAMICS

Jung's description of the child as influenced by parental psychology and psychopathology (the 'unlived life' of the parents) suggests that he had an outline conception of a view of neurosis as caused by family dynamics. Not only do the parents influence the child but, Jung stated, the birth, development and personality of the child influence the parents (*CW* 4, paras. 91-2). Because of these elements in Jung's thought, he has been seen as a precursor of family therapy based on an examination of the dyanamics of the family. Skynner, a leading family therapist, noted:

> from the beginning [Jung] regarded children's psychological problems as usually expressive of difficulties in the total family system, whereby relief of symptoms in

one individual might lead to the development of symptoms in another. (1976, p. 373)

Skynner also noted Jung's willingness to see an educative or re-educative aspect in therapy and his idea of the patient 'working' between sessions, occasionally on tasks set by the analyst. Both these features figure in family therapy.

There are two elements in Skynner's reading of Jung which are particularly interesting. These are *system* and *symptom*. According to Andolfi, 'every organism is a system, a dynamic ordering of parts and processes that interact reciprocally' (1979, p. 6). We may note this use of the word reciprocal which, coming as it does in a book on the 'interactional approach' to family therapy, leads us back to Jung's ambivalent view: child as individual, child as product or victim of parental psychology. The second element from Skynner's appreciation of Jung that we might look at concerns what is implied by 'symptoms'. Hoffman, also a family therapist, defined the symptom *inter alia* as 'the harbinger of change' (1981, p. 347). She goes into this at length; here we may content ourselves with noting the similarity to Jung's conception of the symptom as symbolic, pointing in two ways – back to causation and on to solution.

Family systems theory and therapy make use, as Jung did, of the concept of homeostasis. But in family therapy this is seen as something which often requires shifting if relief is to occur. The family will repeat its hopeless patterns unless something is done about it.

It took a long time for family therapy to move from under the wing of psychoanalysis and develop a 'circular epistemology' stressing reciprocity, feedback and interaction, in contrast to Freud's cause and effect epistemology (Draper, personal communication, 1982). One can only speculate about what might have happened if the prevailing psychodynamic orthodoxy in the 1950s, when family therapy got under way, had been Jungian.

PERSPECTIVES ON INCEST AND OEDIPUS

Earlier I quoted Roazen's remarks that contemporary psychoanalysis would have much in common with many of the positions which Jung took up in 1913. It is particularly interesting to examine this in connection with the Oedipus complex and with incest.

Jung's ideas about incest are often puzzling and tend to be omitted from summaries of his work. Jung used Layard's ideas (1942) to reformulate Freud's notion of incest in terms of a return to the original predifferentiated state to be found in the body of the mother. We have seen that healthy development requires both separation from, and regression to, the mother. Thus, although Jung acknowledged the Oedipus complex as an archetypally determined phase of development, he resisted the idea that it was actual coitus that was desired.

Jung's conception of incest (*CW* 5) is that of a symbol, revealing both the need to move on from mother, father and the family circle (the incest taboo) and, *at the same time*, the opposite, the need to regress (the incest impulse). The symbolic regression to the mother is for regeneration or rebirth, perhaps before moving on developmentally (? refuelling, as in Mahler's theory).

The incest taboo prohibits intercourse and therefore the libido that powers incestuous impulses tends to become imperceptibly spiritualised, so that the 'evil' incestuous impulse leads to creative, spiritual life. Blocked in the realm of instinct by the taboo, energy moves to the opposite of instinctuality, spirituality. It is a striking *enantiodromia* or swing to the opposite.

Shorter's work on the importance of her father to the woman, mentioned earlier, is of importance here. This is because it balances Jung's approach which seems on occasion to speak more of male psychology and predicament. She shows that we can speak of incestuous involvement with the father as regenerative for a girl. This would be different from the daughter's involvement with her mother, more erotic, for one thing. Hence incestuous fantasy around the image of father performs a similar spiritualising function for the girl as fantasies of his mother perform for the boy.

Jung suggested that the psychologically regenerating endogamous tendency (the symbolic attempt to marry within the family) must be considered as a genuine instinct and not as a perversion. This implies that symbolic incest should find expression in fantasy as well as that actual incest be prohibited. It would be pathological to repress either the impulse *or* the prohibition. For example, in Oedipal conflict, we may stress the prohibiting father or, conversely, the son's ability to live with his negative feelings and fantasies about the psychological reality of his father's possession of his mother. The son, if he can attain such acceptance, will have available a substantial amount of frustrated energy. This then can be used for spiritual or creative purposes. There is a similarity here with the psychoanalytic idea of sublimation.

Finally, the incest taboo creates in mankind the need for a working alliance between father and son or mother and daughter without which there would be no culture. In Freudian terms, this is the resolution of the Oedipus complex by identification with the parent of the same sex. Although, for example, father and son may be enemies, they are also allies and, anyway, one day the son will become a father, married to a woman from outside the immediate family (exogamy). Kohut put it thus in his last paper before he died:

> the essence of human experience is not to be found in the biologically inevitable conflict between generations but in intergenerational continuity. (Kohut, 1982, p. 406)

To summarise: the impulse toward symbolic incest has to be balanced with the taboo. Incest may be considered as symbolic because it unites the following pairs of opposites: regression/progression, endogamy/exogamy, instinctuality/spirituality, father-son hostility/father-son alliance (or mother-daughter hostility/alliance).

There is another way altogether of viewing oedipal resolution, first put forward by Searles (1959). This involves emphasising the role of the loved parent of the opposite sex in helping the child acquire enough strength to accept the unrealisability of his oedipal strivings. What is needed is that the child recognise that the loved parent returns that love and, above all, does see the child as a potential love partner but communicates that, regrettably it cannot be. The renunciation is therefore a mutual process, rather different from the conventional stress on the child's acceptance of frustration. The child's ego can be impaired by the beloved parent repressing or suppressing his or her oedipal love for the child. Clinically, one often meets patients with injured oedipal feelings. These may be women whose fathers were incompetent at managing and sharing in the mutual renunciation outlined here; men being more worried by their sexual and loving feelings towards their daughters, on the whole, than women towards their sons.

(A full discussion of differences in the experiences of male and female children is to be found in Chapter 7.)

INCEST AND HUMAN LOVE

This is the title of a remarkable book by R. Stein (1974). Stein, following Layard and Jung, stressed that the incest taboo is as natural a phenomenon as the incest impulse and that there is no point in trying to make the one contingent on the other.

Stein's main emphasis was on the incest taboo as promoting truly *human* love and interpersonal relationships because it makes the individual stop and consider whether he is permitted to proceed with his impulse, while, in turn, this forces him to think about the *person* he desires. The taboo also has the effect of sanctifying the parents and stimulating generational identity:

> the taboo creates a psychological distance which is essential for the development of consciousness. An aura of mystery begins to surround the parents, stimulating the child's imagination to focus on the special qualities of mother and father. Why is the child allowed such intimacy with them except for their sexual organs? And why does one parent have a penis and one a vagina? Perhaps they fit together. If so, why are they allowed such intimacy and not he? Is it not dangerous for them and if not why? How is it that mother and father, so different in every way, seem to belong together? ... the taboo stimulates questions and images of the male-female connection ... and it releases the archetype of human love and sex as a sacred union. (pp. 36-7)

The incest taboo is also intimately linked to an awareness of being incomplete. As we see, prohibiting the boy intercourse with mother or sister forces him, by dint of frustration, to focus on them as persons (and the same applies to the girl in relation to father or brother). This has two implications: first, the unattainable one becomes the human prototype of all unattainable mysteries and life goals. And, second, the taboo forces men and women, within their personal limits and the rules of culture, to *choose* who to love, how to love. Sexual restraint leads to 'the idea of sexual union as ... binding two people together' (ibid., p. 37).

Stein offers some insights into the Oedipus story which can be compared with modern psychoanalytic readings of the myth. He points out that the tale

168

begins with *parental rejection* caused by a fear of incest and parricide. Oedipus fails to realise that he has had substitute parents, hence confusing real and archetypal parents. Therefore what should be symbolic becomes actual. Oedipus's slaying of his father cannot lead to any regeneration; similarly, his regressive connection to Jocasta leads to sex and not to rebirth. The emphasis is therefore on his lack of consciousness rather than on an incestuous sexuality which requires taming. The Oedipus problem is the lack of a sense of renewal and rebirth following the death of the old father and the re-entry into the mother. As renewal and rebirth *are* possible, Oedipus is a portrait of a neurotic rather than Everyman.

Stein's suggestions derive from Neumann (1954) as well as from Jung's formulations. We can see a parallel in Bion's psychoanalytic view of the Oedipus tragedy, as presented by Hamilton (1982). Oedipus is a story of an excessive and one-sided commitment to *knowledge*. This is symbolised in questioning the Oracle twice and then being able to comprehend the Sphinx's riddle. But Oedipus' approach to knowledge is an all-or-nothing one 'suffused with possessiveness . . . and greed . . . An attitude of apprehension little by little has no place' (ibid., p. 245). This damages the chances of any sense of renewal. And the knowledge that Oedipus possesses is not 'a transcendental fact, but the precise details of his own origins' (ibid.). He knows nothing of his own need for regeneration.

Regeneration would involve what Hamilton, using Einstein's words, calls a 'holy curiosity', a capacity to live in uncertainty and to search for constructive possibilities rather than facts. She sees no reason why curiosity should be associated with what is forbidden: 'in my view, sexuality is one aspect of exploratory activity rather than its cause' (ibid., p. 264). In this we hear overtones of Jung's 'instinct to individuate' and his prospective view of psyche.

We now leave the infantile world and go to the other extreme; to a consideration of the psychology of the whole of life.

THE PSYCHOLOGY OF THE WHOLE OF LIFE

From a variety of quarters Jung has been hailed as a forerunner of the modern field of whole of life psychology or adult development (Levinson et al., 1978; Maduro and Wheelwright, 1977; Staude, 1981). From an historical perspective this is probably true, though there are considerable methodological differences between Jung and more formal whole of life psychologists. My argument will be that Jung's innovatory model of 'The stages of life' (*CW* 8) is, in several ways, somewhat problematic and that care must be taken in adopting his insights wholesale.

In this paper, written in 1931, Jung laid great emphasis on the various psychological transitions he saw as occurring at mid-life. This is often described as a 'crisis' or traumatic period and is illustrated by case material demonstrating problems in making an adaptation to the demands of the second half of life. There are two difficulties with this. The first can be put as a question: can we talk of psychological 'stages of life' at all? I do not differ solely on the grounds of cultural relativism and social change (though that is important). My concern is more with what we might lose were we to imply a linear process or progression through separate stages.

The second major problem concerns whether the transition is indeed difficult or traumatic. Jung criticised the psychoanalyst Rank at one point for developing his idea of a 'birth trauma' because the use of the word trauma is inappropriate to depict a normal occurrence. Jung's reiteration that there are *problems* involved in making the transition from the first to the second half of life is a peculiar feature in a psychology that is, in general, not based on psychopathology. I have reached the conclusion that, in this area of his thought, Jung generalised too freely from his own personal experience of his near-breakdown following the separation from Freud when he was thirty-eight years old. I would not go so far as to say that the differing emphases are totally incorrect, but the whole first half/second half division is puzzling.

Jung further divided life into four periods: childhood and up to puberty, youth (from puberty to 35-40 years), mid-life, and old age. In an attempt to define the psychological features of each period, Jung is found sometimes to take up extreme positions. For instance, he asserts that one is not conscious of one's problems in childhood and in old age – there, one is simply a problem to others. In the other two stages one is more conscious of one's own problems (*CW* 8, para. 795).

The psychological achievements of youth involve separation from mother, achieving a strong ego, giving up childhood status, acquiring an adult identity, and, finally, the achievement of a sound social position, marriage and a career. These are necessities if the richness of the second half of life is to be enjoyed. In the second half of life the accent switches somewhat from the interpersonal dimension to a conscious relationship with the intrapsychic, with inner depth processes. Investment in the ego will have to be replaced by the deeper guidelines of the self, and dedication to external success altered to include a concern for meaning and spiritual values. Jung's emphasis for the second half of life is the acquiring and living out of such values: 'Could by any chance culture be the meaning and purpose of the second half of life?' (*CW* 8, para. 787).

But this poses a further question. Why does this further transformation of libido not simply happen? Why are we 'unprepared for such a change?' (*CW* 8, para. 785). Jung's answer was that the social goals of the first half of life which I have been enumerating are attained only at the cost of a 'diminution of personality' (*CW* 8, para. 787). But how can what is said by Jung to be *natural* (namely the stress on external achievement in the first half of life) lead to any damaging effects on personality?

We may also wonder whether social achievement is *always* a product of one-sided development. I would suggest that what is crucial is the person's *attitude* to his career, marriage, and so on. And here the most vital factor will be early development. If career success is based on schizoid retaliatory fantasy, or oedipal rivalry, then personality *is* diminished. But it is far too gloomy a view to say that this is true of everyone. Achievement will always have its shadow in the sorts of pathology I have just mentioned, but Jung was, after all, the first to teach that everything substantial casts a shadow.

Jung's conception of the stages of life was hotly disputed by Glover (1950). Glover noted that, as so often as Jung's work, we find the magic number four. He went on to marvel at Jung's definition of 'youth' extending to the age of forty. During that time, Glover observed, 'most individuals have completed the reproductive phase of family life' (ibid., p. 126). Glover also wondered about Jung's assertion that there are characteristic problems or lack of them during the various stages of life and perceived that Jung's theory is undermined by his idealisation of childhood and of old age.

I mentioned earlier that there are indeed clear differences in task and challenge between the two halves of life. One of these, as Jung noted, is that in the second half of life death becomes more of a reality to be accepted or denied. And recognition of those strengths and weaknesses which have been revealed in earlier years is also a process which may reach fruition in old age, leading to self-acceptance. This would include the coming to consciousness of both the inferior function and the animus or anima, a rounding out of personality in the individuation process. We may speak of a natural fullness or flowering and a sense of a life satisfyingly lived.

Jung's stress on crisis and transition is echoed in the work of Erikson (1951) and Levinson (1978). Erikson talked in terms of eight stages of life; these are well known and do not need summarising as such. It is interesting to note Ellenberger's comment (1970) that, while Freud worked on the first five of Erikson's stages, only Jung worked on the last three. These are: 'intimacy verus isolation, generativity versus stagnation, and ego integrity versus despair' (Erikson, 1951).

Levinson's stages are: early adulthood from 20-40 years, middle adulthood from 40-60 years and late adulthood after 60. But the main stress in Levinson's approach is around the transitional periods of 18-22 years, 38-42 years and 58-62 years.

There is, then, a growing field of research involving cognitive, social and dynamic psychology. And here Jung's pioneering contribution is acknowledged. In spite of these various qualifications, we may agree with much of Staude's positive evaluation of Jung's strengths as a whole of life psychologist (1981). Jung introduced the whole of life perspective, has a model which can include inner and outer worlds, was interested in the cultural context, had a religious viewpoint, and also a capacity to incorporate the phylogenetic aspect. Finally, he attempted to see the whole man.

There is one unexpected way in which Jung's first half/second half dichotomy can be of enormous help. This is as an aid to looking at the culture we live in *now* which, in spite of sporadic signs to the contrary, has a cast of a first half of life type, as Jung described it. We value independence and success; it seems we cannot control our destructiveness. And we have but glimpses of the meaning and purpose of life. The qualities of the second half of life represent what our culture desperately needs to grow toward. In particular, I am thinking of Jung's suggestion that the rigid differentiation between masculine and feminine dissolves in the second half of life. Leaving aside the question of whether there is such a thing as innate femininity until Chapter 7, we do have need of those qualities which seem more accessible to

171

women if we are not to destroy ourselves. A whole of life psychology brings both feminine and masculine to our attention; in that sense, Jung's division of life on a chronological basis seems more and more a description of a division in humankind.

6

The analytical process

We now turn our attention to the clinical application of some of the ideas we have been discussing. In no other chapter of the book have I been as aware of possible disparities in my readers' experience and knowledge. To save confusion, I want to state at the outset that I am assuming a general knowledge of what happens in psychotherapy and analysis and of the better known principles of Freudian analysis. When we examine psychoanalytic parallels we can do so in outline only; though, as throughout the book, detail will be introduced when Jung's individual contribution is discussed. Post-Jungian debates can be seen as occurring within the overall psychotherapeutic milieu; very few Jungian analysts have been unaffected by developments in psychoanalysis.

The use of the term 'patient' and 'analyst' conforms with my habitual use. That this is not as straightforward as it might be may be deduced from the presence of a section in the chapter entitled 'What is Jungian analysis?' The word 'patient' offends some who would prefer the more autonomous sounding 'client' or the more process-specific 'analysand'. It may be worth noting that some, like certain existential analysts, may insist that they work with 'persons'.

AN INDIVIDUAL ART

Jung stressed that analysis is an art and not a scientific or technical procedure: 'Practical medicine is and always has been an art, and the same is true of practical analysis' (Jung, 1928, p. 361). This led him to state that each treatment was an individual business and that there must be no programme or list of 'shoulds' (*CW* 16, para 237).

In fact, Jung did offer much advice to analysts, his main emphasis being the need to adapt to the individual patient. It would be *hubris* for the analyst to know in advance what will happen. Analysts observe the phenomenon whereby the patient assumes that the analyst knows all about what is to occur and is disgruntled and angry or feels betrayed when this is not the case. One meets in practice the strange situation, so different from the stereotype, that it is the *analyst* who is open to all sorts of possibilities while the patient, based on his previous experience of illness, expects to be diagnosed and cured. It is

173

easy to be seduced into inflation by such a patient.

Jung, however, moderated his idea that in each case the analyst should abandon all his existing knowledge of theory, writing:

> This does not mean that he should throw [his theories] overboard, but that in any given case he should use them merely as hypotheses for a possible explanation. (*CW* 16, para. 163)

Jung was surely being narrow minded when he claimed that the therapeutic approaches of Freud and Alfred Adler consisted of 'technical rules' and the 'pet emotive ideas' of their respective authors (*CW* 17, para. 203). Yet his insistence that psychological disturbances are not distinct clinical 'entia' but affect the whole man differs from Freud's earlier approach:

> we must not mind doing tedious but conscientious work on obscure individuals, even though the goal to which we strive seems unattainable. But one goal we can attain, and that is to develop and bring to maturity individual personalities . . . I therefore consider it the prime task of psychotherapy today to pursue with singleness of purpose the goal of individual development . . . only in the individual can life fulfil its meaning. (*CW* 16, para. 229)

Jung perceived a few still points in the endlessly shifting world of treating the neurotic; these concern the 'stock-in-trade' of neurosis:

> every neurosis is characterised by dissociation and conflict, contains complexes, and shows traces of regression and *abaissement du niveau mental*. These principles are not, in my experience, reversible. (*CW* 17, para. 204)

But we should be careful with our generalisations. For example, for every neurosis caused by repression, there is one caused by 'the drawing away' of a content, its 'subtraction or abduction . . . its "loss of soul" ' (ibid.). Similarly, Jung's flexible approach to treatment was also shown in his adage that, for some people, it is a matter of becoming more of an individual while, for others, it is a question of adaptation to the collective.

Jung continually asserted that analysis is a 'dialectical process'. By this he meant that (a) there are two people involved, (b) that there is a two-way interaction between them, and (c) that they are to be conceived of as equals (*CW* 16, para. 289). Each of these propositions seems relatively commonplace to the modern psychotherapeutic outlook but was daring in its time (1951 and before).

To assert that two people are involved obviously means more than that there are two bodies in the room; the implication is that the unconscious of each is involved, together with projection, introjection and ego defences of both analyst and patient (*CW* 16, para. 239). It follows that the analyst may have a transference to the patient and project on to him his own unconscious contents. The second proposition of Jung's, that there is a two-way interaction, means that, as Fordham has put it, Jung is describing analysis as an open rather than a closed system. This permits the interaction to become the centre of interest along with whatever consequences may result from the interaction. A closed system, with 'techniques of diagnosis, prognosis and treatment [would] consider the patient as essentially separate from the physician' (Fordham, 1978a, p. 69). Jung's third proposition, that the participants are 'equal', is somewhat more problematic.

When we say that analyst and patient are 'equal', what do we mean? We clearly cannot mean equal in the sense of identical; both individuals will have different psychologies and backgrounds, may be of different sex, and so forth. We cannot say that both perform similar functions in that one has come to the other with an expectation, whatever that may be. Finally, one participant pays the other, keeps appointments at specified times and at a specified place, is one of several in a similar relationship to the other. No, the equality of patient and analyst implies something else that is best defined in relation to its opposite: an image of analysis in which the patient does what he is told, 'takes the pills', and is respectful to one whom he sees as superior.

At times, because it is the patient's own life that is the centre of attention in analysis, it is only the patient who can know how he feels or set the pace and suggest the rhythms of the work:

> The psychotherapist . . . must decide in every single case whether or not he is willing to stand by a human being with counsel and help on what may be a daring misadventure. He must have no fixed ideas about what is right, nor must he pretend to know what is right. . . . If something which seems to me an error shows itself to be more effective than a truth, then I must first follow up the error, for in it lie power and life which I lose if I hold to what seems to me true. (*CW* 11, para. 530)

At other times, because of his insight or because he is not affected by the patient's defences and resistance in the same way as the patient is affected, the analyst may be the one who takes authority for guiding the analytical process. But, as Jung cautioned, 'if the doctor wants to guide another, or even accompany him a step of the way, he must *feel* with that person's psyche' (*CW* 11, para. 519).

Equality has a further meaning in the sense of equal 'in the eyes of God', spiritually and morally equal. The analyst is not necessarily a better person for having trained or worked analytically on himself. It follows that contact with the patient may enhance the life of the analyst. Sometimes one finds analysts who derive both personal insight and healing from work with their patients. Such work serves their own process of individuation. There is a risk of exploiting the dependence of the patient for the analyst's own ends, perhaps in a gratification of the analyst's desire for power (see p. 187, below).

Jung's word *equality* represents difficulties then. A better word, and one which finds a wide current, is 'mutuality'. The possibility of this term's becoming idealised, with a connotation of cosiness or even exclusiveness, is countered by referring to *asymmetrical mutuality*, suggesting the differing roles of patient and analyst. Other asymmetrical but mutual relationships would be those of mother and child and teacher and student.

Such considerations should be borne in mind when we contemplate Jung's statement that psychotherapy is an encounter, a discussion between two psychic wholes, in which knowledge is used only as a tool. The goal is transformation. . . . No efforts on the part of the doctor can compel this experience. (*CW* 11, para. 904)

or that the analyst is a 'fellow participant' in the analysis. (*CW* 16, paras 7-8).

If the purpose of analysis is transformation, and if analysis is conceived of as a mutual, dialectical procedure, we may conclude that the goal of analysis is mutual transformation. What happens in the treatment may change the analyst, illumine his life, face him with problems and opportunities of which he was not cognisant. Jung took this even further to assert that unless the analyst felt a personal impact arising out of the analysis, nothing would come of it. The analyst must be *affected* by what is happening:

> [Analysis] presupposes not only a specific psychological gift but in the very first place a serious concern with the moulding of one's own character. (*CW* 4, para. 450)

Jung often asserted that the analyst can only work with his patient as far as he has moved himself psychologically. Getting stuck in analytic work often indicates a blockage in the analyst's own psyche (*CW* 16, para. 400). Hence the need for a training analysis of the prospective analyst. We can summarise what this implies in practice. The patient's development is intimately linked with that of the analyst and, *ipso facto* the analyst must be emotionally involved in what is happening.

At some point we need to refer specifically to the 'real relationship' that exists between patient and analyst in order to see it alongside the inner or fantasy relation of transference-countertransference. In psychoanalysis this is referred to as the treatment (or working) alliance (Greenson, 1967, and see p. 186, below). Jung developed this particular theme in 1938 in terms of the personalities involved in analysis: 'in reality everything depends on the man and little on the method' (*CW* 13, para. 4). Fordham pointed out that Jung insisted on the human aspect of analysis being underscored in spite of the fact that, in many respects, analysis is not an ordinary human relationship: 'He was keen to keep this distinction going in the midst of the transference' (Fordham, 1978a, p. 67). Fordham went on to suggest that Jung had anticipated the idea of the treatment alliance.

NEUROSIS

Jung never committed himself to a definition of neurosis, referring generally to 'one-sided development'. That is not to say that he refrained from describing neurotics, but he seemed to want to avoid the trap of having just one answer to any problem. Jung describes neurosis as an 'inner cleavage' that arises out of the feeling that within the patient there are two persons at war with each other (*CW* 11, para. 522). At the same time, neurosis must be understood as 'the suffering of a soul that has not discovered its meaning' (*CW*

11, para. 497). And Jung continually emphasised the potentially positive aspect of neurosis, writing in 1934:

> A neurosis is by no means a negative thing, it is also something positive. Only a soulless rationalism reinforced by a narrow materialistic outlook could possibly have overlooked this fact. In reality the neurosis contains the patient's psyche, or at least an essential part of it. (*CW* 10, para. 355)

Jung has left neither *classification* of neurosis nor a statement about the borderline between neurosis and psychosis. Nor does he link presenting symptoms and aetiology. Post-Jungians, particularly, but not exclusively, of the Developmental School, have had to lean heavily on psychoanalytic expertise in classifying neuroses and upon its skill in delineating the syndromes brought about by early childhood experience. (For a discussion of approaches to psychopathology in analytical psychology since Jung, see p. 204, below.) Some would make a virtue of this lack in analytical psychology, using the absence of criteria as an opportunity to explore each neurotic manifestation individually and *de novo*. My own position is that concern for aetiology need not get in the way of an attempt to envision neurosis positively.

THE FOUR STAGES OF ANALYSIS

Jung developed a model, published in 1929, which he intended as a general picture of the stages of analysis (in 'Problems of modern psychotherapy', *CW* 16). The stages overlap each other but their importance is that they sketch in outline what Jung sees as the features of the analytical process, rather than any schedule of progress.

The first stage is *confession* or catharsis which involves the patient relating what he considers relevant in his history and talking about his problem as he sees it. For many people, this is a tremendous relief because something concealed acts like a 'psychic poison' (*CW* 16, para. 124). There may be some lessening of guilt and the patient can check out the analyst's response to him and to his life story. This in itself provides a widening of perspective.

The second stage Jung referred to as *elucidation*. This he equated with Freud's 'interpretive method' and he referred in particular to the working out of the transference relationship, involving reductive explanation. But Jung saw a limit to what can be achieved via elucidation, which alone does not produce deep change.

Such change is brought about in the third stage, that of *education*. This is said by Jung to derive from Alfred Adler's work and involves extension of the understandings gleaned from elucidation into the social and behavioural realm. But even after the stage of elucidation the patient still needs 'drawing out' into other paths.

The fourth stage is that of *transformation*. It is in this stage that Jung's stress on the involvement of the analyst becomes most pertinent. The second and third stages deal, respectively, with normality and with social adaptation. For some people this will not be enough; it will be limiting or even damaging to them. The changes that might occur during the stage of transformation are changes towards a person's becoming himself rather than 'normal' or 'adapted'; it is, therefore, the stage of analysis most concerned with individuation.

Lambert has made a number of points which facilitate our contemporary use of Jung's initial formulation of the stages of analysis. (I would note that Jung was writing in 1929, before the impact of object relations theory on psychoanalytic technique.) There can therefore be little description in Jung's paper of projective or introjective processes in analysis, nor much account of how the patient's material is absorbed by the analyst and made intelligible. There is also the question of the impact of the analyst's own analysis, which Jung does not go into in this paper. Finally Lambert observes that Jung may have erred in making a distinction between what he refers to as normality and the stage of transformation 'so sharply as to suggest that normality equals false conformity' (Lambert, 1981a, p. 33).

REGRESSION IN ANALYSIS

Jung's tolerant and positive attitude to regression was a sharp contrast to Freud's description of regression as a destructive phenomenon linked to fixation (cf. Laplanche and Pontalis, 1980, p. 388). We saw in the last chapter that Jung wrote of regression as a potentially positive and creative psychological activity. We may see overtones of this when we focus upon regression in analysis: 'therapy must support the regression, and continue to do so until the "prenatal" stage is reached' (*CW* 5, para. 508).

This view is grounded in Jung's conviction that regression is to be seen as an 'adaptation to the conditions of the inner world' (*CW* 8, para. 75). It follows that, as analysis is geared to the inner world, it must be able to contain regression on the part of the patient and hence eventually facilitate the release of energy for psychological development.

As far as analytical procedure is concerned, I would suggest that it does not matter whether the regression is conceived of as an infantile state or as adaptive to the inner world because the external signs of such regressions will be the same. For example, infantile needs and the adult's anxiety at encountering the unconscious will inevitably produce a state of dependence on the analyst. And the mechanism of projection will draw in the analyst in whatever symbolic guise (as mother or, alternatively, psychopomp or soul-guide).

These ideas of Jung's seem very modern. Maduro and Wheelwright summarise Jung as advocating 'creative regression within the transference situation' (1977, p. 108) and we will assess this in relation to developments in psychoanalysis in a later section (see pp. 183-5, below).

THE ALCHEMICAL METAPHOR FOR THE TRANSFERENCE

Jung's investigation led to the discovery that in alchemy was the precursor to his own study of the unconscious. The alchemists described many of the problems of modern psychology in their own language and Jung felt that they had intuitively anticipated and imaginatively projected what has been verified in modern times. The lively imagery of alchemy differed markedly from the stylised and sexless expressions of medieval Christianity. Jung drew the parallel with the way psychoanalysis and analytical psychology contrasted with complacent and rational Victorian views of man.

When non-Jungians study Jung for the purpose of understanding his writings on the transference, they are often struck by the fact that the work of his which most overtly alludes to it (written in 1946) draws heavily on alchemical symbolism as found in the text *Rosarium Philosophorum* dated 1550 ('The psychology of the transference', *CW* 16). Here I do not propose to consider the *Rosarium* itself in much detail, though I do suggest that alchemy is relevant to a consideration of the analytical process and wish to consider why this is so. My experience has been that many students, trainees and readers of Jung do not grasp the nature of the metaphor Jung is using.

It is important to note that, in Jung's own description of what he was attempting, he was trying to interpret a 'grand projected image of unconscious thought-processes' (Jung quoted in Jaffé, 1979, p. 97). Bearing this in mind, we may consider some of the more central alchemical terms that have a symbolic relation to analysis.

Vas. This is the alchemical vessel in which the base elements (*prima materia, massa confusa* are mixed and added to, leading to the hoped-for translation into gold and the revelation of the *lapis*. The *lapis*, or philosopher's stone, became for Jung a metaphor for realisation of the self, the outcome of the process of individuation. The *vas* corresponds to the containment of the patient and analyst in the structure of analysis and the translation of his suffering into lasting changes in his personality. In addition, from the patient's point of view, the analyst's understanding, interpretation and holding of the situation create a *vas*.

The coniunctio. This refers to the mating in the *vas* of disparate elements (what we would today call chemical combination). In alchemy, the base elements to be combined are conceived of as opposites, the combination leading the alchemist to the production of gold. These elements are often represented anthropomorphically by male and female. The fact that humans are used to represent chemical elements showed to Jung that, far from being a strictly chemical investigation, alchemy was concerned with creative fantasy and thus with unconscious projections. In analysis the *coniunctio*, the union of opposites, symbolises: (a) The interaction of the analyst and that of his analytical 'opposite', the patient. (b) The differentiation and integration into his ego of conflicted and warring elements in the patient's psyche. (c) The interpenetration and integration of conscious and unconscious parts of the patient's psyche.

The hierosgamos. Literally translated as 'sacred marriage'. Many forms of this motif, signifying the conjunction of opposites, may be found. For instance, in Augustinian Christianity the sacred marriage is between Christ and his Church and is consummated on the marriage-bed of the cross. In alchemy the sacred marriage is often referred to as a 'chemical marriage' in which opposite elements, designated male or female, unite to produce a third, unsullied

179

substance. As such a substance does not seem to exist in the physical world, alchemy became less important as natural science claimed primacy of place and attention in the Renaissance. But the psychological meaning of the *hierosgamos* serves to illustrate the transformation of chaos and confusion to pattern and integration. In analysis, it is hoped that such transformation will take place in relation to neurotic conflicts and splits.

The transmutability of elements. This idea is central to alchemy because it affirms that the transformation can occur. Similarly, without an image of the possibilities in psychological movement, there would be little point in analysis. This remains true even when the goal of analysis is said to be the deepening of experience or the widening of awareness rather than the changing of attitude and behaviour. Deepening itself represents a change or translation.

Adept-soror. The alchemical adept seems always to have carried out his work in the context of a relationship with a partner of the opposite sex, usually an inner figure but sometimes with a real person, referred to as *soror mystica* or mystical sister (*CW* 14, para. 161). This figure may be regarded from a psychological viewpoint as the alchemist's anima or the analyst's unconscious. But analysis also takes place in an external setting where the analyst (adept) is complemented by an outer world patient (soror).

Nigredo, fermentatio, mortificatio, putrefactio, impregnatio. From the alchemist's viewpoint, these terms refer to stages of the alchemical process. *Nigredo* implies a darkening of the prima materia and a sign that something of significance is to happen. *Fermentatio* suggests a brewing, a mingling of elements which will produce a new substance, different in kind to the original components. *Mortificatio* is the stage when the original elements have ceased to exist in their initial form. *Putrefactio* sees a decay of the dead or dying original elements and the giving off of a vapour which is the harbinger of transformation. *Impregnatio* marks the point where the soul, depicted in the woodcut by a tiny human figure or homunculus, ascends to heaven.

From the analyst's standpoint, these terms symbolise what happens in analysis. *Nigredo* may take the form of an important dream which signals change, or the onset of depression that often precedes change. Sometimes, *nigredo* refers to the end of the honeymoon period of an analysis. *Fermentatio* is an apt term for the mingling of personalities that takes place in the transference-countertransference, in the analytical relationship generally and within the unconscious of both analyst and patient. *Mortificatio* and *putrefactio* describe the ways in which symptoms alter, the analytical relationship develops and changes come about. Finally, the soul as depicted in *impregnatio*, refers to movement within the patient, the emergence of the 'new man'.

The elements used in alchemy are themselves metaphors for personality, according to Hillman's understanding of Jung:

> [the] four basic substances of alchemy (lead, salt, sulphur, mercury) ... [are] archetypal components of the psyche. ... Personality is a specific combination of dense depressive lead with inflammable aggressive sulphur with bitterly wise salt with volatile evasive mercury. (Hillman, 1975a, p. 186)

These alchemical concepts and Jung's proposals as to their psychological

180

meaning need to be borne in mind when Jung speaks of the analytical process as involving the altering of both participants (see p. 176, above). Such alteration takes place because the personalities of analyst and patient are combined like chemical elements, and the result is the same as that met with in both chemistry and alchemy: a new, third substance is produced. The 'third' is the transformed factor for both analyst and patient.

The analyst, in his combining with the patient, is bound to be influenced because 'he quite literally "takes over" the sufferings of his patient and shares them with him' (*CW* 16, para. 358). Once an analysis is under way unconscious contents will be projected leading to an 'atmosphere of illusion' with constant miscommunications. But it is in this atmosphere that both transference and transformation occur.

The woodcuts which illustrate the *Rosarium* form a series which illustrates the transformation of potentials represented by two imaginary figures – king and queen. These, in turn, symbolise psychological opposites. As Jung is writing about transference, he means us to see king and queen on one level as symbolising analyst and patient. Within *analysis*, the opposites which define the field are patient and analyst, even though the two people involved may not actually be 'opposites' in human terms. But on another level and at the same time, the process illustrated in the woodcut could just as well be one of intrapsychic growth and the changes which may occur within an individual. The male king and female queen may be seen as symbolising conflicts within the psyche between opposing impulses, or ways of seeing, or between impulse and super-ego, to suggest a few possibilities.

The interpretive overlap between interpersonal and intrapsychic is quite deliberate, then. Baldly put, without a two-person relationship with an analyst, the patient will not experience and explore movement of the various elements within his own psyche. The analyst, the other, constellates what is 'other' to consciousness – namely, the unconscious. The interaction which we call transference-countertransference and the dynamic within a patient's psyche are close reflections of each other. Inner and outer are related:

> The living mystery of life is always hidden between Two, and it is the true mystery which cannot be betrayed by words and depleted by arguments. (Jung quoted in Jaffé, 1979, p. 125)

Or, put the other way round, 'the "soul" is therefore the very essence of relationship' (*CW* 16, para. 504).

For example, the sixth woodcut, called *the return of the soul*, shows the soul, a baby or child, diving down from heaven to breathe life into the dead body. Jung notes that the reanimation of the body is a transcendental process, cannot happen in reality, and cannot be willed by ego. We might add that the new life depends on the previous stages of analysis having been thoroughly lived and worked through; it is a consequence of what has gone before. The conscious and personal effect is radical. The soul is the one (integrated personality) born of the two (patient and analyst).

The tenth and final woodcut is that of *the new birth*. The two-headed king and queen are alive, standing on a plinth depicting the moon. There is a tree of skulls in the background. This is a difficult picture to understand because the final product of the process is depicted as a hermaphrodite which accentuates rather than diminishes the sexual symbolism. Jung supposed that the combination of opposites would be a hybrid. When Freud stumbled on the symbolism of opposites in the sexual images of primal scene fantasy (masochism/sadism, passive/active, woman/man) he took these as literally sexual. This means that Freud, too, was infected with the symbolic theme that so captivated the alchemists. Thus Freud, and the rest of us, remain confronted with a similar problem:

> how is the profound cleavage in man and the world to be understood, how are we to respond to it and, if possible, abolish it? So runs the question when stripped of its natural sexual symbolism, in which it had got stuck only because the problem could not push its way over the threshold of the unconscious. (*CW* 16, para. 534)

The alchemist, like modern man in general and the analyst in particular, is trying to resolve inner and outer conflict. This applies to Freud's attempt to free sexuality from the shackles of unnecessary repression and also to Jung's pursuit of wholeness.

PERSONAL AND ARCHETYPAL TRANSFERENCE

It should not be assumed that Jung conceived of transference only as an image, however. Throughout his work there appear references of a more conventional sort to transference and, especially, to the difference between archetypal and personal transference. This is one of those theoretical distinctions which is more of a weighting and hence rarely met with as described when one is at work. Jung is referring to the extent to which transference consists of the projection of images derived from innate patterns and structures, or, on the other hand, results from the individual's actual experiences. Either variety of transference is natural, according to Jung, but is accentuated in analysis by the situation and by the analyst's alertness to such phenomena.

The analyst's experience of transference is a subject about which Jung expressed mixed feelings. In the 1935 Tavistock Lectures (*CW* 18), transference is conceived of as primarily erotic and as a 'hindrance'. Transference is 'never an advantage' and 'you cure in spite of transference and not because of it'. On the other hand, Jung recalled that when he first met Freud in 1907 he was asked what he thought of the transference. He answered 'with the deepest conviction' that it was the 'alpha and omega of the analytical method. Whereupon Freud said "Then you have grasped the main thing" ' (*CW* 16, para. 358).

Analytical psychology has had to cope with the tension engendered by these divergent statements of Jung's in its coming to terms with the implication and explication of personal and archetypal parental images lying dormant in the unconscious of an individual. At times the impression has been that Jung had neglected to give sufficient attention to the transference but, as Fordham (1974b) pointed out, Jung's remarks in the Tavistock Lectures need to be taken in context.

In earlier papers of Jung's such as 'The therapeutic value of abreaction' (*CW* 16, written in 1921), there is evidence of a quite different attitude. For example:

> The transference phenomenon is an inevitable feature of every thorough analysis, for it is imperative that the doctor should get into the closest possible touch with the patient's line of psychological development. . . . The transference . . . consists in a number of projections which act as a substitute for a real psychological relationship. They create an apparent relationship and this is very important, since it comes at a time when the patient's habitual failure to adapt has been artificially intensified by *his analytical removal into the past.* (*CW* 16, paras 283-4, emphasis added)

In such earlier works, Jung was stressing analysis of the transference as therapeutic. In one sense, this is a special contribution because, in Fordham's view, psychoanalysis was still, at that time in 1921, valuing the making conscious of what was unconscious above transference analysis.

Suggesting explanations for Jung's playing down transference analysis in favour of dream analysis in 1935, Fordham suggested that, as Jung was trying to present his ideas about the collective unconscious, he may have feared that his emphasis on archetypal material would be lost if he brought in the personal transference issue.

Further, by 1935 Jung was interested in, and saw analysis as, what Fordham characterises as an 'internal dialectic between the ego and the archetype' (1974b, p. 10). This highlights working on material from dreams and active imagination. I would schematise such an approach in the form of a triangle. The patient's previously unconscious material is at the apex and the analyst and patient as observers at each of the corners. The energy flow would primarily be to and from the material and not between patient and analyst.

In 1934 the psychoanalyst Strachey introduced the concept of a mutative interpretation. Usually referring to the immediate situation, such an interpretation was considered to be the effective and change-bringing element in analysis. Mutative interpretations relate to the here and now situation between analyst and patient; they are 'hot' interpretations. Thus the live interaction between patient and analyst is the stuff of transference and its interpretation. The reader will see how Strachey's view is compatible with Jung's formulations, and the concept of mutative interpretation has fallen on fertile post-Jungian ground in the Developmental School.

PSYCHOANALYTIC PARALLELS

Although, once again, there was little or no direct communication, many of the themes that Jung touched on have also received attention in psycho-analysis.

Balint (1968) stressed that throughout life a person could be envisioned in terms of the pattern of his relationships to others. Balint responded to patients suffering from early emotional deprivation, particularly when there seemed to have been a struggle on the patient's part to get into object relations, by abandoning verbal interpretation and by providing the patient with the opportunity to rectify a fault in his early development instead. The analyst had, therefore, to be either an 'object' or an 'environment' which the patient could use as he wished. At times this necessitated valuing regression, recognising it as the precursor of movement or a 'new beginning', to use Balint's phrase (1952).

Balint is one of a considerable number of psychoanalysts who have taken a less negative view of regression in analysis than Freud did himself. We may note the following well-known psychoanalytic catchphrases that indicate something of the same point of view:
- 'regression of ego in the service of ego' (Kris)
- 'the valuable resting place of illusion' (Winnicott)
- 'the need to 'transcend the common-sense ego' (Milner)

(and cf. Plaut, 1966, for a Jungian commentary on these propositions). The psychoanalytic terminology which has most strikingly paralleled analytical psychology is Little's concept of 'R', the analyst's 'total response to the patient', her definition of countertransference (1957).

There seem to me to be two strands in psychoanalytic thinking on this subject. One, centred in England, sees the emotional response of the analyst to the patient in terms of a mother-infant relationship, or at least a symbolic replay of that relationship. In other words, factors such as consistency, reliability, warmth and acceptance are accentuated. An emotionally based response is not ruled out. The key factor is that the mother-infant relationship in the patient's early days is conceived of as having been damaged.

The psychoanalysts who represent this point of view (e.g. Balint, Winnicott, Little, Milner) report their occasional use of 'token care' in which small objects to which the patient has become attached may be taken home to bridge the gap between sessions, especially at weekends and at holiday time. Or simple feeding might be offered: a glass of milk or of water, or a biscuit. Cushions and blankets will be readily available and, on occasion, physical contact will be permitted. The essence is that such behaviour on the part of the analyst, so foreign to 'orthodox' psychoanalytic technique, is helpful to someone for the moment too regressed or too wounded to make use of caring when offered in a less concrete form. This should not be thought of as a technical procedure – the concern is for the quality of relationship prior to the patient's capacity to symbolise. The hope is that eventually the patient will establish a relationship with his own inner world. In that regard, fantasy, even regressive fantasy, is seen as creative.

The work of Langs and Searles in the United States is different, however. Langs uses the concept of a 'bi-personal field' which refers to the 'temporal-physical space within which the analytic interaction takes place' (1979, p. 72). The tone and language is more redolent of systems or communication theory than of the mother-infant relationship. There are, in Lang's view, different forms of the interactional field: for symbolic communication, for discharge of disturbing affect, or for attempts to destroy meaning and communication. Langs, like Jung, stresses that the patient's relationship with his analyst has transference and non-transference elements in it. It follows that the analyst's relation to the patient will also contain elements apart from countertransference. (For an attempt to align Langs and Jung, cf. Goodheart, 1980.)

Langs feels that, even now, many Freudian analysts do not see the patient in a positive light. The 'patient as enemy and as resisting dominates the analyst's unconscious images, while the patient as ally and as curative is far less appreciated' (1979, p. 100). Similarly, it has been just as hard to validate countertransference as an essential therapeutic tool.

Searles, in his paper 'Oedipal love in the countertransference' (1959), develops at length a picture of the analyst as 'in' the analysis. He advances the idea that:

> in the course of a successful psycho-analysis, the analyst goes through a phase of reacting to, and eventually relinquishing, the patient as being his Oedipal love object. (p. 284)

He then puts into words what many of the psychoanalysts we have been discussing seem to have observed: that the analyst can learn about the patient by looking at his own feelings in the analytical relationship. This, Searles notes, has been liberating to psychoanalysts because previously all strong affective reactions towards the patient, sexual or angry, for instance, have been seen as neurotic on the part of the analyst.

I would add that this realisation (that the analyst's feelings about the patient are communications and sources of information) is the greatest advance in analytical thinking in recent years. To consolidate this, psychoanalysts have had to go beyond Freud's negative attitude to countertransference (cf. Laplanche and Pontalis, 1980, p. 92 and Rycroft, 1972, p. 25).

Searles advocates allowing the more severely damaged or regressed patient to see how the analyst is affected by him. This involves acknowledging when feelings are present and what they are. Although Searles is writing in terms of his own childlike feelings, he does not ignore adult emotions. He was the first to stress the adult or parental sense of loss in the Oedipus complex (see p. 167, above). Searles is most concerned not to replicate 'an unconscious denial of the child's importance to the parent' (ibid., p. 302). Like Langs, he asserts that the main job of the analyst is to analyse the transference but he recognises that there is a 'feeling background' in the analyst as he undertakes this.

Racker's work (1968) on classifying the different types of transference and countertransference stands midway between the mother-infant orientation of the first group of psychoanalysts and the more in-the-present communications studies of Langs and Searles. I shall focus on what Racker has to say about countertransference in particular because this shows the parallels with analytical psychology more closely.

Racker distinguishes between neurotic countertransference and countertransference proper. Neurotic countertransference reflects aspects of the analyst's infantile self without the analyst realising that this infantile part of him, which is bound to exist to some degree, is operating. In particular, the infantile feelings of the analyst are directed towards his patient who may function as a parent or as a rival. Neurotic countertransference may take the form of identifying with or idealising the patient. Or the analyst may see the patient as a parent figure and try to impress him or her. The analyst may be unable to disentangle his own problems from those of the patient or work to defeat his own therapeutic intention by manic overinterpretation. Finally, the analyst may forgo his analytic attitude and respond to the patient's angry attacks by retaliation or, on the other hand, to the patient's erotic communication by sexual activity.

Moving on to non-neurotic countertransference, Racker makes a distinction between what he refers to as *concordant*, and then *complementary*, countertransferences.

The concordant countertransference involves the analyst's feeling what the patient is feeling, but does not *know* he is feeling. This can happen because the analyst's own psyche is in empathic concord with the feeling state of the patient. For example, if after seeing a particular patient the analyst feels depressed, this may be the patient's depression, of which the patient is still unconscious.

The complementary countertransference occurs when the analyst finds himself behaving in a way which he feels is foreign to him (i.e. is connected in some manner with the patient). The analyst, in Racker's formulation, has become involved and incorporated in the patient's inner world and is feeling, or behaving, like the inner world figure (mother or father, perhaps) that the patient felt he had had. In the example mentioned in the previous paragraph, the analyst's feeling of depression would be his expression of the depressed parent the patient felt he had had – an incarnation of an inner world figure.

Racker's stress on countertransference and transference is counterbalanced in psychoanalysis by the emphasis laid by Greenson and others on the treatment alliance or non-transference relationship. We noted the parallel with Jung briefly earlier; here we might add that the treatment alliance leads readily to the idea of a 'therapeutic contract' (Menninger, 1958) which is applicable in many helping situations. The treatment alliance has been defined as:

> the non-neurotic, rational, reasonable rapport which the patient has with his analyst and which enables him to work purposefully in the analytic situation. (Greenson and Wexler, 1969, quoted in Sandler *et al.*, 1973, p. 27)

Sandler went on to point out that the treatment alliance should not be idealised. It does not mean only the patient's conscious wish to get better and certainly it does not infer only a positive, harmonious relationship between analyst and patient. In fact, the essence of the treatment alliance may well be that the patient goes on working even when he hates the analyst and consciously wishes to leave the analysis.

Finally, in the review of psychoanalytic parallels to Jung's thought, we should note Bion's use of the image of the container (analyst) and the contained (patient) (1963). This means something more than physical containment in infancy. The idea is that emotions and anxieties are projected by the infant into the mother and returned to him in a milder, more tolerable form. The modification of the uncontainable emotion is what is meant by containment.

THE WOUNDED HEALER

Turning back to post-Jungian analytical psychology, there are basically two approaches to understanding what happens in analysis. The first uses material from the collective unconscious in an archetypal approach to understanding the interaction of an analytical session. The second emulates the psycho-analytic tradition which we have been discussing. We look at these in turn.

Meier (1949) drew parallels between the ancient healing practices of the temples of Asclepius and modern analysis. Two points are relevant here. Healing practices and rituals took place within a closed setting, the *temenos* or temple precinct, and fostered sleep in the hope of the 'patient' having healing dreams. The teacher of the healing arts, Chiron the centaur, is depicted as suffering from an incurable wound. The analogy with analysis is clear. The analyst becomes the wounded healer, the analytic setting, which permits regression and the giving up of over-consciousness, functions as the *temenos*.

Although Meier does show how the material of contemporary patients bears resemblance to both positive and negative patterns that were known to the healer-priests, his aim was to demonstrate historical continuity within the collective psyche. What actually happens in analysis is not described and there is little in his book concerning what we would now call countertransference.

Guggenbühl-Craig (1971) continued to explore the image of the wounded healer – but as applied to the practice of analysis and more widely in the helping professions. His theory may be summarised as follows: the image of the wounded healer, with its inherent contradiction, is an archetypal image and, therefore, the *bipolarity* of the archetype is constellated. But we tend to split the image so that the analyst figure in the therapeutic relationship becomes all-powerful; strong, healthy and able. The patient remains nothing but a patient; passive, dependent and prone to suffer from excessive dependency (cf. Goffman's *The Asylum*, especially on hospitalisation, 1961).

In addition to the split in the image of the wounded healer into healer analyst and wounded patient, we must also consider, in Guggenbühl-Craig's view, the split that this involves *within* both analyst and patient. If it is the case that all analysts have an inner wound, then to present oneself as 'healthy' is to cut off part of one's inner world. Likewise if the patient is only seen as 'ill' then he is also cut off from his own inner healer or capacity to heal himself. That analysts are in some sense wounded is scarcely to be doubted, and there seems to be a growing body of opinion that psychological factors play a part in a choice of a helping profession and that doctors, for example, suffer greatly from stress-related syndromes (cf. Ford, 1983, for a summary of the evidence).

Guggenbühl-Craig goes on, stating that, when a person becomes sick, the healer-patient archetype comes into operation. The outer man *is* sick but there is also an inner healer. When the patient meets a doctor he knows with his conscious mind that this *is* a doctor because of the social setting (white coat, instruments, etc.). But unless there is also a projection on to the doctor of the inner healer of the patient there will be less chance of a cure. Yet while the projection may be necessary to get the treatment moving, it must be withdrawn at some point so that the patient's self-healing capacities may flourish.

In the same way, the analyst 'knows' he has a patient by external signs. But he, too, will have to project his own inner wounded part into the patient in order to know the patient in an emotional sense. There is a parallel here with Kohut's definition of empathy as 'vicarious introspection'. The analyst knows what it is like to be the patient because, in a sense, he is treating an amalgam of the patient and himself.

It is easy to say that when projections which serve to define who is analyst and who patient have done their work, they should be withdrawn. But, until Groesbeck's paper on 'The archetypal image of the wounded healer' (1975) this had not been worked out in practice. Groesbeck is continuing to particularise the mythic theme hinted at by Meier and applied to the contemporary analytical setting by Guggenbühl-Craig.

Groesbeck posits the possible reconstitution of the split archetypal image of the wounded healer in the psyche of both patient and analyst. I am grateful to Groesbeck for permission to adapt a series of diagrams he devised to illustrate the making and withdrawing of projections during analysis. The commentary is my own. In my view, the diagrams most clearly illustrate what happens in the early stages of an analysis, and demonstrate a pattern that is repeated over and over during the course of an analysis.

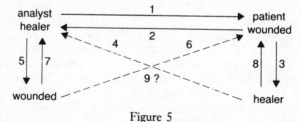

Figure 5

In Figure 5, the first diagram, we can see that there is a two-way interaction between analyst and patient (1 and 2). In addition, the analyst and patient each have in their unconscious a wounded and a healer capacity respectively and there is an interplay between the conscious role and the unconscious component (5, 7, 8, 3). The analyst projects his wounds into the

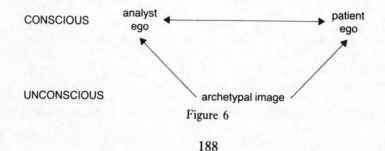

Figure 6

188

patient and the patient his healer into the doctor (4 and 6). But, as yet, there is no link between the patient's inner, unconscious healer and the doctor's inner, unconscious wound (9).

In Figure 6 the early stages of an analysis is also represented. The analyst and patient are in interaction. And the ego of the analyst together with the ego of the patient are looking at the patient's material which contains, among other things, images and themes which, because archetypal, activate and affect the analyst, pulling him into the treatment.

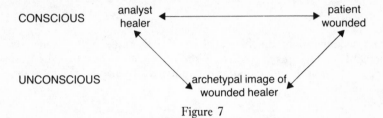

Figure 7

Moving on to Figure 7, the archetypal image of the wounded healer is present. The analyst has started, and is continuing, to assess the patient's weaknesses and strengths. These latter concern the patient's inner healer. And the patient will have been exploring the skills of the analyst, what he has to offer and, given the inevitability of some negative transference, what his weaknesses seem to be. So both participants are relating to the image of the wounded healer.

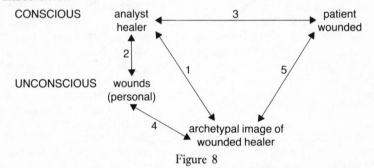

Figure 8

In Figure 8 we see the analyst struggling with the balance between what Racker called neurotic countertransference and countertransference proper. His wounds facilitate empathy with the patient (2, 4, 5) but the danger is identification (2, 3). Nevertheless, the diagram portrays what it is like to be an analyst. The patient's personality is being appreciated, explored, empathically filtered through the analyst's psychopathology (1, 2, 4, 5); the hope is for as little distortion as possible.

Figure 9 rests on Figure 8. If the analyst has been moved by his patient, then the patient is more aware of the analyst as a healing presence. In addition, the analyst is reflecting to the patient that he is acceptable, mirroring the transference. This frees the patient to have communication with his inner healer, identified as his potential. It would follow that the inner healer might

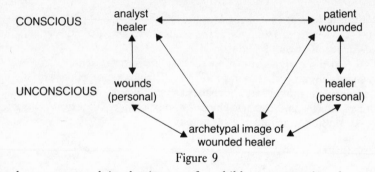

Figure 9

first be encountered in the image of a child or some other form of new beginning. Both Figures 8 and 9, it should be noted, involve the bipolar archetypal image of the wounded healer rather than separate images of illness and health.

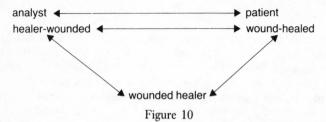

Figure 10

By the time the stage of Figure 10 is reached both analyst and patient have progressed beyond the paranoid-schizoid tendency to split the image of the other into 'all-wounded' and 'all-healing'. Neither participant is splitting himself; so, therefore, there is a whole object basis to the analysis. This does not rule out regressions to the stages portrayed in earlier diagrams and it should not be taken for granted that Figure 10 is achieved in every analysis.

It may be asserted that the idea of an inner healer is nothing but a Jungian fancy. We need to consider what psychoanalysts have to say that alludes to this same factor. We have already noted Langs' designation of the patient as an 'ally' and as 'curative', and Greenson's concept of the treatment alliance.

Money-Kyrle, in a paper entitled 'the aim of psychoanalysis', stated that he regarded as one aim of analysis as being

> to help the patient understand, and so overcome, emotional impediments to his discovering what he *innately already knows*. (1971, p. 104, emphasis added)

Rycroft tell us:

> the human ego is not a passive entity . . . but an active agent, capable of initiating behaviour, including those ultimately self-defeating forms of behaviour known as neuroses. (1972, p. xxiv)

Finally, Sterba (1934) saw as fundamental to the analytical process that the patient must split his ego, identifying one part with the analyst, so observing and reflecting on the material he produces as patient – the other part of his ego. We might adapt this to the language of analytical psychology, describing it as activation of the inner healer of the patient which performs a healing function for him.

THE USE OF THE COUNTERTRANSFERENCE IN ANALYTICAL PSYCHOLOGY

I mentioned a second approach to understanding what happens in analysis by analytical psychologists who, like their psychoanalytic colleagues, examine the detail of transference-countertransference interaction during analysis. In fact, though Jung never stressed the point, he was amongst the first to see the clinically positive side of the analyst's countertransference, referring to it as a 'highly important organ of information' in 1929 and stating explicitly:

> You can exert no influence if you are not susceptible to influence.... The patient influences [the analyst] unconsciously.... One of the best known symptoms of this kind is *the counter-transference evoked by the transference*. (*CW* 16, para. 163, emphasis added)

Jung also contrasted his approach with Freud's attempts to avoid the effects of countertransference (*CW* 16, para. 358n). To illustrate the effects of neurotic countertransference, Jung used the image of 'psychic infection', concentrating in particular on those clinical situations where, because of a similarity in the nature of their personal wounds, the analyst identifies with the patient (*CW* 16, paras 358, 365). In general, Jung simply accepts that benign and malign forms of countertransference are, respectively, professional benefits and hazards (ibid.).

The use of the countertransference by members of the Developmental School of post-Jungians is particularly interesting. At the same time as Racker was first developing his work on countertransference, but without knowledge of it, Fordham introduced and elaborated his concepts of illusory and syntonic countertransference (1957).

Concisely, illusory countertransference is similar to what Racker refers to as neurotic countertransference and may be seen in the various forms I listed (see pp. 185-6, above). Fordham noted that illusions are truly symptoms of the analyst's but to refer to them as such runs the risk of pathologising all of countertransference (1960, p. 244). In addition, countertransference illusions can be corrected.

Syntonic countertransference corresponds to Racker's 'complementary' countertransference. The term 'syntonic' is used in radio communications to describe the accurate tuning of a receiver so that transmissions from one particular transmitter may be received. In Fordham's usage, the unconscious of the analyst is tuned into what emanates from the patient's transmitter. His own unconscious, says Fordham following Jung, becomes an 'organ of information' for the analyst (1960, p. 247).

In the same way that Kohut had to distinguish empathy from intuition (by stating that empathy is rationally comprehensible), Fordham distinguished a syntonic countertransference from intuition by drawing attention to the way in which emotion and projective/introjective processes play a part; this is not something which can be said with certainty of intuition.

In the syntonic countertransference the analyst's feeling and behaviour fit in with or are in tune with the patient's inner world:

> through introjection, an analyst perceives a patient's unconscious processes in himself and so experiences them often long before the patient is near becoming conscious of them. (Fordham, 1969b, p. 275)

Fordham revealed that a vital step in his evolution of the concept was his realisation that it was *necessary* to incorporate the content of the syntonic countertransference into the analyst's understanding of the patient's material and of the transference. In this way, excessive dwelling on the subjective aspects of the countertransference experience may be avoided. Syntonic countertransference then becomes part of a ceaseless cycle of projection and introjection, the unconscious part of the whole communication process.

Taking this further, if the analyst feels himself projecting something on to the patient, having a fantasy about the patient perhaps, he need not rush to withdraw his projection, fearing to damage the patient with it. The advantage of a concept like syntonic countertransference is that it permits the analyst's consideration of the possibility that this feeling towards the patient is something the patient may have engendered in him and may have felt in the past in relation to inner-world or outer-world figures. Thus the analyst's projection takes on a new light.

To reach this position, Fordham had to move beyond the prevailing psychodynamic orthodoxy of his time in which the analyst's projecting on to his patient was a cardinal sin and, if the patient stirred a feeling in the analyst, this was regarded as revealing a blind spot to which the analyst should pay attention.

Syntonic countertransference consists, then, of exceedingly rapid affective processes. These happen anyway. The issue is whether they are recognised for what they are: communications. But syntonic countertransference cannot be taught as a technique, though it can be passed on to trainees as an ethos or attitude.

We should note that Fordham has based this idea on the functioning of the self and not on ego functioning. The self, in its transpersonal guise (see p. 99, above) provides the essential context and condition for syntonic countertransference. The concept of the self in analytical psychology may have strengthened efforts to look at whatever it is that links analyst and patient. Fordham emphasised that while countertransference is not the only source of information about the patient's unconscious functioning, the analyst can use this particular information 'as part of technique' (1969b, p. 286).

Before going on to consider Fordham's more recent revision of his views, I want to accentuate a point that he made in relation to the personal qualities of the analyst, so stressed by Jung. In Fordham's view, within certain limits, it is less important to identify these personal qualities than to note *how they are managed*. It was this realisation that helped Fordham to use the affects of the analyst as a response to the patient rather than simply as a source of self-knowledge; the whole bias has become less subjective and introspective (ibid., p. 267).

More recently (1979b), Fordham has proposed the following question as a logical development of his thought: if interaction is the basis of analysis, if the analyst's affect and behaviour are part of that interaction, then why do we still refer to the analyst's side of the business as 'countertransference'? Perhaps what Fordham has in mind is that, as a word, 'countertransference' has intimations of illusion, delusion and fantasy, whereas, in fact, it is simply a normal part of analysis. Fordham proposes that the term 'countertransference' should be restricted to what is now usually referred to as illusory or neurotic countertransference:

> I believe the theory of countertransference has performed its main function. It has had the desirable effect of taking analysts out of their ivory towers, making it possible for them to compare notes on what they really do during analytic psychotherapy. The pathological reactions of the analyst ... may be called countertransference. I would call the rest part of the *interactional dialectic*. (1979a, p. 208, emphasis added)

In the case illustration in Chapter 10, examples of the various kinds of countertransference may be found.

These ideas on countertransference, though formulated largely by the Developmental School, are influential throughout contemporary analytical psychology. As McCurdy (an analyst trained in Germany and Zürich, but working in the United States) commented on Fordham's work:

> these observations have led to more precision about details of the technical procedure of analysis and to a great appreciation and valuation of transference/ countertransference phenomena, not only as therapeutic and diagnostic tools, but also as the immediate situational structure in which neurotic behaviour and ideation can be observed, experienced and worked through. (1982, p. 55)

From other Schools we have already noted Dieckmann's work in Germany on the sharing of images in transference-countertransference (see pp. 122-3, above). And, while his methodology is quite different, an analyst of the Classical School such as Fierz can write of 'the hypnotic effect on the analyst of the transference projection'. The analyst has then to find out what is happening, and what, if anything, has gone wrong:

> During the treatment of difficult cases the analyst may become noticeably tired, even exhausted, and exceedingly moody. This is an indication that important factors are not sufficiently conscious and that the corresponding complex is drawing the energy to itself and into the unconscious. (1977, p. 8)

Fierz focuses in an interesting manner on the various negative uses to which the analyst's theory may be put. This would be a special case of neurotic countertransference. The analyst may collude with a patient when that patient attempts to deal with his disorientation and loneliness by finding out something about the school of analysis adhered to by the analyst and becoming a champion of it. Fierz's idea is that such championing is a false attempt to deal with a painful human problem in that the feeling of belonging to a group or school lessens a sense of isolation. I think this has special relevance to psychologically 'sophisticated' patients and to training candidates in particular. It is this championing of the parent figure's ideas (as they are perceived by the patient or ex-patient) rather than the development of an independent point of view that makes so much analytical discussion sterile or rigid.

WHAT IS JUNGIAN ANALYSIS? (1) INTRODUCTION

I mentioned at the start of the chapter that the use of the words 'analyst' and 'patient' in connection with Jungian analysis was emotive. This is because, in recent years and most especially since Jung's death, the Jungian community *has questioned what Jungian analysis is*, how it should be conducted, whether techniques are identifiable and useful, and so on. The charge that such-and-such a procedure is not analytical has been countered by the assertion that the other's practice is not Jungian.

As far as the method of conducting analysis is concerned, post-Jungian analytical psychology divides into two camps. The Developmental School constitutes one camp and, in this chapter, we have seen its focus on interaction between patient and analyst and on the clinical use of countertransference. Using Fordham's phrase, we can refer to a method of *interactional dialectic* (ID). Members of the Classical and Archetypal Schools form the other camp. *Three* schools fall into *two* camps as far as analytical *method* is concerned because, as Hillman says, archetypal psychology has departed from classical Jungian analysis 'less in the form of therapy than in its focus' (Hillman, 1983, p. 44). In this chapter, the theme of the wounded healer is a contribution from this second camp. Far less concerned with interaction, as it is, we can follow McCurdy (1982, p. 50) in referring to the method of these practitioners as *classical-symbolic-synthetic* (CSS).

There has been a certain amount of cross-fertilisation, as I noted earlier when discussing McCurdy's evaluation of Fordham's work. (And see my apologia for introducing the notion of schools, pp. 17-19, above.) Nevertheless, a comparison of the ID and CSS approaches is illuminating.

WHAT IS JUNGIAN ANALYSIS? (2) ANALYTICAL STRUCTURE
AND PROCEDURE

Whilst there would be no disagreement that analysis is, or should be, an *experience* as contrasted to learning, there is a considerable divergence of view as to how that experience should be structured.

Fierz (1977) pointed out the paradox in analysis by which formalised structure serves as the background to a release of elusive and fluid psychic contents. The structure of analysis facilitates a shift in which the process becomes less peripheral and more central to the patient's life. This includes regularity of appointments, an appropriate setting and agreed payment – factors over which there is no disagreement between a CSS practitioner such as Fierz and the ID group.

A key and contentious aspect of analytical structure may be expressed in the tag: *couch or chair?* Jung opposed Freud's suggestion of providing a couch for the patient behind which the analyst would sit because of his (Jung's) emphasis on equality and mutuality. The insistence upon the arrangement of analyst and analysand seated and face to face is central to CSS, and the active involvement of the analyst is stressed. For example, Adler (1966) objected to placing the patient on the couch for a number of reasons (unless the patient is 'very strung up and tense' (p. 27) and so needs to relax). He felt that the couch emphasises the passivity of the patient; it is as if an operation was being performed on him. The couch enables the patient to talk about himself in an 'artificial manner'. And the couch hinders the patient, in Adler's view, from bridging the gap which separates him from the analyst. Crucially, the couch enables the patient to see his experiences in analysis as cut off from everyday life. Sitting face to face produces a more human situation and 'makes it more difficult for the patient to use the analyst as a lay figure on which to hang his projections without testing the degree of reality they possess' (ibid., pp. 27-8).

Fordham (1978a), arguing in favour of the couch, made a number of points which take a diametrically opposite line. Fordham's opening remark was that Jung was too literal in his understanding of the importance of face-to-face communication. Fordham, continuing, pointed out that although the couch was once used by physicians, that does not mean it is so used in today's analysis. The couch *does* emphasise that the patient *is* a patient seeking treatment and, usefully, that analysis is not a social occasion dealing only in the interpersonal. From the analyst's point of view, he does not have to pretend an absolute equality with his patient and his professional attitude is maintained.

In Fordham's view, it is true that the couch is not a 'natural' factor; but then neither is the process of analysis itself. Behaviour of a sexual or aggressive kind is proscribed and this itself alters the feeling of 'naturalness'. Therefore to worry about the couch damaging what is 'natural and human' is to make much of an issue already resolved. In Fordham's opinion, it may not always be desirable for the patient to see the analyst. From the patient's perspective, he may need to feel alone or explore something without intrusion. Or, quite reasonably, the patient may wish to dissemble. Of course the patient on the couch may turn to look at the analyst and, in any event, he sees him upon arrival and departure.

In my own practice I do use a couch and place my chair beside the head of the couch, not behind it. Thus the patient can look at me or look away; I, too, can look straight ahead or make eye contact with the patient, or, should I wish, simply observe. The couch is not compulsory and, with some patients who come infrequently, I do not advocate its use. I would agree with Fordham that the stereotype of the silent, cold analyst sitting behind the couch is probably a historical curiosity even in psychoanalysis.

Above all, Fordham argued, there is no reason why the analyst should be out of touch with a patient on the couch. In Fordham's opinion, the monitoring of his reactions, which forms the operant part of his counter-transference, and which links the analyst to the patient, is aided by the patient using the couch.

We may note from this controversy something more than an argument about furniture. What is central is the attitude to transferences of infantile origin, and to regression. Those who use the couch work with these at length; those who use the chair may seek to dissolve them.

In psychoanalysis there has been less debate. But Fairbairn spoke up in 1958 against the use of the couch, saying that he had stopped using a couch in his practice. Fairbairn felt that the use of a couch in analysis was an anachronism from Freud's days as a hypnotist and also stemmed from his dislike of being stared at. In Fairbairn's words:

the couch technique has the effect of imposing quite arbitrarily upon the patient a positively traumatic situation calculated inevitably to reproduce such traumatic situations of childhood as that imposed on the infant who is left to cry in his pram alone, or that imposed upon the child who finds himself isolated in his cot during the primal scene. (quoted in Jackson, 1961, p. 37)

In other words, the use of the couch is not 'neutral' and Fairbairn suspects that its use has much to do with the defensiveness of the analyst and his desire to be protected from the demands of his patient. As far as I know, Fairbairn's abandonment of the couch has not been widely adopted in psychoanalysis; though for treatments of lesser intensity or duration its use is governed by caution lest an uncontainable regression takes place.

Continuing to compare CSS and ID, a second procedural point of disagreement has been over *the frequency of sessions*. The issue is this: if analysis is defined in such a way that it implies or requires treatment of a certain intensity and duration, then it follows that treatment not conforming to those requirements cannot be analysis. At least, this is what has been said by proponents of ID; it is the definition of analysis that is disputed and the argument has become tautological (i.e. if analysis is defined as 4-5 sessions weekly, then only treatment of such frequency constitutes analysis).

Jung seems to have been flexible over the frequency of sessions. Analysis requires that:

the patient be seen as often as possible. I content myself with a maximum of four consultations a week. With the beginning of synthetic treatment it is of advantage to spread out the consultations. I then generally reduce them to one or two hours a week, for the patient must learn to go his own way. (*CW* 16, para. 26)

What this suggests is that the first three of Jung's four stages of analysis require frequent attendance by the patient but that when the stage of transformation (synthesis) is reached this may tail off. Jung is often quoted as advocating 'holidays' from analysis.

But what sort of patients did Jung see? He himself admitted that he had an unusual practice (a 'peculiar composition'):

new cases are decidedly in the minority. Most of them already have some form of psychotherapeutic treatment behind them, with partial or negative results. About a third of my cases are not suffering from any clinically definable neurosis, but from the senselessness and aimlessness of their lives. I should not object if this were called the general neurosis of our age. Fully two thirds of my patients are in the second half of life. (*CW* 16, para 83)

I think that patients suffering such 'general neurosis' are even more common now than when Jung was writing in 1929. But a practice with a preponderance of patients in the second half of life who have had previous treatment is definitely unusual.

It is considerations such as these that have led ID proponents to insist that a high frequency of sessions is a prerequisite, if the treatment is to be called analysis. Less intensive treatment is referred to as a type of psychotherapy. As in psychoanalysis, some form of compromise has been proposed and we would then refer to 'analytical psychotherapy' to describe treatment of less than analytical intensity but with analytical methodology and goals (cf. Paolino, 1981, pp. 22-48 for a psychoanalytic comparison).

But definitions of analysis do not *have* to refer to frequency of sessions, though frequency may be implied. If we were to accept a definition of analysis as 'the sorting out and breaking down of complex structures and images into their components, i.e., archetypal forms and patterns of ego-archetype interactions' (Society of Analytical Pyschology discussion paper, 1966), then we still have to consider whether or not this could be achieved at a frequency of, say, once-weekly sessions. The definition above can also be used in another way. Rather than define the whole of a process, the definition might be used to point up those parts of psychotherapy in general which are analytical in particular. Thus we would talk of doing *analysis* at one point of a session or for one period of a prolonged treatment. It follows that, in most, but not all, instances, that the more sessions available, the more space for analysis proper. The caveat has to be entered because *analysis* as just defined may take place in a one-off interview and prolonged and intensive treatment may be *supportive* rather than analytical.

Such issues are more than a numbers game. They must be set alongside such assertions as that of Mattoon in her overview of analytical psychology that 'the frequency of Jungian sessions is usually once or twice a week' (1981, p. 228). As with the couch-versus-chair issue, the question of frequency may be seen as a symbolisation of deep ideological differences.

WHAT IS JUNGIAN ANALYSIS? (3) THE INPUT OF THE ANALYST

Memories of those who worked with Jung often present him as a sort of analytical trickster: master of insights, wisdom, intuition and one who did not demur from admonishing, instructing or suggesting. He comes over in these descriptions (e.g. Henderson, 1975a) as the paradigm of the *active, interventionist therapist*. No doubt some of this was due to the 'peculiar composition' of his caseload. For those who may be thought of already to have had 'reductive' analysis, as Jung hints, such input coming from the analyst seems more appropriate.

Jung's analytical input centred on his psychological elucidation of his patient's images using 'the history of religion in its widest sense, mythology, folklore and primitive psychology'. This 'treasure-house of archetypal forms' enables the analyst to '*draw helpful parallels and enlightening comparisons*' (*CW* 12, para. 38, emphasis added).

Jung went on:

> It is absolutely necessary to supply these fantastic images that rise up so strange and threatening before the mind's eye with some kind of context so as to make them more intelligible. Experience has shown that the best way to do this is by means of comparative mythological material. (*CW* 12, para. 38)

It is on this that the CSS method rests. For example, Adler notes that sometimes the analyst is 'required to enlarge upon the patient's associations by means of his own knowledge' (1966, p. 51). This is, continues Adler, legitimate if 'the dreamer is in complete agreement with it' (ibid.). Adler feels that it is the patient's assent to the interpretation that avoids the improper use of the analyst's authority. But, in fact, it may be the other way round; immediate assent to the analyst's speculations may indicate excessive patient suggestibility. Adler is careful, though, to indicate that 'intervening because of our knowledge of collective symbolism' only comes into play when associations have dried up (ibid., p. 95) which would be the point when a practitioner of the ID style would hope to interpret the resistance.

In an illustration of his method of dream interpretation, Adler suggested to the patient that he make a picture that would extend a dream image. This had striking and undoubted therapeutic effects. What is important for us to enquire is whether the caution shown by Adler in making the suggestion only in the absence of associations is followed by other CSS practitioners. In Adler's example the area of collective symbolism which came into play after the suggestion was mythology; Adler could use his knowledge of this to illumine what the patient had produced in response to Adler's initial suggestion.

In principle, there is no reason why the use of amplification should necessarily take the form of a forced feeding of the patient with images. The analyst may amplify silently, to himself (*unamplification*, to adapt Masud Khan's term 'uninterpretation'). Or the analyst may allow his amplificatory knowledge to guide him in his intervention, for example in connection with on what to focus. It is also possible that knowledge of a mythologem may enable the analyst to see where things may be leading. Sometimes a patient will say that he is reminded of, say, Hansel and Gretel, or will introduce a modern version of an ancient myth figure, e.g. Superman. Such remarks from patients invite amplification. And there are, of course, patients with their own knowledge of collective symbolism. Similarly, working with the infantile material of an adult patient and making use of models of psychological development in infancy may also be seen as a form of amplification.

I have developed this point because, as with reductive interpretation, amplification has much to do with the way the analyst functions as a person. This, and the atmosphere he creates, is as important as application of a technical procedure.

We may wonder what has become of the image of the *reticent and reserved psychoanalyst*, waiting for patient material to which he might react and initiating very little not germane to the translation of what was unconscious into consciousness. In analytical psychology the ID approach incorporates such an analytical ethos far more than the CSS approach does.

But even in psychoanalysis the reserved analyst, passive to the point of silence, has been criticised. Anna Freud wrote:

> With due respect for the necessary strictest handling and interpretation of the transference, I feel still that we should leave room somewhere for the realisation that analyst and patient are also two real people, in a real relationship to each other. I wonder whether our – at times complete – neglect of this side of the matter is not responsible for some of the hostile reactions which we get from our patients and which we are apt to ascribe to 'true transference' only. (Quoted in Malcolm, 1982, p. 40)

Anna Freud was commenting on a paper of Stone's, written in 1961, in which Stone wondered what possible damage could be done to the transference by the patient knowing where the analyst plans to spend his holidays or whether he knows more about sailing than about golf. Kohut was even blunter: 'To remain silent when one is asked a question is not neutral but rude' (quoted in Malcolm, 1982, p. 40).

If analytical psychologists look solely for impressive, archetypal, numinous material, then they will be tempted to be over-active and over-suggestive. If we consider, for instance, a patient who does not take off his coat, or one who sits in a session listening to his personal stereo on headphones, we may conclude that he is not producing myth-like material. Or could he be? I do not propose to suggest mythologems relevant to such highly charged behaviour, merely to stimulate thought around the proposition that the unconscious is unpredictable and its imagery changes over time. We may be receptive to it with a store of amplification, or even a 'store of interpretations' (Fordham, 1978b, p. 127), but we cannot forecast what will transpire. It follows that possession of a theory of development is just as likely to over-organise the patient's material, if it is misused, as adherence in an unselective way to a myth based approach.

WHAT IS JUNGIAN ANALYSIS? (4) THE TRANSFERENCE IN ANALYTICAL PSYCHOLOGY

Continuing this survey and discussion of ideological differences, we arrive at the question of *transference*. The title of this section is taken from a paper by Plaut (1956). There he discussed the historical beginnings of the clinical dichotomy (in our terms between CSS and ID approaches). This concerned, in particular, 'the handling of transference phenomena' (ibid., p. 155).

Plaut acknowledged that both schools of thought do agree that transference occurs and is important. However, the CSS method

> will deal with it by a mainly educative procedure centred on the elucidation and differentiation of archetypal contents. (ibid., p. 156)

The adherents of ID, on the other hand (of whom Plaut is one):

> accept the projection in a wholehearted manner, making no *direct* attempt to help the patient sort out what belongs to him, what to the analyst and what to neither as well as to both. On the contrary, they will allow themselves to become this image bodily, to 'incarnate' it for the patient. (pp. 156-7)

Plaut went on to note that it is not simply a question of timing interpretation of transference phenomena, but 'a *totally* different attitude to the transferred image' (ibid., p. 157, emphasis added). The analyst who incarnates the image is doing so in response to the transference. The analyst should not state that he is incarnating the image in this way, but when he becomes aware of it the implication is that he must 'be able to recognise the boundaries of his own ego' (ibid.).

The skill required by an analyst to let the patient make him what the patient's unconscious insists he be does not necessarily correlate with an intent to amplify. Then the material is, as I suggested earlier, more likely to be conceived of as 'on the table' for consideration by analyst and patient. It follows that those ID practitioners who work like Plaut do not think in terms of an early introduction of 'reality' to the analytical situation; this may be contrasted with Adler's CSS remarks (see p. 195, above). The transference fantasy *is* the sought after field of work for the ID practitioner.

WHAT IS JUNGIAN ANALYSIS? (5) INTERPRETATION AND TECHNIQUE

I was struck by the fact that in the indexes to three of Adler's publications (1961, 1966, 1979) there is no mention of 'interpretation'. Similarly, Mattoon's *Jungian Psychology in Perspective* shows a CSS bias with but one entry – and then as a synonym for 'elucidation'. Hillman is against interpretation altogether, particularly where this means 'translation' or 'dissection'. Both of these distort the image and injure the psyche. He prefers to talk, for instance, of 'befriending' a dream or an image (1967, p. 57).

On the other hand, in the ID view, *interpretation is the cornerstone of analytical technique* (Fordham, 1969b, p. 270). But the idea that there could be a 'technique of analysis' is, for some Jungians, quite foreign to Jung's conception of analysis as an art, as defying formulation, and ignoring Jung's admonitions against the excessive use of theory (cf. Henderson, 1975b).

But it is not reasonable to postulate that Classical analytical psychology and the CSS method are devoid of theory or technique. Then there is no reason for analytical psychologists to turn aside from ID attempts to define technique and to delineate techniques. Hillman, on the other hand, objects to the placement of the analyst's technique at the *centre* of the analytical process. In a personal communication (1976) he wondered why the Developmental School had to choose what were, to him, provocative titles for their two volumes of papers (Fordham *et al.*, 1973, 1974). The titles were *Analytical Psychology: A Modern Science* and *Technique in Jungian Analysis*. The provocative words were 'science' and 'technique'.

Therefore there has been a gut reaction amongst some post-Jungians to what they see as the extremism of the ID approach as practised by the Developmental School and, in particular, to what Fordham has referred to as a 'microscopic' study of the analyst-patient interaction' (1969b, p. 260).

MEDIAL PRACTITIONERS

Sometimes one experiences the temptation to dismiss the differences we have been reviewing as nothing more than temperament, language, theoretical pomposity or empire building. And it is an erroneous distinction to separate apparently 'technical' approaches from a mutual or dialectical attitude to analysis. The advantage of the possession of analytical technique is that such a mutual relationship between patient and analyst may become a *deeper* one. Nevertheless, the contrasts between CSS and ID are striking enough to prevent any easy conclusion that all post-Jungians are attempting much the same in analysis. We may test this out by examining the possibility of *a medial position*, one which combines classical-symbolic-synthetic ideology with that of interactional dialectic.

What I propose to do is to look at the views of two potentially medial analytical psychologists. First, Davidson's attempt in 1966 to combine Jung's ideas about active imagination with the transference analysis of her overall ID method. Second, Schwartz-Salant's approach to the treatment of narcissistic personality disorder, where he modifies the CSS tradition in which he trained to incorporate analysis of transference-countertransference interaction (1982).

Davidson's idea was that transference can be seen as an imaginary dialogue between the patient and a figure, apparently the external analyst, but largely derived from the patient's inner world. In this respect, there is an instant resemblance to the dialogue in active imagination between the patient's ego and his unconscious contents. In analysis, according to Davidson, the analyst may function for the patient as the patient's ego would in an active imagination, allowing the unconscious material of the patient to 'come through'. The transference-countertransference is then in one sense, an active imagination.

To many Classical Jungians and CSS practitioners, these ideas are anathema, because they seem to offend the usual groundplan for active imagination. For example, von Franz (personal communication, 1977) informed me that one should never practise active imagination involving a living person, and certainly not one's analyst or patient. Nevertheless, if we examine closely Weaver's authoritative summary of what is involved in active imagination (1964), we may see that Davidson's thesis is justified.

Weaver felt that the first step in active imagination is that the ego pays attention to psychic fragments and images. The ego can initiate fantasy and also be the conscious recorder of such fantasy. Fantasy can be enlarged by participation and intervention of the ego. The more the involvement in the drama, the more the ego participates. But there are areas where the ego may participate but not understand. Finally, and most important, it is the fact that the ego undergoes 'meaningful participation' rather than the 'form in which such participation is expressed' that is crucial (ibid., pp. 17-18).

Returning to Davidson, we can see that it is the analyst who is the representative of the observing ego as in Jung's original schema for active imagination. The analyst, when she incarnates the images in the patient's transference, enters into the patient's inner drama, but retains her own boundaries just as the ego does when participating in the more usual kind of active imagination.

Schwartz-Salant, the second potentially medial analyst, is writing about patients who are cut-off, lack real self-love, have little empathy and function emotionally in an over-concrete way, though they may make an apparently successful social adaptation. Such narcissistically disordered patients require long and painful periods before what is usually thought of as analytical work may commence. The analyst is trying to create a warm and empathic environment in which trust can develop. Schwartz-Salant writes of attempting to transform archetypal reality, in which the narcissistic patient, cut off from human contact, is enmeshed, into 'personal historical life in a manner that retains some degree of archetypal rootedness' (1982, p. 25). To achieve these aims, he eschews his normal technique.

For our purpose, we must focus in some detail on what Schwartz-Salant has to say about CSS technique in relation to the treatment of narcissistic disorder. He states:

> The clinical picture, especially in the early stages of transformation, is dominated by the specific nature of the transference-countertransference process. Consequently, the failure to relate to the narcissistic character through an understanding of this process and especially the objective nature of the countertransference, frequently results in a failure to constellate a healing process. (ibid., p. 25)

This means avoiding working with amplification and, above all, *not* using the model of mutuality and equality that Jung proposed because:

> [the] encounter between two individuals giving expression to the unconscious is often appropriate when the interacting individuals are capable of somewhat equal participation. But in the narcissistic character disorders this is precisely not the case, a situation often blurred by the seeming authority of the patient. (ibid.)

The two important points from what Schwartz-Salant has said are: concentration on transference-countertransference, not amplification, and suspension of the mutuality/equality model. Does this mean that Schwartz-Salant has become an ID practitioner?

Schwartz-Salant depicts narcissism as a disorder of the self and as an attempt to function in a new way. For instance, the various features of an archetypal figure such as Mercurius (or Hermes) suggest both the negative and positive aspects of narcissism and its connection to creativity (ibid., pp. 36-7). Mercurius, according to Jung, encompasses a whole series of psychic roles, ranging from trickster, thief, cheat and rapist to messenger of the Gods, and hence guide of souls. Hermes suggests both an archetypal base for narcissistic disorder and a positive connotation for it. Schwartz-Salant underscores Jung's contention that the self wants to live its 'experiment in life' and if this does not happen the self will manifest negatively; this is what is happening in narcissism.

But in contrast to ID writers on narcissism such as Ledermann (1979, 1981, 1982) Schwartz-Salant offers a historical, cultural perspective on narcissism because this 'broadens the easily myopic view that clinical approaches can yield' (1982, p. 105). This leads Schwartz-Salant to assert that there is bound to be a positive, spiritual emphasis in both the aetiology of narcissistic disorder and in its treatment.

Do these statements mean that Schwartz-Salant is still, in fact, a CSS practitioner? Or, taking his work as a whole, is he a medial practitioner? If we compare his work to Ledermann's, we see that both regard empathy as vital in treatment and as having been missing in the real infancy of the patient. A difference is that, though both practitioners postulate a 'pre-analysis' stage, there is a less radical switch in Ledermann's treatment methodology when the first stage of analysis is concluded, leaving a viable ego in the patient with which to work (Ledermann, 1982, p. 311). Although Ledermann does state that the normal analytical work of interpretation can then commence, this is a less sharp delineation than that which Schwartz-Salant makes between *his* first stage of analysis and the second stage. Then the phenomenology of the self with its creative self-regulating function is apprehended through the usual CSS approaches, using the symbolism of mythology.

I am sure that Schwartz-Salant would not consider analysis as a process in which the infantile 'stuff' is first 'dealt with' by 'transference' before the real McCoy of the archetypes is reached. But there is an impression of a more recognisable continuity of style in the work of an overtly ID analyst of the Developmental School such as Ledermann. Perhaps post-Jungians like Schwartz-Salant (and Davidson) are bound to appear less of a piece than more extreme practitioners. And perhaps this is their strength – the capacity to be more flexible, and with a wider range of patients than is the norm.

I mentioned that Schwartz-Salant resumes the use of amplification using mythological material when the patient is ready for this. The question of the relevance of myth to our understanding of infancy and childhood is an interesting one – the *Oedipus* complex, the problem of *Narcissus*; what do we mean by evoking such myths?

I do not think that any analytical psychologists still claim that myth reveals how a child's mind functions (i.e. children do not have minds full of mythological material). The contemporary emphasis is upon myth as expressive in a metaphorical way of something to do with typical patterns of emotional behaviour throughout life. We know that studying 'typical' patterns is difficult because the observer is also immersed in what is being studied; the myth offers a respite from subjectivity, a chance to stand back from experience and foster ideas. And at the same time, the myth may be a culvert to emotional experience. That is why I have constantly equated the study of myths and the empirical observation of infant and mother behaviour. Both may be designated 'objective' enterprises that encompass emotional activity.

It may be said that myth, when borne in mind, saves us from a too-literal approach (what Schwartz-Salant calls 'clinical myopia') and connects us to the imaginal. The danger is that, as Giegerich says of Neumann's work, myths may also be taken over-literally and as concrete, thus 'literalising the imaginal' (Giegerich, 1975, p. 128).

If we plough these reflections back into our discussion about mediality, I think that we must conclude that this does exist and that, for some analytical psychologists, what radiates from their work is a desire to bridge the divide that has grown up between the classical-symbolic-synthetic approach and that of interactional dialectic.

FURTHER DISCUSSION ON PSYCHOPATHOLOGY

I would like to single out two other clinical syndromes in addition to narcissistic disorder. These are psychosis and the *puer aeternus*.

Jung anticipated the work of Laing and his school who detected both cause and meaning in the words and behaviour of psychotic patients. Laing noted Jung's statement that the schizophrenic ceases to be schizophrenic when he meets someone by whom he feels understood (Laing, 1967, p. 165). Jung also commented that, for some psychotics, breakdown may be psychological breakthrough. This also finds echoes in Laing's work. Jung saw psychosis as a movement into the collective unconscious from which a 'normal' person is separated and protected by ego-consciousness. He would therefore agree with Laing that psychosis is a frustrated form of a potentially natural process and that such psychosis may be an 'initiation', 'ceremonial' or 'journey' (Laing, 1967, p. 136). It would be interesting to know what Jung would have made of the modern concept of a 'schizophrenogenic family'. His idea that a family member can 'carry' psychological conflicts for other family members tends in this direction.

Post-Jungian work has concentrated on the developmental aspects of psychosis (e.g. Redfearn, 1978) or an attempt to codify and organise typical psychotic material (e.g., Perry, 1962).

The other specific example of psychopathology that I want to mention was named by Jung as the *puer aeternus*, the eternal youth who will not, or cannot, grow up. This idea has been developed by von Franz (1970) to refer to a general immaturity, characterised by a lack of being grounded and an inability to make any personal or other commitments; the *puer* lives what has been called a 'provisional life'. The puer (and there are *puella*s too) may express his lack of rootedness either in excessive spirituality and a head-in-the-clouds attitude, or, conversely, in daredevil risk-taking in dangerous sports or in war. His lack of reality sense blinds him to danger. The *puer*'s problem, in von Franz's view, stems from an attachment to the mother and a failure to separate from her and hence make any other commitment. As Mattoon (1981,

p. 99) notes, such a person may get away with this style of life until middle age when an acute emptiness and loneliness may be experienced. The *puer aeternus* syndrome bears a resemblance to certain psychoanalytic descriptions of the schizoid personality (e.g. Guntrip, 1961).

Jung stated that the remedy for the *puer* was work; von Franz adds to this the need to strengthen ego-consciousness. Sometimes the routine of analysis, felt as boring or insufficiently elevated, becomes an important feature in the *puer*'s or *puella*'s coming to terms with living in the present (cf. Samuels, 1980a, pp. 40-1).

Neither Jung nor von Franz denied that the *puer aeternus* has positive features. Such people are searching for authentic experience of a spiritual nature, their problem is all too easily being satisfied with a bogus and shallow version leading to a dreary, lassitudinous style of life – or to the manic over-activity noted earlier. Hillman's positive assessment of the *puer* is also captured in such statements as: 'the *puer* is not meant to walk but to fly . . . the *puer* captures psyche. . . . It is to the *puer* that psyche succumbs' (1979a, pp. 25-6).

It is the *puer* in them that leads many to choose Jungian analysis, only to find that

> it is analytically tough-minded and mostly devoid of cultic or mystical qualities, that it is not always supportive of lofty spiritual strivings, and that it is usually geared more towards mundane psychological conflicts than toward purely symbolic inward journeys. (M. Stein, 1982, p. xii)

As other Jungian analysts have noted (e.g. Clark, 1978), there is no reason why grounding should damage spirit, though such risk will always be there.

DIFFERENT MODALITIES

Applications of analytical psychology have been made to group therapy, child analysis and marital therapy; the last of these will be examined in the next chapter.

Jung's theory of the self as containing and regulating all the disparate parts of the personality is applicable to group psychology, and the archetypal base of group process and themes has been elaborated (e.g. Hobson, 1959; Whitmont, 1964; Fiumara, 1976).

Jungian child analysis is a separate and thriving field and the spectrum of approaches used may be appreciated in the growing literature (Wickes, 1966; Fordham, 1969a; Kalff, 1980). Very broadly, the classical-symbolic-synthetic versus interactional dialectic debate is also to be found in child analytic discussion. A recent development has been for child analytical psychologists from the different schools of analytical psychology to meet together. A complicating factor in the discussions going on amongst analytical psychologists who work with children is Jung's ambivalent attitude to the psychology of children which was noted in the last chapter.

CURING AND HEALING

It seems appropriate to conclude this chapter with a few words about what makes analysis work and what the goals of analysis are. Gordon proposes a distinction between curing and healing, both of which take place in analysis. The former is concerned with ego development and the integration of the drives and archetypes. Healing, on the other hand, is a 'process in the service of the whole personality towards ever greater and more complex wholeness' (1979, p. 216).

This accent on individuation brings us to a paradox noted by Fordham (1978a) when discussing the criteria for ending an analysis. (By ending is implied a mutual decision by patient and analyst as opposed to unilateral 'stopping'.) Fordham looks for evidence that the patient can live through, and function in, periods when he is *not* in charge of what is happening. So any fantasy that analysis enables the patient to control completely what is happening to him is dispelled and the relativity of the concluding state of analysis is underlined.

Still, this leaves open the part played in analysis by decisions having to do with selection of patients, assessment and diagnosis, for example. The problem here is that, by accentuating the 'chemistry' and empathy between analyst and patient, analytical psychology has restricted its contribution. Analytical psychology has tended to work on a growth model rather than a cure model. Hence, as far as selection of patients is concerned, many have been taken on who might be rejected by classical psychoanalysis (for reasons of age, or because deemed too ill). Latterly, criteria such as ego-strength, depth of damage, motivation, and the favourable or unfavourable impact of the patient's current environment have been taken more into account.

Psychoanalysts, too, ask from whence comes the healing. Paolino gives an utterly conventional definition as to how healing and cure is to be achieved in psychoanalysis: 'a constructive mobilisation of drives . . . a more adaptive ego function . . . a reduction of intrapsychic conflicts' (1981. p. 87). He then goes on to quote with approval this from another psychoanalyst, Gitelson:

> One of the as yet unsolved problems of psychoanalysis is concerned with the essential nature of psychoanalytic cure. It is not insight; it is not the recall of infantile memories; it is not catharsis or abreaction; it is not in the relation to the analyst. Still, it is all of these in some synthesis which it has not yet been possible to formulate explicitly. Somehow, in a successful analysis the patient matures as a total personality. (quoted in ibid., p. 87)

No wonder that Jung suggested that the words *deo concedente* hovered over an analysis, or that the alchemists used to have an *oratorium* in which to contemplate and pray for success in their work in the *laboratorium* (*CW* 13, para. 482).

7

Gender, sex, marriage

In my teaching work with Jungian, non-Jungian and eclectically oriented trainees, I have found that it is Jung's views on gender and sex that excite the most passionate feelings. Partly this reflects a general cultural interest, but I have become convinced that something more specific is at stake. There is an impression that, locked up in Jung's copious writings on masculinity and femininity, there may lie clues to an understanding of our current conundrum. But, at the same time, I have also detected an immense dissatisfaction – with Jung's concepts and not just some of his expressed attitudes. The tension between anticipation and frustration has been so striking that I almost entitled this chapter 'Jung: feminist or chauvinist?'.

The divergence of opinion extends to sophisticated commentators on Jung's ideas. Maduro and Wheelwright felt that these were well ahead of their time in their positive evaluation of femininity, and that Jung had anticipated contemporary interests (Maduro and Wheelwright, 1977). Goldenberg, on the other hand, calls for a 'feminist critique to examine the inequity of [Jung's] basic model' (Goldenberg, 1976, p. 445).

In a nutshell, my argument will be that Jung's formulations of Logos and Eros and animus and anima can be stripped of their connections, not only to *sex*, but also to *gender*. That done, we are left with superb tools for an approach to *psyche*. And, moreover, such an endeavour finds its own links with present-day psychoanalysis.

TERMS

Before embarking on any serious discussion, definition will be helpful. Because Jung never specifically made the distinction, he was often unaware that at times he was speaking of sex and sex differences (male and female) and at other times of gender differences (masculine and feminine). More recently, Stoller, in his seminal psychoanalytic work *Sex and Gender* (1968) has suggested that we restrict the term *sex* to biology: chromosomes, genitalia, hormones and secondary sexual characteristics. Stoller notes that 'one's sex is determined by an algebraic sum of all these qualities and most people fall under one of two separate bell curves, the one of which is called "male", the other "female" ' (ibid., p. 9). *Gender*, on the other hand, is a cultural or psychological term, referring to the quantity of masculinity or femininity found in a person and, adds Stoller, 'while there are mixtures of both in many humans, the normal male has a preponderance of masculinity and the normal female a preponderance of femininity' (ibid., pp. 9-10).

Stoller then introduces two further terms: *gender identity* and *gender role*. The former refers to an awareness of which sex one belongs to and, more importantly, to the personal and cultural aspects of that awareness. Thus one may sense himself as a 'masculine man' or an 'effiminate man', or dispute with some feeling what society expects of women. This leads us to the second term – gender role. This refers to overt behaviour in society, especially in relation to others and, crucially, includes the individual's *evaluation* of his gender.

The problem with this neat division into sex and gender is that gender behaviour (conceived by Stoller as mainly *learned* from the time of birth onwards) plays a vital part in sexual behaviour which is, of course, markedly biological. Further, it is possible to observe the extent to which gender behaviour may be influenced by changes in sexual composition; for example, after castration. There may even be distinct behavioural differences at birth between boys and girls; for instance, boys have been said to be more restless before feeding but become calmer more readily whereas girls display the opposite behaviour. But, to put the counter-argument, Stoller suggests that some of this may be due to learning which commences immediately after birth. Mother-infant interaction may be affected by the mother's emotional attitude to the sex of her baby as well, and this leads to differences both in handling and in expectation.

Stoller's synthesis has two conclusions. First, that there is a biological substrate to gendered behaviour, though it is hard to define this precisely. Second, because sexual relations include 'the most intense of human communications' we need to look at what happens between people and, even more, at what happens inside a person – what 'neuroses, fantasies, and wishes are stirred up in the individual' (ibid., p. 16), and this, according to Stoller, leads inevitably to a turning to psychology as 'an essential *methodology* in our understanding of sexuality' (ibid., p. 16, emphasis added).

By now it is apparent that debate concerning sex and gender revolves around notions of what is innate and what is encultured. When we discuss sex and gender we will find ourselves in the footsteps of Freud who, as Gallop summarised, developed a concept of sexuality that is not 'inscribed within the bounds of actual interpersonal relations' (1982, p. 2). In other words, though marriage and personal relations may be discussed, the field is first one of *identity and internal balance* and only secondarily about man and woman in relationship.

A further consideration is the extent to which the early experiences of the individual play a part in his or her subsequent gender identity. In this connection, we may ask if there are any general observations to be made about possible differences between male and female development. For instance, a boy does not have to switch his love object as he moves from two-person to three-person relating; the feeding mother and the oedipal mother are the same person. In Western culture, a girl will have to make a switch. Different problems are presented to a boy in developing his gender identity from those presented to a girl. The relationship of a boy to his mother makes a feminine identification a distinct possibility, and one to be overcome; a girl does not have to surmount her relationship to her mother in the same way to achieve femininity. But the more established notion that the boy has this difficulty in his relationship with his mother should be looked at alongside a claim from femininist psychoanalysis that, precisely because they are of the same sex, a girl and her mother also have special problems.

In their book on women's psychology, the founders of the London Women's Therapy Centre argue that the ego development of a woman is shaped within the mother-daughter relationship. This is affected by females being 'second-class citizens within patriarchal culture' and alongside the fact that

all mothers learned from their mothers about their place in the world. In each woman's experience is the memory – buried or active – of the struggles she had with her mother in the process of becoming a woman, of learning to curb her activities and to direct her interests in particular ways. (Eichenbaum and Orbach, 1982, p. 31)

We might also add to this the possibility that sameness may fuel envy between mother and daughter in a way that gives the former an unconscious motive to limit the scope of the latter who, in her turn, may be driven to go beyond her mother.

Taking this feminist psychoanalytic view further, Chodorow asserts that

the greater length and different nature of their pre-oedipal experience, and their continuing preoccupation with the issues of this period, means that women's sense of self is continuous with others and that they retain capacities for primary identification both of which enable them to experience the empathy and lack of reality sense needed by a cared-for infant. In men, these qualities have been curtailed, both because they are early treated as an opposite by their mother and because their later attachment to her must be repressed. (Chodorow, 1978, p. 26)

Jung's perspective on the mother-daughter relationship emphasised that fighting with the father may well not be destructive for the girl, but that the daughter who fights with her mother may 'injure her instincts' because 'in repudiating the mother she repudiates all that is obscure, instinctive, ambiguous, and unconscious in her own nature' (*CW* 9i, para. 186).

That we can think at all of possible differences between the boy's and the girl's development points up the part played by heterosexuality. The special dynamics mooted above are based on the prevalence of otherness or sameness in sex relationships. But we also need to question whether heterosexuality itself should be taken as innate and therefore as something fundamental and beyond debate, or whether it, too, has a cultural dimension. I am thinking of Freud's perception of an innate *bisexuality* followed later by heterosexuality. Jung's view was that man and woman are each incomplete without the other:

heterosexuality is therefore a given. In this sense he differs from Freud's emphasis on bisexuality as the natural state of mankind (though see below, p. 223). In Freud's approach, sexual identity arises from the enforced twin demands of reproduction and society. However, Jung's belief that what we have come to call the 'masculine' and the 'feminine' co-exist in a complementary relationship in the psyche is the psychological extension and application of bisexuality.

The cultural institution which reflects heterosexuality most clearly is marriage. In Western societies this is coupled with the nuclear family. Whether this pattern is universal or local is a matter for debate. Mead's material on cultural variation must be weighed together with new evidence that the nuclear family has a far longer history and is more widespread than had been previously thought (Mead, 1949; Macfarlane 1978; Mount, 1982).

Taking all these factors into consideration, it seems that males and females do have early experiences that differ, perhaps markedly. But it is a huge step from that to a claim that they actually *function* quite differently psychologically. The scientific evidence concerning this is confused and difficult to assess (pp. 220ff., below). For instance, observations that boys build towers and girls enclosures when they are given bricks can be taken to show a similarity of functioning rather than difference (which is what is usually claimed). Both sexes are interested in their bodies and, possibly, in the differences between male and female anatomies. Both sexes express that interest in a similar way – symbolically, in play with bricks. Or, put another way, both sexes approach the differences between the sexes in a similar way. Differences in gender role and gender identity can then be looked at as having arisen in the same way. The psychological processes by which a male becomes an aggressive businessman and the female a nurturing housewife are the same and one should not be deceived by the dissimilarity in the end product. A recent summary of the available experimental evidence strongly supports the 'similarity' argument, bringing out the enormous influence of the cultural factor (Nicholson, 1984).

MASCULINE AND FEMININE PSYCHOLOGY

Jung refers to the existence of two quite different and archetypally determined principles of psychological functioning. The masculine principle he terms Logos ('the word', hence rationality, logic, intellect, achievement), and the feminine principle Eros (originally Psyche's lover, hence relatedness). His aim may have been to underline the need for both these principles to exist in harmony within an individual. But the lines of his theory tend to be clouded by the gender terminology. It is important to see that Jung was speaking in symbolic terms of psychological factors that are independent of anatomical sex. Logos and Eros exist within a person of either sex. The balance and relation between the two separate principles regulates the individual's sense of himself as a sexed *and* as a gendered being, his sense of wholeness and completion: 'it is the function of Eros to unite what Logos has sundered' (*CW* 10, para. 275).

Eros and Logos are 'intuitive concepts' (*CW* 9ii, para. 29) which 'mark out a field of experience which it is difficult to define' (*CW* 14, para. 224). Jung speaks of a man possibly having a 'finely differentiated Eros' (*CW* 9i, para. 164) or a 'poorly developed Eros' (*CW* 9ii, para. 37) or a 'passive Eros' (*CW* 9ii, para. 20). A woman may have an 'overdeveloped Eros' (*CW* 9i, para. 168) or require Logos (*CW* 9ii, para. 33). Even Yahweh may be described as having 'no Eros' (*CW* 11, para. 621).

But sometimes Jung's claim seems to be that Eros and Logos are not only measurable and quantifiable but also inhabit, as it were, real men and women:

> The concept of Eros could be expressed in modern terms as psychic relatedness, and that of Logos as object interest.... A man is usually satisfied with 'logic' alone. Everything 'psychic', 'unconscious', etc., is repugnant to him; he considers it vague, nebulous, and morbid.... To a woman it is generally more important to know how a man feels about a thing that to know the thing itself. (*CW* 10, paras 255, 258)

What are we to make of this discrepancy? Although, as Mattoon suggests, Jung is trying to describe 'values rather than behaviours' (1981, p. 101), he sometimes manages to give a quite different impression. Jung's basic perception was that there is a fundamental dichotomy in humankind, human culture and psychology – and 'Logos' and 'Eros' express this. Eros and Logos are equally valuable – there is no suggestion of otherwise in Jung's writings. But when he attempts to attach gender to these two principles he invites confusion and prejudice.

Consider: Logos implies active, assertive, intellectual, penetrative, objective interest; Eros implies passive, submissive, emotional, receptive, psychic relatedness. But there are many other ways of denoting this basic dichotomy, and none of these involve questions of gender at all: Apollonian-Dionysian, Classical-Romantic, secondary and primary process, digital and analogic thinking. Yang and Yin may be the exception that proves the rule (they come already gendered) and were in any case one basis for Jung's putting forward any notion of gender as innate in the first instance.

Rossi (1977) suggested that this general dichotomy reflects and stems from differences between right and left hemispheric brain functioning; however, as both sexes have both hemispheres, the question still remains: why bring in gender at all? If we are talking about *reproduction* then the divide is appropriately expressed in terms of men and women – otherwise, all we can conclude is that there is some kind of basic division or difference within us.

It may be objected that, because the traditional cultural split between masculine and feminine does follow the Logos-Eros pattern, it is reasonable to assign gender to each member of the pairs I have mentioned. However, customary usages have a way of becoming definitions and, even if Jung's doubts about women who think fit some, there are, of course, numerous women who hold emotion and intellect in balance.

But what if we choose to emphasise Jung's vision of Eros and Logos as complementary, available to both sexes and constructive only in partnership? On this reading, Jung, writing in 1927, seems almost to be a modern feminist, for his position is that all qualities and abilities are available and that it is the blend that is crucial. To reach this conclusion, it is necessary to see that Jung, in common with many others, has chosen (perhaps unconsciously) to represent the basic dichotomy in human psychological functioning *in a symbolic form* – man and woman.

ANIMUS AND ANIMA

Traditionally, Jung's theory of animus and anima has been expounded to non-Jungians in terms of the 'biological fact that . . . the smaller number of contrasexual genes seems to produce a corresponding contrasexual character, which usually remains unconscious' (Jaffé in Jung, 1963, p. 410). In over-simple form, this may tempt some to behave as if men and women really were inside them. But Jung's use of animus and anima can be better understood by regarding them as archetypal structures or capacities. In that sense, anima and animus promote images which represent an innate aspect of men and women – that aspect of them which is somehow different to how they function consciously; something *other*, strange, perhaps mysterious, but certainly full of possibilities and potentials. But why the 'contrasexual' emphasis? This is because a man will, quite naturally, image what is 'other' to him in the symbolic form of a woman – a being with an-other anatomy. A woman will symbolise what is foreign or mysterious to her in terms of the kind of body she does not herself have. The contrasexuality is truly something 'contrapsychological'; sexuality is a metaphor for this.

This explains why animus and anima become personified easily so that an imaginary figure forms. When such a figure is encountered in dream or fantasy he or she can be interpreted as representative of alternative modes of perception and behaviour and as differing value systems. For example, animus has been linked to focused consciousness and respect for facts, anima to imagination, fantasy, play. The crucial issue is that these are images of general principles which pertain to all humans and, if unavailable to a person for the moment, this is on individual and not sexual grounds. Perhaps the penumbra of gender associations to animus and anima is by now unavoidable and, since this is also undesirable, it would be better to talk simply in terms of 'focused consciousness', or 'fantasy', or whatever qualities we wish to examine.

To carry out this function of portraying alternatives, anima and animus figures often act as guides or sources of wisdom and information. They help a person on his or her journey (a common dream theme). When Jung met with this phenomenon at a time of maximum stress in his personal life following the break with Freud, he termed such a figure a 'soul-guide' or 'psychopomp', destined to play a vital role in analysis in connecting the person as he or she is (ego) with what he or she may become (self). He described his dialogues with the female figures encountered in his own psyche in his autobiography (1963). Later he felt he recognised the same pattern in women, but because the figures were male he gave them the general name of animus (from the Latin for 'mind' or 'intellect'); this in contrast to the man's anima (from the Latin for 'soul' or 'breath' as in 'breath of life').

Animus and anima often appear in projection on to a real man or woman; here they may spark attraction between the sexes for they carry the seed of an understanding of, or communication with, the opposite sex. Via projection, man and woman recognise and are attracted to each other. As archetypal structures, animus and anima precede and condition experience. This leads to an interesting problem: the extent to which animus and anima archetypal structures influence our earliest perceptions of father and mother via projection of certain qualities (hypothetically innate) on to the real parents. Or the reverse – the extent to which father and mother give shape and tone to the individaul's nascent animus or anima. Jung was careful to distinguish 'anima' from 'mother' (e.g.. *CW* 9ii, para. 26) but we shall see in our later discussion of marital problems that this is easier to do in theory than in practice (pp. 224ff., below).

Projection is of the utmost importance to the life of animus and anima. Jung anticipated this as normal and healthy up to a point, and it is certainly pathological if no projection of animus or anima takes place at all. In 1921 Jung regarded this as one explanation of narcissism – in the absence of projection, all psychic energy is caught up in the subject (*CW* 6, para. 810).

But projection of animus and anima involves more than a facilitation of heterosexuality. Projection of what is contrasexual is a projection of unconscious potential: 'soul-image'. Thus the woman may first see or experience in the man parts of herself of which she is not yet conscious and yet which she needs. The man draws her soul (willingly) out of her. And the reverse will apply for a man. Jung's use of the word 'soul' is in contradistinction to the persona, which is conceived of as less deep or personality enriching. He speaks of soul as an 'inner personality', the true centre of the individual.

The last two paragraphs stress the positive side of projection. However, excessive projection is problematic and the recipient may not be able to flesh out the idealised projection, with resultant disappointment and emergence of negative feelings when love at first sight crumbles into an awareness that the other partner has feet of clay. Jung comments that one should try to find a midway position between insensate projection and no projection at all (see section on marriage, below).

The fact that animus and anima act as a channel or avenue of communication between ego and unconscious can lead to a person's projecting his shadow via his animus or anima, and hence experiencing in a partner that which he most fears and despises in himself. A further psychopathological possibility is that the ego may be overwhelmed by animus or anima, leading to a state of possession. Identification with one's anima or animus often exhibits in behaviour as a stereotypical portrayal of the supposed deficiencies of the opposite sex. A man will become moody, irrational, lazy, effeminate; a woman over-assertive, disputational, obsessed by facts, literalness and insistence upon what is correct. An animus-possessed woman can be described as 'a poor edition of a man' and vice versa.

Funnily enough, the student 'howler' in which everyone is stated to have an animus *and* an anima may turn out to be exceedingly useful. If we go back to the earlier example, every person may be said to possess enough focused consciousness or capacity for fantasy to round out whatever imbalance might exist in their personality. In such an approach we would still be making use of

213

Jung's concept of *syzygy* in which animus and anima are linked to give an approximation of wholeness. To talk of the one without the other is fruitless but stating that a combination of focused consciousness with fantasy can be achieved by all still leaves open questions of tension, reconciliation, development of these opposites – but in a pragmatic manner, evacuated of gender-engendered confusion.

Reviewing these differing uses of animus and anima, I am particularly struck by the way in which the actual sexual relation between men and women is seen psychologically, as enriching psychological processes within the individual. (And this may be one reason why humans need more than simply functional relationships.) The reverse is quite true as well: internal processes promote sex relations. But Jung, it may be argued, has produced a psychological model in which a necessary rectification of concentration on the interpersonal dimension has taken place.

We may also note that a modern reading of animus and anima has somewhat muted the drumbeat of oppositionalism. Animus and anima are ways of communicating otherness, difference, that which is momentarily unavailable because of unconsciousness. Animus and anima speak, then, of the unexpected, of that which is 'out of order', which offends the prevailing order. We shall return to this theme in a closing passage.

Goldenberg is particularly concerned to dispute the symmetry of Jung's theory. The animus theory is much more of an artificial construction, was developed by Jung later and much less well thought out. The parallel is to Freud's introduction of the Elektra complex to balance Oedipus (Goldenberg, 1976, p. 446). Goldenberg suggests that it may well be that, whereas a man (Jung himself?) may urgently need to integrate his unconscious, feminine, soul side, women can live more equably with the divide in themselves perhaps, or heal it without much dialogue with an internal, male figure. Then the symmetry would be broken; a man's struggle with his anima need not necessarily lead us to conclude that all women must struggle in that way with animus.

While Goldenberg's position is logical, the experience of women that they do indeed have to work with something inside – which we might call animus – so parallels that of men that we may assume for the purposes of argument that, if there is an unconscious contrasexual component, it operates in the same way in both sexes.

However, there is little doubt that Jung saw the anima as a more pleasant figure than the animus. In his books anima seems to soften and render a man more full of soul, whereas animus, on the other hand, he more often portrayed as leading a woman into aggressive *ex cathedra* pronouncements, mania for facts, literalness and so on. This prejudice is indeed problematic and has had to be redressed by post-Jungian writers such as Binswanger (1963)

There is a difficulty in reconciling Jung's ideas about Eros and Logos with his theory of anima and animus. Having established that Eros and Logos are available to all, he then emphasises that anima and animus are secondary and unconscious ('inferior', *CW* 10, para. 261):

> since masculine and feminine elements are united in our human nature, a man

can live in the feminine part of himself and a woman in her masculine part. None the less, the feminine element in man is *only something in the background* as is the masculine element in woman. If one lives out the opposite sex in oneself one is living in one's own background, and one's real individuality suffers. A man should live as a man and a woman as a woman. (*CW* 10, para. 243, emphasis added)

There is a danger of overlooking what we know from clinical experience: images of masculinity, once unconscious, abound in the material of men. Similarly, for a woman her femininity is not, as Jung states it to be, a purely conscious concern. Jung has hoist himself on the petard of oppositionalism, in this case between consciousness and the unconscious. Women and men also express an *unconscious* femininity and masculinity respectively.

GENDER AND SEX: JUNG IN CONTEXT

Inevitably, Jung's approach to gender and sex was affected by both his personal situation and the context in which he lived, and also by his whole cast of thought, his *conceptual bias*. Let us examine this conceptual bias first and then look at Jung's cultural bias.

We have observed that Jung envisioned man's psychological make-up in terms of complementary opposites and that, for him, the opposites tend to polarise and form a spectrum. He saw masculine and feminine as psychologically complementary. He extended the oppositional principle even further in the way in which he places gender in a map of psychic structure. Specifically, this extension or application of the oppositional principle involved visualising animus or anima as occupying the opposite place in relation to ego to that taken by persona. Animus and anima mediate between the ego and the inner world, whereas persona mediates between the ego and the outer world (*CW* 6, para. 804). Moreover, unconscious gender potential is seen by Jung as the opposite of gender limited to sex, and different from that laid down by the culture. The effect of this is to over-compartmentalise the relation between what is internal (unconscious) and what is outer (conscious).

In mentioning Jung's *cultural bias* I include the conscious or unconscious influence on his theory exercised by his personal attitudes to men and women, sex and gender. He himself asks:

What can a man say about a woman, his own opposite? I mean of course something sensible, that is outside the sexual programme, free of resentment, illusion, and theory. Where is the man to be found capable of superiority? Woman always stands just where the man's shadow falls, so that he is only too liable to confuse the two. (*CW* 10, para. 236)

But Jung does not seem to have been as aware of how much he also reflected the cultural consciousness, including the general prejudices of his time, his views often being no different from those of any other Swiss burgher. He seemed surprised and concerned that women should think rather than feel, work rather than mother – and even, or so it has been rumoured, wear trousers rather than skirts. And in his marriage Jung seems to have applied the conventional double standard regarding sexual licence. To understand Jung's viewpoint it is essential to keep the context in mind.

Sometimes Jung's cultural bias affects his conceptual formulations. For instance, in his general description of the various psychological types, Jung claims that introverted feeling is mainly to be found among women. He asserts that the catchphrase here should be 'still waters run deep' (*CW*, 6, paras 640-1). We are presented with a stereotype, caricature even, of the woman who really has got lots of good qualities but does not dare to reveal them.

Even in later writers – and there have been many books on feminine psychology by women analysts including Jung's wife (E. Jung, 1957) – we find considerable conservatism. For example, Harding, discussing the question of women and work, suggests that only by being more masculine can a woman work and that even this should not interfere too much with the 'life of wife and mother which would fulfill her feminine and biological needs' (1933, pp. 70-1, but republished in the author's lifetime in 1970). The one exception Harding makes is when the woman's job is to pay for her husband's training! To be fair to Harding, she writes about the tension many women feel nowadays between home and work – but her adherence to her understanding of Jungian principle sounds unsympathetic to present-day ears.

Another example of Jung's cultural bias may be found in his insistence that men and women view relationships, and especially marriage, quite differently. According to Jung, 'a man thinks he possesses a woman if he has her sexually'; but for a woman the quality of relatedness is completely different. For her, 'marriage is a relationship with sex thrown in as an accompaniment' (*CW* 10, para. 255). There is no need to labour further the point that generalisations like these reflect a particular personal and historical context and, whilst possibly true for some, should not be taken as absolute statements.

I am not alone in having been struck by the discrepancies between these attitudes of Jung's (and of his close followers) on the one hand and, on the other, the life in Zürich between the wars. In the sub-culture of analytical psychology, at least, the city was home to several high-achieving women analysts. These women, often without children or husbands, do not appear to have felt any anxiety or conflict between their career orientation and what they had to say about being feminine.

Perhaps excepting where marriage problems are being discussed in terms of *interaction* between man and woman, Jung's statements should not be taken as literal or applicable to behaviour but rather to one of a number of intrapsychic psychological perspectives. This is a distinction which Jung himself fails to make, however, and we are faced with a theoretical confusion between the outer world of men and women and the inner world of psychological imagery. While there is a link between these, Jung's repeated shifting of viewpoints is not deliberate and hence confusing.

In my view, what is now needed is restriction in the use of the oppositional theory and clarification of gender terminology. The latter should be used only when absolutely necessary and warranted by the subject under discussion. For example, if differing expectations of active and passive behaviour in the sex act are being discussed or fantasised about, then both sex and gender terminology

216

are relevant. But much active and passive behaviour has nothing to do with sex or gender. Active and passive define a spectrum of psychological possibilities around *activity and passivity* – nothing more.

These arguments do not do away with the need to distinguish men from women and, for an infant, to discriminate father from mother. Coping with the fact of a division into two sexes is important, not only for external reality testing, but also as a first approach to reconciling internal psychological diversity and conflict.

In summary, questions in regard to animus/anima, Logos/Eros, may be expressed as follows:
(1) whether there can be absolute definitions of masculine and feminine, or that gender terms can be as widely applied as in Jung's perspective;
(2) even if there were something absolutely masculine or absolutely feminine, it is not necessarily the case that men have more of the former, women of the latter;
(3) not all of what seems to be masculine is to be found in the consciousness of a man; not all of what seems to be feminine is available to the consciousness of a woman. We have to speak in terms of multifarious potentials that are not yet available.

THE SEARCH FOR THE FEMININE

In the preceding passages I have been discussing the relationship of gender to psyche. Jung's idea that gender has its archetypal component (Eros and Logos) has been examined in detail by several post-Jungian writers, most of them women. From a historical perspective, there seem to be three broad groupings.

The *first* grouping continues to explore Jung's dictum that Eros implies 'psychic relatedness'. Apart from Emma Jung and Harding, who have already been mentioned, this group includes Wolff and Claremont de Castillejo (1973). Wolff wrote a short paper entitled 'Structural forms of the feminine psyche' (1951) which had vogue among Classical analytical psychologists. In this paper she identified four forms, naming them: mother, hetaira (or companion), amazon, and medial woman. All express relatedness to men, or at least to others – the mother to her child or husband, the hetaira to her consort, the amazon the world of work and objective, external goals. The amazon is not psychologically involved with or dependent on a man, though she may come to resemble one, at least as it is expressed in the culture of Wolff's time. The medial woman acts as a bridge between personal and collective forces, modulating the dynamic between consciousness and the unconscious. She senses what is 'on' at any moment and communicates it. As such, she is a personification of (a man's) anima.

Wolff's paper is primarily an analysis of interpersonal relations, of relatedness outwards and to others – to husband, children, objective goals. This is true even for the medial women whose modulation of the dynamic between consciousness and the unconscious is for the benefit and protection of the former.

Further, as Mattoon has pointed out (1981, p. 90), Wolff is really writing about the *female* psyche (i.e. a woman's psyche) because men are simply not under consideration. Although Whitmont has attempted a parallel classification for men (1969), the confusion between sex and gender remains.

Wolff does not say that her categories are mutually exclusive but that, as in typology, one may speak of a superior or an auxiliary form (and presumably an inferior form, the most troublesome because most unconscious). Thus her model does contain the possibility of movement and change.

The *second* grouping of post-Jungians who have written about feminine psychology have moved away from a position in which woman is viewed as one who 'relates' and they look at her, as she is, in her own right (Woodman, 1980; Perera, 1981; Ulanov, 1981). These writers explore what it means, and has meant historically, to be a woman. They feel this has been neglected in a 'patriarchal' psychology.

Here I must question whether the basic thesis of the work is flawed; whether there is not too great an emphasis on the *innately* feminine with the consequence that 'the feminine' is idealised. For instance, although such a concept as a 'primal feminine energy pattern' is surely an *internal* hypothesis (and hence pertains to men and women), Perera suggests we consider the 'implication for modern *women*' (1981, p. 94, emphasis addd). However, there is no doubt that something which may be termed 'feminine' has been both repressed and undervalued in Western culture and that something is happening to redress the balance (see pp. 228-9, below).

Sometimes these modern Jungian women who write on the feminine are at pains to differentiate themselves from political feminism. For example, Woodman states that:

> The powerful Feminist Movements in the West are demanding recognition, but too often their approach is a mere parody of masculinity. Many thousands of women are taking up arms against patriarchal dominance; many others rejoice in the new rights for women which governments are being forced to recognise. Many others feel lost. They are appalled by the aggression of the militant Feminist leaders, but they recognise some profound emptiness in themselves. They try to be good wives and good mothers and good career women. But something is missing. They do not know how to be true to their own femininity. (1980, p. 103)

To call a *third* grouping 'feminist' over-simplifies their position. Nevertheless, these post-Jungians are expressing views compatible with contemporary feminism. We saw that Jung did allow for Eros and Logos in both men and women but lost sight of this in certain statements. This facet of his theory has been taken up by these writers. A fundamental psychological bisexuality is proposed – not just as a starting point but also as a goal. For example, in her book *Androgyny* (1977), Singer writes of a '*conscious* recognition' of the masculine and feminine potential in every individual. She states that this recognition comes about through a struggle to bring masculine and feminine elements into harmony. She prefers the word *androgyny* to bisexuality because this emphasises an innate, primary unity and leaves open the question of later

218

division, whereas bisexuality, as a word, suggests an aggregate of two elements. Singer's vision is of the androgyne as the carrier of a new attitude to gender and sex.

Though Singer may be thought to have overlooked the question of gender differences, she emphasised that polarities do deserve attention; they cannot be wished away. But such differences are to be seen as emanating from one source, *neutral as regards gender*. So, although Goldenberg disagrees with Singer's notion of androgyny, she also calls for general consent that we are in truth discussing a psychic force that is in itself neutral and the same within both males and females:

> It is less important, in my view, whether the basic human drive is labeled 'male' or 'female'; what matters is that the *same* primary impetus in human libido exists for men and women alike. In future work this model might be developed more profitably than the petty anima-animus division of the psyche. (1976, p. 447)

In a similar, though slightly less extreme, vein several writers (e.g. Mattoon, 1981; Moore, 1983) have suggested that animus and anima should not be regarded as two separate archetypes so that we may speak of relating to the anima-animus; and, hence, be able to verbalise more freely the possibility of experiencing or integrating a wide range of options.

IS CONSCIOUSNESS MASCULINE?

In our discussion of ego-consciousness in Chapter 3, (p. 67, above), we noted the connection made by Neumann between consciousness and masculinity (1954). Although Jung never designates consciousness as masculine *per se*, he does make a sharp and somewhat tenuous distinction between masculine and feminine consciousness. To feminine consciousness, Jung grants the realm of the 'infinite nuances of personal relationships which usually escape the man entirely.' But to the man he grants the 'wide fields of commerce, politics, technology, and science, the whole realm of the applied masculine mind' (*CW* 7, para. 330).

There is a way to understand why consciousness has been traditionally expressed in masculine terms. This has to do with early separation from the mother. Both sexes have to be assertive and adventurous, learn to say 'no', and so on. Mother is female and may come to represent all that is feminine because of the cultural equation female=feminine. It follows that separation from her, and hence ego development, has to be conceived of by the child in terms of that which is opposite to her. This will be as male and, via the working of the same cultural equation, ultimately masculine.

On the other hand, the prevalence of images with masculine bias, said to represent consciousness (hero, sun-god, etc.) may mean nothing more than an equation between what our culture values (consciousness) and a superior group within it (males); the imagery then symbolises the *status quo*.

THE SCIENTIFIC DEBATE

It is with some hesitation that I suggest we examine the scientific evidence available to speak to the question of whether there are innate gender differences just as there are innate sex differences. The hesitation is due to the fact that one is forced to attempt the enormous task of evaluating 'science' at the same time: objective study, or influenced by prevailing social relations and values? As a non-scientist, all I can offer my readers is my understanding of the strands in the debate. I am drawing largely on two books. The first is by a Jungian-oriented psychiatrist, Anthony Stevens, and the book is entitled *Archetype: A Natural History of the Self* (1982). The other book is called *Biological Politics* by Janet Sayers, an academic psychologist (1982).

To give a flavour of the differences of opinion, Stevens clearly thinks that:

> male dominance is a manifestation of the 'psychophysiological reality' of our species. In addition [there is] genetic and neurophysiological evidence relating to the biology of sexual differentiation. . . . Patriarchy, it seems, is the natural condition of mankind. . . . Society, through its representatives the parents, may modify, repress or exaggerate patterns of sexual behaviour and consciousness, but what these influences modify, repress or exaggerate are gender predispositions which are already there. (1982, pp.188-92)

Sayers, on the other hand, has identified the ways in which those opposed to changes in women's social role have 'appropriated' biology for their cause. In addition to presenting an at times devastating attack on the experimentally derived data, Sayers suggests that:

> When one examines these supposedly purely biological accounts of sex roles one finds that they are rooted in appeal to social, not biological, considerations. This is true not only of recent biological analyses of sexual divisions in society but also of the analogous biological explanations of these divisions advanced [in] the nineteenth century. The similarity between earlier and current versions of the thesis that 'biology is women's destiny' is striking. (1982, p. 3)

Stevens draws on the work of Hutt, who observed behavioural differences according to sex from a very early age, and from the sociobiology of Wilson and Goldberg, who attempt to show how our cultural and social organisation is genetically determined in its hierarchy. A typical experiment of Hutt's (quoted in Stevens, p. 181) is to give a toy to both boys and girls. She observed that boys put it to more original and inventive use. Teachers also reported that such ingenuity was linked to disruptiveness in the classroom. Stevens agrees with Hutt's conclusion that 'creativity, assertiveness and divergent thinking are linked masculine characteristics' (ibid.).

These, and other observations of sex differences lead Stevens to conclude that there is a biologically determined complementarity of sex differences and sex roles. He means 'gender' rather than 'sex', for his idea is to bring in biology to substantiate Jung's idea of innate gender qualities. So, for example, the preponderance of men in positions of political power is seen as a 'direct expression of [the male's] biological nature. . . . By contrast, women display a marked lack of enthusiasm for public affairs' (Stevens, 1982, p. 187).

This is surely an example of an incorrect conclusion from data (and one which Sayers would certainly point out). Stevens goes on to add that 'for many years now it has been possible for [women] to enter politics as well as professional and business organisations, but seldom do they reach the pinnacles of power' (ibid.). Stevens appears to assume this is because of lack of interest or some innate deficiency.

Taking the biological approach further, a key area for dispute is provided by the findings that followed administration of large doses of male sex hormones to female foetuses *in utero*. If this happens, a degree of 'masculinisation' is said to occur. This involves increased aggression and other factors (which will be discussed). The argument is apparent: such behaviour is linked to the sex hormone, and hence genetically determined.

Sayer's position, however, is that such data proves very little. For instance, even the sociobiologist Wilson suggests that these changes in behaviour might have been due to the cortisone the girls were receiving after birth rather than to what happened *in utero*. Moreover, the evidence is based on reports by the mothers of the girls who knew of their daughters' medical situation and may have reacted to the presence of male-like genitalia present at birth. However, the 'androgenised' girls were said by Goldberg to demonstrate

a greater interest in a career and a lesser interest in marriage, showed a preference for 'male' toys like guns and little interest in 'female' toys like dolls. (quoted in Sayers, 1982, p. 75)

Sayers is contemptuous of this conclusion. She writes:

Career interest in childhood does not, however, necessarily lead to achievement of upper positions in hierarchies in adulthood. But Goldberg has to assume that it does if he is to use this data on foetally androgenised girls, as he tries to, in support of his thesis that patriarchy is determined by 'male hormonolization'. (ibid., pp. 75-6)

Another example of the way in which the sociobiological case may be countered is shown in Sayers's treatment of Wilson's data regarding differing skills in the sexes. Wilson quoted studies that showed that boys were consistently more able than girls at mathematics but that girls have a higher degree of verbal ability. And boys are, in Wilson's view, more aggressive in social play. From these bases, Wilson concluded that 'even with identical education and equal access to all professions men are likely to continue to play a disproportionate role in political life, business, and science' (quoted in Sayers, 1982, p. 77).

Sayers wryly remarks that it is hard to see how men's lesser verbal ability leads to their being better 'fitted' for political life and to their dominant role there. Surely it should be the other way round if biology really does determine social role. It is also hard, adds Sayers, to see how mathematical skill is linked to political dominance.

An even more fundamental criticism of sociobiology concerns the use of the term 'masculine' in connection with aggression. The basic idea is that, as aggression flows from the male sex hormone testosterone, and as aggression leads to male social dominance, therefore testosterone leads to social dominance. Much of the data on aggression derives from work with monkeys. If injected with male hormones, female monkeys display more 'rough and tumble play', 'aggression' and 'dominance'. But is there a necessary connection between these things and political or occupational life? This is not to say that present-day politics or occupational life is altogether different from the play of injected monkeys, merely that the connection is situational and not scientific.

To sustain the sociobiological viewpoint, female aggression (evidenced by the lioness who hunts and the mother who protects her offspring) has to be overlooked or minimised. What is more, there is a conceptual confusion in sociobiology between the terms 'aggression' and 'dominance'. Not all human (or primate) patterns of dominance depend on aggression. Sayers:

> the biological determinist claim that male dominance is essentially the effect of male aggression . . . collapses. The evidence suggests, rather, that, as in baboon societies, so in human societies male dominance is a learned phenomenon, a response to the material conditions of life; conditions that vary both historically and cross-culturally. (ibid., p. 82)

Perhaps Sayers has in mind the phenomena of altruistic or self-sacrificing behaviour, of conscience, of the checks placed on the power of a leader, or even the voluntary granting of power to a leader at a time of crisis. A leader may acquire *status*, which is not the same as dominance. Finally, there is a potential in humans for collective decision-making.

The reader will have his or her own view of this matter. My purpose in this brief resumé is to show that the subject is not yet clarified. We must recognise that much of the so-called scientific evidence is contaminated by the inadequacy of methodology and pre-existent values on the part of the investigators.

DISCUSSION

What we have been talking about in this chapter is not a relation to an innate masculinity or to an innate femininity or to both. Rather we are talking of a *relation to the phenomenon of difference*. Then we have considered the social or cultural structures erected on the basis of that difference. Each of us lives his life in a relation to such difference. This may lead to questions of gender role (how a woman can best assert herself in our culture, for example) but these will not be couched in terms of innate femininity or masculinity, nor in terms of a masculine-feminine spectrum. Rather they will be expressed in terms of *difference* (in the example, between assertion and compliance).

The problem with this seemingly more flexible approach is that, if one is attempting to describe the entire masculine-feminine spectrum, one has to be sure why terms with sexual or gendered associations are used at all. Otherwise we end up with bland and misleading conclusions (such as that 'masculine' assertion is available to women via their relation to the animus). Again, let us speak merely of assertion.

Singer's 'androgyny', Goldenberg's 'primary impetus in human libido', my 'relation to difference', all take analytical psychology close to contemporary psychoanalysis and its development of Freud's bleak but brilliant insight that infantile sexuality is polymorphously perverse. In fact, though Jung disputed the term 'perverse' (something universal cannot be said to be perverse), his preferred phrase 'polyvalent germinal disposition' expresses the same point.

We may compare the three terms just introduced with the viewpoint of Lacanian psychoanalysis. As Mitchell and Rose (in an introduction to Lacan's work) put it:

> [We are speaking] of adamant rejection of any theory of the difference between the sexes in terms of pre-given male or female entities which complete and satisfy each other. Sexual difference can only be the consequence of a division; without this division it would cease to exist. (1982, p. 6)

Now is the time to play back these ideas into analytical psychology. From Jung's overall theory of opposites we may extract the themes of difference, otherness, division. Perhaps this is the principle on which the debate about sex and gender should be based: not 'opposites' but *definition through difference*. I see this as of the utmost importance and as something which may be extracted from Jung's generalising about gender. If we add to a perception of difference part of an earlier quotation from Jung ('masculine and feminine elements are united in our human nature') we have a workable base from which to proceed (*CW* 10, para. 243).

For Lacan, the question of division and difference is paramount and in his expression this revolves around the phallus as the 'absolute signifier of difference' (1958). The parallel with post-Jungian analytical psychology is expressed vividly in this quote from Mitchell and Rose's work on Lacan:

> All speaking beings must line themselves up on one side of [the] division, but anyone can cross over and inscribe themselves on the opposite side from that to which they are anatomically destined. It is, we could say, an either/or situation. (1982, p. 49)

Each person remains a 'man' or 'woman' but what that *means* becomes relative. The picture is of fluidity within a structure of otherness.

This shifts the concept of bisexuality from being something undifferentiated (polymorphous or polyvalent) into a vision of there being available to all a variety of positions in relation to sex and gender differences and divisions (ibid.). I would add that these positions may stay divided or united – and all the time the issue of 'masculine' and 'feminine' is in suspension. Whatever position is taken may call into being another position; the two may divide the spectrum or remain just two positions on it. Or one position may eliminate the other. One might even combine with another to produce a third, new, position! Such a plurality of possibilities is what Hillman had in mind when he introduced the idea of a 'polytheistic' psychology deriving from, and leading to anima (1971, 1981).

MARRIAGE AS A PSYCHOLOGICAL RELATIONSHIP

Though he often refers to the subject, 'Marriage as a psychological relationship' is the main paper that Jung wrote on marriage (in 1925, *CW* 17). Here we find an application of his ideas about animus and anima to a live, continuous relationship, and also an outline of theory.

Jung commenced by acknowledging that young people of marriageable age are subject to unconscious motivational influences deriving from unresolved unconscious ties to their parents. Here he restates his idea that children suffer from the unlived psychological life of their parents. He also noted that the marriage tie stimulates unconscious regressive propensities in a search for harmony. On the personal level, then, he recognises that there is a regressive infantile element in all marriages.

Because of the connection to reproduction, marriage may also be seen as a collective relationship; we have noted how animus and anima play their part in this. Jung then proceeds to tease out an overall pattern in which he sees men and women as capable of performing interchangeable psychological roles. This has to be said because the English version seems to imply that Jung is giving one specific role to women and another to men. (The translator notes that this is 'due entirely to the exigencies of English grammar, and is not implied in the German text' – *CW* 17, para. 333n).

As Jung perceived it, marriage often involves the partnership of a simpler and a more complicated personality. In marriage the simpler personality is surrounded and encapsulated by the more complex. Thus a relation is set up between what Jung refers to as the 'container' (the more complicated) and the 'contained' (the simpler):

> The one who is contained feels himself to be living entirely within the confines of his marriage; his attitude to the marriage partner is undivided; outside the marriage there exist no essential obligations and no binding interests. (*CW* 17, para. 332)

On the other hand, the container, the more complicated personality, strives to unify or harmonise his or her tremendous psychological dissonance and his multi-faceted nature. He/she cannot do this in relationship with the contained because the latter is too simple to accommodate the former's diversity and complexity. The simpler, contained partner, in his or her turn, asks for simple answers – and it is quite impossible for the container to provide these. Although the contained may seem to be satisfied by the marriage, the problem is dependency on the container with a resultant insecurity. But at least the contained possesses his or her unity.

The container needs a more complicated person to aid in the quest for integration and tends to 'flee from simplicity'. This will lead to feelings of being outside the marriage and ultimately to 'unfaithfulness' (para. 334); as Jung puts it, to a tendency to 'spy out of the window' (para. 333).

The crucial observation that Jung went on to make is that the more complicated container suffers from an unmet need to be contained. It is in search of just that containment that the container moves outside the marriage and 'always plays the problematic role' (para. 333). The more the contained partner demands containment, the less can it be provided for the so-called container – and hence the greater the latter's need to look for unity and harmony elsewhere.

This problematic pattern resolves when the contained sees that he/she must seek solutions in himself/herself, that the container cannot be expected to do everything and that marriage is not the be-all and end-all. The container may have to experience a degree of breakdown before also realising that the integration which is sought lies within.

When I first encountered this model of Jung's I felt that the description could not be universally valid. My current feeling is that this dynamic applies to a great number of marriages but that Jung's somewhat abstract schema needs to be looked at in terms of numerous small-scale, everyday interactions. Then the idea that the one who is apparently doing the containing is in secret search for containment comes to life.

Although Jung is writing about marriage, his model is remarkably useful in examining other relationships such as that between mother and baby and, especially, the relation of individual to group. Jung's thesis may once again be compared with Bion's use of the same terms: Bion also connected the relation of container and contained to the question of transformation, seeing the former as transforming experience for the latter.

What Jung means by 'container' seems to involve setting the emotional tone and pace, dominance and so forth. Thus, this part of his theory is of use in attempting to move beyond cultural oppression of women by understanding that a squashing husband (container) has his own pressing needs to be contained.

Williams (1971), taking the orientation of a marital therapist, argued that Jung's container-contained model is similar to the modern marital therapeutic concept of unconscious collusion, in which the illusions which may have underpinned the original partner choice are protected by the marriage. Williams, using object relations theory, takes Jung's observations somewhat further to encompass the idea of a married couple as prone to be dominated by a shared, single image. This dominant shared image may emanate from the unconscious of one partner (often from the container) or be a jointly produced image. The image, to which both partners relate, may, in a sense, contain the marriage.

Williams is emphatic that the link with infancy is the central one in marital disharmony. Both the mother-infant and the husband-wife relationships involve physical intimacy and the mouth orifice/nipple connection is paralleled by that between vaginal orifice/penis.

Jung's main thesis concerning choice of partner is that people tend to choose one who will activate unfulfilled factors within themselves. Pathologically, this may lead to a marriage with a partner who plays the part of the parent of the opposite sex (para. 328). But, according to Jung, the unconscious impulse to round out the personality leads an individual to be attracted to a display of different characteristics to his own. Two interesting pieces of evidence are relevant here and show that this might not always be the case. An examination of data submitted by applicants to a large computer dating firm shows that the applicant's self-description personality profile and that of their 'ideal' partner are remarkably similar (Wilson and Nias, 1977, pp. 53-6). The other study was of the typology of the spouses of Jungian analysts (Bradway and Wheelwright, 1978). The authors comment:

> The data does not support the contention that we had previously held that one tends to marry one's psychological opposite. Apparently this is not true for a majority of analysts, at least not as they perceive their spouses. (p. 189)

It may be objected that the two groups of computer dating applicants and Jungian analysts are hardly typical (cf. Samuels, 1980a).

Still other evidence suggests that people marry opposites and similars in about equal numbers. Marital success seems to be based on being similar *enough* but not *too* similar (Mattoon, 1981, pp. 217-18).

MARRIAGE AND INDIVIDUATION

In my comment on Jung's paper I noted that he felt that it was necessary for both partners to realise that solutions to problems lay inside them and not in relation to the other. Until relatively recently that was the consensus in analytical psychology. This has led some post-Jungians to complain of a split in the theory of individuation between interpersonal factors and intrapsychic growth. Prominent amongst these dissidents is Guggenbühl-Craig in his book *Marriage – Dead or Alive* (1977).

Guggenbühl-Craig admits that the odds are stacked against marriages working and feels that it does seem absurd at first sight to expect young people to commit themselves for a lifetime which, with modern life expectancy, could easily exceed 50 years. An anti-marriage *Zeitgeist* would, therefore, be expected. Yet marriage, in spite of critiques, is as prevalent today as ever and we know that divorced people tend to remarry. From comparative studies with other cultures we can see that the institution is capable of almost infinite variety of expression or form.

Guggenbühl-Craig points up a crucial distinction in our varying ideologies of marriage – between 'well-being' and 'salvation'. The former approximates to material security, physical health and what might loosely be termed happiness. Salvation, on the other hand, 'involves the question of life's meaning' (ibid., p. 22) and may even contradict well-being. For salvation may involve suffering which cannot be included in the concept of well-being.

With suffering and salvation in mind, Guggenbühl-Craig invokes the question of individuation. As normally developed, there is something missing in 'individuation':

Individuation and soteriological (*i.e., concerned with salvation*) questing seem to be something autistic and self-centred. It seems to happen to individuals as they work on their own souls in the stillness of their private rooms. (ibid., p. 34)

Guggenbühl-Craig's suggestion is that the 'dialectic' (meaning dialogue or communication) in marriage may also be a path of individuation, a 'special path for discovering the soul' (ibid., p. 41). Partners in an *interpersonal* relationship function for each other as the *intrapsychic* opposites to be reconciled in individuation. One is reminded both of Buber and of Zinkin's use of Buber in which we noted how 'dialogue precedes self-awareness' (see p. 81, above). This also ties up with our explication of alchemy and the transference, where the interpersonal and the intrapsychic communicate with one another (see p. 181, above).

Guggenbühl-Craig has taken an intrapsychic conception and extended its use into the interpersonal area. We are offered a paradox: *individuation through adaptation to the other.* This is a Protestant (or even Talmudic) individuation in which a satisfying social accommodation, if achievable, is the greatest good. This involves both partners in a great tolerance of the attributes and behaviour of the other, including what might usually be seen as sexual perversions. Guggenbühl-Craig sees sexuality itself as one special form of individuation:

I would like to emphasise . . . . that sexual life, above all as it shows itself in fantasy, is an intense individuation process in symbols. (ibid., pp. 83-4)

Guggenbühl-Craig is concerned to separate sex from reproduction so that the former may become a mode of self-expression but, and hence the paradox, self-expression involving another person. Gugenbühl-Craig is moved to talk of an 'instinctual individuation' which may come about if both partners in the marriage fully 'confront' each other; only then do they really 'enter' the marriage and experience the enhancement of soul that may be there in potential.

It is difficult to evaluate Guggenbühl-Craig's impassioned book. In one way, he is merely describing what happens already in many marriages. At the present time there is a far greater tolerance within marriage than there used to be and many, possibly after some struggle, have come to terms with the separation of sex from reproduction. The value of the book is that it is a further demonstration that the conventional distinction between interpersonal relatedness and intrapsychic individuation requires examination (see Chapter 11).

A NOTE ON SEXUAL BEHAVIOUR

In much the same way that Jung freely used Freud's insights, post-Jungian analytical psychologists have drawn extensively on psychoanalytic understanding of sexually deviant behaviour. In the Developmental School there has been a favouring of those theories which see such deviancy as stemming from disturbances in the primary mother-infant relationship as opposed to theories stressing the part played by the Oedipus complex in sexual psychopathology. (For instance, *The Forbidden Love* ed. Kraemer, 1976, a series of papers on paedophilia.)

Storr (1957) applied Jungian theory to fetishism and transvestism. In particular, he illustrated the positive, compensatory value of symptoms. I would see a simple example of this in the powerful man, too dependent on his status, who wishes to be humiliated by a prostitute. Genet's play *The Balcony* involves the same idea: the terrorist leader and the police chief play out each other's lives in fantasy in the brothel.

Homosexuality has received little attention in analytical psychology. So far as I know there has never been a suggestion that homosexuality is either a mental illness or biologically determined. Jung saw homosexuality in the man as resulting from over-involvement with the mother. Further, the masculine side of the homosexual man, which is underdeveloped in reality, is experienced in the idealisation of, and fascination by, the penis. Jung has very little to say about female homosexuality, save that there is also over-involvement with the mother. In general, then, his account is somewhat sketchy.

My own approach is that there are two quite different kinds of homosexuality. The first results from an intense narcissistic wound resulting from an oppressively unempathic parent and leading to a search for a partner who will fill the gap in relation to the self. Thus the partner is not experienced as a separate person – which is aided by the anatomical sameness. We might call this narcissistic homosexuality.

Narcissistic homosexuality can be compared with homosexuality of a more Oedipal character and reached by the same *dynamics* as heterosexual sexual identity save, in Anna Freud's words, for 'the influence of excessive love for and dependence on either mother or father or extreme hostility for either of them' (1966), p. 161). The point is that an oedipal account of *heterosexual* sexual identity would also emphasise what is felt and fantasised about the parents.

In general, analytical psychology recognises that it is extremely difficult to say anything definite about sexual behaviour. A considerable amount of analytical work centres on the patient's acceptance that deep feelings for a person of the same sex are not 'homosexual' in any sense that implies a fixed sexual orientation. They are healthy and enriching and arise out of psychological bisexuality. Finally, when we talk about the sexual behaviour of an individual we have also to consider this from the point of view of ego strength and, in particular, take note of the frequency and intensity of anxiety caused for an individual by his sexual impulses.

ANIMA-TION

The cultural changes of our times are focused on gender, sex and marriage. There is what seems to be a new atmosphere and perhaps the social and political struggles of women are part of this. I think we can adapt the idea that animus and anima exist equally for both men and women and say that, increasingly, we live in an anima world, an anima-ted world. If we detach anima from syzygy (where it will always be linked with animus), from persona (where it will always be an 'inferior', unconscious factor), from ego (where it will always be 'employed'), from self (where it will always pale by comparison), then we may have a tool, even a methodology, for understanding our cultural vicissitudes.

Jung was alive to this new atmosphere. He felt that the proclamation by the Pope in 1950 of the dogma of the Assumption of the Blessed Virgin Mary, implying an incorporation of the feminine into the divine, was of immense significance. This development had been brewing for more than a thousand years, was brought about by collective pressures, but the way had been prepared by the alchemists: their symbolic representations of psychological division *and* unity by using male and female figures (*CW* 14, paras 662-8).

Our culture is still patriarchal though, and Jung and his analytical psychology are a part of that patriarchy. Here I am not referring to Jung personally but to ways in which analytical psychology is coloured, structured and controlled by a patriarchal perspective. The essence of patriarchy is having and needing to have things in their places. It is characterised by order, perhaps rank, certainly discipline. Even our use of language buttresses this for we hardly conceive of one element without something in contradistinction. Patriarchy does not like 'diffuse awareness' (Claremont de Castillejo, 1973, p. 15); it does not search for 'wisdom in change' (Perera, 1981, p. 85); it disdains a sense of 'elemental being' (E. Jung, 1957, p. 87); 'moonlike reflection' is not approved of (Hillman, 1972, p. 111). This is *anima*.

8
Dreams

Working with the patient and his dreams plays an important part in Jungian analysis. Jung never organised his ideas about dreams into a general theory but he did give very clear indications of his attitude to dreams and dreaming. Inevitably, some of Jung's concepts are cast in the form of disagreement with Freud. This reflects both an acknowledgment of debt to Freud and the limitations which he found in using Freud's approach.

BASIC PRINCIPLES

Concisely, Jung's main disagreement with Freud was over the question of manifest and latent dream content. Jung did not regard the dream as a potentially deceptive message requiring careful decoding. He wrote:

> *I take the dream for what it is.* The dream is such a difficult and complicated thing that I do not dare to make any assumptions about its possible cunning or its tendency to deceive. The dream is a natural occurrence, and there is no earthly reason why we should assume it is a crafty device to lead us astray. (*CW* 11, para. 41)

Jung looked at dreams and dream content as psychic facts (*CW* 13, para. 54). But against his claim that dreams can be taken as they are, we must set a good deal of work by him on the structure, language and meaning of dreams. It would be a mistake, as Mattoon has pointed out, to think that Jung 'did' less with a patient's dream than Freud (1981, p. 248). He most certainly did interpret dreams but not in terms of what Mattoon defines as 'one-to-one representations', relatively fixed in meaning, and disclosing sexual conflict (ibid.). For Jung, Freud did not work with symbols but rather *signs* which do not, as symbols do, point the way ahead or express a complicated situation in a unique way, but rather refer to something already known (penis, father, mother). A sign is therefore 'always less than the concept it represents, while a symbol always stands for more than its obvious and immediate meaning' (Jung, 1964, p. 41).

I am not sure whether Freud's more evolved method of interpreting dreams was so rigid. Hence, how much should Jung's differentiation from

Freud be seen as serving Jung's own development? For example, there seems substantial evidence that aggression figured as much in Freud's interpretation as as did sexuality (cf. Jung, 1963, pp. 182-3, where Jung records that Freud interpreted a dream of his in terms of a death-wish). On the other hand, post-Freudian psychoanalytic work on dreams does seem to have moved away from Freud's starting point to a position closer to that of Jung (e.g. Rycroft, 1979; Gill, 1982). This would only have happened if something of a rigid attitude had existed in fact. All things considered, then, Jung's approach appears to be quite different from that of Freud.

We might also bear in mind that analytical psychology has had its own problems with fixed interpretation based on a pre-existing symbological lexicon. It is still common, if a man's dream has a woman in it, to hear talk of an 'anima figure' before any real entry into the dream has been achieved. Still, in general terms, analytical psychology has accepted Jung's statement that:

> The dream is a little hidden door in the innermost and most secret recesses of the soul, opening into that cosmic night which was psyche long before there was any ego-consciousness, and which will remain psyche no matter how far our ego-consciousness extends. (*CW* 10, para. 304)

There is a tension between this openness and Jung's technique of 'directed association' (drawing the dreamer's attention to important elements in the dream, in contrast to the free association of Freud's approach).

Against Freud's concept of *wish-fulfilment*, Jung set his own theory of *compensation* to explain the function of dreams. There are two aspects to this. First, Jung states that:

> the dream is a *spontaneous self-portrayal, in symbolic form, of the actual situation in the unconscious*. (*CW* 8, para. 505)

Second:

> The dream rectifies the situation. It contributes the material that was lacking and thereby improves the patient's attitude. That is why we need dream-analysis in our therapy. (*CW* 8, para. 482)
> Every process that goes too far immediately and inevitably calls forth compensations.... The theory of compensation [is] a basic law of psychic behaviour.... When we set out to interpret a dream, it is always helpful to ask: What conscious attitude does it compensate? (*CW* 16, para. 330)

The reader will note the logic of this: if the dream both states the unconscious situation *and* is a compensation (i.e. in some sense opposite) to consciousness, then Jung is saying that the conscious attitude, on the one hand, and the unconscious as expressed in dreams on the other, are always in a complementary relationship. We shall see in a moment how this conclusion, though logically derived from Jung's premises, has been found unacceptable by some post-Jungians (e.g. Dieckmann, Hillman, below).

One requirement arising out of Jung's conscious-unconscious polarity is that it then becomes of paramount importance to have a thorough knowledge of the conscious situation at that moment. The dream is full of 'material which the conscious situation has constellated in the unconscious'. Without knowledge of the personal situation, 'it is impossible to interpret a dream correctly, except by a lucky fluke' (*CW* 8, para. 477). We really need to bear in mind this concern of Jung's for the conscious situation when considering amplification of dreams, and later in the chapter when looking at modifications to Jung's approaches by post-Jungian analytical psychologists.

In addition to his insistence upon the compensatory nature of dreams and dreaming, Jung also thought that his synthetic approach to psychological material such as dreams was more appropriate than Freud's reduction. We saw earlier how the line between synthetic and reductive orientations is rather blurred (see pp. 135ff., above). For now, we may note that Jung agrees that the dream's causes may be taken to be the same by both a synthesist and a reductionist, but the criteria by which they are understood alter. Jung wants to know:

> What is the purpose of this dream? What effect is it meant to have? These questions are not arbitrary inasmuch as they can be applied to every psychic activity. Everywhere the question of the 'why' and the 'wherefore' may be raised, because every organic structure consists of a complicated network of purposive functions, and each of these functions can be resolved into a series of individual facts with a purposive orientation. (*CW* 8, para. 462)

The final area of disagreement with Freud concerns whether dreams are to be seen from a 'subjective' or an 'objective' viewpoint. If the former, then all the elements of the dream are taken as referring to the dreamer or to parts of the dreamer's own psyche (though not necessarily when the image is of an actual person well known to the dreamer). From the objective perspective, figures in the dream are taken to stand, for example, for real people, or aspects of them, in the dreamer's life or from a life situation with which he is confronted. The point is not that Jung adopted a subjective view in preference to an objective one but that he used both – and argued that Freud was limited only to an objective methodology.

THE INTERPRETATION OF DREAMS

Jung felt that dreams have a typical structure and that, by paying attention to the way any particular dream fitted or deviated from this structure, the analyst would become more certain of not missing an important element of the dream. The four divisions in dream structure are: exposition, development, culmination and solution (*CW* 8, paras 560-6).

Exposition includes an indication of place, of the main protagonists, the initial situation, hinting at the questions the dream will raise. *Development* involves a complication of the plot and a 'definite tension develops because one does not know what will happen' (ibid., para. 562). In the *culmination*, something quite definite happens or the situation changes. Not all dreams have a *solution* but this will be a final situation (final in narrative terms that is, because nothing may actually be settled).

We may apply this structure to a dream brought by an anorexic patient, M. Her mother and father separated when she was fifteen months old and her father subsequently rejected her. Her step-father died when she was a teenager. At the time of the dream M. had no boyfriend (and had had no lasting relationship and minimal sexual experience). She was 28 years old and, for apparently good reasons, worked for the same organisation and in the same role as her mother. She had heard me being interviewed on the radio about dreams and had tracked me down, which, as we shall see, may have been important.

I have divided the dream in accordance with Jung's schema:

Exposition: *I am in a hospital for an operation on my hip. A nurse comes in and tells me that a mistake has been made.*
Development: *I have now got cancer because of this mistake.*
Culmination: *I am very upset and angry but I decide not to say or do anything*
Solution: *because I do not want to upset the nurse's feelings.*

Jung's further concern is to work on the dream, both through personal associations and by amplification with archetypal parallels. It is crucial for our subsequent discussions to remember that Jung is concerned with amplification of both these levels:

> always ask the patient how *he* feels about his dream images. For dreams are always about a particular problem of the individual about which he has a wrong conscious judgment. (*CW* 18, para. 123)

and:

> Together the patient and I address ourselves to the 2,000,000-year-old man that is in all of us. In the last analysis, most of our difficulties come from losing contact with our instincts, with the age-old unforgotten wisdom stored up in us. And where do we make contact with this old man in us? In our dreams. (Jung, 1978, p. 100)

I do not think Jung is saying that the archetypal is not personally relevant, but rather that such material does not arise from the dreamer's personal situation. Indeed the task of analysis is to make 'age-old unforgotten wisdom stored up in us' of use in our personal situation.

In M.'s dream described just now, the nurse figure was identified by the patient to 'be' her mother, the cancer the result of their relationship. On a more general level, her further associations included: mistakes made in hospitals, the one-sidedness of modern medicine and possible links between psyche and soma. She did not mention me in connection with the dream at that time.

A Classical Jungian might have gone on to work with metaphors derived from the heritage of the collective unconscious, such as that of the wounded healer, the wound being his fallibility. In fact, because of my knowledge of the patient's history and, above all, some reconstruction of her early sensing of her mother's vulnerability to criticism or protest, I interpreted the dream objectively. Thus the nurse who must not be offended in spite of her professional status symbolised 'mother' rather than the more subjective 'defective inner healer'.

The patient told me in the next session that when she had got home that evening she had experienced an explosion of anger and banged her bed in an intense expression of rage. This was quite uncharacteristic behaviour. I said to her that she had managed (just) to keep this strong feeling out of our session. Did she perhaps also mistrust me? Or feel that I had made mistakes along the line? Not a mistake, she responded, but she did doubt I could help her – and *was worried about saying this and hurting my feelings*. We could then discuss this transference aspect of the dream.

Strangely enough, the interpretation of the dream I thought of but did not make (that the nurse represented a defective inner healer) became more and more relevant. I found myself wanting her to help herself and we looked together at why she could not be active in relation to her problems and at what hidden gain there was for her in helplessness. So, over time, that nurse 'was' her mother, the analyst, a defective inner healer, and even a nurse (see below, p. 239).

Jung stressed that both the dream and the amplifications should be approached without preconceptions:

> The art of interpreting dreams cannot be learnt from books. Methods and rules are good only when we can get along without them. Only the man who can do it anyway has real skill, only the man of understanding really understands. (*CW* 10, para. 153)

But at the same time, 'wide knowledge is required, such as a specialist ought to possess' (ibid.). This knowledge must be 'living' and 'infused with the experience of the person who uses it' (ibid.). If we couple this with Jung's overall attitude to therapeutic interaction we can see that dream interpretation requires the full emotional involvement of the analyst.

It is often important to see whether the dream is part of a series and, if so, how the thematic material has developed or not. In addition, Jung gave considerable importance to initial dreams as presented in analysis. These often summarise the situation, giving, as it were, diagnosis and prognosis. Not all dreams are compensatory; some are oracular or prophetic, and are said by Jung to anticipate future events.

Jung was flexible about there being 'correct' dream interpretation. Although he does use the word, he also seems to have taken his interpretation as a *hypothesis* that needed to be tested out in relation to the whole life of the dreamer and, if necessary, modified. Dream interpretation, for Jung, seems to have been a response to a creative phenomenon in spite of his warnings against the aesthetic approach to psychological material (1963, p. 210).

For those interested in learning more about Classical Jungian approaches to dreams, there are now available comprehensive accounts (Hall, 1977; Mattoon, 1978) but these do not deviate in any marked way from Jung's position. I would like to look at three important modifications to Jung's theses that have been proposed. They are: (a) more stress on the importance of the dream ego, (b) making sure that one analyses the patient and not just the dream, and (c) drawing a quite different distinction from Jung's between the nightworld of dreams and the dayworld of consciousness.

THE IMPORTANCE OF THE DREAM EGO

Dieckmann (1980) wonders if analytical psychology has not over-estimated the differences between dreams and waking experiences. He is reacting, I would think, to views of Jung's such as:

> I would not deny the possibility of *parallel* dreams, i.e., dreams whose meaning coincides with or supports the conscious attitude, but, in my experience at least, these are rather rare. (*CW* 12, para. 48)

Dieckmann points out that the behaviour of the dreamer in the dream (dream ego) is often similar to that when awake. The dream ego tends to deploy the same defences and have the same feelings as the waking ego and, like the waking ego, is seeking to maintain itself, to survive. Dieckmann acknowledges, of course, that dreams convey repressed experience or experience that is new to the ego. But he feels that he has spotted a third way to envision dreams, different from wish-fulfilment and from compensation. In other words, Dieckmann suggests that dreams express what is happening in the dreamer's waking life but, for the moment, not available (perhaps because unpalatable) to the dreamer's waking ego.

The continuity that Dieckmann perceives between the dream and the waking state provides clinical advantages. The patient can talk about his experience in the dream and discover

> recognisable qualities in dreams which were to him unintelligible. On this basis the first bridge of relationship and understanding can be built to dreams. The ego feeling which very clearly occupies the dream ego facilitates this process. (1980, p. 50)

The patient, in this methodology, can move into the inner world by seeing and experiencing *himself* in the strange dream context. This itself brings insight. Dieckmann admits that his approach is an objective one if placed on an objective-subjective spectrum. However, the 'object' is the dreamer himself, the 'subject'.

Let's look at the dream that was reported earlier and examine it from Dieckmann's vantage point. M. did, in her waking life, have enormous difficulty in being angry or even assertive and a huge reservoir of blaming feelings towards her mother had been built up. She was not consciously aware of this, only that she was tending to avoid contact with her mother. She could not let go of these feelings because unconsciously she saw her mother as exposed and vulnerable. She seemed, from our reconstructions of her childhood, always to have done so. In fact, without my knowing it at the time, we used Dieckmann's approach with that dream because there was a consistency between her daily behaviour and her dream behaviour. Compensation did not seem especially relevant to the dream in this instance (though the dream itself did lead to a compensatory *experience* – the angry explosion). I was able to say to her 'Look: how you were in the dream when you had real grounds for complaint and felt angry but could not express it, is how you are in real life. And you do feel you have to defend yourself against your mother's bad mothering of you (giving you cancer) by not feeding from her rather than acknowledging your anger.'

ANALYSING THE PATIENT NOT THE DREAM

The second modification to Jung's basic approach that I want to discuss is Lambert's critique of the Classical Jungian approach to dreams. He is concerned with problems in 'practical handling of patients' dreams by analysts in the daily clinical situation' (1981a, p. 173). Lambert identifies four problems with the Classical approach.

First, if dreams are *elicited* from the patient by asking for them, then the spontaneous flow of material is interrupted and the analyst will hear what he wants rather than what the unconscious of the patient is trying to say.

Second, a consequence of this is that an analyst may become nothing more than an interpreter of dreams and lose sight of the whole person he is working with. The dream, often typed in duplicate, may be, in the Classical approach, laid on a metaphorical table between patient and analyst for a rather detached examination of the dream which avoids the experiencing of deep emotions.

Third, the Classical practitioner may fail to see the introduction of dreams (and also their content, to some extent) as a product of transference-countertransference interaction. The dream may be introduced out of compliance. Knowing analysts like dreams, the patient may feel he *should* produce some. Dreams may also come in such profusion that the analyst will be swamped and overwhelmed. Conversely, the patient may obtain gratification by denying the analyst dreams. Sometimes the patient may tantalise the analyst by bringing scraps of dreams or old dreams or seek to fight the analyst and express negative feelings in the form of a seemingly safe disagreement with the analyst's interpretation.

Fourth, the Classical approach pays insufficient attention to the way in which ordinary psychological mechanisms (e.g. projection, introjection) operate *within* dreams so that, for instance, threatening figures may be manifestations of projected rage on the dreamer's part.

Lambert suggests that analysts should not ask for dreams and should remember that dreams are

one aspect of a wide range of communications on the part of the patient, out of which central or nodal points of meaning can be isolated and interpreted (in other words the patient is being analysed rather than the dream). (1981, p. 186)

Lambert's point is a crucial one but most analytical psychologists are, nowadays, aware of transference-countertransference implications of the introduction of dreams. For instance, Berry refers to how a 'process-orientated analyst' will pay attention to the way the dream is told, whether it is 'properly' presented or not, how active or passive the patient was in relation to interpretation and so forth (1974, pp. 59-70).

Blum (1980) wondered if Lambert may have over-reacted to the Classical emphasis on the primacy of dream and drawn a false distinction between analytical process and dream process. Blum is against seeing any one dream in isolation from other dreams of the patient and I am reminded of what Jung said in relation to a possible accusation that he ignored the dream's context. He felt that a series of dreams was its own context and that, in such a circumstance, personal data was sometimes of lesser importance (*CW* 12, paras 49-50).

The question remains: are dreams special in any way? Lambert does not rule out a special role for dreams, referring to the 'remarkable' way they sum up the dreamer's psychological situation. Nevertheless, Lambert gives the impression of wanting to dethrone the dream as far as analytical practice is concerned and, because of that, may have over-reacted, as Blum suggests. But in noting an unhealthy idealisation of dreams, and the way they can *stop* analysis from taking place, he does pose some awkward questions for the practice of analytical psychology.

If we apply Lambert's points to M.'s dream, we can see that, without my knowledge and reconstruction of her history, I would not have been quite so confident of interpreting 'nurse' as 'mother' rather than as 'defective inner healer'. M. certainly knew of my interest in dreams and it was this that led her to consider working with me. Nevertheless, there was also ample non-dream material.

DAYWORLD AND NIGHTWORLD

The third modification is that of Hillman. He, too, searches for a differing path from 'repression or compensation' (1979a, p. 1). Hillman uses the metaphor of the underworld to suggest that dreams are phenomena that emerge from a precise archetypal location. By stressing the underworld, the nightworld of dreams, as something quite different to the dayworld, Hillman demonstrates that he is not in pursuit of any increase in consciousness *per se*. That, he believes, is the goal of some interpreters, both Freudian and Jungian. Hillman is not concerned to *interpret* the dream, or to translate it, because he sees the dream as having purposes of its own.

Further, Hillman is not trying to bridge the gap between consciousness and unconsciousness:

We must reverse our usual procedure of translating the dream into ego-language and instead translate the ego into dream-language. This means doing a dream-work on the ego, making a metaphor of it, seeing through its 'reality'. (ibid., p. 95)

Hillman wants to avoid any causal rendering of the dream, getting anything moral out of the dream, seeing the dream as having to do with personal life, placing the dream in a temporal mode (looking back or forward), seeing the dream as a guide for action, and, above all, taking the dream literally. Thus:

> The more I dream of my mother and father, brother and sister, son and daughter, the less these actual persons are as I perceive them in my naive and literal naturalism and the more they become psychic inhabitants of the underworld. (ibid., p. 96)

That implies that 'right' interpretation is not achievable; instead we must have a plural, multiple approach. But there does seem to be a contradiction here. Plural and multiple *what?* In the end, though doubtless in a unique way, Hillman does make use of interpretation. But his vision of 'interpretation' is more of a *deepening* than a translation into 'surface reality'. Hillman is trying, through dream, to reach the archetypal layers of the psyche. So we may reflect, contemplate, play with the images and metaphors of the dream and see where they lead.

Where they lead, in Hillman's view, is into the nightworld, the underworld. And in that underworld there is no harmony or balance (compensation) between conscious and unconscious, no 'self-regulation':

> What is this 'original harmony', this ideal balance that must be restored? . . .
> The result of it in the consulting room of the analyst is that it requires the interpreter to 'do something' and appeals to the dreamer to 'correct something'. Theory of compensation appeals to the dayworld perspective of ego and results from its philosophy, not from the dream. (ibid., p. 78-9)

For Hillman, each dream is complete in itself, there is no reason to talk of compensating anything. Hence, in earlier writings, he refers to 'befriending the dream' (see p. 200, above).

If we look at what Hillman does with dreams in practice we find that he is actually using what amounts to the classical Freudian methodology of free association. In the underworld the rules are quite different (Freud's primary process), the laws of nature altered (Freud's substitution, condensation, displacement). Hillman shows a love of parapraxis, semantic reversal, experimentation and play that constantly puts one in mind of Freud's *The Psychopathology of Everyday Life* (1901). Naturally, Hillman does not have Freud's sexual programme, nor repression, in mind and his conclusions are altogether different. But in his certainty that unconscious language is different from conscious language and his observation of the total breakdown of the laws of nature in dream, Hillman is in a sense closer to Freud than he is to Jungian ideas of compensation.

Hillman himself is a source for these suggestions, referring to Freud's 'underworld experience' with his own dreams and claiming that Freud to a very great extent 'built a world upon the dream' (1979a, p. 8). In addition,

Hillman states that Freud's conception of dream-work, evacuated of some of ego's prejudices, is the concept to which he feels most sympathetic (ibid., p. 94).

But Freud 'ruined' his own ideas, in Hillman's evaluation, by taking the undoubted connection between the residues of the day's events and the dream in a literal manner and hence seeing the dream in terms of the dayworld. The day's events are, for Hillman, only raw material employed by the dream, they are not the dream. Hillman's detailed reading of Freud is that this is at times his position as well. Why, when the dream is in essence completely foreign to waking life, interpret dreams in such a way as to make them relevant for the dayworld, 'reclaiming' them, to use Freud's word?

Hillman's method involves a rapid moving round of the dream elements which has the effect of temporarily stunning consciousness like the Cabbalistic technique of rapidly moving letters around. This opens up the metaphorical dimension of the dream. Reverting to M.'s dream, the image *hip* thrust itself forward for attention. A hip, she said, is what a woman rests her baby on; it is therefore something to do with being female. Being 'hip' also has the meaning of being cool or laid back and not expressing strong emotions such as anger. Hillman's perspective was therefore of use *en route* to the type of formulation or interpretation he eschews. M.'s psyche had connected lack of emotion with femaleness – and, we might add, was concerned with the image of *nursing* not of *mothering*. In the next chapter, which looks at archetypal psychology, Hillman's manner of linking image and feeling will become clearer.

DISCUSSION

There is a conundrum here: how to move in the underworld and also keep a connection to the personal life of the patient in the dayworld. I do not want to lose the benefits of either perspective but, as presented by Hillman and Lambert, the two are inimical.

My attempt to resolve this conundrum involves an extension of what we normally take to be the dream. Hillman adopts what I would call a *literary* approach to the dream. What is taken as the dream is limited to what could be written down (the dream text), no more and no less. In this Hillman shows his background in Classical analytical psychology. My suggestion is that the dream be regarded as both the 'official' dream and also whatever that dream manages to pull into its orbit. This would include relevant parts of the patient's history, subsequent events in his or her life related to the dream – and, above all, those parts of the therapeutic interaction connected to, and informed by, the dream.

In our example, the dream would *include* the patient's evasion of her mother in her waking life, her strong angry reaction to the dream, and also her doubts about my efficacy. Including this extra material and counting it as *dream* paves the way for an interior exploration, consistent with an underworld perspective, but also acknowledging the whole person of the patient together with their pain, and incorporating relevant transference-countertransference.

The dream may be regarded as incorporating all that it touches emotionally

239

and all that touches on it. Then Hillmanesque focus on image can accompany Lambertian attention to process. Both may be seen to connect to Dieckmann's concern that the patient learn from observing himself in the dream. The paradox that we noted earlier in Dieckmann's perspective serves to promote a blend of these various approaches. Here again, however, we must not minimise differences.

THE DREAM IN CONTEMPORARY PSYCHOANALYSIS

Rycroft, in his book *The Innocence of Dreams* (1979), agrees with Jung that a dream is not a deception. He asserts that symbolisation is a natural, general capacity of the mind and not a method of disguising unacceptable wishes. According to Rycroft, primary and secondary process coexist throughout life so that dreaming is completely de-pathologised (and see Plaut's ideas about primary and secondary process coexisting throughout life, p. 77, above). When Rycroft refers to dreams as 'innocent' he means that dreams 'lack knowingness, display an indifference to received categories, and have a core which cannot but be sincere and is uncontaminated by the self-conscious will' (ibid., p. 7).

Rycroft's approach is essentially subjective, in contrast to Freud's objectivity. (In fact most modern approaches to dreams use the subjective approach pioneered by Jung; for instance, Gestalt psychology which sees the dream elements as part of the dreamer). Dreaming, according to Rycroft, is

> a form of communicating or communing with oneself and is analogous to such waking activities as talking to onself, reminding oneself, frightening oneself, entertaining oneself or exciting oneself with one's own imagination – and perhaps to such waking meditative imaginative activities as summoning up remembrance of things past or envisaging the prospect of things future. (ibid., p. 45)

The language of dreams is metaphorical. Rycroft states in unequivocal terms that dreaming is an imaginative activity (ibid., p. 71) and that dream imagery should be understood metaphorically. But, as he does intend to *relate* the imagery of dreams to a 'subject or theme' outside the dream, his approach is closer to Jung's than, say, to Hillman's.

To find a parallel to Hillman's seemingly extreme attitude, we may reflect on the French psychoanalyst Pontalis's remark that 'when the dream *dreamt in images* is converted into the dream *put into words*, something is lost' (quoted in Gill, 1982, p. 476). In the same psychoanalytic paper Gill also quotes Khan's aphorism that 'there is a dreaming experience to which the dream text holds no clue.' Finally, Gill understands Lacan as saying that language distorts dreams by trying to organise and control them (ibid., pp. 475-6).

In general, there seems to be a move in psychoanalysis away from seeing the dream as a disguise or forbidden wish. The psyche emerges as more creative than deceptive. To continue to suspect dreams of deceit may, as Gill suggests, be like an Englishman in Paris who knows no French and assumes that the Parisians are talking gibberish just to make a fool of him.

9

Archetypal psychology

Throughout this book there have been references to the Archetypal School of analytical psychology which has been furthered principally by James Hillman (and also Avens, 1980; Berry, 1982; Giegerich, 1975; Lopez-Pedraza, 1977; M. Stein, 1973; R. Stein, 1974). In this chapter we will be concentrating on describing this controversial psychological ideology. The thesis of the present book which has stressed a common ideological future for analytical psychology is further developed in Chapter 11.

The term *archetypal psychology* was first used by Hillman in 1970 (Hillman, 1975a, pp. 138ff.). In his view, archetypal theory is the most fundamental area of Jung's work but this could not have been apparent at the time when the term 'analytical psychology' was coined. The archetype underpins psychic life, is both precise and indefinable, and is central to Jung's conception of therapy. Hillman went on to point out that the archetypes owe nothing to analytical endeavour, as it were, and that the substitution of the more fundamental for the more limited term opens up the area of psychological examination to what lies beyond the consulting room. In sum, 'after all, analysis too is an enactment of an archetypal fantasy' (ibid., p. 142). We shall have to discuss the implication of this claim; it is one that Hillman repeats in a later and didactic summary of the School's approach. There he says that archetypal psychology is an attempt to 'connect to the wider culture of Western Imagination beyond the consulting room' (Hillman, 1983, p. 1).

Although Jung is a major influence, perhaps *the* major influence, other writers who are not analytical psychologists are seminal. For instance Corbin, who first used the term *mundus imaginalis* (1972), and saw archetypes as basic structures of the imagination is, in fact, a scholar of Islam. From philosophy, Casey has made an important contribution, perhaps because unhindered by the humanistic dimension that most analysts take for granted. Casey speaks of the 'extrapersonal' (1974, p. 21) and emphasises that 'what we come to experience in archetypal imagining is . . . rooted outside of human consciousness, whether this consciousness presents itself in the form of the ego or in the more expansive format of the Self' (ibid.). Casey developed a topography in which imagination lies midway between the senses on the one hand and, on the other, cognition. This arrangement clearly gives a medial place to imagination – but body and intellect are acknowledged and so possible bridges are created to a psychology emphasising instinct or to one concentrating on cognitive development.

Stress on the imaginal leads to focus on the image itself. Avens makes the claim that Jung, and then Hillman, resuscitated images and turned our attention to the spontaneous image-making capacity of the psyche (1980, p. 32). In archetypal psychology, images are not representations, signs, symbols, allegories or communications. They are simply images and part of the realm of psychic reality. The directness of this approach implies that images must be *experienced*, caressed, played with, reversed, responded to – in short, related to (felt) rather than solely interpreted or explained (thought). Were it not for long-standing inhibitions and prohibitions to an aesthetic approach, images might be responded to as if works of art, with the proviso that such aestheticism be emotional, gutsy, passionate, ahistorical and, perhaps, simple. It was Jung himself who argued against an aesthetic approach. How can the products of the psyche, which are *natural*, be judged as if they were created by artistic man? (1963, p. 210).

The way in which images live, involve with one another, and enact stories leads archetypal psychology away from the image *an sich*. It penetrates far into another province in which stories from deep in human psychological experience are to be found: mythology. For Hillman, 'the primary, and irreducible, language of . . . archetypal patterns is the metaphorical discourse of myths' (1983, p. 2).

It is the word *metaphorical* that is crucial. That is well summarised by Miller:

> the Gods and Goddesses are the names of powers or forces which have autonomy and are not conditioned by or affected by social and historical events, by human will or reasoning, or by personal and individual factors . . . they are felt to be informing powers that give shape to social, intellectual, and personal behaviour.(1981, pp. 28-9)

In similar vein, Hillman observes that he looks at myths to *open* things and not to ground the issue. The suggestion is that such grounding is what happens in the Classical School. The charge of mythological reductionism on his part is thus refuted by Hillman. For him, myth leads to ever more productive circumambulation and experience of the image. Greek mythology, in particular, deriving from a polytheistic pantheon, and in our time overshadowed by the monotheistic Judaeo-Christian world view and story, carries for archetypal psychology a locked-up store of what Freud called 'the antiquities of human development'. It is worth reflecting on Miller's demonstration of his thesis. For instance, the impact of technology on our culture

> is playing itself out according to the stories of Prometheus, Hephaestus, and Asclepius. . . . The military-industrial complex is Hera-Heracles-Hephaestus. . . . Activism – whether in the form of altruistic do-good-ism or revolutionary movements – is the work of Heracles. . . . Urbanisation bears the imprint of Athena . . . the ever-presence of outbreaks of the irrational is the work of Pan. . . . Can anyone doubt that the doctrine of God is the work of

242

Zeus? (ibid., pp. 83-8)

The concentration of attention on a polytheistic culture is not accidental and is directly connected to the question of the resuscitation of the image *qua* image. We have seen how a restrictive view of the psyche, deriving partly from Jung's 'theological' temperament, placed the self in a pre-eminent position compared, for example, to animus/anima, and this stimulated Hillman to dispute the primacy of the self, quaternity, mandalas, etc. (cf. pp. 106-8, above). Hillman accents a psychological parity of the self and other so-called archetypes of psyche.

Miller and Hillman interpret the rise of monotheism and of a monotheistic world view as metaphors for the limitation on imagination and variety in contemporary Western culture. In social terms, this expresses itself as totalitarianism. In Miller's view, though some societies strive for pluralism, it is more desired than achieved. So it is for the contemporary psyche – godless, split, one-sided and neurotic. On one level, these phenomena are traced to worship of *a* Being rather than to the placing of trust in a *principle* of being. Divinity, as a layer of existence, can no longer be truly expressed in a single God – as Nietzsche first prophesied. Monotheism has got where it has, in Miller's reading of the situation, by undermining and destroying the Greek Gods who were much more variegated and particularised, as well as being somehow closer both to man and nature. Gradually the notion of one God has grown from its Jewish source and also from Greek *philosophical* speculations on the divine as a single sphere with an omnipresent centre and no circumference. This is an image that appealed to Jung (as we saw in his definition of the self, pp. 91-2, above) and is one factor in his connection of the *imago dei* to the self.

Miller charts the links between a spherical, single God, Western over-rationalism and dependence on technology, and a certain theological simplification leading to moral either/or-ness. He maintains that the absence of a single Devil figure in the Greek pantheon does not seem to have damaged seriously their capacity for moral philosophy.

So we enact the patterns of the Gods and they express our natures for us. Polytheism involves making, seeing and living plural patterns of behaviour but not making morality out of myth (as in the Classical Jungian tradition and even in Freudian ideas about work and genitality). Polytheism is claimed to permit non-ego experience – i.e. challenging our conventional notion of the necessity of an experiencing ego. Polytheism is an approach to the imaginal world leading to the emergence of the individual symbol formation that Jung always claimed could healthily follow the breakdown of Christianity. There are many modes of perception and experience in the psyche and each man must work out for himself whether the content represents 'good' or 'evil'.

Miller defines his own attitude as that of a *henotheist*: one who worships a single God at a time out of a large pantheon. The slogan seems to be 'one God at a time but, in its time, many Gods' (ibid., p. 87). The polytheistic perspective leads directly to imaginal personification. We can even say that Jung's tendency to personify psychic contents makes him a closet polytheist. So the pluralistic personification of the polytheistic pantheon is not necessarily foreign to Classical analytical psychology. And we should not forget that a place is reserved for temporary monotheism.

So far, in our survey of the main tenets of archetypal psychology, we have looked at its basal concept (archetype), its area of interest (image), its vehicle (mythology), and its *Weltanschauung* (pluralism and polytheism). We now turn our attention to the issue of where all this is happening, at what level of experience. Clarifying this will suggest the *value and purpose* of having an archetypal psychology at all.

To give the answer at the outset: the ideogram 'soul' tells us where and at what level we are operating. The usage of 'soul' has become somewhat controversial: for some it is a cliché, used simply to answer all problems (Laughlin, 1982, pp. 35-7). And it is certainly difficult to summarise what Hillman and the archetypal psychologists are getting at.

Hillman stated that when he used the word 'soul' he was referring to a perspective or viewpoint that is essentially reflective between us and events or deeds. Soul is not to be found in any one phenomenon in particular but also cannot be grasped in isolation from phenomena. Perhaps because of this paradox soul is often 'identified with the principle of life and even of divinity' (1975b, p. x).

Hillman is also referring to what it is that grants meaning, enables love, and motivates the religious instinct. In particular, he stresses the 'deepening of events into experiences' ('soul making') and the connection of soul to death. Finally, he envisions soul as subsuming 'the imaginative possibility in our natures, the experiencing through reflective speculation, dream image, and fantasy – that mode which recognises all realities as primarily symbolic or metaphorical' (ibid.).

Hillman sees fantasy images as underpinning everything we know and feel and every statement we make, and, because fantasy images lie in the soul, it follows that it is soul that may indeed be the principle of life. The key image in this psychology of image is 'depth' and the term 'depth psychology', though largely abandoned by psychoanalysis, is apt (the term *is* still used, cf. Yorke, 1982). Soul is about depth, not the heights attainable by spirit. We may add that *depth* is surely both a *condition* and an *expression* of our phylogeny. This is an important point to bear in mind: imagery, even poetic imagery, is as old as man and not a product of the civilised or over-civilised version of *homo sapiens*. In other words, images are not only phylogenetic but are phylogeny itself.

The connection between soul and death is reminiscent of the healthy fusion Freud perceived between eros and thanatos, the life and death instincts. Soul then approximates to that aspect of the death instinct involving a desire for merger, regression and an 'oceanic' state. Such features are in constant conflict with ego attributes such as analysing, developing, separating.

Continuing with Hillman's use of 'soul', we may note that to depth he adds intensity (1975b, p. xii), which involves an agency of experience, at the very least, and the addition of an agency of meaning. This justifies the retention of ego-self language though archetypal psychology disputes that there is only one kind of ego (as we saw in Chapter 3). Is ego the only way to experience something? Ego may be necessary to *integrate* an experience but many experiences are not asking for integration, merely to be experienced. There is an epistemological problem here. If I refer to experiencing something, who is the 'I' of which I speak? It could be argued that this has to be the ego and that it is ego strength and not soul that is the key factor in experience. Separating the two (ego and soul) makes for a good debate but here, once again, we need to conceive of an interaction.

To summarise: *soul* includes life, death, divinity, love, meaning, depth and intensity. But soul is, when all is said and done, as much a way of being and perceiving as it is a datum. In this sense, soul is as dependent on man for incarnation as man is on soul for depth. It follows that the business of analysis is not to *cure* the soul but rather to facilitate that *soul-making* mentioned just now – not to 'deal with' deep problems but rather to let problems become deeper.

We may gain a further insight into archetypal psychology's use of 'soul' by a consideration of its opposite, namely 'spirit'. If soul is down there in the depths, spirit is up there in the heights, idealistic, exclusive, high-minded. Archetypal psychology detects (and is wary of) spirit in science as much as in theology, in rationalism and apparent common sense as much as in metaphysics. Spirit is not denied existence but it is disputed *as the subject of psychology*. Hillman points out that 'spirit' is chasing ultimates and this rules out many things – especially fantasy. Analysis is not a spiritual business:

> There is a difference between Yoga, transcendental meditation, religious contemplation and retreat, and even Zen, on the one hand, and the psychologising of psychotherapy on the other. (1975b, p. 67)

Succinctly, soul is about dreams, spirit about miracles or wishes. It is the difference between *inside* and *outside*; as science looks at what is outside (or, if inside, as if it were outside), it is a spiritual business. The problem is, as Hillman observes, that spirit (science) wants to discipline and harness soul (fantasy images). So interpretation of images may be seen as the imposition of spirit on to soul and, in addition, if we speak of 'correct' interpretation, of monotheism on to polytheism. Hillman also links 'spirit' with the self, heroism, and 'the rhetoric of unity, ultimacy, identity' (1983, p. 28).

Where this leads us is to a consideration of the relativity of fantasy and reality. Hillman suggests that conventional notions of reality and fantasy might swap places or at least not be regarded as opposed (1983, p. 23). Fantasy, according to Hillman, is never merely mentally subjective but is always being enacted and embodied. And behind what is concrete and actual lies an image, a fantasy image. When we resume our discussion of the parallels between the Archetypal and Developmental Schools we will return to this, for here we can see a possible bridge between the two schools.

The non-clinical pursuits of archetypal psychology lead to a re-evaluation of what is normally accepted about our cultural tradition; this is manifested in an interest in Mediterranean thinkers – Southern, and hence differing from the Northern, humanist tradition. Hillman:

> The Northern approach is overtly called 'psychology'; it is systematic and written in an objective voice ... Southern psychologising is not called such; it is episodic and written subjectively. (1975b, p. 260)

Hillman regards Plotinus, Ficino and Vico as precursors of archetypal psychology (1975a, pp. 146ff.). Plotinus, though 'officially' a philosopher of the third century AD, 'wrestles with such psychological questions as anger, happiness, suicide' and, moreover, Hillman finds a number of themes in Plotinus' work that parallel archetypal and analytical psychology. For example, man can act unconsciously, can be partially conscious and partially unconscious at the same time. For Plotinus, like Jung, there is one universal psyche. Then consciousness is mobile and multiple and is not identical with ego-consciousness but, rather, depends on imagination. Finally, the rhetoric of Plotinus, his attempt to win one over to his argument, and that of Jung are similar. Rhetoric is an important thread in this because it is so different from the sober, 'rational' way of communicating exemplified by Erasmus, Bacon, Freud.

A second example of the Southern tradition is Ficino, a Renaissance Florentine who developed a schema in which the psyche is divided into three. First there is mind or rational intellect. Second comes imagination or fantasy, which connects us to fate. Third we find body, which connects us to nature. Hillman comments:

> The relation between fantasy and body corresponds remarkably with Jung's idea of the relation of archetypal image and instinct. In both men fantasy shows the capacity of the psyche to dominate and direct the compulsive course of nature – 'body' in Ficino's language, 'instinct' in Jung's. (1975a, p. 156)

A third figure that Hillman wishes to acknowledge was from eighteenth-century Naples: Vico. Vico is of importance because his work, which has received considerable attention from philosophers of late, stresses metaphor or fantasy-thinking. Vico speaks of *universali fantastici*, or universal images such as those found in myths. He set out the twelve Gods of Olympus as fundamental structures 'each with his historical, sociological, theological, and I would add, psychological, significance' (Hillman, 1975a, pp. 158-9). Vico is therefore part of that tradition of polytheistic imagination that has never been completely suppressed by monotheism or science and in which Hillman sees himself and archetypal psychology.

This is doubtless an inadequate summary of a central concern of archetypal psychology. Perhaps the point can be made even more clearly by drawing attention to Jung's well-known inability to visit Rome. He fainted while buying the tickets and, more than once, sabotaged his expressed conscious desire (Jung, 1963, pp. 318ff.). The Southern tradition may be seen as filling out gaps in Jungian thought, functioning as an unconscious compensation to Jung's Protestantism and theological cast of mind (Hillman, 1975a, p. 160).

But archetypal psychologists do have consulting rooms and patients and do belong to professional societies of analysts. It is therefore appropriate to conclude this survey with a few words on psychopathology, archetypal psychopathology, and the practice of analysis.

Hillman has stressed the 'essential infirmity of the archetype'. That is to say, each archetype contains a pathological element or potential and this, too, can be elaborated in myth: 'pathology is mythologised and mythology is pathologised' (Hillman, 1983, p. 23). Archetypal psychology claims, therefore, to function close to the shadow and to have continued Jung's emphasis on the reality of evil. This approach is somewhat different from a psychodynamic psychopathology in which what the individual experiences in his early life, and his way of using that experience, are the determining factors. At the same time, though, psychodynamics and the archetypal approach do share a vision of pathology in which what is healthy at one time, in one context, for one person, may be unhealthy when the parameters shift. Too much conscious-ness in a neonate may be pathological; later on, awareness of dependence and boundary is vital. Psychopathology is a circular business from whichever school the subject is considered. Psychodynamic psychopathology nowadays does not use a rigidly linear model of growth but, like archetypal psychology, sees the elements of psychic life as neutral until vivified by age, context and individuality.

A demonstration of the archetypal approach to psychopathology may be found in Lopez-Pedraza's study *Hermes and his Children* (1977). The author does more than merely *point out* the links between Hermes as trickster, his mendacity, criminality, perversion – and his role as 'the spirit Mercurius', agent of alchemical transformation, messenger of the Gods, and guide of souls to Hades. *The link itself is celebrated* and made central. I have tried elsewhere (1982) to move fluidly within both psychodynamic and archetypal language so that Hermes' criminality, for instance, may be seen as the pattern of psyche in which a baby has grandiose and omnipotent fantasies before morality and the reality principle raise their heads. Hermes is an amoral figure and so is a baby; both possess the power to transform and to be transformed.

As far as the practice of therapy and analysis is concerned, Hillman stays within the classical-symbolic-synthetic (CSS) tradition discussed in Chapter 6 (Hillman, 1983, p. 48). What is different, in his view, is that the focus has switched on to the patient's images. Hillman's credo is that images should not be 'reduced to [the patient's] feelings'. Feelings are not 'merely personal but belong to imaginal reality' (1983, p. 48). In other words, images are not communications in code about something else which could be made conscious but are valid in and as themselves. Hillman goes further than this: he wishes to see through feelings, conventionally regarded as gold dust by the analyst, to perceive and experience the underlying images.

In particular, attention must be paid to the way in which parts of the personality and also clinical abstractions (shadow and anima, or drive and conflict) express themselves in the form of personifications. This is not so much a theory as a statement about what ordinarily happens to us. It is derived from Jung who counselled that one should differentiate oneself from unconscious contents by personifying them, and added that, as such contents are relatively autonomous anyway, this is not hard to do. Hillman's elaboration is that it is our relations with these inner persons, or rather with images of them, that constitute what we mean by *feelings*:

> These persons keep our persons in order, holding into significant patterns the segments and patterns of behaviour we call emotions, memories, attitudes, and motives. (1975b, p. 128)

These personifications derive from archetypal structures, hence their power, their universality and our tendency to experience them as Gods and call them such. Thus archetypal psychology's tendency to work with personifications can build a link between our everyday consulting room material and our theory without reifying that theory or taking it too literally.

10

Theory in practice: an illustration

I am conscious that many readers may not be practising analysts or psychotherapists so I propose to discuss aspects of analytic work with a patient which illustrate some of the theoretical matter introduced. I am not attempting to give an account of a whole analysis, but, rather, selecting vignettes to point up links between practice and theory to orientate those readers who cannot refer to their own clinical experience. Of necessity, all analysts work differently with different cases; this chapter concerns my own way of working, evolved out of my training in the Society of Analytical Psychology. Narrative appears in italics, commentary (some of it *ex post facto*) in roman type.

D. was 28 years old, female, unmarried when she came to see me. She said that her main problem was an inordinate fear of what would happen were she to vomit; this would be disintegrating or otherwise disastrous for her personality. She had had this fear since the age of nine though she had never actually been sick. After the four years of analysis reported here, this symptom had virtually disappeared. At that initial interview, the patient also complained that there was no direction to her life. She felt an inability to carry through any project, described herself as a 'middle-aged hippy' with a room full of discarded symbols such as a deck of tarot cards, a guitar, a loom, etc. and she admitted that she saw herself as childish and pathetic, prone to 'wingeing' instead of taking action to solve her problems.

This irrational, obsessional fear suggests a complex. But why does she not manage to be sick? Is it infantile attention seeking, or is there something in the act of being sick that would disturb psychic homeostasis? Is this an example of a desperate attempt at psychological self-regulation, concerning survival rather than harmony, fear without actual disintegration? Her various activities (by now all discarded) indicate a lack of rootedness or a weakness in ego-consciousness. There was also an overdeveloped concern for persona, of how she looked to others. But there is also a prompting from an internally directed impulse to undertake self-fulfilling activities. In fact she became a potter and by now has her own pottery. In other words, she has added solidity and consistency (ego) to the 'instinct' for self-development (self) and, in retrospect, this could be seen as evidence of individuation. Indeed, otherwise she would not have undertaken analysis.

Wingeing was her word to describe how she exerted an influence on others. The impression she must give is of a pathetic and weepy dependence and vulnerability; the effect is extraordinarily powerful in that others tend to fit in with her wishes. So wingeing is, more accurately, an expression of her omnipotence,

In appearance she is slight, extremely thin, with a boyish figure and strong features. When I first met her she moved with great precision, like a mechanical doll, and on the couch she usually lay rigid. Her dress was unusual; perhaps typical was a cut-down one-piece man's working overall, covered by an old mini-dress from the 1960s, combined with a black silk scarf and wellington boots. She did not wear make-up or jewellery, rolled her own cigarettes, ate macrobiotic and vegetarian food, read Jung, hated London. My immediate personal reaction was that she looked like a refugee from the Portobello Road.

Was she identified with this persona? The androgynous clothing leads one to think of her relation to her animus, to gender identity, to femininity in particular and, hence, to her image of man.

D. is the youngest of four and her mother was over forty when she was born. D.'s mother died of cancer of the breast when D. was thirteen and her father remarried several years later. During her childhood (and into adult life) she experienced her father as a dominant figure, tyrannical and driving, knowing what was best for his children. D. always felt that his attitude to life was expressed in prohibitions and this led to numerous disagreements, particularly after the death of her mother. Disagreements centred upon the courses she should take at school, what clothes she should wear, her choice of dates and so on.

The father image was so stereotyped that it appeared to be a representation of the archetypal father in negative guise. The death of the mother established the primitive symbolic equation: to be female = to die. Adolescence reiterates Oedipal struggles and her mother's dying at that time might be seen as an Oedipal fantasy come true. She was deprived of her mother as a role model, as a confidant or guide into adult female sexuality.

Analytically speaking, intergenerational alliance just never took place. Similarly, the image of the father was such a negative one that any refuelling, regressive, 'incestuous' movement towards him was out of the question. However, when her analysis was well under way and she needed money to pay for tuition, she asked him for this and it was forthcoming. From that moment additional energy was available to her for pottery-making and for life in general.

She felt her father pushed her towards an ideal of hard work, particularly in a technical or a practical field as he was an engineer. She was forced to give up dancing and art. Not surprisingly, she insisted on attempting to become an actress and studied arts at university.

Her claim was that her father had interfered with her use and development of her individual gifts. Her choice of subject could be seen as an over-determined response to the image of the authoritarian father.

Between the death of her mother and her departure for college at eighteen she was

virtually alone in the house with her father.

The ego defence of denial has been operating here. Father is portrayed as unlovable, preventing the emergence of her more positive feelings. She is not aware of this denial, however. There is an unconscious flight from incest involvement.

She experienced her mother as competent but unattractive. A 'farmyard mother',
she called her.

I think she was communicating the lack of a personal relation to her mother which predated her mother's death. Her real mother when alive did not mediate the image of a powerful, bountiful, agricultural 'Goddess'. A farmyard mother is vastly superior to the animals (babies) she is feeding and caring for. And she is not very sexy. An overbearing, un-giving, non-erotic image of mother becomes established (and see Figures 11, 12, 13, below).

From the start D. was unhappy with the structure of analysis, experiencing the
routine of daily sessions as an expression of my unlimited power. She struggled with
me over the time of the sessions, the fees and over the purpose of the analysis.

In her transference fantasy, I am both farmyard mother and tyrant father, while she is forced into a little girl role. Although she was regressed, depressed and agoraphobic before she started analysis, at the moment she sees me as the cause of her problems.

She said she had chosen the Jungian approach because of its cosmic outlook,
reaching upwards and outwards, and because the analyst would be less distant, even
become a friend in time.

I think she meant that she did not want Freudian sexual emphasis. Once when discussing orgasmic problems she said 'an orgasm a day keeps the analyst away.' There is no doubt that many people still choose Jungian analysis hoping to avoid working on instinctual material. D. needed to stress the 'equality' in her envisioning of a Jungian analysis because she felt so unequal to almost anyone. She was torn by feelings of superiority and inferiority neither of which she had integrated.

Then she had a dream (her initial dream):

I am standing in a ruined cottage in Wales, planning to rebuild it. I realise
that it is not going to be as easy as I thought because I do not know how to put
in the basics, such as plumbing and electricity. I look up, and I see a power
station on a distant hilltop. I feel that, though this building is ugly, it will
somehow help to solve the problem. The power station has two enormous
chimneys.

The interpretation was primarily subjective: the plumbing connected with her vomiting fears; the ruined cottage her self-image; the realisation it would not be easy is self-explanatory and relates to the analysis; the connection between her conscious loathing of all things industrial and the dream fact that it is a power plant that will help is an example of the unconscious producing a compensatory symbol – she will have to use what she consciously does not like. After this she was more co-operative with me for a while. But she did not accept the objective interpretation that the two chimneys represented my breasts and that particular interpretation was probably mistimed.

After a further nine months' work her struggle with her fantasy of my control took the form of repeated absences, culminating in a three-week unofficial 'holiday' at a cottage in Wales (see her initial dream) spent with a recently acquired boyfriend. As it turned out, the time was exactly equal to a just-past holiday of mine; I felt very uncomfortable and deserted.

She was retaliating against what felt like my cruelty, but also letting me know how she felt and had felt. My countertransference reaction, which I kept to myself though I saw it as a communication from her, helped me to empathise with her emotional state.

Three weeks went by without any word. Eventually I telephoned her London flat, got the Wales address and wrote asking for an explanation. I then received a postcard with a picture of a sheep on the front and a one line message indicating she did not know when she would be back. I wrote back at once trying to draw some boundaries. I said I might have to end the analysis if she did not return and presently she came back.

I had become the inner world heavy-handed father who could not let her alone or, possibly, live without her. This was a valuable clue as to her perception of her father's mental state when they were together after her mother's death. This was a syntonic countertransference in that she seemed to need this father-image to live in me, hence her provoking of it.

The sheep summed things up. On her return she told me that the sheep was symbolic of how *she* had felt all her life, patiently waiting in a docile way for people to tell her what to do, how to live. In other words, she had gone to Wales to break open, grow out of, crack or 'transform' that image of herself – as well as get revenge on me for my desertion of her when I went on holiday. The retaliation was the shadow of the transformative aspect of her behaviour.

D.'s struggle with me shifted from an attempt to acquire 'equality' into an attempt by her to change and improve my life. The idea was that I should move so as to be closer to her geographically and then that we should start to see one another socially, go to parks and the country together. She referred to this fantasy as 'ruffling' me.

She presented herself as a revolutionary anima figure for me but not, as yet, as a potential lover.

She dreamt:

I visit a doctor who is ill in bed. He begs me to stay.

Then she remembered how lonely and broken her father had been after his wife's death and fantasised about my sickness, my weakness, my personal wound.

Here I appear in the guise of the wounded healer, but this is also a manifestation of personal transference, given her childhood memories. It would indicate that we were getting closer to the repressed oedipal material –

she can 'handle' it in a dream. I did not interpret incestuousness at this point.

Surrendering any of her internal control was hard for D. because of her difficulty in facing the feeling of inner emptiness that lay behind her struggle with me. Her journal suggested the problem. This is a thick diary dating back many years. The journal was being told things I was not – and she made sure I knew that. The problem for me was how to point this out without, in effect, prohibiting her from writing it. She offered to let me read what she had written since the start of the analysis two and a half years before. I accepted the offer.

I understood this as a first manifestation of her productiveness and generosity in relating. It also represented a definition of individual (personal) boundary. At the same time, and defensively, it tantalised me by demonstrating how much of her life lay outside our relationship.

In the journal she appeared as lovelorn, emotionally impoverished and ontologically non-existent. The handover of the journal signalled the break-up of the pattern of struggle and withholding.

Handing the journal to me could be seen as symbolic of an increase of trust within the transference. This may be rather an over-simplification but approximates to what was going on. The part played by objects, such as this journal, produced voluntarily in analysis, lends itself to many interpretations and varies with each case. When I had the journal given to me I had to be careful not to analyse it rather than her.

Her relations with men (most of the journal was about these) had always been characterised by idealisation. In adolescence she had invented a wholly fictitious man to whom to relate. He was a poet, consumptive, but acclaimed as a genius and so on. She would talk with him of 'all the mysteries' . . .

. . . but not sleep with him. This was a projection of the idealised (spiritualised) animus image. But it was also the first suggestion of her ego's capacity to work with personification. I 'unamplified' the mythological parallel of Apollo and Artemis.

Almost immediately after this, she saw Ken Russell's film 'Savage Messiah'. This is about the young romantic sculptor, Henri Gaudier, who fell deeply in love with an older woman, Sophie Brzeska. As a sign of their intimacy (and it was a non-sexual relationship) they agreed to add each other's name to their own; hence, the artist is known as Gaudier-Brzeska. After telling me about this film, D. said she had worked out a list of the qualities of their relationship which, she said, applied to her own life. The list ran: 'idealised, platonic, spiritual, incestuous, doomed'.

Indeed, it is not easy in real life to confine heterosexual activity to something idealised, platonic, spiritualised and incestuous, without being doomed. There is a split between the spiritual aspect of the archetypal (image) and the libidinal impulse (instinct).

Working with D., I felt what can only be described as incestuous pressure. On three occasions I found it necessary to bring this into the open. On each occasion, I committed myself to an intense interaction and was strongly affected by what transpired. These three instances exemplify the dialectical process of analysis and illustrate the way in which the psyches of analyst and patient combine to produce something different.

D. often referred to a group of friends from the arts and hippy worlds who, she claimed, liked her and understood her in a way that I did not. She did not underfunction with them the way she felt she did with me. But it so happened that I knew several of this group who, she supposed, were quite antipathetic to me. After a time, the regularity with which these people were mentioned convinced me that she knew of the coincidence and was using the knowledge in an omnipotent and sadistic way. I asked her if she knew that I was acquainted with these people and she said not.

This probably contained elements of a neurotic, or even psychotic countertransference but gradually my reactions became more manageable and, hence, clinically effective.

The second instance occurred after she saw me at the theatre. The play was Oscar Wilde's 'Salome' performed in an experimental style with an all-male cast. During the performance I had the strong fantasy that the actor playing Salome reminded me of D. So after she had told me of her feelings about the incident when she had seen me, I told her of this fantasy. She replied that Salome had always been an important figure for her and that she had moved heaven and earth to capture the part when the play was staged at university and she had successfully played the role. She was particularly attracted to the alliance against Herod between Salome and Herodias (Salome's mother and the wife of Herod's predecessor on the throne). Another important theme for her was the rejection of Salome by the handsome and spiritual John the Baptist. But the crux of her involvement came when Salome refused to dance for Herod unless he acceded to her every request (eventually for John's head).

In D.'s life there had never been a Herodias to help her in her struggle to dethrone Herod, her father/king. Indeed, her mother had paid loving attention to father. At this point I remembered my supervisor's saying that neither D. nor I seemed to realise that the woman in my life was more important to D. just now than I was. This, appropriately adapted, I put to D. which released her to explore fantasies about this woman (whom she had seen at the theatre) and my relationship with her (see below).

The third interaction occurred when D. was attacking the materialism and concern for their 'image' of some psychotherapists she had met at a party. As it happened, I knew those she mentioned. I became very angry. I suggested with some feeling that clothes and way of life were most certainly matters of extreme concern for D. herself. In fact, she saw herself and others very much in terms of appearance, jobs and achievement. For example, she had told me she tended to introduce herself as 'I'm D., I'm a potter.'

Looking back, it was necessary for me to draw certain boundaries by facing the incestuous omnipotence implied in all these events. Up to that point I had been frightened to offend D.'s sensibilities, whereas, in reality, she had been looking for 'firm love'. Early in the analysis, D. said she felt ours was a one-sided relationship. On the surface she meant that she provided all the raw material, and did all the feeling and suffering. At a deeper level, she was finding it impossible to experience a sense of two-ness, or mutuality, with me. The analysis can be looked at as a progression from her omnipotent oneness towards a sense of boundary and twoness. My revelations of my Salome fantasy and of my impression that she knew I knew her friends, leading to my confrontation of her, constellated this twoness. We were no longer merged. She has said that these occurrences marked the point at which she began to have confidence and hope in the analysis.

Gradually over the next six months, she consolidated her career and entered a stable relationship with a man. This relationship was difficult for her, but the progress she has been making is summed up in a report that once, after a bitter argument, as he stalked out of the room she felt a sudden and quite new feeling of loss, of losing him as a person. She said 'not losing control and wingey but full of disappointed love.' The shift is to a feeling for the man as another person and not anxiety over possible loss of control. Talking about wingeing one day, she commented on how she had really pushed this man around. I compared this to a bossy mother and her naughty child, to which she replied, 'If I'm a mother I'm a stone mother.' This marked the beginning of work on the developing image named by her the Stone Mother.

The important thing to me here is the conscious use of personification. She named the image; I did not.

The first stage of work with this image involved her being in a state of identity with the Stone Mother. As she described herself, she *is* the Stone Mother. In a drawing she brought she tries to prevent her boyfriend from going off with a group of his friends to follow a signpost marked 'self' (Figure 11). The man is attached to her by a chain which passes through a crying child (her wingeing, powerful self).

Then we moved on to consider the Stone Mother as an image of the mother she felt she had had. In a second picture (Figure 12) a sinister, hard-faced woman looms over a tiny D. figure, naked and vulnerable, curled into a foetal position. But the mother takes no notice of the child; the two are unrelated. This drawing produced feeling-memories in D. of her mother's preoccupation and abandonment of her. Memories centred on her mother carrying bucket after bucket of boiling water to the bathroom for her father when he had a digestive upset. 'The house revolved around his stomach', D. said angrily. She wished it had been hers and she had been able to attract similar attention.

Figure 13 shows D. taking a hammer to a statuesque female figure who has already started to disintegrate. The body of the young woman in the picture radiates life and energy. A man waits for her.

The drawings were produced spontaneously outside the session and were done over quite a short period. She brought them all at the same time.

Still, D. did not like the fact that I had outside relationships. For example, she referred to the woman who lived with me in my flat as the 'him-her', thus avoiding a feeling of too much jealousy. Gradually, she became able to accept that there was a woman and this person became, unconsciously, very important to D. in a new way. First, she had a fantasy that her agency (D. was doing casual jobs at this time) sent

Figure 11

Figure 12

Figure 13

her to clean our flat. She enjoyed playing with the idea of helping my partner, much as a little girl helps Mummy. She did not find the cleaning idea demeaning; quite the reverse.

She had a dream:

> *I am cleaning Andrew's flat when I am visited by my boyfriend. We start to make love in the bedroom when Andrew's partner comes in. In a firm but kind way she remonstrates with me; she points out that a room has been provided for me to make love in. She asks me to use it.*

The purposive element here is that a mother-figure with a positive attitude to her sexuality has come into being, thus making up for the earlier lack. My partner provides the raw material to flesh out an archetypal potential. A place for D.'s own sexual activity is provided but with a firm sense of boundary. Clearly, sex will be something for *her* and not an incestuous complication. My partner symbolises a mother with whom D. can have the whole range of mother-daughter relationships from identification to rivalry over the father/ lover.

We can observe the progress from (a) dead mother to (b) farmyard mother to (c) stone mother (victorious) to (d) stone mother (vanquished) to (e) sexually accepting mother. The analytical relationship, and my interventions, enabled her to withdraw the projection of her own omnipotent control, first from me, and then from Stone Mother. This released the archetypal potential of a mother who facilitates psychosexual development. After this, the transference became markedly erotic.

A final dream:

> *I am at an exhibition at the art college. There is a cupboard in the corner and on a wall inside the cupboard is a large biological diagram of the clitoris – this has been hidden from us students. It is very detailed and I can see the nerve endings and cross-sections of the flesh. It looks like an insect. Through a window in another wall of the cupboard, I see a skull that has been cracked and mended with silver. The skull is of prehistoric antiquity. I remember seeing the skull before sometime. A middle-aged woman comes in and removes the partition between the diagram and the skull. She seems to understand what is going on. Then the scene shifts to a lake. Three men beckon me onto a raft but I decide to choose another raft for myself. I am frightened. I remember various childhood dreams. They seem to be some sort of preparation or rehearsal for this. I know that my raft will spin round and round until it stops against the shore of the lake. I consider trying to steer the raft.*

We interpreted this dream as follows: for years she has been cut off from direct experience of the clitoris, symbol of orgasmic sexual pleasure for a female. The drawing *is* rather technical but it is also very clear and nothing is murky or guardedly concealed. The drawing is given another dimension by the insect motif, for an insect is a vigorous repository of instinctual life and, in D.'s association, virtually indestructible.

There is a need to link the clitoris-insect drawing with the ancient skull, repaired in silver. We felt this was a self symbol; her core, stripped of outer covering – coverings which had been damaged in some way (? in infancy) and had been repaired (? by analysis).

The middle-aged woman removing the dividing wall is significant in the light of what has been said about her mother. This leads to the lake, functioning here as a matrix for the action and not merely as a social grouping. She elects to travel apart from the men, saying 'no' to them. Conciously, she was anxious at her audacity in turning these men down and was thus reassured by the feeling that earlier dreams from childhood have prepared her for what is to come.

She embarks on a giddying, spiralling journey. Early in the analysis the image of the spiral was mentioned as justifying going over the same ground in the sessions again and again but each time a little further along, or higher on the spiral. It is therefore a symbol of hard-won growth and conscious achievement. At some point she will reach terra firma, but meanwhile she begins to think that she can contribute to the process by steering her raft.

11

Comparison and evaluation

The reader will recall that a main premise of the first chapter was that differences between the Schools of analytical psychology can enable us to see the discipline as a whole. A common tradition is not enough to hold a group together. It also needs areas of dialogue in order to avoid the twin illusions of consensus and schism and assure continued movement into the future. For this reason I propose to summarise some of the areas in which I observe the apparently opposed Developmental and Archetypal Schools reacting similarly in an iconoclastic, revisionary way to the expressed tenets of Classical analytical psychology. The two wings appear to be attacking the centre. I am not claiming that developmentally and archetypally oriented analytical psychologists agree upon their differences; they most certainly do not. But they share a common process.

For example, in Chapter 4 we saw how both schools find the Classical concept of the self to be overweighted by emphasis on potential and a view of conflict conditioned by possibilities of resolution. And the notion of individuation has been 'earthed', seen to be a lifelong process, starting in infancy and discoverable in the infirm. This is another view shared by both Developmental and Archetypal Schools, both of which eschew striving for 'wholeness' as a psychological goal. Instead, a differentiation of psychic contents is stressed, illustrated both by Hillman's 'polytheism' and Fordham's 'part-selves'. If a person gives honest and full attention to his part-selves or energetically explores the dimensions of a particular myth, unity takes care of itself. This is similar to Plaut's conclusion that investment in things less than perfect, whole or complete, may constitute a viable alternative form of psychological functioning, and also to Guggenbühl-Craig's rejection of a 'cult of perfection'.

To take the parallels that have emerged further, when discussing archetypes in Chapter 2 we stated that what contemporary analytical psychology requires of an image before the appellation *archetypal* is bestowed has undergone a radical change. In both the Schools we are examining the archetypal images no longer need to conform to pre-existing criteria. I suggested then that what is archetypal is to be found in the eye of the beholder and not in a particular image itself. With this assumption it becomes possible to set aside preconceived schemes or hierarchies of archetypes. The archetypal experience is more a state of mind.

It may be objected that the language of the two Schools is so different that observations of common ground such as these are forced. There are certainly vast differences between the poetic rhetoric and cultural contents employed by Hillman, Berry and Lopez-Pedraza and the sober, empirical, scientific tenor of expression used by some members of the Developmental School. But I wonder if the conventional distinction between metaphorical and scientific language does not break down completely when it comes to psychology. We have already seen how the language even of Kleinian psychoanalysis lends itself to talk of internal 'Gods' (p. 113, above), and, in fact, the Kleinian approach is essentially a mythological one.

As a colleague from the Developmental School said, Klein stopped using the 'scientific' world view promulgated by Freud and simply started telling stories about the inner life of children. While she worked backwards from behaviour, even adult behaviour, in pursuit of the story, her conclusion was that inner stories (myths, unconscious phantasies) are the dominant powers, or Gods, in personal development. The moment that such a viewpoint is adopted is, to my way of thinking, the moment when the metaphorical-scientific dichotomy becomes less meaningful. *To experience another from inside that other takes us into the imaginal and metaphorical.* Shades of a Klein-Hillman hybrid?

Light may be shed on the linguistic differences by a recent development in psychoanalysis. Bettelheim has argued that Freud's apparently scientific outlook and style are more the product of Strachey's English translation than a true reflection of Freud's original German, and hence his aim and purpose has been distorted (1983). The English-speaking world has not met the real Freud. Bettelheim claims that Freud's conception of psychoanalysis was, as a liberal and human discipline, concerned more with people and culture and less with scientific abstraction.

For example, Bettelheim suggest that *ego* is not an accurate rendering for *ich* (I), *id* for *es* (it), *instinct* for *Trieb* (impulse or drive). In his review of Bettelheim's book, the philosopher Hampshire makes the point that, had we had to consider a death *impulse*, or the existence of twin impulses, we would not have concluded that this was a *biological improbability* but rather a *psychological fact*: 'death is the cool night, rescuing us from the sultry day' (Hampshire, 1983).

According to Bettelheim, the distortion is shown most clearly in Strachey's mistranslation of *Seele* as *mind* rather than as soul. A mechanistic overlay has thereby been created which disfigures Freud's interest in man's inner being. Bettelheim acknowledges that, to an atheist like Freud, the word soul would have a religious connotation and would, in many respects, be more satisfactorily rendered as *psyche*. It must be said that Freud may have been more enamoured of objective science than Bettelheim admits.

However, Bettelheim's thesis is important both for the relation of analytical psychology and psychoanalysis and also for that between the Developmental and Archetypal Schools of analytical psychology. Terms such as 'soul-making' may be seen as compatible with the language of drive theory, or the impact of archetypes in early development.

But what of the absence of a model of individual development in archetypal psychology? Surely, it will be argued, this wrecks any attempt to see parallels. The answer is that the child under consideration is, for the most part, an inner child, a child of psychic reality, a metaphor of child, image of child, a symbolic child. And, of course, a 'real' child! Events in infancy and childhood have consequences, but these consequences cannot be expressed in the language of causality, certainty and determinism. Increasingly, and in the Developmental School, the infant under consideration is seen as a psychological infant located within an adult and facing in two directions: towards archetypal beginnings and towards experiential outcomes. We may begin to speak of a myth of development. This fits well with Jung's choice of the phrase 'personal myth'.

Sometimes archetypal psychologists dismiss the wholly or partly personal or condemn 'psychodynamics' and it is important to speculate why this might be so. I think that the problem is that fantasy about Freudian reductionism which, as we noted earlier (p. 135, above), infected Jung. In fact, in the Developmental School, save when a deliberate process of reconstruction is under way, the infantile material may be regarded as present in the transference in the here and now, and not a subject for an historical analysis. The psychological child is a child of the imagination, a *version* of the historical child, a symbolic personification of primitive affects. And to round out the picture, the historical child, as Jung pointed out, is a version of the archetypal child.

Jung was fond of quoting Goethe's axiom that what is inside is also outside, which would justify attending to the historical child. Frankly, however, I doubt whether many Freudians are nowadays as crudely reductive as archetypal psychology fantasises them to be. In brief, there is a flavour of contrivance to Hillman's attacks on the developmental approach (e.g. in his paper 'Abandoning the child', 1975a, pp. 5ff.).

We may explore the parallels between Schools further by considering the relation of image to feeling. Hillman argues that, in conventional approaches, images are used as ways of reaching feelings which cannot be more directly expressed. In his view, feelings are themselves the result of the action and interplay of images. But in the Developmental School much work has also been done to resolve the question of how unconscious imagery leads to emotion and affect and how these in turn interfere with or facilitate relationships (e.g. Newton, 1965). So here, too, image is not seen simply as an encoded feeling but as an active agency of psyche.

COUNTERTRANSFERENCE AND THE *MUNDUS IMAGINALIS*

There are also mutual misconceptions concerning the words actually used during the interchange of analysis. Although an analyst of the Developmental School may use the 'scientific' language of drives, instincts, processes, when he is with a patient personification is the basic mode of work. Parts of the personality, tendencies, emotional traits, may all acquire a name. Jung's perception that 'personality' is an illusion and that the psyche speaks through its figures is therefore utilised in both schools.

We may conclude this discussion by asking how and whether the transference-countertransference core of interactional dialectic (ID) may be seen as compatible with the imaginal perspective of archetypal psychology. Hillman, discussing the question of psychological unity, speaks of an 'outlook which sees all *events* as psychic realities' (1975a, p. 138, emphasis added). This is precisely what informs the 'microscopic' approach to patient-analyst interaction as evolved in the Developmental School. So how a dream is introduced by the patient *may* be as important as the dream itself – or, more accurately may be regarded as seamlessly interwoven with the dream, as was suggested earlier (pp. 239-40, above).

We can place the interaction of patient and analyst firmly within the imaginal realm without forgetting that there are two people present. Illusion, fantasy and imagery are the stuff of transference and the analyst is rarely what the patient claims or feels he is. I wonder whether, in the analytical setting, we may speak of a shared, two-person *mundus imaginalis*.

The factor that makes possible the idea of a two-person *mundus imaginalis* is countertransference. We have seen how an analyst can think, feel or behave as if he were the patient, and also how he can become a part of the patient's inner world. For example, M., the anorexic patient of mine introduced earlier, stimulated in me mental pictures of bodily corruption and decay. She had a pallid complexion, and was extremely thin and wasted. The phrase 'living dead' came into my mind. She later told me she thought of maggots a great deal but had been inhibited from telling me. We talked about why food repelled her, what it meant to be eaten away from within, that eggs (in the sense of larvae, or reproduction) were obnoxious, and related issues. I did not need to share with her my images of her because, in this instance, her material took up the themes. Yet, what happened (and every analyst has had experiences of this) was that the *mundus imaginalis* had become a *shared* dimension of experience.

I am suggesting that current views of countertransference force us to consider our attitude to the division between internal and external in analysis. There is no need to fear an abandonment of the interpersonal dimension, or that we might lose the idea that psychological consequences of early development need analysis. In fact, I would suggest that, in the same way that our notion of the internal world may be enlarged to include interpersonal dynamics, our notion of what is interpersonal may also be redefined and expanded to the extent that internal imagery becomes seen as linking patient and analyst (two persons) in the analysis. It follows that to divorce work on the apparently imaginal and work on the apparently interpersonal is conceptually in error and practically limiting.

It is not simply a question of opposing interpersonal communication, and the examination of that, to an imaginal approach. If the idea of a two-person *mundus imaginalis* is taken seriously then we must regard the interpersonal in terms of psyche speaking, and the imaginal in terms of an avenue of communication between two people. Persons may be expressions of internal dynamics, and inner images may originate, to some extent, in persons. From a pragmatic point of view, blurring this distinction in evaluating the material of patients may be what analysts of all schools do already when they use the concept of complex (archetypal core plus personal experience, part of psychic reality). At times, it is very important to stress the distinction but this would be a response to a particular situation.

Yet, in analytical psychology generally, a tension exists between working with the person and with the image. This tension has sometimes been expressed in terms of a split between 'clinical' and 'symbolic' approaches. I have been arguing that even though there may be immense methodological and expository differences, such a divide can be bridged. Otherwise analytical psychology would cease to exist as a discipline.

We need to envision our field of reference as seamless and continuous so that ostensible 'images' and ostensible 'interpersonal communications' do not get separated, nor one gain ascendency over the other on the basis of a preconceived hierarchy of importance.

THE FIELD OF REFERENCE: TOWARDS A POST-JUNGIAN ETHOS

But even, or rather particularly, with a seamless field of reference, we need to reflect upon our reasons for paying attention to certain factors and not to others. Earlier, I gave the example of how *wordy* had archetypal impact while *bombing* did not, though apparently a more profound issue (p. 53, above). We might ask what it was that caused such a powerful fluctuation of attention to take place, a fluctuation that constellated the archetypal. In that instance, attention was generated by depth of feeling and, above all, by a *shift of feeling*.

The shift of feeling was felt as an alteration in the sensory condition of the group and the individuals in it. In its turn, that alteration arose from an incongruity, a use of metaphor (*the group is wordy*). In analysis, the analyst works with such things, finding their psychological implication, adopting a minimalist approach. The analyst's discourse to his patient is also redolent of fluctuation, incongruity and metaphor. An interpretation or intervention, even one based on reconstruction, is a metaphor designed to shift the patient's feeling.

When we speak of shifts of feeling, two influences are discernible. First, what Poincaré called the 'selected fact'. In psychological terms this is an image or an idea which brings about a momentary sense of understanding in an atmosphere of incoherence by acting as a special nodal point of attention.

The second influence is, in Bion's term, the 'vertex' of the subject. This implies point of view, angle, or perspective and includes assumptions, value-judgments, preconceptions and lessons learned from experience. It is from one's vertex that attempts to understand phenomena radiate. This is not to be thought of as solely intellectual. Bion writes of 'using the inward eye', 'visualising', and of 'seeing in imagination' in connection with vertex (Bion, 1965).

Many disagreements over theory and practice reflect the differing vertices of analysts. Though, as Bion points out and as this chapter intends to demonstrate, 'two analysts belonging to different psychoanalytic schools can communicate and understand each other if they share a vertex, even though their theories and conceptual schemes may differ' (quoted in Grinberg, *et al*, 1977, p. 108). Thus we can now look back to the six categories in the grid, introduced in Chapter 1 (pp. 15-17, above), which defined the discipline of analytical psychology and provided a *post-Jungian vertex*. The theories and conceptual schemes of analytical psychologists do differ but, by relating to the debates implied in giving greater or lesser emphasis to the six headings, post-Jungians share a vertex and a common ideological future. Importantly, this indicates that they are able to communicate and understand each other.

A vertex implies a point of view or perspective, but a perspective on what? Presumably on psyche. Schematic, hierarchical and classificatory approaches to psyche have been superseded by a neutral, functional ethos involving themes, patterns, behaviour, images, emotions, instincts. The key words now are *interaction* (of those elements), *relativity* (archetypes in the eye of the beholder) and *systemic*. A systemic (not systematic) view implies that changes in any one element under consideration bring about changes in all the other elements to which it might be connected. Hence studying any one element becomes a difficult, even fruitless, undertaking.

Eventually, inner and outer, innate and personal, image and instinct, interpersonal and intrapsychic can be seen to be just that seamless field of references with no pre-existing or prescribed focus or locus of attention. It is to this that the vertex is applied.

There is also a link to be established between this vision of analytical psychology and what has happened in physics, linguistics and anthropology during the twentieth century. In those fields there has also been a shift away from thinking in terms of mass, substance or entity towards thinking and imagining in terms of pluralistic relations, hypotheses and other attempts to capture momentarily the fluidity of the universe. Overall, Jung hints at this, though the false rendering of his psychology as literal, concrete and static is a reading for which he must also be seen as responsible.

Our orientation is quasi-phenomenological. By this I mean that the phenomenological search for what is the case is also turned on to the inner world, on to images and fantasies, expanded to include a concern for meaning but only where such a concern is truly elected by the individual or the context. Meaning is not a given, an obligation or a requirement imposed by the outer world.

Analytical psychology seems no longer to march in fours (functions, stages of analysis, phases of life, forms of the feminine psyche), or in reliably computable patterns of opposites. In this sense post-Jungian analytical psychology has something in common with psychoanalysis whose elegant, pioneering metapsychological stuctures are now seen as reifications (Schafer, 1976), as personally defensive on Freud's part (Atwood and Stolorow, 1979) or, for English speakers, as the unfortunate results of mistranslation (Bettelheim, 1983).

THE PRIVACY OF THEORY

To talk of selected facts, vertices, shifts of feeling and attention brings both the analyst's personality and his theoretical position into focus, for these influence what he attends to, what he selects. There is an influence exerted upon the analyst's subjective response in the session by his pre-existing theory. This may be set alongside the better-known impact of his personality upon his theoretical views, and noted by Jung in 1951 as the 'personal equation, a subjective confession' (*CW* 16, para. 235). But it should not be thought that there is always a fit between the analyst's personality, his theory and the patient's material, and it may be that inflexibilities and inadequacies in personality and theory are responsible for a proportion of those cases that do not respond to analysis.

If we believe that theory is an extension of personality, and if we hold the view that the personality of the analyst is crucial in healing (Jung, *CW* 8, paras 1070-2), then why is so much energy expended on ideological dispute between analytical psychologists? Part of the answer lies in our remembering that a theory really has to be *held*, believed with conviction to explain certain facts, given up only when proven false. In this sense it is different from a model, which is more of a temporary and expedient device for organising information. Now, if personal integrity underpins analytical efficacy, and if strongly held convictions are part of personal integrity, it follows that possession of a theory is necessary for analytical efficacy. Though Jung rails against the rigid and unintegrated use of theory, he also states:

> the art of psychotherapy requires that the therapist be in possession of *avowable, credible, and defensible convictions* which have proved their viability either by having resolved any neurotic dissociations of his own or by preventing them from arising. (*CW* 16, para. 179, emphasis added)

Elsewhere, Jung gives his opinion that it is unnecessary to worry when psychotherapists cannot reach agreement about theory for 'agreement could only spell one-sidedness and desiccation.' We need many theories before we get 'even a rough picture of the psyche's complexity' (*CW* 16, para. 198).

After writing nearly all of this book, I read an article by the psychoanalyst Sandler. The article explored the distance and tension between what he referred to as 'standard', 'official', 'public' formulations of theory, and something described as 'private' and 'implicit' theory (1983).

Analytical psychology and psychoanalysis have been developing organically since the early days. Developments in theory put strain on other areas, both of theory and of practice. What happens is that the original concepts are stretched, or new concepts emerge, which conflict with standard, official and public formulations. Though we know that conceptual terms have multiple meanings, we tend to operate otherwise. We easily forget that a term 'is pliable in its usage, having a whole spectrum of context-dependent meanings' (ibid., p. 35).

Sandler's suggestion was that we should abandon searching for 'the pot of theoretical gold at the end of the rainbow' (ibid, p. 36) and, rather, value elasticity in our concepts. For it is elasticity that holds a depth psychology together. Analytical psychology (or psychoanalysis) is composed of part-theories and ideas at different levels of abstraction – it is not a complete theory, not even a complete clinical approach, but rather a *body of ideas*. As Sandler says, it is less important what our ideas should be than what we select from amongst them to stress or emphasise.

As an analyst becomes more experienced, he utilises bits of theory in an individual way, unconsciously or semi-consciously, when a patient's material requires it. These bits of theory often contradict each other logically but that does not matter. However, when the contradictions become conscious, the resultant hybrid may clash with official, standard or public formulations – and therefore tends to remain private.

We need to say something about these private and implicit theories. Analytical psychology has, on the surface, experienced less tension between what is private and what is public and official because of Jung's having been less of a dogmatic leader than Freud. But such tension does exist and the process outlined by Sandler has taken place. In his paper, Sandler went on to look at three areas in psychoanalysis where the distance between private and implicit theory and standard, official, public theory is, in his opinion, very wide. (These areas were drives and motives, conflict and object relations and transference.)

I would like to carry out the same exercise for analytical psychology, remembering that the issues have been discussed throughout the book. The three areas are (a) the theory of opposites, (b) the archetypal, and (c) images.

Is the *theory of opposites* a boon or a curse? The interplay of opposites serves to describe psychological movement and development and also to underpin ontology and psychic structure. But the theory is also too rigid an imposition, Hegelian, and too dependent upon a specified and questionable definition of psychic energy. We need to explore and test our use of the theory of opposites.

The work done on *archetypal structures* in analytical psychology is considerably in advance of any other clinical methodology. The problem is to scale this down to the level of everyday life without losing the impact of the archetypal experience. If archetypes are the psychological aspect of phylogeny, then working with them must be at this everyday, emotional level; hence my assertion that the archetypal is in the eye of the beholder. The area of theory where such a down-to-earth attitude may be taken is the concept of the complex. In particular, it would be interesting to work out more details about how experiences earlier in life, attached to an archetypal core, evolve into the adult complex.

At one point, Jung placed concepts and *images* in opposition: 'concepts are coined and negotiable values, images are life' (*CW* 14, para. 226), which serves to underline the central importance of imagery in analytical psychology. It is in the experience of image, and experience initiated by image, that analysis becomes a deep and living event. The personal, the subjective, even the intimate, involve the free passage and expression of image. Enjoying the image for itself, or as part of a therapeutic relationship, is different from symbological interpretation or amplification. Yet no analyst would discard what he knows of symbols, particularly if he has personally experienced their healing power.

In these three areas there are differences and similarities to be found in the approaches of the Schools. But there is also evidence of the particular tension that Sandler has codified: between what is standard, official and public, and what is private and implicit. Perhaps the tension also results from something the mathematician Poincaré wrote in 1902 about the development of science: at one and the same time we are advancing 'towards variety and complexity' and also 'towards unity and simplicity' (quoted in Carr, 1961, p. 90). Poincaré wondered if this apparent contradiction might be a necessary condition of knowledge.

JUNG AND THE POST-JUNGIANS

Three main threads run through this book. The first is a consideration of the work of the post-Jungians. As this theme evolved, I found that to delineate the starting point for present-day analytical psychologists, a critical account of Jung's own ideas was also needed. At that point the pursuit ran the risk of becoming somewhat parochial. It was easily extended to embrace the third theme, comparison between analytical psychology and psychoanalysis, past and present. Thus I have incorporated the 'unknowing Jungians'. Jung emerges not only as a relevant source for but also, in many respects, as *the* precursor of contemporary analysis and psychotherapy.

The supposition that the best way 'in' to an understanding of post-Jungian analytical psychology is by way of the debates within it derived from Karl Popper and from William James. The debates illuminate the foundation upon which analytical psychology rests. Thinking of the future, one wonders how the process of formation into schools will proceed. Though this process is likely to intensify, for all the reasons that have been put forward (see pp. 19-20, above), individuals will wish to express themselves by drawing on the work and ethos of all the schools. Jung's own striving in the direction of eclecticism took the form of active participation in the propagation of the fourteen points, known colloquially as *Views Held in Common*, according to the sole surviving author (Meier, personal communication, 1983). As previously mentioned, this was an attempt in the late 1930s by psychotherapists with differing orientations (Freudian, Adlerian, Jungian and others) to see if a unification of all the depth psychologies might be possible. I thought it might be useful to see whether and how the fourteen points could be applied to the Schools of post-Jungian analytical psychology.

Most of the points deal with the basic tenets of depth psychology and analytical work – for example, that there is such a thing as psychological disorder with aetiology and symptoms, etc. A number of points concern the relations between analyst and patient – transference, professional ethics and so forth.

One particular point is of considerable interest, however. It is called 'Significance of Fixation' and I reproduce it in full:

> The fixations appear on the one hand as *causae efficientes* [i.e. actual causes – A.S.] of the ensuing pathological states. On the other hand they appear as *causae*

finales, in as much as they set aims for the individual that exercise a decisive influence on his later conduct of life. This would be the prospective aspect of the initial situation in childhood.

The drives and their development (*causae materiales*) are to be taken into consideration together with symbols and ideas (*causae formales*).

Fixations can work pathogenically from the beginning, or they can be so animated through regression that they appear as dynamic causes, although are not such in reality.

This is the clearest statement that I have come across which links the so-called symbolic and the so-called clinical, the reductive-causal and the synthetic-prospective methods. The last sentence is fascinating because here, in a few words, is the suggestion that the child in the adult is *both* an historical and a symbolic child – a point which I take to be the fulcrum of communication between the Schools (see p. 263, above).

Turning now to Jung's own work, I would like to record a specific reaction. This concerns the way in which Jung constantly describes and faces up to the darker side of mankind, particularly as revealed in the analyst's consulting room. In theoretical language we refer to integration of the shadow or the reality of evil and destructiveness. But it is the figure to whom Jung related and upon whom he drew in his confrontation with darkness who interests: Hermes. Hermes has made an entry several times in this book in the form of what Jung referred to as

the Mercurius duplex who on the one hand is Hermes the mystagogue and psychopomp and on the other hand is the poisonous dragon, the evil spirit and 'trickster'. (*CW* 9i, para. 689)

Jung wrote that in connection with an artistically gifted patient who produced a 'typical tetradic mandala' and stuck it on a sheet of thick paper. On the other side there was a matching circle packed with drawings of sexual perversions. Jung saw this as demonstrating the 'chaos' that hides behind the self.

Elsewhere, and referring to the trickster stories of the Winnebago Indians, Jung insists that the trickster mythologem is actively sustained and promoted by consciousness as a reference point. He pointed out that the trickster does become more civilised and even 'useful and sensible' (*CW* 9i, para. 477). The Winnebago trickster, with his vaguely defined body capable of the utmost pliability, his obscenity, his tendency to enact his fantasy, is sometimes regarded as a symbol of an omnipotent infant. Maybe so, but to my mind he represents psyche itself.

Returning to Hermes, Jung sees him as a united entity 'in spite of the fact that his innumerable inner contradictions can dramatically fly apart into an equal number of disparate and apparently independent figures' (*CW* 13, para. 284). That, too, is psyche.

In analysis, Hermes 'flits' from analyst to patient; he is the 'third party in the alliance' (*CW* 16, para. 384). Analytic interaction is fast-moving; analytic attention is to minimal stimuli; philosophical expertise is not a requirement for the analyst. Yet how to take these realities and render them deep, make them soul? That is where Hermes makes his contribution. In addition, no author can afford to avoid acknowledging the connection between Hermes' thievery and creativity.

Finally, what of the claim that Jung anticipated much of what has developed in psychoanalysis? At this juncture, the arguments do not need reiterating. What might need restating is the original intent to try to do something about the credibility gap that has attended Jung.

The credibility gap is not a fantasy. For instance, in an appreciative review of a selection of Jung's writings (Storr, 1983), Hudson, an academic psychologist, explains that the credibility gap exists because Jung was 'banished comprehensively by the good burghers of British academic life [as] a charlatan.' Doubts about Jung's work, leading to a 'comprehensive rejection of it', has already been stiffened by the psychoanalytic 'secret committee set up by Ernest Jones to ensure that defectors ... were not taken seriously' (Hudson, 1983).

In some senses, Jung was never 'banished' at all. However, writing as a Jungian analyst, it is Jung the analyst who has occupied me. If he can now be seen as a reliable inspiration and to have had good judgment, then a different response to his work and to that of the post-Jungians will evolve.

Practical information

SOME JUNGIAN JOURNALS

Journal of Analytical Psychology, 1 Daleham Gardens, London NW3.
Spring, 2719 Routh Street, Dallas, TX 75201.
Psychological Perspectives, 10349 W. Pico Blvd., Los Angeles, CA 90064.
Quadrant, 28 East 39th Street, New York, NY 10016.
Harvest, 20 Canonbury Park North, London N1.
San Francisco Jung Institute Library Journal, 2040 Gough Street, San Francisco, CA 941090.
Zeitschrift für Analytische Psychologie, S. Karger AG, Postfach, CH-4009 Basel.
Rivista di Psicologica Analitica, Via Severano 3, 00161 Roma.
Cahiers de Psychologie Jungienne, 1 Place de l'École Militaire, 75007 Paris.
Chiron, 400 Linden Avenue, Wilmette, IL 60091

TRAINING

*Training institutions marked * are constituent members of the International Association for Analytical Psychology.*
Society of Analytical Psychology*, 1 Daleham Gardens, London NW3.
Association of Jungian Analysts (Alternative Training)*, 18 East Heath Road, London NW3.
British Association of Psychotherapists, 121 Hendon Lane, London NW3. (Has a separate training in analytical psychology.)
Westminster Pastoral Foundation, 23 Kensington Square, London W8. (Counsellor training oriented towards analytical psychology.)
Chicago Society of Jungian Analysts*, 550 Callan Avenue, Evanston, IL 60202.
Inter-Regional Society of Jungian Analysts*, c/o 1673 Canyon Road, Santa Fe, NM 87501. (Organises training for those not in other US localities listed.)
Society of Jungian Analysts of Southern California*, 10349 W. Pico Blvd, Los Angeles, CA 90064.
Society of Jungian Analysts of Northern California*, 2049 Gough Street, San Francisco, CA 94109.
New England Society of Jungian Analysts*, 264 Beacon Street, Boston, MASS 02116.
New York Association for Analytical Psychology*, 28 East 39th Street, New York, NY 10016.
Society of Jungian Analysts of San Diego*, c/o 12350 Oak Knoll Road, Poway, CA 92064.

Practical information

For details of training in other countries contact International Association for Analytical Psychology, Postfach 115, 8042 Zürich. (Australia and New Zealand, Austria, Belgium, Brazil, France, Germany, Switzerland, Israel, Italy; other training programmes may exist by publication date – check with IAAP in Zürich.)

Selected further reading (by School)

DEVELOPMENTAL

Fordham, M. (1978), *Jungian Psychotherapy: A Study in Analytical Psychology*, Wiley, Chichester.
Fordham, M. *et al.* (eds) (1973), *Analytical Psychology: A Modern Science*, Heinemann, London.
Fordham, M. *et al.* (eds) (1974), *Technique in Jungian Analysis*, Heinemann, London.
Lambert, K. (1981), *Analysis, Repair and Individuation*, Academic Press, London.

CLASSICAL

Adler, G. (1979), *Dynamics of the Self*, Coventure, London.
Frey-Rohn, L. (1974), *From Freud to Jung*, C.G. Jung Foundation, New York.
Jacobi, J. (1959), *Complex/Archetype/Symbol in the Psychology of C.G. Jung*, Princeton University Press.
Whitmont, E. (1969), *The Symbolic Quest*, Barrie & Rockliff, London.

ARCHETYPAL

Hillman, J. (1975), *Revisioning Psychology*, Harper & Row, New York.
Hillman, J. (1983), *Archetypal Psychology: A Brief Account*, Spring, Dallas.
Lopez-Pedraza, R. (1977), *Hermes and his Children*, Spring, Zürich.
Miller, D. (1982), *The New Polytheism*, Spring, Dallas.

References

Abenheimer, K. (1968), 'The ego as subject', in *The Reality of the Psyche*, ed. Wheelwright, J., Putnam, New York.

Adler, G. (1961), *The Living Symbol*, Routledge & Kegan Paul, London.

Adler, G. (1966), *Studies in Analytical Psychology*, Hodder & Stoughton, London.

Adler, G. (1967), 'Methods of treatment in analytical psychology', in *Psychoanalytical Techniques*, ed. Wolman, B., Basic Books, New York.

Adler, G. (1971), 'Analytical Psychology and the principle of complementarity', in *The Analytic Process*, ed. Wheelwright, J., Putnam, New York.

Adler, G. (ed.) (1973-4), *C.G. Jung Letters* vols 1 & 2, Routledge & Kegan Paul, London.

Adler, G. (1979), *Dynamics of the Self*, Coventure, London.

Andolfi, J. (1979), *Family Therapy: An Interactional Approach*, Plenum, New York.

Apter, M. (1982), *The Experience of Motivation*, Academic Press, London.

Atwood, G. and Stolorow, R. (1975), 'Metapsychology, reification and the representational world of C.G. Jung', *Int. Rev. Psychoanal.*, 4:1.

Atwood, G. and Stolorow, R. (1979), *Faces in a Cloud: Subjectivity in Personality Theory*, Jason Aronson, New York.

Avens, R. (1980), *Imagination is Reality*, Spring, Dallas.

Balint, M. (1952), *Primary Love and Psychoanalytic Technique*, Hogarth, London.

Balint, M. (1968), *The Basic Fault: Therapeutic Aspects of Regression*, Tavistock, London.

Bateson, G. (1979), *Mind and Nature: A Necessary Unity*, Dutton, New York.

Berry, P. (1974), 'An approach to the dream', *Spring*, 1974.

Berry, P. (1982), *Echo's Subtle Body*, Spring, Dallas.

Bettelheim, B. (1983), *Freud and Man's Soul*, Chatto & Windus, London.

Bion, W. (1963), 'Elements of psychoanalysis', in Bion, 1977.

Bion, W. (1965), 'Transformations', in Bion, 1977.

Bion, W. (1977), *Seven Servants*, Jason Aronson, New York.

Binswanger, H. (1963), 'Positive aspects of the animus', *Spring*, 1963, pp. 82-101.

Blomeyer, R. (1982), *Der Spiele der Analytiker: Freud, Jung und die Analyse*, Walter, Olten.

Blum, F. (1980), Comment on 'The use of the dream in contemporary analysis' by Lambert, K., *J. Analyt. Psychol.*, 25:3, pp. 275-8.

Bowlby, J. (1969), *Attachment and Loss*, vol. 1, *Attachment*, Hogarth Press, London.

Bradway, K. and Detloff, W. (1976), 'Incidence of psychological type among Jungian analysts classified by self and by test', *J. Analyt. Psychol.*, 21:2, pp. 134-46.

Bradway, K. and Wheelwright, J. (1978), 'The psychological type of the analyst and its relation to analytical practice', *J. Analyt. Psychol.*, 23:3, pp. 211-25.

Brome, V. (1978), *Jung: Man and Myth*, Macmillan, London.

Brown, J. (1961), *Freud and the Post-Freudians*, Penguin, Harmondsworth.

275

Burlingham, D. (1973), 'The pre-oedipal infant-father relationship', *Psychoanal. Stud. Child*, 28, pp. 23-47.

Capra, F. (1975), *The Tao of Physics*, Wildwood House, London; Fontana, London, 1976.

Carr, E. (1961), *What is History?* Penguin, Harmondsworth, 1965.

Carvalho, R. (1982), 'Paternal deprivation in relation to narcissistic damage', *J. Analyt. Psychol.*, 27:4, pp. 341-56.

Casey, E. (1974), 'Towards an archetypal imagination', *Spring*, 1974.

Chodorow, N. (1978), *The Reproduction of Mothering: Psychoanalysis and the Sociology of Gender*, University of California Press, Los Angeles.

Cirlot, J. (1962), *A Dictionary of Symbols*, Routledge & Kegan Paul, London.

Claremont de Castillejo, I. (1973), *Knowing Woman: A Feminine Psychology*, Harper & Row, New York.

Clark, G. (1978), 'A process of transformation: spiritual puer, instinctual shadow and instinctual spirit', *Harvest*, pp. 24-39.

Corbin, H. (1972), '*Mundus imaginalis*, or the imaginary and the imaginal', *Spring*.

Dare, C. and Holder, A. (1981), 'Developmental aspects of the interaction between narcissism, self-esteem and object relations', *Int. J. Psychoanal.*, 62:3, pp. 323-37.

Davidson, D. (1966), 'Transference as a form of active imagination', in *Technique in Jungian Analysis*, ed. Fordham, M. *et al.*, Heinemann, London, 1974.

Dieckmann, H. (1974), 'The constellation of the countertransference', in *Success and Failure in Analysis*, ed. Adler, G., Putnam, New York.

Dieckmann, H. (1977), 'Some aspects of the development of authority', *J. Analyt. Psychol.*, 22:3, pp. 230-42.

Dieckmann, H. (1980), 'On the methodology of dream interpretation', in *Methods of Treatment in Analytical Psychology*, ed. Baker, I., Bonz, Fellbach.

Dry, A. (1961), *The Psychology of Jung: A Critical Interpretation*, Methuen, London.

Edinger, E. (1960), 'The ego-self paradox', *J. Analyt. Psychol.*, 5:1, pp. 3-18.

Edinger, E. (1962), 'Symbols: the meaning of life', *Spring*, 1962.

Edinger, E. (1972), *Ego and Archetype*, Penguin, New York.

Eichenbaum, L. and Orbach, S. (1982), *Outside In . . . Inside Out: Women's Psychology: A Feminist Psychoanalytic Approach*, Penguin, Harmondsworth.

Ellenberger, H. (1970), *The Discovery of the Unconscious*, Allen Lane, London; Basic Books, New York.

Erikson, E. (1951), *Childhood and Society*, Imago, London.

Fiedler, L. (1955), *An End to Innocence*, Beacon Press, Boston.

Fierz, H. (1977), Translated as 'Methodics, theory and ethics in analytical psychotherapy', *Die Psychologie der 20. Jahrundert*, vol. 3, Kindler, Frankfurt.

Fiumara, R. (1976), 'Therapeutic group analysis and analytical psychology', *J. Analyt. Psychol.*, 21:1, pp. 1-24.

Ford, C. (1983), *The Somatizing Disorders: Illness as a Way of Life*, Elsevier, New York.

Fordham, M. (1949), 'Biological theory and the concept of archetypes', in *New Developments in Analytical Psychology*, Routledge & Kegan Paul, London, 1957.

Fordham, M. (1957), *New Developments in Analytical Psychology*, Routledge & Kegan Paul, London.

Fordham, M. (1960), 'Countertransference', in *Technique in Jungian Analysis*, ed. Fordham, M. *et al.*, Heinemann, London, 1974.

Fordham, M. (1963), 'The empirical foundation and theories of the self in Jung's works', in *Analytical Psychology: a Modern Science*, ed. Fordham, M. *et al.*, Heinemann, London, 1973.

Fordham, M. (1969a), *Children as Individuals*, Hodder & Stoughton, London; Putnam, New York, 1970.

Fordham, M. (1969b), 'Countertransference and technique', in *Technique in Jungian Analysis*, ed. Fordham, M. *et al.*, Heinemann, London, 1974.

Fordham, M. (1971), Comment on 'Psychology: monotheistic or polytheistic?' by Hillman, J., *Spring*.

Fordham, M. (1972), 'Note on psychological types', *J. Analyt. Psychol.*, 17:2, pp. 111-15.

Fordham, M. (1974a), 'Defences of the self', *J. Analyt. Psychol.*, 19:2, pp. 192-9.

Fordham, M. (1974b), 'Jung's conception of transference', *J. Analyt. Psychol.*, 19:1, pp. 1-21.

Fordham, M. (1975), 'Memories and thoughts about C.G. Jung', *J. Analyt. Psychol.*, 20:2, pp. 102-13.

Fordham, M. (1976), *The Self and Autism*, Heinemann, London.

Fordham, M. (1978a), *Jungian Psychotherapy: A Study in Analytical Psychology*, Wiley, Chichester.

Fordham, M. (1978b), 'Some idiosyncratic behaviour of therapists', *J. Analyt. Psychol.*, 23:1, pp. 122-34.

Fordham, M. (1979a), 'The self as an imaginative construct', *J. Analyt. Psychol.*, 24:1, pp. 18-30.

Fordham, M. (1979b), 'Analytical psychology and countertransference', in *Countertransference*, ed. Epstein, L. and Feiner, A., Jason Aronson, New York.

Fordham, M. (1980a), 'The emergence of child analysis', *J. Analyt. Psychol.*, 25:4, pp. 311-24.

Fordham, M. (1980b), Review of *The Kleinian Development* by Meltzer, D., *J. Analyt. Psychol.*, 25:2, p. 201-4.

Fordham, M. (1981), 'Neumann and childhood', *J. Analyt. Psychol.*, 26:2, pp. 99-122.

Fordham, M. *et al.* (eds) (1973), *Analytical Psychology: A Modern Science*, Heinemann, London.

Fordham, M. *et al.* (eds) (1974), *Technique in Jungian Analysis*, Heinemann, London.

Freud, A. (1937), *The Ego and the Mechanisms of Defence*, Hogarth, London.

Freud, A. (1966), *Normality and Pathology in Childhood*, Penguin, Harmondsworth, 1973.

Freud, S. (1901), *The Psychopathology of Everyday Life*, Std Edn, 6, Hogarth, London.

Freud, S. (1912), 'Recommendations to physicians', Std Edn, 12, pp. 109-20, Hogarth, London.

Freud, S. (1916-17), *Introductory Lectures on Psychoanalysis*, Std Edn, 15 & 16, Hogarth, London.

Freud, S. (1918), 'From the history of an infantile neurosis', Std Edn, 17, Hogarth London.

Frey-Rohn, L. (1974), *From Freud to Jung*, C.G. Jung Foundation, New York.

Gallop, J. (1982), *Feminism and Psychoanalysis: The Daughter's Seduction*, Macmillan, London.

Gammon, M. (1973), 'Window into eternity', *J. Analyt. Psychol.*, 18:1, pp. 11-24.

Giegerich, W. (1975), 'Ontogeny=phylogeny? A fundamental critique of Erich Neumann's analytical psychology', *Spring*, pp. 110-29.

Gill, H. (1982), 'The life-context of the dreamer and the setting of dreaming', *Int. J. Psychoanal.*, 63:4, pp. 475-82.

Glover, E. (1939), 'The psychoanalysis of affects', *Int. J. Psychoanal.*, 20, pp. 299-307.

Glover, E. (1950), *Freud or Jung*, Allen & Unwin, London.

Goffman, I. (1961), *The Asylum*, Doubleday, New York.

Goldberg, A. (1980), Introduction to *Advances in Self Psychology*, ed. Goldberg, A., International Universities Press, New York.

Goldenberg, N. (1975), 'Archetypal theory after Jung', *Spring*.

Goldenberg, N. (1976), 'A feminist critique of Jung', *Signs: J. of Women in Culture and Society*, 2:2, pp. 443-9.

Goodheart, W. (1980), 'Theory of analytic interaction', *San Francisco Jung Institute Library J.*, 1:4, pp. 2-39.

Gordon, R. (1978), *Dying and Creating: A Search for Meaning*, Society of Analytical Psychology, London.

Gordon, R. (1979), 'Reflections on curing and healing', *J. Analyt. Psychol.*, 24:3, pp. 207-19.

Gordon, R. (1980), 'Narcissism and the self: who am I that I love?' *J. Analyt. Psychol.*, 25:3, pp. 247-62.

Greenson, R. (1967), *The Technique and Practice of Psychoanalysis*, Hogarth, London.

Greenson, R. and Wexler, M. (1969), 'The non-transference relationship in the psychoanalytic situation', *Int. J. Psychoanal.*, 50, pp. 27-39.

Greenstadt, W. (1982), Letter in *Int. Rev. Psychoanal.*, 9:4, pp. 485-6.

Grinberg, L. *et al.* (1977) *Introduction to the Work of Bion*, Jason Aronson, New York.

Grinnell, R. (1971), 'In praise of the instinct for wholeness: intimations of a moral archetype', *Spring*, 1971.

Groesbeck, C. (1975), 'The archetypal image of the wounded healer', *J. Analyt. Psychol.*, 20:2, pp.122-45.

Guggenbühl-Craig, A. (1971), *Power in the Helping Professions*, Spring, New York.

Guggenbühl-Craig, A. (1977), *Marriage – Dead or Alive*, Spring, Zürich.

Guggenbühl-Craig, A. (1980), *Eros on Crutches: Reflections on Psychopathy and Amorality*, Spring, Dallas.

Guntrip, H. (1961), *Personality Structure and Human Interaction*, Hogarth, London.

Hall, J. (1977), *Clinical Uses of Dreams: Jungian Interpretation and Enactments*, Grune & Stratton, New York.

Hamilton, V. (1982), *Narcissus and Oedipus: Children of Psychoanalysis*, Routledge & Kegan Paul, London.

Hampshire, S. (1983), Review of *Freud and Man's Soul* by Bettelheim, B. (*q.v.*), in *The Observer* 17 July London.

Hannah, B. (1967), 'Some glimpses of the individuation process in Jung himself', privately printed and circulated to members of the Analytical Psychology Club, London.

Hannah, B. (1976), *Jung: His Life and Work*, Putnam, New York.

Harding, E. (1933), *The Way of All Women*, Harper & Row, New York, 1975.

Hartmann, H. (1939), 'Psychoanalysis and the concept of health', *Int. J. Psychoanal.*, 20, pp. 308-21.

Heimann, P. (1952), 'Certain functions of introjection and projection in early infancy', in *Developments in Psychoanalysis*, ed. Riviere, J., Hogarth, London.

Henderson, J. (1975a), 'C.G. Jung: a reminiscent picture of his method', *J. Analyt. Psychol.*, 20:2, pp. 114-21.

Henderson, J. (1975b), Review of *Analytical Psychology: a Modern Science* and *Technique in Jungian Analysis*, both ed. Fordham, M. *et al.* (qq.v.), in *Psychological Perspectives*, 6:2, pp. 197-203.

Henry, J. (1977), Comment on 'The cerebral hemispheres in analytical psychology' by Rossi, E. (*q.v.*), in *J. Analyt. Psychol.*, 22:2, pp. 52-8.

Hillman, J. (1962), 'Training and the C.G. Jung Institute, Zürich', *J. Analyt. Psychol.*, 7:1, pp. 3-19.

Hillman, J. (1967), *Insearch: Psychology and Religion*, Spring, Dallas, 1979.

Hillman, J. (1971), 'Psychology: monotheistic or polytheistic?', *Spring*.

Hillman, J. (1972), *The Myth of Analysis*, Northwestern University Press, Evanston, Illinois.

Hillman, J. (1973), 'The Great Mother, her son, her hero, and the puer', in *Fathers and*

Mothers, ed. Berry, P., Spring, Zürich.

Hillman, J. (1975a), *Loose Ends*, Spring, Dallas.

Hillman, J. (1975b), *Revisioning Psychology*, Harper & Row, New York.

Hillman, J. (1977, 1978), 'An enquiry into image', *Spring*, 1977, 1978.

Hillman, J. (1979a), *The Dream and the Underworld*, Harper & Row, New York.

Hillman, J. (1979b), 'Senex and puer', in *Puer Papers*, ed. Giles, C., Spring, Dallas.

Hillman, J. (1981), Expanded version of Hillman (1971) in Miller (1981) (*q.v.*).

Hillman, J. (1983), *Archetypal Psychology: A Brief Account*, Spring, Dallas.

Hobson, R. (1959), 'An approach to group analysis', *J. Analyt. Psychol.*, 4:2, pp. 139-52.

Hobson, R. (1961), 'The archetypes of the collective unconscious', in *Analytical Psychology: A Modern Science*, ed. Fordham, M. *et al.*, Heinemann, London, 1973.

Hoffman, L. (1981), *Foundations of Family Therapy*, Basic Books, New York.

Hubback, J. (1973), 'Uses and abuses of analogy', *J. Analyt. Psychol.*, 18:2, pp. 91-104.

Hubback, J. (1980), 'Developments and similarities, 1935-1980', *J. Analyt. Psychol.*, 25:3, pp. 219-36.

Hudson, L. (1983), Review of *Jung: Selected Writings* ed. Storr, A. (*q.v.*), in *Sunday Times*, 13 March, London.

Humbert, E. (1980), 'The self and narcissism', *J. Analyt. Psychol.*, 25:3, pp. 237-46.

Isaacs, S. (1952), 'The nature and function of phantasy', in *Developments in Psychoanalysis*, ed. Riviere, J., Hogarth, London.

Jackson, M. (1961), 'Chair, couch and counter-transference', in *J. Analyt. Psychol.*, 6:1, pp. 35-44.

Jacobi, J. (1942), *The Psychology of C.G. Jung*, Kegan Paul, Trench, Trubner, London; Yale University Press, New Haven, 1962 (6th ed.).

Jacobi, J. (1959), *Complex/Archetype/Symbol in the Psychology of C.G. Jung*, Princeton University Press.

Jacobson, E. (1964), *The Self and the Object World*, Hogarth, London.

Jacoby, M. (1981), 'Reflections on H. Kohut's concept of narcissism', *J. Analyt. Psychol.*, 26:1, pp. 19-32.

Jacoby, M. (1983), Comment on 'Ego and self: terminology' by Redfearn, J., *J. Analyt. Psychol.*, 28:2, pp.107-10.

Jaffé, A. (1971), *The Myth of Meaning*, Putnam, New York.

Jaffé, A. (ed.) (1979), *C.G. Jung: Word and Image*, Princeton University Press.

James, W. (1911), *Pragmatism*, in Fontana Library of Philosophy, London, 1962.

Jarret, J. (1981), 'Schopenhauer and Jung', *Spring*, 1981.

Jones, E. (1927), 'Early development of female sexuality', in *Papers on Psychoanalysis*, Baillière, Tindall & Cox, London, 1950.

Jones, E. (1931), 'The concept of the normal mind', *Int. J. Psychoanal.*, 23, pp.1-8.

Joseph, E. (1982), 'Normal in psychoanalysis', *Int. J. Psychoanal.*, 63:1, pp. 3-14.

Jung, C.G., References are to the *Collected Works* (*CW*) and by volume and paragraph number, except as below, edited by Read, H., Fordham, M., Adler, G., McGuire, W., translated in the main by Hull, R, Routledge & Kegan Paul, London; Princeton University Press.

Jung, C.G. (1928), *Contributions to Analytical Psychology*, Kegan Paul, London.

Jung, C.G. (1963), *Memories, Dreams, Reflections*, Collins and Routledge & Kegan Paul, London; Fontana, London, 1972; Pantheon, New York.

Jung, C.G. (1964), *Man and his Symbols*, Dell, New York.

Jung, C.G. (1978), *C.G. Jung Speaking*, ed. McGuire, W., Thames & Hudson, London; Picador, London, 1980.

Jung, C.G. (1983), *The Zofingia Lectures. CW* Supplementary Volume A, ed. McGuire, W., translated by van Heurck, J., Routledge & Kegan Paul, London; Princeton University Press.

Jung, E. (1957), *Animus and Anima*, Spring, New York.
Kalff, D. (1980), *Sandplay: A Psychotherapeutic Approach to the Psyche*, Sigo, Santa Monica.
Kay, D. (1981), 'Paternal psychopathology and the emerging ego', *J. Analyt. Psychol.*, 26:3, pp. 203-19.
Keutzer, L. (1982), 'Archetypes, synchronicity and the theory of formative causation', *J. Analyt. Psychol.*, 27:3, pp. 255-62.
Klein, M. (1960), 'On mental health', *Brit. J. Med. Psych.*, 33, pp. 237-41.
Kohut, H. (1971), *The Analysis of the Self*, International Universities Press, New York.
Kohut, H. (1977), *The Restoration of the Self*, International Universities Press, New York.
Kohut, H. (1980), 'Reflections', in *Advances in Self Psychology*, ed. Goldberg, A. (*q.v.*).
Kohut, H. (1982), 'Introspection, empathy, and the semi-circle of mental health', *Int. J. Psychoanal.*, 63:4, pp. 395-408.
Kraemer, W. (ed.) (1976), *The Forbidden Love: The Normal and Abnormal Love of Children*, Sheldon Press, London.
Lacan, J. (1949), 'The mirror stage as formative of the function of the I as revealed in psychoanalytic experience', in *Écrits*, trans. Sheridan, A., Tavistock, London, 1977.
Lacan, J. (1958), 'The significance of the phallus', in *Écrits*, trans. Sheridan, A., Tavistock, London, 1977.
Laing (1967), *The Politics of Experience*, Penguin, Harmondsworth.
Lambert, K. (1977), 'Analytical psychology and historical development in Western consciousness', *J. Analyt. Psychol.*, 22:1, pp. 158-74.
Lambert, K. (1981a), *Analysis, Repair and Individuation*, Academic Press, London.
Lambert, K. (1981b), 'Emerging consciousness', *J. Analyt. Psychol.*, 26:1, pp. 1-18.
Langs, R. (1979), 'The interactional dimension of countertransference', in *Counter-transference*, ed. Epstein, L. and Feiner, A., Jason Aronson, New York.
Laplanche, J. and Pontalis, J.-B. (1980), *The Language of Psychoanalysis*, Hogarth, London.
Layard, J. (1942), *Stone Men of Malekula*, Chatto & Windus, London.
Leach, E. (1974), *Lévi-Strauss*, Fontana, London.
Ledermann, R. (1979), 'The infantile roots of narcissistic personality disorder', *J. Analyt. Psychol.*, 24:2, pp. 107-26.
Ledermann, R. (1981), 'The robot personality in narcissistic disorder', *J. Analyt. Psychol.*, 26:4, pp. 329-44.
Ledermann, R. (1982), 'Narcissistic disorder and its treatment', *J. Analyt. Psychol.*, 27:4, pp. 303-22.
Lemaire, A. (1977), *Jacques Lacan*, Routledge & Kegan Paul, London.
Levinson, D. *et al.* (1978), *The Seasons of a Man's Life*, Knopf, New York.
Little, M. (1957), ' "R": the analyst's total response to his patient's needs', *Int. J. Psychoanal.*, 38:3.
Loomis, M. and Singer, J. (1980), 'Testing the bipolar assumption in Jung's typology', *J. Analyt. Psychol.*, 25:4, pp. 351-6.
Lopez-Pedraza, R. (1971), Comment on 'Psychology: monotheistic or polytheistic?' by Hillman, J., *Spring*.
Lopez-Pedraza, R. (1977), *Hermes and his Children*, Spring, Zürich.
Loughlin, T. (1982), *Jungian Psychology*, Panarion, Los Angeles.
Lyons, J. (1977), *Chomsky*, Fontana, London.
McCurdy, A. (1982), 'Establishing and maintaining the analytical structure', in *Jungian Analysis*, ed. Stein, M., Open Court, La Salle.
Macfarlane, A. (1978), *The Origins of English Individualism*, Blackwell, Oxford.
McGuire, W. (ed.) (1974), *The Freud/Jung Letters*, Hogarth and Routledge & Kegan Paul, London; Princeton University Press.

References

Maduro, R. and Wheelwright, J. (1977), 'Analytical psychology', in *Current Personality Theories*, ed. Corsini, R., Peacock, Itasca.

Mahler, M. (1975), *The Psychological Birth of the Human Infant*, Hutchinson, London.

Malcolm, J. (1982), *Psychoanalysis: The Impossible Profession*, Pan, London.

Marais, E. (1937), *The Soul of the White Ant*, Methuen, London.

Mattoon, M. (1978), *Applied Dream Analysis: A Jungian Approach*, Winston, Washington.

Mattoon, M. (1981), *Jungian Psychology in Perspective*, Free Press, New York.

Mead, M. (1949), *Male and Female: A Study of the Sexes in a Changing World*, Penguin, Harmondsworth, 1981.

Meier, C. (1949), *Ancient Incubation and Modern Psychotherapy*, Northwestern University Press, Evanston, 1967.

Meier, C. and Wozny, M. (1978), 'An empirical study of Jung's typology', *J. Analyt. Psychol.*, 23:3, pp. 226-30.

Meltzer, D. (1981), 'The Kleinian expansion of Freud's metapsychology', *Int. J. Psychoanal.*, 62:2, pp. 177-86.

Menninger, K. (1958), *Theory of Psychoanalytic Technique*, Basic Books, New York.

Metzner, R. *et al.* (1981), 'Towards a reformulation of the typology of functions', *J. Analyt. Psychol.*, 26:1, pp. 33-48.

Miller, D. (1981), *The New Polytheism*, Spring, Dallas.

Mitchell, J. (1974), *Psychoanalysis and Feminism*, Allen Lane, London.

Mitchell, J. and Rose, J. (1982), *Feminine Sexuality: Jacques Lacan and the École Freudienne*, Macmillan, London.

Money-Kyrle, R. (1968), 'Cognitive development', in *Collected Papers*, ed. Meltzer, D., Clunie Press, Strath Tay, Perthshire, 1978.

Money-Kyrle, R. (1971), 'The aim of psychoanalysis', in *Collected Papers*, as above.

Money-Kyrle, R. (1977), 'On being a psychoanalyst', in *Collected Papers*, as above.

Moore, N. (1983), 'The anima-animus in a changing world', unpublished.

Mount, A. (1982), *The Subversive Family*, Cape, London.

Myers, I. (1962), *The Myers-Briggs Type Indicator*, Consulting Psychologists Press, Palo Alto.

Neumann, E. (1954), *The Origins and History of Consciousness*, Routledge & Kegan Paul, London; Pantheon, New York, 1964.

Neumann, E. (1959), 'The significance of the genetic aspect for analytical psychology', *J. Analyt. Psychol.*, 4:2, pp.125-38.

Neumann, E. (1973), *The Child*, Hodder & Stoughton, London.

Newton, K. (1965), 'Mediation of the image of infant-mother togetherness', in *Analytical Psychology: A Modern Science*, ed. Fordham, M. *et al.*, Heinemann, London, 1973.

Newton, K. (1975), 'Separation and pre-oedipal guilt', *J. Analyt. Psychol.*, 20:2, pp. 183-93.

Newton, K. (1981), Comment on 'The emergence of child analysis', by Fordham M., *J. Analyt. Psychol.*, 26:1, pp. 69-78.

Newton, K. and Redfearn, J. (1977), 'The real mother, ego-self relations and personal identity', *J. Analyt. Psychol.*, 22:4, pp.295-316

Nicholson, J. (1984), *Men and Women: How Different Are They?* Oxford University Press.

Offer, D. and Sabshin, M. (1973), *Normality*, Basic Books, New York.

Paolino, T. (1981), *Psychoanalytic Psychotherapy*, Brunner/Mazel, New York.

Perera, S. (1981), *Descent to the Goddess: A Way of Initiation for Women*, Inner City, Toronto.

Perry, J. (1962), 'Reconstitutive process in the psychopathology of the self', *Annals of the N.Y. Academy of Sciences*, vol. 96, article 3, pp. 853-76.

Plaut, A. (1956), 'The transference in analytical psychology', in *Technique in Jungian Analysis*, ed. Fordham, M. *et al.*, Heinemann, London, 1974.

Plaut, A. (1959), 'Hungry patients: reflections on ego structure', *J. Analyt. Psychol.*, 4:2, pp.161-8.

Plaut, A. (1962), 'Some reflections on the Klein-Jungian hybrid', unpublished.

Plaut, A. (1966), 'Reflections on not being able to imagine', in *Analytical Psychology: A Modern Science*, ed. Fordham, M. *et al.*, Heinemann, London, 1973.

Plaut, A. (1972), 'Analytical psychologists and psychological types: comment on replies to a survey', *J. Analyt. Psychol.*, 17:2, pp. 137-51.

Plaut, A. (1974), 'Part-object relations and Jung's "luminosities" ', *J. Analyt. Psychol.*, 19:2, pp.165-81.

Plaut, A. (1975), 'Object constancy or constant object?', *J. Analyt. Psychol.*, 20:2, pp. 207-15.

Plaut, A. (1979), 'Individuation: a basic concept of psychotherapy' (English resumé), *Z. Analytische Psychologie*, 10, pp. 173-89.

Plaut, A. (1982), Review of *Analysis, Repair and Individuation* by Lambert, K. (*q.v.*), *J. Analyt. Psychol.*, 27:3, pp. 285-8.

Popper, K. (1972), *Conjectures and Refutations: The Growth of Scientific Knowledge*, Routledge & Kegan Paul, London.

Racker, H. (1968), *Transference and Countertransference*, Hogarth, London.

Raglan, Lord. (1949), *The Hero*, Watts, London.

Redfearn, J. (1969), 'Several views of the self', *J. Analyt. Psychol.*, 14:1, pp. 13-25.

Redfearn, J. (1974), 'Can we change?', unpublished.

Redfearn, J. (1978), 'The energy of warring and combining opposites: problems for the psychotic patient and the therapist in achieving the symbolic situation', *J. Analyt. Psychol.*, 23:3, pp. 231-41.

Redfearn, J. (1979), 'The captive, the treasure, the hero and the "anal" stage of development', *J. Analyt. Psychol.*, 24:3, pp. 185-206.

Redfearn, J. (1982), 'When are things persons and persons things?', *J. Analyt. Psychol.*, 27:3, pp. 215-38.

Riviere, J. (1952), 'On the genesis of psychical conflict in earliest infancy', in *Developments in Psychoanalysis*, ed. Riviere, J., Hogarth, London.

Roazen, P. (1976), *Freud and his Followers*, Penguin, London; Knopf, New York, 1975.

Rossi, E. (1977), 'The cerebral hemispheres in analytical psychology', *J. Analyt. Psychol.*, 22:1, pp. 32-58.

Rycroft, C. (1972), *A Critical Dictionary of Psychoanalysis*, Penguin, London.

Rycroft, C. (1979), *The Innocence of Dreams*, Hogarth, London.

Rycroft, C. (1982), Review of *Archetype: A Natural History of the Self* by Stevens, A. (*q.v.*), *New Society*, 20 May, London.

Samuels, A. (1976), 'The psychology of the single parent', unpublished.

Samuels, A. (1979), 'Diagnosis and power', in *The Jung Symposium*, Group for the Advancement of Psychotherapy in Social Work, London.

Samuels, A. (1980a), 'Incest and omnipotence in the internal family', *J. Analyt. Psychol.*, 25:1, pp. 37-58.

Samuels, A. :1980b), 'Incesto e onnipotenza', *La Pratica Analitica*, vol. 2, pp. 113-36.

Samuels, A. (1981a), 'Fragmentary vision: a central training aim', *Spring*.

Samuels, A. (1981b), 'Fragmentarische Vision: Ein zentrales Ausbildungsziel', *Gorgo*, 9, 1984.

Samuels, A. (1982), 'The image of the parents in bed', *J. Analyt. Psychol.*, 27:4, pp. 323-40.

Sandler, A.-M. (1982), 'The selection and function of the training analyst in Europe', *Int. Rev. Psychoanal.*, 9:4, pp. 386-97.

References

Sandler, J., Dare, C. and Holder, A. (1973), *The Patient and the Analyst*, Allen & Unwin, London.

Sandler, J. (1983), 'Reflections on some relations between psychoanalytic concepts and psychoanalytic practice', *Int. J. Psychoanal.*, 64:1, pp. 35-46.

Sayers, J. (1982), *Biological Politics: Feminist and Anti-Feminist Perspectives*, Tavistock, London.

Schafer, R. (1976), *A New Language for Psychoanalysis*, Yale University Press, New Haven.

Schwartz-Salant, N. (1982), *Narcissism and Character Transformation: The Psychology of Narcissistic Character Disorders*, Inner City, Toronto.

Searles, H. (1959), 'Oedipal love in the countertransference', in *Collected Papers on Schizophrenia and Related Subjects*, Hogarth, London, 1968.

Segal, H. (1973), *Introduction to the Work of Melanie Klein*, Hogarth, London.

Segal, H. (1979), *Klein*, Fontana, London.

Seligman, E. (1982), 'The half-alive ones', *J. Analyt. Psychol.*, 27:1, pp. 1-20.

Shorter, B. (1983), *Woman and Initiation*, part 2, 'Growing a woman', unpublished.

Singer, J. (1972), *Boundaries of the Soul: The Practice of Jung's Psychology*, Gollancz, London.

Singer, J. (1977), *Androgyny: Towards a New Theory of Sexuality*, Routledge & Kegan Paul, London.

Skynner, R. (1976), *One Flesh, Separate Persons*, Constable, London.

Spitz, R. (1965), *The First Year of Life*, International Universities Press, New York.

Staude, J.-R. (1981), *The Adult Development of C.G. Jung*, Routledge & Kegan Paul, Boston and London.

Stein, L. (1957), 'What is a symbol supposed to be?', in *Analytical Psychology: A Modern Science* ed. Fordham, M. *et al.*, Heinemann, London, 1973.

Stein, L. (1958), 'Analytical psychology: a modern science', in *Analytical Psychology: A Modern Science*, as above.

Stein, L. (1967), 'Introducing not-self', *J. Analyt. Psychol.*, 12:2 pp. 97–114.

Stein, M. (1973), 'Hephaistos: a pattern of introversion', *Spring*.

Stein, M. (1982), Editor's preface to *Jungian Analysis*, Open Court, La Salle.

Stein, R. (1974), *Incest and Human Love*, Penguin, Baltimore.

Sterba, R. (1934), 'The fate of the ego in analytic therapy', *Int. J. Psychoanal.*, 15, pp. 117-26.

Stevens, A. (1982), *Archetype: A Natural History of the Self*, Routledge & Kegan Paul, London.

Stoller, R. (1968), *Sex and Gender*, Hogarth, London.

Storr, A. (1957), 'The psychopathology of fetishism and transvestism', *J. Analyt. Psychol.*, 2:2, pp. 153-66.

Storr, A. (1973), *Jung*, Fontana, London.

Storr, A. (1979), *The Art of Psychotherapy*, Heinemann, London.

Storr, A. (1983), *Jung: Selected Writings*, Fontana, London.

Strachey, J. (1934), 'The nature of the therapeutic action of psychoanalysis', *Int. J. Psychoanal.*, 15, pp. 127-59.

Strauss, R. (1964), 'The archetype of separation', in *The Archetype*, ed. Guggenbühl-Craig, A., Karger, Basle.

Sutherland, J. (1980), 'The British object relations theorists: Balint, Winnicott, Fairbairn, Guntrip', *J. Amer. Psychoanal. Assn.*, 28, pp. 829-59.

Tolpin, M. (1980), Contribution to 'Discussion' in *Advances in Self Psychology*, ed. Goldberg, A. (*q.v.*).

Ulanov, A. (1981), *Receiving Woman: Studies in the Psychology and Theology of the Feminine*, Westminster, Philadelphia.

von der Heydt, V. (1973), 'On the father in psychotherapy', in *Fathers and Mothers*, ed.

Berry, P., Spring, Zürich.

von Franz, M.-L. (1970), *The Problem of the Puer Aeternus*, Spring, New York.

von Franz, M.-L. (1971), 'The inferior function', in *Jung's Typology*, Spring, New York.

von Franz, M.-L. (1975), *C.G. Jung: His Myth in Our Time*, Hodder & Stoughton, London; Putnam, New York.

von Franz, M.-L. (1980), *Projection and Recollection in Jungian Psychology*, Open Court, La Salle.

Weaver, R. (1964), *The Old Wise Woman*, Vincent Stuart, London.

Westmann, H. (1961), *The Springs of Creativity*, Routledge & Kegan Paul, London.

Wheelwright, J. *et al.*, (1964), *Jungian Type Survey: The Gray-Wheelwright Test Manual*, Society of Jungian Analysts of N. California, San Francisco.

Whitmont, E. (1964), 'Group therapy and analytical psychology', *J. Analyt. Psychol.*, 9:1, pp. 1-22.

Whitmont, E. (1969), *The Symbolic Quest*, Barrie & Rockliff, London.

Wickes, F. (1966), *The Inner World of Childhood*, Appleton, New York.

Wilden, A. (1980), *System and Structure: Essays in Communication and Exchange*, Tavistock, London.

Willeford, W. (1976), 'The primacy of feeling' (part 1), *J. Analyt. Psychol.*, 21:2, pp. 115-33.

Williams, M. (1963a), 'The indivisibility of the personal and collective unconscious', in *Analytical Psychology: A Modern Science*, ed. Fordham, M. *et al.*, Heinemann, London, 1973.

Williams, M. (1963b), 'The poltergeist man', *J. Analyt. Psychol.*, 8:2, pp. 123-44.

Williams, M. (1971), 'The archetypes in marriage', unpublished.

Wilson, G. and Nias, D. (1977), *Love's Mysteries*, Fontana, London.

Winnicott, D. (1958), *Collected Papers: Through Paediatrics to Psychoanalysis*, Tavistock, London.

Winnicott, D. (1965), *The Maturational Processes and the Facilitating Environment*, Hogarth, London.

Winnicott, D. (1967), 'Mirror role of mother and family in child development', in *Playing and Reality*, 1971.

Winnicott, D. (1971), *Playing and Reality*, Tavistock, London.

Wise, P. (1971), *The Schlemiel as Modern Hero*, Chicago University Press.

Wolff, T. (1951), 'Structural forms of the feminine psyche; a sketch', privately printed, Zürich, 1956.

Woodman, M. (1980), *The Owl was a Baker's Daughter: Obesity, Anorexia Nervosa and the Repressed Feminine*, Inner City, Toronto.

Yorke, C. (1982), 'Freud rediscovered', *The Listener*, 28 October, London.

Zinkin, L. (1969), 'Flexibility in analytic technique', in *Technique in Jungian Analysis*, ed. Fordham, M. *et al.*, Heinemann, London, 1974.

Zinkin, L. (1979), 'The collective and the personal', *J. Analyt. Psychol.*, 24:3, pp. 227-50.

Index

Page numbers in bold type indicate where in the text Jung's main concepts are introduced and defined.

285